German Colonialism

German Colonialism

Race, the Holocaust, and Postwar Germany

Edited by
Volker Langbehn and Mohammad Salama

COLUMBIA UNIVERSITY PRESS   New York

Columbia University Press
Publishers Since 1893
New York   Chichester, West Sussex
Copyright © 2011 Columbia University Press
All rights reserved

Library of Congress Cataloging-in-Publication Data
German colonialism : race, the Holocaust, and postwar Germany /
edited by Volker Langbehn and Mohammad Salama.
  p.   cm.
Includes bibliographical references and index.
ISBN 978-0-231-14972-3 (cloth : alk. paper) —
ISBN 978-0-231-14973-0 (paper : alk. paper) — ISBN 978-0-231-52054-6 (ebook)
1. Germany—Colonies—Africa—History. 2. Africa—Colonial influence. 3. Racism—
Germany—History. 4. Racism—Africa—History. 5. Nationalism—Germany—History.
6. Continuity—Political aspects—Germany—History. 7. Holocaust, Jewish (1939–1945)
8. World War, 1939–1945—Atrocities. 9. Germany—History—1945– 10. Imperialism—
Social aspects—Germany—History. I. Langbehn, Volker Max, 1959–
II. Salama, Mohammad. III. Title.

DT34.5.G46   2011
325'.343—dc22

2010023533

Columbia University Press books are printed on permanent and durable acid-free paper.
This book is printed on paper with recycled content.
Printed in the United States of America

References to Internet Web sites (URLs) were accurate at the time of writing.
Neither the editors nor Columbia University Press is responsible for URLs
that may have expired or changed since the manuscript was prepared.

Contents

Acknowledgments *vii*
Introduction: Reconfiguring German Colonialism *ix*
Volker Langbehn and Mohammad Salama

Part I. Colonial (Dis)Continuities: Framing the Issue   1

1. Borrowed Light: Nietzsche and the Colonies   3
   Timothy Brennan
2. German Colonialism: Some Reflections   29
   on Reassessments, Specificities, and Constellations
   Birthe Kundrus

Part II. *Lebensraum* and Genocide   49

3. Against "Human Diversity as Such":   51
   Lebensraum and Genocide in the Third Reich
   Shelley Baranowski
4. Hannah Arendt, Imperialisms, and the Holocaust   72
   A. Dirk Moses

5. Caesura, Continuity, and Myth: The Stakes of 93
Tethering the Holocaust to German Colonial Theory
Kitty Millet

Part III. Looking East: Poland, the Ottoman Empire, 121
and Politicized Jihadism

6. Germany's Adventures in the Orient: 123
A History of Ambivalent Semicolonial Entanglements
Malte Fuhrmann

7. Arguing the Case for a Colonial Poland 146
Kristin Kopp

8. Colonialism, and No End: The Other Continuity Theses 164
Russell A. Berman

Part IV. Of Missionaries, Economics, 191
and Intranational Self-Perception

9. The Purpose of German Colonialism, or 193
the Long Shadow of Bismarck's Colonial Policy
Hartmut Pogge von Strandmann

10. Christian Missionary Societies in the German Colonies, 215
1884/85–1914/15
Ulrich van der Heyden

11. German Colonialism and the British Neighbor in Africa Before 254
1914: Self-Definitions, Lines of Demarcation, and Cooperation
Ulrike Lindner

Part V. Postcolonial German Politics 273

12. "Kalashnikovs, Not Coca-Cola, Bring Self-Determination 275
to Angola": The Two Germanys, Lusophone Africa, and
the Rhetoric of Colonial Difference
Luís Madureira

13. Germany, Palestine, Israel, and the (Post)Colonial Imagination 294
Martin Braach-Maksvytis

Contributors 315
Index 321

Acknowledgments

The initial idea for this collection of essays emerged from our conference "Germany's Colonialism in International Perspective: International Interdisciplinary Conference on German Colonialism and Post-Colonialism," held in September 2007 at San Francisco State University. Presentations at the conference revealed many different and, at times, contested assessments of Germany's colonial past. We decided to follow up on some of the heated debates, especially the ones surrounding what has been referred to as "the continuity thesis" and the possible link(s) between the Holocaust and Germany's imperial history in Africa. Apart from several contributors who attended the conference, we solicited additional contributions from colleagues to offer a wide range of responses to this topic.

The conference was generously sponsored by the College of Humanities and the College of Behavioral and Social Sciences at San Francisco State University, the Goethe-Institut of San Francisco, the Friedrich-Ebert-Stiftung, the German Academic Exchange Service (DAAD), the Heinrich Böll Foundation of North America, and the Holocaust Center of North America. We express our special appreciation to Paul Sherwin, Joel Kassiola, and Ulrich Everding for their unfailing support of our project from its very inception.

We would also like to acknowledge the faculty and staff of the College of Humanities and, particularly, our home Department of Foreign Languages and Literatures at San Francisco State University.

We would like to thank Bradley Naranch for his support. We are deeply indebted to Birthe Kundrus, Shelley Baranowski, Timothy Brennan, and A. Dirk Moses for their invaluable feedback. Bryan Aja, now a graduate student of German at the Department of Germanics at the University of Washington, offered a masterful English translation of Ulrich van der Heyden's essay. Rachel Friedman, now a UC Berkeley graduate student, provided superb editing of the introduction and the essays at the volume's early stages. Paul Listen, desktop editor of the first phase, offered his excellent skills in polishing the essays. In addition, we thank Kelly McGuire of Trent University (Canada), who has read the introduction and essays repeatedly and offered insightful feedback, and the anonymous reviewers, who offered us much advice in "getting it right." We also wish to thank Philip Leventhal and Anne McCoy at Columbia University Press, as well as our copy editor, Joe Abbott, for expertly assisting us at every stage of the publication process.

Finally, we wish to express our deepest appreciation and gratitude to our extended family: our wives—Noreen and Kelly—and our children: Salma, Isabelle, Otto, Malachi, Oliver, and Aliya.

DANKE / SHUKRAN for all your love and support.

Stade / Toronto

Introduction

Reconfiguring German Colonialism

Volker Langbehn and Mohammad Salama

> Only he who is oppressed by a present need, and who wants to throw off this burden at any cost, has need of critical history, that is to say a history that judges and condemns.
> —Friedrich Nietzsche

Holocaust historiography has undergone major changes in recent years. Discussions in the 1960s and 1970s centered on models of fascism, totalitarianism, or the historiography of Nazi Germany rather than the Holocaust per se. Beginning in the 1980s, historical research viewed either Nazi anti-Semitism or alternative concepts such as modernity, technology, race, and eugenics as the primary cause of the Holocaust.[1] In the past decade colonial aspects of the Nazi project have become an important research focus. Newly established frames of reference, which include genocide and globalization, have triggered a reevaluation and redefinition of the parameters within which to understand the Holocaust. Along the lines of delineating possible connections or similarities between the German colonial empire and Hitler's empire, historians are now increasingly locating the Holocaust within a broader frame of inquiry, notably the history of genocide.[2] Furthermore, the reemergence of Hannah Arendt's writings in contemporary research has fueled the interest in possible links between colonial genocide and the Holocaust.[3]

A new wave of historians reads the Herero and Nama war from 1904 to 1907 as a precursor to the National Socialist war of extermination. The historian Jürgen Zimmerer, for example, has argued that the type of warfare conducted in southwest Africa was fully realized in Europe only decades later.[4] Similarly, the sociologist George Steinmetz views the war as the first genocide of the twentieth century,[5] and even more directly, the anthropologist and political scientist Mahmood Mamdani argues that race was the link between the genocide of the Herero and the Nazi Holocaust.[6] These scholars advocate the view that Germany's colonial rule and the history of the Nama-Herero war have to be seen in a wider context of genocide in the twentieth century.[7] Challenging this argument, the historian Birthe Kundrus questions any continuity between colonialism, Nazism, and the Holocaust. Kundrus argues that there are fundamental differences in both the nature of the envisioned colonial orders and the means to achieve them.[8] She is not alone in her point of view. In her book *Absolute Destruction* Isabel Hull examines the German conduct of war from 1870 through 1918, including the Herero genocide. Even though she situates Germany's colonial practices in a broader European context of violence and calls the campaign against the Herero a war of "destruction," Hull does not think *genocide* is an appropriate term. Like Kundrus, Hull is hesitant to draw a direct link or a cause-effect relationship between the empire and the Holocaust.[9] Along the same lines, Pascal Grosse cautions against accepting the argument of a direct linkage between German colonialism and National Socialism. Instead, he advocates examining the biopolitical intellectual foundation, which he calls "racial order."[10] More recently, the historians Robert Gerwarth and Stephan Malinowski have suggested that the German war of annihilation constituted a break with European traditions of colonialism rather than their continuation. Both Gerwarth and Malinowski join Kundrus and Hull in questioning the merits of the term *genocide* for assessing the Herero uprising because the United Nations General Assembly only mandated the term in a declaration in 1946 and a convention in 1948. They also argue that using a more recent understanding of warfare to assess the Herero uprising is anachronistic and irrelevant.[11]

As these different viewpoints reveal, a serious approach to German colonialism cannot dissociate itself from the wider political, social, and cultural European and non-European contexts embedded in the contours of various economic, philosophical, historical, and anthropological traditions. Here we delineate the significance of the debates to set the frame for the following contributors' responses regarding the discontinuities, continuities, ruptures, or parallels between the German Empire and Nazi Germany. Our approach does not aim to be comprehensive but rather identifies the broad patterns and commonalities in the debates. Although we situate the debate within a larger context, we foreground the inherent tensions and differences among contributing scholars.

In his summary of the *Sonderweg* (special path) debate in German historical research in the 1970s and 1980s, the social historian Jürgen Kocka contends that "the proper place of National Socialism in German history and in a universal context continues to be one of the most crucial problems, perhaps the most crucial problem in German historical self-understanding."[12] As an advocate of the Sonderweg explanation of German history, Kocka's call to research National Socialism in German history within a universal context remains tied to delineating German peculiarities, not to advocating a broader conceptual or methodological approach to German historiography.[13] Historiographical restrictions also characterize the *Historikerstreit* (historian's dispute) of 1986 and 1987, about the uniqueness of Nazi crimes in comparison with Soviet atrocities. The suggested comparability of the "Final Solution" touches on a very important aspect of German *Vergangenheitsbewältigung* (coming to terms with the past), namely, the fear that comparability to other genocides would invite apologetics for Nazi crimes and evasion of responsibility and thereby burden any concept of German nationhood.[14]

Debates about the legacy of the Nazi past have resurfaced frequently over the past forty years, starting with the Auschwitz Trial during the early 1960s and further exemplified in the Bitburg controversy (1985), the *Wehrmachtsausstellung* (army exhibition) of the 1990s, the publication of Daniel Jonah Goldhagen's *Hitler's Willing Executioners* in 1996, and the heated debates surrounding the Holocaust memorial in Berlin in the early 2000s.[15] Although the debates represent important junctures in German national self-interrogation, they nonetheless underscore the difficulty of studying the Holocaust and its complex ramifications. After all, debates about the legacy and meaning of the Third Reich often cross the barriers of the academic environment and become imbricated in public culture because of Germany's continual preoccupation with its Nazi past since the 1960s.[16]

Without dwelling on the widely studied Sonderweg thesis and other debates, it is relevant to invoke Mark Levene's observation that the German Sonderweg thesis applies equally to other countries, such as Britain, France, and the United States, "on the grounds that their prototypicality made them a great deal more unusual than a Germany whose *dirigiste* response was very much the example adopted by other modernizing latecomers."[17] Levene's general study of genocide in the age of the nation-state suggests that genocide is a "function of empire and even intrinsic to its very nature."[18] Levene's provocative and insightful work analyzes the Holocaust as part of Nazi imperial visions that include eastern occupied territories. Nevertheless, placing the Holocaust within a broader framework of the history of genocide and European imperialism is not without opposition. Such highly contested visions of the Holocaust raise a crucial question: why do scholars in various disciplines differ so widely over the topic at hand?[19]

It is noteworthy that the latest investigation of the wider historical context of Nazi racialism in its connection to German colonialism has increasingly challenged established interpretative frameworks.[20] Numerous subdisciplines have begun to shape and influence the historiography of the Holocaust. The increasing fragmentation of historiography into subfields, especially genocide studies, one of the fastest-growing disciplines in academia, and modern anthropology, a conglomerate of disciplines, has assumed a central role in the study of colonialism.[21] It appears that the reliance on the political and economic relationships as the primary analytical focus for understanding colonialism has partially exhausted itself. A reading of the increased fragmentation into subdisciplines suggests diversity in the study of a possible similarity or continuity between Nazi Germany and the German Empire. One possible "framing" of these developments reflects an overall crisis of the "older cognitive and epistemological scientific world view" as characteristic of the postmodern condition, a challenge Saul Friedländer recognized more than a decade ago.[22] While the postmodern condition appears to have signified a turn from metanarratives to micronarratives, the recent surge in scholarship with an emphasis on race as a conceptual or methodological framework to measure genocides outside of Europe against the Holocaust seems to suggest a return to grand narratives, a return that has a different philosophical underpinning yet the same results.

The debates about "uniqueness," "singularity," or "unprecedentedness" of the Holocaust have reached an "unproductive intellectual and moral stalemate."[23] How are we to address the topic of genocide, and how do we write about German colonialism and the Holocaust? We must situate the apparent conundrum of continuity and discontinuity. As the contributors to this volume demonstrate, we must approach the question of continuity and discontinuity from a transnational, transcultural, and interdisciplinary perspective that is not contained within geographical, political, or cultural boundaries. After all, the notion of continuity and discontinuity derives its impetus and definitions from mutual interdependencies of and influences by other imperial cultures. Colonialism has always been imbricated in the cultural process, a process whose boundaries are permeable.[24] As Edward Said has maintained, culture is not a matter of ownership "but rather of appropriations, common experiences, and interdependencies of all kinds among different cultures. This is a universal norm."[25] The mutual interdependencies of European imperial cultures direct our attention to the unevenness of the processes of social, cultural, and political transformation. Considering the mutual interdependencies disable a comprehensive view of "real" history, the idea of being able to determine "how it really was," and demonstrates that there are neither authentic cultures nor authentic cultural realities, nor even cultures that are wholly organically unified or traditionally continuous.[26]

The debate about "continuity" and "discontinuity" between German colonialism and the genocide of Nazi Germany has to reflect on and move beyond existing structures of established historiographic boundaries. We evaluate history neither as the progression toward a purported goal nor as the unfolding of a comprehensible whole. We define history as a text that constitutes itself *only* in relation to other texts and historical contexts and thereby defines its unity as relative and variable.

A different way to address the volume's main theme is to invoke a Freudian play between the uncanny and familiar from the past to the present. Because of the continuous reinscription of the past through its relevance for the present, a new structure of knowledge emerges; our understanding of the past undergoes changes. The ghost of "continuity" will not fade away; it is here to stay, for better or worse, but with many different faces and within variable (con)texts. Nietzsche summarizes our discussion when he advocates a critical history. For Nietzsche a critical history recognizes the misdeeds of the past and concurrently liberates people from dominant forms of historical representation. The interpretation of a possible link between colonialism and the genocide of the Third Reich must always include the investigation of one's own cultural, intellectual, and ideological position vis-à-vis the multiple imbrications of these events outside their familiar grounds (to insist on the Freudian trope). If we follow Nietzsche's and Freud's lead, critical history disrupts our understanding of history anchored within the binary frame of a rather homogenous notion of change or discontinuity, and even of colonialism as a coherent object of inquiry.

German Colonialism contextualizes the rise of German overseas protectorates within the history of late-nineteenth- and early-twentieth-century globalization. The chapters extend and complicate arguments that Germany's early colonial retirement is either a finale to an age of imperial expansionism or a prelude to Nazism. Yet both the history and the functional analysis of existing literature on German colonialism, especially following 1966, show careful critical approaches attempting to balance different and conflicting interests that move far beyond the colonial discourse itself. While there is a risk—and there is always a risk—that our own collection might itself be a microcosm of such inherent interdisciplinary tensions, it is today's Germany that is also implicated in light of those tensions. As Geoff Eley adeptly puts it in *A Crooked Line*, historians are inevitably influenced by the settings in which they operate.[27] This axiom prompts us to investigate what kinds of present intradisciplinary and interdisciplinary shifts are capable of assimilating or consolidating Germany's colonial past in light of the continuity thesis. Some history is always useful in this context. For example, when the Sonderweg thesis came under attack in the 1980s, many historians argued that critiques of Germany's colonial experience had been distorted in comparison with those of England and France.[28] Now, more than three decades later, and after dwelling on the complexities of such crucial events in Germany's recent past, it is difficult to make the same argument, especially after a new generation of German historians and scholars has taken up the task of radically investigating and questioning the traditional picture of Germany's imperial history.

We have asked contributors to consider the continuity thesis in broad and pluralistic terms and to challenge, where appropriate, forms of conventional wisdom regarding its place within the historical contexts of transnational imperialism and cultural modernity in the late nineteenth and twentieth centuries. The resulting collection is a balanced set of chapters by scholars who specialize in cultural, intellectual, or gender history and who are versed in postcolonial discourse analysis, among other various fields. The volume incorporates topics of great relevance to German imperial history, such as Malte Fuhrmann's intriguing argument that the difficulty in historicizing the *Kaiserreich*'s involvement with the Ottoman Empire lies in historians' almost futile task of constructing a valid and sustained narrative of Germany's relation to the East while ignoring the very volatility that characterized Germany's relationship to Turkey, Greece, Armenia, and the former Yugoslavia. As reflected in this volume, debates over the sociopolitical implications of Germany's colonial past indicate that accurate assessments of this sensitive period in the country's modern history cannot be reached outside historical specificities, and then only within definite parameters inside those specificities. The discursive possibilities of this task are understandably colossal and involve many epistemic fields: anthropology, sociology, race and gender studies, religion, economics, national politics, international competition, and philosophy. Such imperial varieties have led to substantial modifications of the role of the German historian and cultural theorist and have further redefined political affiliations.

The chapters in the volume fall into five thematic parts: (1) Colonial (Dis)Continuities: Framing the Issue, (2) *Lebensraum* and Genocide, (3) Looking East: Poland, the Ottoman Empire, and Politicized Jihadism, (4) Of Missionaries, Economics, and Intranational Self-Perception, and (5) Postcolonial German Politics. All five parts engage from various angles the central question of this volume: Are there any possible connections between acts of colonial genocide in German Southwest Africa during the early 1900s and Nazi genocidal practices on the eastern and western fronts during the Second World War, including the Holocaust?

The contributors shed a different historical light on late-nineteenth-century and twentieth-century Germany, approaching its coloniality both vertically and horizontally at the same time—vertically, by introducing racial, religious, cultural, sociopolitical, and philosophical issues at the heart of Germany's transitions from the colonial to the postcolonial (Brennan, Millet, Moses, Baranowski); and horizontally, by looking at Germany through the broader scope of comparative colonialism (Kundrus, Lindner, Fuhrmann, Berman, Kopp, Braach-Maksvytis, Madureira).

The chapters bring together diverse attempts by active and influential scholars from North America, Great Britain, Australia, and Germany to reevaluate existing perceptions in the study of Germany's colonial regime. This is one of the main reasons this volume is unique and timely. Even though the study of Germany's colonial past has experienced a dramatic transformation in its scope of inquiry and significance, such interest did not take place until the 1980s. As Russell A. Berman points out in his contribution, this epoch was not necessarily productive of full-fledged and developed theories on German colonialism, an epoch where "high literary theory, the critique of colonialism, understood as the imperial practices of Western states during the nineteenth century, was rapidly conflated with a deconstructive critique of Western metaphysics." This critique, reflected in the works of Michel Foucault, Michel de Certeau, Robert Young, and others,[29] did open the door to a reconsideration of Western metaphysics, but what was most urgently needed was "a profound reconfiguration of anticolonial discourse, the association of which with deconstructive philosophical paradigms," Berman contends, "was surely counterintuitive."

While there have been some monographic attempts and effective studies on German colonialism since then, they have had little or nothing to say about what may have existed in nineteenth-century Germany in the way of larger political visions. All of those works nicely encapsulate the regional context of Germany's colonial adventures, but they do not offer anything whatsoever about the wider horizontal and vertical connections between Germany's colonial past and the unfolding expansion of the Third Reich, the full panoply of Germany's postcolonial ideological and cultural inclinations, or the relationship of Germany to the overall framework of imperial policy making in Europe.

The desire to manage Germany's colonial experience is prompted by the desire to understand, come to terms with, and in some cases complicate a past that has until very recently been repressed or considered insignificant. This "management" has yielded a range of results that are reflected in this volume. The question of race, for instance, has received considerable attention. After Hannah Arendt's inaugural work *The Origins of Totalitarianism*, the question of genocide received pointed critical attention from different historical perspectives. Arendt has argued that race as a political device "was discovered in South Africa." The Boers' extermination of Hottentot tribes, the brutal Maji Maji Rebellion massacres in German Southeast Africa, and the decimation of the Congo population were an "escape into irresponsibility where nothing human could any longer exist."[30] Scholars such as Hajo Holborn, Mahmood Mamdani, and Sven Lindqvist have made similar arguments, the latter even describing the Holocaust as an event "born at the meeting point of two traditions that marked modern Western civilization: the anti-Semitic tradition and the tradition of genocide of colonized peoples."[31] New studies in this volume further complicate the question of race, as well as the contested existence of a subtle line between the Congo and Auschwitz.

The assembled chapters come together through a historically nuanced and detailed framework for future investigation of the putative links connecting the genocidal campaigns of colonial wars, the brutal and destructive campaigns of the First World War, and later manifestations of Nazi expansionism, racial politics, and colonial practices. Although all chapters are brought together by their attempts to understand the question of continuity and discontinuity, a major source of tension is still apparent in the disagreement over the nature and purpose of German colonialism among eminent German historians. For example, in the volume's first section, Framing the Issue, Timothy Brennan opens a new chapter in the continuity thesis and brings us face-to-face with deeper roots of the colonial expansionism underlying Nietzsche's philosophy.

Brennan revisits Nietzsche not just to extend existing arguments but, more important, to radically reexamine Nietzsche's writings on colonialism. Brennan acknowledges Adorno's and Horkheimer's argument in *Dialectic of Enlightenment* that Nietzsche viewed German colonialism as embracing world-historical missions. He identifies Carl Schmitt's enthusiastic support of Nietzsche's view of foreign conquest and the subjugation of lesser peoples as a "fundamental philosophical doctrine,"[32] a position Adorno and Horkheimer opposed. Ultimately Brennan maintains that some of Nietzsche's writings on the subject either remain neglected or have been misunderstood. For example, Brennan shows that Nietzsche's passion for colonialism goes hand in hand with his position on the "lower classes" and early "communist movements" in Germany. In fact, Brennan finds in Nietzsche startling proof of a larger rhetorical posture on the European right that was later developed in the interwar era." Brennan goes on to show how scholars writing on colonialism in Germany today are unaware of or unwilling to acknowledge their strong dependence on and continuation of Nietzschean modes of thought. Brennan's critique of Nietzsche raises important questions of political and moral responsibility, as well as identity and self-assurance in a postcolonial and unified Germany looking forward to political and economic stability among its European counterparts.

While "continuity" arguments depend on an understanding of a complex set of relationships between colonial past and postcolonial desire for normalcy in a multicultural age, "discontinuity" arguments, especially the one Kundrus presents here, are concerned mainly with situating Germany's brief colonial venture in relation to a long period of global imperialism. Like the position taken by Ulrike Lindner in this volume, Kundrus places the German experience within the larger context of European colonialism. But unlike Lindner, who compares Germany's and Great Britain's relationships mainly to their respective African colonies, Kundrus advocates a careful use of the discriminatory power of the colonialism concept. Kundrus's "reflections" aim chiefly to explain how, when, and why such a "fleeting... phase" of German colonialism took place in terms of changes within Europe that led to the emergence of hierarchical and race-oriented systems around 1900.

It should be noted that whereas "continuity" and "discontinuity" advocates view German colonialism from different perspectives, their studies are similarly admonitory in tone. Brennan's chapter implies that the trivialization of Germany's colonial past may lead to present and future abandonment of political responsibility. Kundrus insists on a contextual understanding of German colonialism that—though concerned with comparing Germany to more established European empires—does so only to warn against the dangerous effects of the abuses and misapplications of the term *colonialism* to the German experience.

Another source of disagreement concerns a notable difference between historians, on the one hand, and literary critics, on the other. German historians are frequently ambivalent toward the aforementioned influence of theory and tend to use it cautiously and infrequently. By contrast, literary critics are bound to consider German colonialism in relation to an existing body of theory. For these reasons discussions between historians and littérateurs often arrive at an insuperable impasse. A. Dirk Moses takes aim at the heart of the well-established tradition among historians to regard Hannah Arendt's seminal work *The Origins of Totalitarianism* as espousing a continuity thesis of German colonialism and Nazism. Moses argues, instead, that Arendt held the Holocaust to be unprecedented because it was governed by a nonutilitarian logic of extermination as an end in itself. Any continuity between imperialism and Nazism, Moses contends, does not lie with Germany's colonial scene in Africa but with continental German imperial aspirations in the form of the Pan-Germans. Moses critiques what he considers to be Arendt's provincial perspective on the Holocaust by highlighting how the event can be understood as a secular happening in world history, governed by the logics of race, security, and paranoia common to all genocides. Like Kundrus, Moses sees British and other Western imperial cultures as the source of the German thought that produced Hitler's Nazis. Meanwhile, Kitty Millet's chapter invokes the philosopher and literary critic Philippe Lacoue-Labarthe's literary theory of the "caesura" in her argument for the uniqueness of the Holocaust and her critique of theories that tend to subsume it under the grander history of German colonialism. Aiming to make visible the stakes of tethering the Holocaust to German colonial theory as it is understood in the continuity thesis, Millet manages to demonstrate that the values underwriting the Reich are not reducible to the historical precedents of imperial Germany. In offering an interesting perspective on Jews in the Nazi imagination and vision, Millet ultimately attempts to differentiate between this and

German colonialism through an analysis of smaller-scale phenomena within Germany that she sees as being essentially representative of the same patterns of thinking that resulted in Nazi attitudes toward Jews. Like Kundrus, Millet opts for discontinuity. Unlike Kundrus, whose discontinuity thesis springs from a recognition of the relatively small extent of Germany's colonial adventures when compared to colonial avatars like Britain and France, Millet's call for discontinuity, informed in part by Wlad Godzich's "never-forget" position on the topic, emerges from an inalienable postwar Jewish identity that is formed and informed by the brutality of the Holocaust.

Steering away from the continuity and rupture thesis, Luís Madureira breaks new ground in revealing a coloniality of power in Germany in its whole colonial and postcolonial historical development. A strong advocate of historical specificity, Madureira addresses West and East Germany's relations with Mozambique from a peripheral and therefore "non-German" perspective. By closely examining Germany's foreign and trade policies with Portugal before and after the independence of its African colonies, Madureira argues that a comparative historical reassessment of Germany's colonial past and present with regard to commercial ties to Portugal, on the one hand, and similar nations in Africa, on the other, is crucial for a better understanding of the German colonial experience in Africa.

What Madureira does with Portugal, Kristin Kopp does with Poland, albeit from a different perspective. Citing references to Poland in Germany's imperial rhetoric as a "colonial country," Kopp interrogates the National Socialists' reorganization of eastern Europe during World War II and its ramifications for Germany's "internal" colonial discourse throughout Europe. In contrast to research that seeks to link the Herero uprising to eastern Europe in 1939, Kopp focuses her investigation "from late-nineteenth-century inner colonization to the *Generalplan Ost*, from precolonial overseas colonial fantasies to postcolonial irredentist claims, and, indeed, from German Southwest Africa to Poland." The expansion of the temporal and spatial frame of inquiry enables her to illuminate the possible link between Africa and eastern Europe and to assist in a comparative study of both genocides.

Shelley Baranowski and Russell A. Berman discuss other variations on the continuity-rupture thesis. Baranowski uses *Lebensraum* and genocide in the Third Reich as axiomatic references to draw attention to the importance of incorporating National Socialism and its radicalization of notions of race and identity into the larger context of German and European colonialism. Baranowski takes this continuity position while aware of Kundrus's forceful argument that in the Nazi regime the Jews occupied a much different imaginative space than Africans. Baranowski insists, however, that taken together, the priority list of the Nazi regime, the case of *Lebensraum* in the East, and the annihilation of the Jews "demand at least equal attention to National Socialism's dissimilarities from previous colonial experience." Berman draws on Arendt's *The Origins of Totalitarianism* to emphasize two continuities linking German colonialism to the aftermath of the Holocaust: communist internationalism and the rise of Nazi-inspired Islamism in the Middle East. Berman's reading of German colonialism through a cultural and literary studies lens gives him an excellent opportunity to investigate such continuities in the works of Bertolt Brecht. He expands on research done by Matthias Küntzel on the relationship between Nazi foreign policy and the incipient Islamism of the Muslim Brotherhood during the 1930s and 1940s.

A growing interest in postcolonial studies that borrows from social and cultural history, anthropology, literary criticism, religious studies, philosophy, and political psychology has opened new methodological and theoretical possibilities in the field of German colonialism. In this volume the discussion of German colonialism is not limited to traditional historical approaches, nor is colonial and postcolonial culture regarded as a variable that can be measured and quantified to establish causality, continuity, or rupture. Yet one of our major aims is to introduce new avenues of inquiry in areas where further research seems particularly promising. Among those chapters, the contributions by Hartmut Pogge von Strandmann and Ulrich van der Heyden share a common demand for historical specificity in German colonialism. At the outset, Pogge von Strandmann takes issue with Ronald Robinson's and J. A. Gallagher's seminal contribution to the early studies of European colonialism and their oft-cited distinction between "formal" and "informal" empire. Attempting to explain the process of decolonization as a response to a failure to find willing local "collaborators," Robinson and Gallagher purposefully set out to provide an anti-Marxist rationale for the establishment of British (and European) colonies in Africa.[33] This argument has led to unresolved and heated debates between opposing schools, especially in connection with the importance both writers ascribe to the economic dictates of colonialism at the expense of the political and nationalist imperatives. Pogge von Strandmann uses the case of German colonialism to argue that Robinson and Gallagher are inaccurate in their general assessment of British and European colonialism. He dismisses Robinson's and Gallagher's conclusions as hurried and unfounded, especially when they claim there is no substantial documentation demonstrating the influence of business circles on the decision-making process leading to imperialist policies and that there was no "unofficial mind" of imperialism. Pogge von Strandmann provides evidence that in the case of Germany's business interests, missionary societies and pressure groups worked together with the government to acquire colonies in Africa and the Far East in the 1880s. He further argues that the creation of Germany's so-called protectorates followed in the footsteps of business interests after the government had been alerted to their special needs. According to Pogge von Strandmann, it was evident that economic arguments provided the main rationale for Germany's overseas expansion. This entrepreneurial expansion led to the acquisition of what he refers to as "a haphazard collection of the colonial territories" and to the subsequent establishment of a *Kolonialrat* (colonial council), which Pogge von Strandmann defines as the communication channel between the interests concerned and the Colonial Department.

Pogge von Strandmann's passing reference to missionary societies receives pivotal attention in Ulrich van der Heyden's chapter, which finds startling connections between German colonialism and Christian missionary work. Heyden's outlook on Germany's Protestant Christian missionary work (as both a record of civilization and barbarism) constitutes the heart of his argument. He uses case studies from Germany's colonies in Africa, in the South Pacific, and in China to argue that German missionary societies were part of a whole civilizing process that amounted to nothing other than a continuation of the colonial exploitation and oppression of the native labor force. Heyden argues that, consciously or unconsciously, German Protestantism was a tool of Germany's colonial expansion from 1884 to 1914 and that despite the occasional critiques of the principles of their Christian mission, few if any missionaries questioned their colonial imperative. Heyden concludes by demonstrating how German Protestant missionaries served as henchmen of the colonial administration regardless of their subjective desires. German missionary societies were thus purveyors of colonialism.

Martin Braach-Maksvytis presents a provocative perspective on Germany's postcolonial relationship with Israel. In this relationship Germany continues what Braach-Maksvytis refers to as a "*redemptive proxy-colonialism*" that complicates the postcolonial and postnationalist German psyche. If Germany's ties with Israel stem from a surrogate search for lost colonies and excessive compensation for the Holocaust, then this special relationship must be based vicariously on a "common colonial imagination that the debates about German post-colonialism have so far overlooked." Assuming that the major components of this relationship are post–World War II German guilt and colonial imagination, Braach-Maksvytis explains the special forms it took in terms of the rise of orientalism and the changing relationship between Europe and the Middle East. Braach-Maksvytis's thesis is that after the Second World War, "the political and cultural functionality of a 'rapprochement' with Israel bears similarities to the German quest for the return of its colonies in the course of the Weimar Republic." This provocative argument makes one wonder if, indeed, there is a political "proxy" at work on a deeper psychological level between Germany and Israel.

Each study in this volume has been crafted to investigate literary or historical aspects of Germany's colonial heritage. Broadly speaking, one can distinguish four general approaches to this inquiry. Some contributors (Moses, Madureira, Berman) attempt new theories of German colonialism. Others (Millet, Fuhrmann, Kopp, Braach-Maksvytis) employ and extend existing theories to support their arguments. A third group (Kundrus, Baranowski) addresses the topic while avoiding theory altogether. In the fourth group (Moses, Berman, Pogge von Strandmann, Heyden, Brennan) the analysis itself rereads and challenges existing theories. While the chapters presented here by no means exhaust the topic of German colonialism, they do contribute something new and essential to the core of the subject in a manner that has never before been addressed in a single volume.

In setting the scope and thematic objectives for this volume, we have drawn inspiration from the pioneering 1998 collection *The Imperialist Imagination: German Colonialism and Its Legacy*, as well as from *Tensions of Empire: Colonial Cultures in a Bourgeois World* and other recently published anthologies.[34] In their introduction the editors of *The Imperialist Imagination*, devoted to the literary analysis of colonial texts, allude to existing debates on the possible connections between colonialism and National Socialism, without, however, providing substantial engagement. Susanne Zantop, in her other writings, has alluded to a possible link between the racial imagination of the empire and the Holocaust. In her cautiously worded reference to the topic, she framed the issue as follows: "We need to analyze and explain why it was *not* the enlightened models of tolerance and assimilation that prevailed, but racism, xenophobia, sexism, and aggressive expansionism."[35] In contrast to these works, a primary emphasis in this volume is the cross-disciplinary inquiry into the social, political, and military (dis)continuities of German colonialism.[36] Our goal is not only to advance and extend earlier discussions surrounding previous controversies such as the Historians' Debate and Goldhagen's *Hitler's Willing Executioners* but also to open new horizons in the field of German colonialism. All of the chapters in this volume confirm one thing: placing the debates about the singularity and uniqueness of the Holocaust in relationship to colonialism provides new ways of reading Germany's colonial history.

German Colonialism constitutes a *Standortbestimmung* (current state of research) that counters the widespread assumption that German colonialism was merely a marginal episode in German history that did not have ramifications for political and cultural life. It also documents how German colonialism in its various forms was intertwined with the inner workings of modern German life and society, revealing *how* German colonialism played a significant role in shaping German perceptions of racial difference and contributed to the construction of German nationalism. It is the editors' hope that the chapters in this volume will add an extensive sociohistorical and cultural perspective to the continuity debates. Despite the different approaches and methods adopted, the volume reveals why Germany's colonial past should be viewed as an important historical presence in debates over German identity and history.

We understand that the life of a nation is a continuum, and Germany is no exception. But we try to show that continuity has larger implications, as well as interpretations. Some theories in this volume regard German colonialism and the Holocaust only as ruptures and catastrophes that destroy all that is past and shatter all connections with the great and glorious; such theories run counter to other evolutionary theses of historical reformism also represented in this volume. The latter see nothing but continuity; the former see nothing but ruptures, fissures, and catastrophes. We choose to present both sides of the coin, with the understanding that any valid argument depends on a substantiated appreciation of content while history remains an inaccessible living dialectic of both continuity and discontinuity. At the heart of this volume is the question of whether the Holocaust can be understood, at least in part, as a result of aspects of colonialism (Madureira, Berman) or whether it should be perceived from a different perspective altogether, one that questions the pertinence of sequential logic of cause and effect for the singularity of the event (Kundrus, Millet).[37]

In the end we choose to emphasize the dialectic of break and continuity, aware that the choice between continuity and rupture is understandably one of critical inclination. Nevertheless, we are equally cognizant that it is also one of deciding beginnings and endings. This choice cannot simply be justified by historical evidence or (post)colonial "material," so to speak, since it is in the nature of the choice to organize and select its own evidence and material, as it is reflected in the volume's opening arguments by Brennan and Kundrus. We contend, however, that such critical choices can themselves be reconstructed as facts that generate their own causalities. In Germany today this debate reflects an oscillation between the perception of the Holocaust as a singular and unprecedented historical event and the apprehension of it as a cultural outcome of a short but intense isolated period in Germany's colonial history. The same logic applies to Germany's colonial experience with assessments both locally, on domestic levels including postcolonial German culture, race, and identity, and globally, on an international and comparative level, especially the consideration of German colonialism vis-à-vis the British or French examples. In both cases the choice between continuity and rupture is a sign of Germany's unresolved historical tensions and of the postcolonial condition in general. The choice between continuity and rupture thus evokes not only the temporality of historical thought in contemporary Germany but also the succumbing to colonial guilt and the critique of the present. The volume localizes the question of causality in German colonialism, a question that involves the construction of a new narrative with different beginnings and with different ways of seeing them.

Notes

We would like to acknowledge the invaluable feedback offered by Birthe Kundrus, Shelley Baranowski, and especially A. Dirk Moses.

1. See the excellent summary of research by Dan Stone, "The Holocaust and Its Historiography"; see also Burleigh and Wippermann, *The Racial State*.
2. See Mazower, *Hitler's Empire*; and Moses, *Empire, Colony, Genocide*.
3. See King and Stone, *Hannah Arendt and the Uses of History*.
4. Zimmerer and Zeller, *Völkermord in Deutsch-Südwestafrika*, 70; available in translation as *Genocide in German South-West Africa*. See also Zimmerer, "Colonialism and the Holocaust"; and Zimmerer, "The Birth of the *Ostland* Out of the Spirit of Colonialism." One of the early proponents on the topic was Smith, *The Ideological Origins of Nazi Imperialism*.
5. Steinmetz, "The First Genocide of the 20th Century and Its Postcolonial Afterlives."

6. Mamdani, *When Victims Become Killers*.

7. Other advocates of the continuity thesis are Trotha, "Genozidaler Pazifizierungskrieg"; and Gewald, *Herero Heroes*. Many other recent publications respond in different ways to the continuity argument. See Furber and Lower, "Colonialism and Genocide in Nazi-Occupied Poland and Ukraine"; Smith, *The Continuities of German History*; Benz, *Ausgrenzung, Vertreibung, Völkermord*, 27–53; Madley, "From Africa to Auschwitz"; Madley, "Patterns of Frontier Genocide, 1803–1910"; Brehl, "'Ich denke, die haben Ihnen zum Tode verholfen'"; Dabag, Gründer, and Ketelsen, "Einleitung"; Brehl, "(Ein) Geborene Feinde"; Dabag, "National-koloniale Konstruktionen in politischen Entwürfen des Deutschen Reiches um 1900"; Böttger, "Zivilisierung der Vernichtung."

8. Kundrus, *Phantasiereiche*.

9. See Hull, *Absolute Destruction*; see also her "Military Culture and the Production of 'Final Solutions' in the Colonies."

10. Grosse, "What Does German Colonialism Have to Do with National Socialism? 118.

11. Gerwarth and Malinowski, "Der Holocaust als 'kolonialer Genozid'?"; and Gerwarth and Malinowski, "Hannah Arendt's Ghosts."

12. Kocka, "German History Before Hitler," 11. The German *Sonderweg* thesis was articulated by Fritz Fischer in the 1960s.

13. The leading advocates of the Sonderweg thesis are Hans-Ulrich Wehler (see his *Deutsche Gesellschaftsgeschichte, 1849–1914*, 1109–68; and *Das Deutsche Kaiserreich, 1871–1918*); Thomas Nipperdey (see his *Deutsche Geschichte, 1800–1918*); and Klaus Hildebrand (see his *Das vergangene Reich*).

14. See Charles Maier's succinct summary of the Historians' Debate in Maier, *The Unmasterable Past*; and Theodor Adorno's 1959 essay "The Meaning of Working Through the Past," which exposes the oxymoronic nature of the term.

15. Moses, *German Intellectuals and the Nazi Past*; Goldhagen, *Hitler's Willing Executioners*; Shandley, *Unwilling Germans?* For the Historians' Debate see Knowlton, *Forever in the Shadow of Hitler?*

16. See Eley, "Ordinary Germans, Nazism, and Judeocide."

17. Levene, *The Meaning of Genocide*, 184.

18. Levene, *The Rise of the West and the Coming of Genocide*, 217.

19. Stone, introduction to *The Historiography of Genocide*, 2. See also Moses, "Conceptual Blockages and Definitional Dilemmas in the 'Racial Century.'"

20. Notable changes have taken place in anthropology; see, e.g., Hinton, *Genocide*.

21. Stone, introduction to *The Historiography of Genocide*, 1. See also Bloxham and Moses, *The Oxford Handbook of Genocide Studies*.

22. Jameson, foreword to *The Postmodern Condition*, by Jean-François Lyotard, xi. See also Friedländer, *Probing the Limits of Representation*; and Lyotard, *The Postmodern Explained*.

23. Moses, "Conceptual Blockages and Definitional Dilemmas in the 'Racial Century,'" 10. For a quasi summary of the debate see Rosenfeld, "The Politics of Uniqueness"; Rosenbaum, *Is the Holocaust Unique?*; and Margalit and Motzkin, "The Uniqueness of the Holocaust."

24. See Langbehn, *German Colonialism, Visual Culture, and Modern Memory*.

25. Said, *Culture and Imperialism*, 217.

26. See Clifford, *The Predicament of Culture*, esp. chap. 11, "On *Orientalism*."

27. Eley, *A Crooked Line*.

28. See Eley and Blackbourn, *The Peculiarities of German History*.

29. See Foucault, *The Archaeology of Knowledge*; Certeau, *The Writing of History*; and Young, *White Mythologies*.

30. Arendt, *The Origins of Totalitarianism*, 207.

31. Lindqvist, *"Exterminate All the Brutes"*; Holborn, *A History of Modern Germany*.

32. Schmitt, *Glossarium*, 309.

33. See Robinson and Gallagher, *Africa and the Victorians*; see also Pogge von Strandmann, *Imperialismus vom Grünen Tisch*.

34. See Friedrichsmeyer, Lennox, and Zantop, *The Imperialist Imagination*; and Cooper and Stoler, *Tensions of Empire*. More recent publications include Conrad and Sachsenmaier, *Competing Visions of World Order*; Wendt, *Kolonialismus zur Globalisierung*; Conrad, Eckert, and Freitag, *Globalgeschichte*; and Dirlik, *Global Modernity*.

35. Zantop, *Colonial Fantasies*, 16 (our italics).

36. See also Ballantyne and Burton, *Bodies in Contact*; and Honold and Scherpe, *Mit Deutschland um die Welt*.

37. See Godzich, "The Holocaust."

Bibliography

Adorno, Theodor W. "The Meaning of Working Through the Past." In *Critical Models: Interventions and Catchwords*, translated by Henry W. Pickford, 89–103. New York: Columbia University Press, 1998.

Arendt, Hannah. *The Origins of Totalitarianism*. Orlando: Harvest Books, 1976.

Ballantyne, Tony, and Antoinette Burton, eds. *Bodies in Contact: Rethinking Colonial Encounters in World History*. Durham, NC: Duke University Press, 2005.

Benz, Wolfgang. *Ausgrenzung, Vertreibung, Völkermord: Genozid im 20. Jahrhundert*. Munich: Deutscher Taschenbuch, 2006.

Bloxham, Donald, and A. Dirk Moses, eds. *The Oxford Handbook of Genocide Studies*. Oxford: Oxford University Press, 2010.

Böttger, Hans Henning. "Zivilisierung der Vernichtung: Hererokrieg, Eingeborene und Eingeborenenrecht im Kolonialdiskurs." *Zeitschrift für Genozidforschung* 4, no. 1 (2002): 22–63.

Brehl, Medardus. "(Ein) Geborene Feinde: Der Entwurf existentieller Feindschaft im Kolonialdiskurs." In *Feindschaft*, edited by Kerstin Platt and Medardus Brehl, 157–77. Munich: Wilhelm Fink, 2003.

———. "'Ich denke, die haben Ihnen zum Tode verholfen': Koloniale Gewalt in kollektiver Rede." In Dabag, Gründer, and Ketelsen, *Kolonialismus*, 185–215. Munich: Wilhelm Fink, 2004.

Burleigh, Michael, and Wolfgang Wippermann. *The Racial State: Germany, 1933–1945*. Cambridge, UK: Cambridge University Press, 1993.

Certeau, Michel de. *The Writing of History*. Translated by Tom Conley. New York: Columbia University Press, 1988.

Clifford, James. *The Predicament of Culture: Twentieth-Century Ethnography, Literature, and Art*. Cambridge, MA: Harvard University Press, 1988.

Conrad, Sebastian, and Dominic Sachsenmaier, eds. *Competing Visions of World Order: Global Moments and Movements, 1880s–1930s*. New York: Palgrave Macmillan, 2007.

Conrad, Sebastian, Andreas Eckert, and Ulrike Freitag, eds. *Globalgeschichte: Theorien, Ansätze, Themen*. Frankfurt: Campus, 2007.

Cooper, Frederick, and Ann Laura Stoler. *Tensions of Empire: Colonial Cultures in a Bourgeois World*. Berkeley: University of California Press, 1997.

Dabag, Mihran. "National-koloniale Konstruktionen in politischen Entwürfen des Deutschen Reiches um 1900." In Dabag, Gründer, and Ketelsen, *Kolonialismus*, 19–66. Munich: Wilhelm Fink, 2004.

Dabag, Mihran, Horst Gründer, and Uwe-K. Ketelsen. "Einleitung." In Dabag, Gründer, and Ketelsen, *Kolonialismus*, 7–18.

———, eds. *Kolonialismus: Kolonialdiskurs und Genozid*. Munich: Wilhelm Fink, 2004.

Dirlik, Arif. *Global Modernity: Modernity in the Age of Global Capitalism*. Boulder, CO: Paradigm, 2007.

Eley, Geoff. *A Crooked Line: From Cultural History to the History of Society*. Ann Arbor: University of Michigan Press, 2005.

———. "Ordinary Germans, Nazism, and Judeocide." In *The "Goldhagen Effect": History, Memory, Nazism—Facing the German Past*, edited by Geoff Eley, 1–31. Ann Arbor: University of Michigan Press, 2000.

Eley, Geoff, and David Blackbourn. *The Peculiarities of German History: Bourgeois Society and Politics in Nineteenth-Century Germany*. Oxford: Oxford University Press, 1984.

Foucault, Michel. *The Archaeology of Knowledge*. London: Routledge, 1989.

Friedländer, Saul, ed. *Probing the Limits of Representation: Nazism and the "Final Solution."* Cambridge, MA: Harvard University Press, 1992.

Friedrichsmeyer, Sara, Sara Lennox, and Susanne Zantop, eds. *The Imperialist Imagination: German Colonialism and Its Legacy*. Ann Arbor: University of Michigan Press, 1998.

Furber, David, and Wendy Lower. "Colonialism and Genocide in Nazi-Occupied Poland and Ukraine." In Moses, *Empire, Colony, Genocide*, 372–400.

Gerwarth, Robert, and Stephan Malinowski. "Der Holocaust als 'kolonialer Genozid'? Europäische Kolonialgewalt und nationalsozialistischer Vernichtungskrieg." *Geschichte und Gesellschaft* 33, no.3 (2007): 439–66.

———. "Hannah Arendt's Ghosts: Reflections on the Disputable Path from Windhoek to Auschwitz." *Central European History* 42 (2009): 279–300.

Gewald, Jan-Bart. *Herero Heroes: A Socio-Political History of the Herero of Namibia, 1890–1923*. Oxford: James Currey, 1999.

Godzich, Wlad. "The Holocaust: Questions for the Humanities." *Partial Answers: Journal of Literature and the History of Ideas* 7, no.1 (2008): 133–48.

Goldhagen, Daniel Jonah. *Hitler's Willing Executioners: Ordinary Germans and the Holocaust*. New York: Knopf, 1996.

Grosse, Pascal. "What Does German Colonialism Have to Do with National Socialism? A Conceptual Framework." In *Germany's Colonial Pasts*, edited by Eric Ames, Marcia Klotz, and Lora Wildenthal, 115–43. Lincoln: University of Nebraska Press, 2005.

Hildebrand, Klaus. *Das vergangene Reich: Deutsche Außenpolitik von Bismarck bis Hitler*. Berlin: Ullstein, 1999.

Hinton, Alexander L., ed. *Genocide: An Anthropological Reader*. Oxford: Blackwell, 2002.

Holborn, Hajo. *A History of Modern Germany, 1840–1945*. Princeton, NJ: Princeton University Press, 1982.

Honold, Alexander, and Klaus R. Scherpe, eds. *Mit Deutschland um die Welt: Eine Kulturgeschichte des Fremden in der Kolonialzeit*. Stuttgart: J. B. Metzler, 2004.

Hull, Isabel. *Absolute Destruction: Military Culture and the Practices of War in Imperial Germany*. Ithaca, NY: Cornell University Press, 2005.

———. "Military Culture and the Production of 'Final Solutions' in the Colonies." In *The Specter of Genocide: Mass Murder in Historical Perspective*, edited by Robert Gellately and Ben Kiernan, 141–62. Cambridge, UK: Cambridge University Press, 2003.

Jameson, Fredric. Foreword to *The Postmodern Condition: A Report on Knowledge*, by Jean-François Lyotard, vii–xxi. Translated by Geoff Bennington and Brian Massumi. Minneapolis: University of Minnesota Press, 1984.

King, Richard, and Dan Stone, eds. *Hannah Arendt and the Uses of History: Imperialism, Nation, Race, and Genocide*. Oxford: Berghahn, 2007.

Knowlton, James, ed. *Forever in the Shadow of Hitler? Original Documents of the "Historikerstreit," the Controversy Concerning the Singularity of the Holocaust*. Atlantic Highlands, NJ: Humanities Press, 1993.

Kocka, Jürgen. "German History Before Hitler: The Debate About the German Sonderweg." *Journal of Contemporary History* 23, no. 1 (1988): 3–16.

Kundrus, Birthe, ed. *Phantasiereiche: Zur Kulturgeschichte des deutschen Kolonialismus*. Frankfurt: Campus, 2003.

———. "Von den Herero zum Holocaust? Einige Bemerkungen zur aktuellen Debatte." *Mittelweg 36*, no. 4 (2005): 82–89.

Langbehn, Volker, ed. *German Colonialism, Visual Culture, and Modern Memory*. New York: Routledge, 2010.

Levene, Mark. *The Meaning of Genocide*. Vol. 1 of *Genocide in the Age of the Nation State*. London: I. B. Tauris, 2005.

———. *The Rise of the West and the Coming of Genocide*. Vol. 2 of *Genocide in the Age of the Nation State*. London: I. B. Tauris, 2005.

Lindqvist, Sven. *"Exterminate All the Brutes": One Man's Odyssey into the Heart of Darkness and the Origins of European Genocide*. New York: New Press, 1997.

Lyotard, Jean-François. *The Postmodern Explained: Correspondence, 1982–1985*. Translated by Don Barry et al. Minneapolis: University of Minnesota Press, 1992.

Madley, Benjamin. "From Africa to Auschwitz: How German South West Africa Incubated Ideas and Methods Adopted and Developed by the Nazis in Eastern Europe." *European History Quarterly* 35, no.3 (2005): 429–64.

———. "Patterns of Frontier Genocide, 1803–1910: The Aboriginal Tasmanians, the Yuki of California, and the Herero of Namibia." *Journal of Genocide Research* 6, no. 2 (2004): 167–92.

Maier, Charles. *The Unmasterable Past: History, Holocaust, and German National Identity*. Cambridge, MA: Harvard University Press, 1988.

Mamdani, Mahmood. *When Victims Become Killers: Colonialism, Nativism, and the Genocide in Rwanda*. Princeton, NJ: Princeton University Press, 2001.

Mann, Michael. *The Dark Side of Democracy: Explaining Ethnic Cleansing*. Cambridge, UK: Cambridge University Press, 2005.

Margalit, Avishai, and Gabriel Motzkin. "The Uniqueness of the Holocaust." *Philosophy and Public Affairs* 25, no. 1 (1996): 65–83.

Mazower, Mark. *Hitler's Empire: How the Nazis Ruled Europe*. London: Penguin, 2008.

———. "Violence and the State in the Twentieth Century." *American Historical Review* (Oct. 2002): www.historycooperative.org/journals/ahr/107.4/aho402001158.html (accessed June 9, 2009).

Moses, A. Dirk. "Conceptual Blockages and Definitional Dilemmas in the 'Racial Century': Genocides of Indigenous Peoples and the Holocaust." *Patterns of Prejudice* 36, no. 4 (2002): 7–39.

———, ed. *Empire, Colony, Genocide: Conquest, Occupation, and Subaltern Resistance in World History*. New York: Berghahn, 2008.

———. "Empire, Colony, Genocide: Keywords and the Philosophy of History." In Moses, *Empire, Colony, Genocide*, 3–54.

——. *German Intellectuals and the Nazi Past*. Cambridge, UK: Cambridge University Press, 2008.

——. "Theoretical Paper: Toward a Theory of Critical Genocide Studies." In *Online Encyclopedia of Mass Violence*. www.massviolence.org/Toward-a-Theory-of-Critical-Genocide-Studies?artpage=5-5 (accessed June 12, 2009).

Nipperdey, Thomas. *Deutsche Geschichte, 1800–1918*. Munich: Beck, 1998.

Pogge von Strandmann, Hartmut. *Imperialismus vom Grünen Tisch: Deutsche Kolonialpolitik zwischen wirtschaftlicher Ausbeutung und "zivilisatorischen" Bemühungen*. Berlin: Christoph Links, 2009.

Robinson, Ronald, and John Gallagher. *Africa and the Victorians: The Official Mind of Imperialism*. London: Macmillan, 1961.

Rosenbaum, Alan S., ed. *Is the Holocaust Unique?* Boulder, CO: Westview Press, 2001.

Rosenfeld, Gavriel D. "The Politics of Uniqueness: Reflections on the Recent Polemical Turn in Holocaust and Genocide Scholarship." *Holocaust and Genocide Studies* 13, no. 1 (1999): 28–61.

Said, Edward. *Culture and Imperialism*. New York: Vintage Books, 1994.

Schmitt, Carl. *Glossarium: Aufzeichnungen der Jahre 1947–1951*. Edited by Eberhard Freiherr von Medem. Berlin: Duncker und Humblot, 1991.

Shandley, Robert, ed. *Unwilling Germans? The Goldhagen Debate*. Minneapolis: University of Minnesota Press, 1998.

Smith, Helmut Walser. *The Continuities of German History: Nation, Religion, and Race Across the Long Nineteenth Century*. Cambridge, UK: Cambridge University Press, 2008.

Smith, Woodruff D. *The Ideological Origins of Nazi Imperialism*. New York: Oxford University Press, 1986.

Steinmetz, George. "The First Genocide of the 20th Century and Its Postcolonial Afterlives: Germany and the Namibian Ovaherero." *Journal of the International Institute* (Oct. 2005): www.umich.edu/news/MT/NewsE/10_05/steinmetz.html (accessed June 15, 2009).

Stoler, Ann Laura, and Frederick Cooper. "Between Metropole and Colony: Rethinking a Research Agenda." In Cooper and Stoler, *Tensions of Empire*, 1–56.

Stone, Dan, ed. *The Historiography of Genocide*. New York: Palgrave Macmillan, 2008.

——. "The Holocaust and Its Historiography." In Stone, *The Historiography of Genocide*, 373–99.

——. Introduction. In Stone, *The Historiography of Genocide*, 1–7.

Trotha, Trutz von. "Genozidaler Pazifizierungskrieg: Soziologische Anmerkungen zum Konzept des Genozids am Beispiel des Kolonialkrieges in Deutsch-Südwestafrika 1904–1907." *Zeitschrift für Genozidforschung* 4, no. 2 (2003): 30–57.

Wehler, Hans-Ulrich. *Das Deutsche Kaiserreich, 1871–1918*. Göttingen: Kleine Vandenhoeck Reihe, 1980.

——. *Deutsche Gesellschaftsgeschichte, 1849–1914*. Vol. 3. Munich: C. H. Beck, 1995.

Weiss-Wendt, Anton. "Problems in Comparative Genocide Scholarship." In Stone, *The Historiography of Genocide*, 42–70.

Wendt, Reinhard. *Kolonialismus zur Globalisierung: Europa und die Welt seit 1500*. Paderborn: Schöningh, 2007.

Young, Robert. *White Mythologies: Writing History and the West*. London: Routledge, 1990.

Zantop, Susanne. *Colonial Fantasies: Conquest, Family, and Nation in Precolonial Germany, 1770–1870*. Durham, NC: Duke University Press, 1997.

Zimmerer, Jürgen. "The Birth of the *Ostland* Out of the Spirit of Colonialism: A Postcolonial Perspective on the Nazi Policy of Conquest and Extermination." In *Colonialism and Genocide*, edited by A. Dirk Moses and Dan Stone, 101–13. London: Routledge, 2007.

——. "Colonialism and the Holocaust: Towards an Archeology of Genocide." In *Genocide and Settler Society: Frontier Violence and Stolen Indigenous Children in Australian History*, edited by A. Dirk Moses, 49–76. New York: Berg, 2004.

Zimmerer, Jürgen, and Joachim Zeller, eds. *Völkermord in Deutsch-Südwestafrika: Der Kolonialkrieg (1904–1908) in Namibia und seine Folgen*. Berlin: Christoph Links, 2003. Translated by E. J. Neather as *Genocide in German South-West Africa: The Colonial War of 1904–1908 in Namibia and Its Aftermath* (London: Merlin Press, 2008).

German Colonialism

PART I

Colonial (Dis)Continuities

Framing the Issue

1

Borrowed Light

Nietzsche and the Colonies

Timothy Brennan

Many of Nietzsche's most vivid remarks on colonialism have circulated underground for some time. Hardly unknown, they are eagerly seized on as evidence of his antinomian spirit. To take one recent example, Massimo Cacciari's *Geofilosofia dell'Europa* links the decline of European Empire (a corollary of the fall of European Man) with the emergence of a new and welcome concept of the "West."[1] In the book's epigraph Cacciari summons Nietzsche's words in prophetic support: "I have absorbed in myself the spirit of Europe—now I want to strike back!"[2] We have here, in microcosm, the kind of riposte to European humanism that many theorists find throughout Nietzsche's work, proving his proleptic capture of our widespread anticolonial convictions. In this view he is the philosopher who articulated above all restlessness, demobilization, and wandering—a dissatisfaction with all end points.

But Cacciari stops short of finishing the idea—strike back, Nietzsche meant, against the deadwood of Europe, on Europe's behalf, in the name of what Europe might become! His intentions are expressed most clearly perhaps in his admiration for Napoleon, whose greatness for Nietzsche lay in the general's hatred of modernity and his bringing a "slab of antiquity" back, allowing Europe to resume the decisiveness and will of ancient conquerors. What Napoleon wanted, Nietzsche explains, "was one unified Europe . . . —as *mistress of the earth*."[3]

Here I want to rethink Nietzsche's reception in colonial discourse and the doubling influences it has had there. Passages like the one on Napoleon, when not hiding in the light, are frequently recuperated as not meaning what they say or as signifying their opposite. This doubling, or inversion, is significant, and not simply as a case study of interpretative ambiguity. It is in Nietzsche's strategy of double entendre and the wearing of masks ("Every philosophy is . . . a secret and involuntary set of personal memoirs")[4] that critics find protection from his sentiments. No reading of Nietzsche is possible without dwelling on his illocutionary strategies and rhetorical feints,[5] both of them devised—as Geoff Waite, the critic who has written the most on this topic, points out—in the name of an *esoteric writing* that Nietzsche considered "an anti-Liberal necessity."[6]

Even a symptomatic reading, though, requires philological support, and one can never get around the problem (as Waite goes on to say) of "making use" of Nietzsche without such support. For doing so simply keeps critics "safe in the *a priori* belief that *their* 'recontextualization,' at least, is inoculated from any possibly hallucinatory effects."[7] There is no safe interpretive place of this sort and therefore no escape from the repetitive, and strangely literal, set of propositions on colonialism in Nietzsche, which are remarkable not because they are ambiguous but because they are so crude.

This awareness of Nietzsche's affinity with a colonialist mentality is at least as old as Theodor Adorno's and Max Horkheimer's observation in the "Juliette" chapter of *Dialectic of Enlightenment* (1944) that Nietzsche "maliciously celebrates the mighty and their cruelty when it is directed . . . against everything alien to themselves."[8] Preferring this to the fake compassion of bourgeois sentiment, Adorno and Horkheimer nevertheless see Nietzsche himself as being caught up in a bourgeois contradiction based on "biological idealism."[9] His vaunted praise for the "beautiful terribleness of the deed" ends up "elevating the cult of strength to a world-historical doctrine." The German philosopher's "master morality," they argue, quite against his intentions, "places itself entirely in the service of the civilizing powers" by being unable to "shake off the idealistic habit of wanting to see the petty thief hanged while imperialist raids are transfigured into world-historical missions."[10]

Others had no trouble identifying in Nietzsche an identical outlook—for example, Carl Schmitt, whose writing in 1950 on the concept of "just war" looks admiringly to Nietzsche's arguments of the 1880s on behalf of "the battle for the domination of the earth ... in the name of fundamental philosophical doctrines."[11] The charge is, in fact, glancingly made much earlier in Wilhelm Carl Becker's *Der Nietzschekultus* (The Cult of Nietzsche) but with little to back it up and without appreciating how influential Nietzsche's structured ambivalence toward "Europe" would later become in left cultural theory and postcolonial studies.

From the mid to the late 1880s—the time both of Germany's intrepid advances in southwest Africa and of Nietzsche's own *anni mirabili*—Nietzsche wrote of the need for a united Europe to recover its vital life by territorial expansion. He urged Europe to take over England's role as global sovereign (although not in the name of German nationalism but of a new European "cosmopolitanism") and declared the spiritual imperative to slough off *Recht* as "justice" in the name of a more basic *Recht*, seen now as the right to resume the role of heroic predator by displacing shopkeeper Europe in the degraded age of democracy.[12] Although his direct involvements with *German* colonialism were ambiguous—he was the brother-in-law of a fervent German colonialist who set up business schemes in Paraguay—there is ample evidence of his enthusiasm for the colonial project as a "fundamental philosophical doctrine" (in Schmitt's words). Debates over emigration, race, and colonial conquest that raged in Switzerland and Germany during the 1880s find many echoes in the writing of Nietzsche—the "free spirit" who (as Peter Bergmann has shown) closely followed the political fashions of an era for which he claimed to be "untimely."[13]

Even more consequential was the manner in which Nietzsche's enthusiasms created an ambiguous left-right amalgam that, as with everything else Nietzschean, became a model for discourse. Colonialism as an unfettering of the European spirit and a vital reawakening of "life" was enmeshed (in his mind) with the early communist movements, whose assertive rise took place during his most productive decade of writing.[14] This is not to say that the mobilization of the European citizenry of various national states under the banner of imperialist privilege was for him anything but a new fettering. Imperialism of this sort was the dangerous expression of a premature *große Politik*, which he regarded with enmity.[15]

But the influence of early social democracy on Nietzsche's reading and thinking has been severely understated. In his preoccupation with socialist thinkers and movements—a neglected story in Nietzsche studies—there is startling proof of a larger rhetorical posture on the European right that was later developed in the interwar era: to think of these two problems (socialists, colonial natives) as being interconnected, raising similar theoretical questions, and demanding related solutions. The new politically active laborers placed alongside the "barbarians" of the global periphery were in this discourse interdependent, although not interchangeable—a fusing that was prompted by the considerable rise of social democratic parties and vocal public claims of other radical tendencies (above all, anarchism) during the period in which Nietzsche's influence on European philosophy was consolidated.

The main currents of writing about colonialism and its aftermath today are conversant with Nietzschean modes of thought, which they generally celebrate, but unaware of the contexts of Nietzsche's antihumanism. From the start his encounter with socialist ideas sharpened and gave direction to his posthumanist conviction, which found expression not in the name of combating the false universalism of European Man (as postcolonial theory might suppose) but because humanism was afflicted with the disease of moral restraint: "We should never dare to permit ourselves to speak of our 'love of humanity'; our kind is not actor enough for that. Or not Saint-Simonist enough."[16] In just this vein there are extensive parallels between Nietzsche's philosophical themes and political causes célèbres found in popular political books and journal articles of the time, as well as in the newspapers. As discussed below, these obsessions included problems of German emigration, the threat (or promise) of socialist government, and German competition with other European countries, especially England. What appear to the casual reader as enigmatic evocations of the artist in his Olympian mode are frequently aphoristic responses to current events. Given Nietzsche's place in postcolonial studies, it is not surprising that the field also acquires his tendency to portray socialism as an undesirable option—the wrong turn, as it were, taken by the global periphery. This view is evident in the field's general indifference to the Bandung intellectuals and in its almost total lack of commentary on the remarkable role of early social democracy in launching the first organized resistance to European imperial attitudes and policies. So we are confronted with something of a scandal. How did a field created to combat Euronormativity and promote the values of peripheral cultures adopt the frameworks and themes of the German political right in the person of someone who endorsed colonialism both literally and metaphorically?

Nietzschean conceptual leads have a special relationship to the left/right amalgam of contemporary theory in general—including its postcolonial wing. As Waite observes, "more books were published about Nietzsche in the last *five* years (1991–1996) than at *any* other comparable length of time previously."[17] Nietzsche's initial influence, moreover, "was not on the Right or Center but rather on what many historians of this phenomenon call 'the Left.'" Advocating cosmopolitanism rather than nationalism ("we who are homeless"),[18] insisting on the virtues of nomadism, asserting the need for intellectuals to abandon analysis in place of living the "bodies" of the racial other,[19] denouncing any politics focused on states or state power, seeing the "self" as a recent creation, rejecting all versions of the "whole" (universalism, totality), and advocating historical "forgetting"—all of these derive from Nietzsche and form many of the principal points of departure for postcolonial cultural studies.

Although many in the field would resist this identification, seeing themselves as activists without particular theoretical allegiances, the language and frameworks of the field have clearly depended very heavily on the leads of Derrida and Foucault, whose debt to Nietzsche is programmatic. Most introductions to the field, moreover, find this arc of influence uncontroversial. In *Postcolonial Studies: A Critical Introduction*, for example, Leela Gandhi refers to the field's "theoretical firmament," observing that all three of the field's leaders "invoke the . . . figure of Nietzsche to bolster their onslaught on the epistemological narcissism of Western culture."[20] If the Western humanist reveals his or her fatal flaw in believing the "origin" a "place of plenitude, presence and truth, the Nietzschean archaeologist . . . can only find the residual traces of malice, theft, greed and disparity at the start of human history. . . . The very idea of Genesis—of unadulterated origins—is shown as a supplement, or as a mythical compensation for an originary lack."[21]

Many have noticed "later Subaltern Studies' devotion to Nietzsche and Heidegger," as well.[22] In his introduction to postcolonial studies Bill Ashcroft points to one of its foundational ideas: the "discovery of the provisionality and circularity of [modernity's] basic premise, the 'providential' power of reason" exemplified in "Nietzsche's realization that the Enlightenment replaced divine providence with the equally transcendental providence of reason. . . . In effect, providence was replaced by the temporally and spatially empty dominance of the European subject."[23] And it is Nietzsche, ultimately, who is responsible—by way of a well-marked heritage—for the philosophical emphasis on the "thought-body." The original form of the concept is captured succinctly in a quotation from Nietzsche found in Joachim Köhler's important study on the philosopher's childhood and sexuality: "The philosopher," wrote Nietzsche, "cannot do other than convert his physical condition into the most highly intellectual of forms—this act of transformation *is* philosophy. We philosophers are not at liberty to distinguish between soul and body."[24] Seized on by Georges Bataille (and later Foucault), this principle supplied the warrant for an identity of being from which a postcolonial "epistemology of the body" was fashioned.[25] In Derrida's words, "Is not all of Nietzsche's thought a critique of philosophy as an active indifference to difference?"—difference, that is, of race, gender, nationality, and sexual preference (of the *body*, that is, as a genealogical inheritance).[26] With these words Derrida instantiates Nietzsche at the center of postcolonial theory, a gesture that informs both the content and style of the field's most commonly cited leaders.

Occasional obstacles stem the momentum of Nietzsche's influence somewhat, although they are rarely commented on. The response to Nietzsche was harsh, for instance, among several intellectuals during the period of decolonization (Alejo Carpentier and Aimé Césaire, for example). In the clearest case Césaire, in *Discourse on Colonialism*, angrily denounced the "hoodwinkers" he considered to be the *faux amis* of the anticolonial movements—the ones who took the form of "chattering intellectuals born stinking out of the thigh of Nietzsche." Colonization itself, Césaire argued, worked by first "decivilizing" the colonizer in order to "awaken him to buried instincts."[27] The project of decivilization on behalf of instinct was, in his mind, precisely Nietzsche's.

Ultimately, we can trace the postcolonial mode of expression to its heavy canonical borrowing from the quizzical European attitudes toward the global periphery in early-twentieth-century literary modernism. Flaubert, Rimbaud, Poe, and later Heidegger and Eliot were distrustful of political optimism, sardonic toward human perfectibility, and drawn to what they considered the redemptive backwardness and simplicity of colonial natives. The affective milieu in which these sentiments thrive are mainstream today and are so permeating that they are hardly noticed. They find their way, with some modulation, into Hannah Arendt's *The Origins of Totalitarianism* and *The Human Condition*. Solitary exile and subterranean inventiveness are called forth to evoke a supposedly new pioneering outlook—a new way of being without ends, free of patriotism, and modest in the face of the uprooted, scattered peoples of the colonial aftermath with whom European and American intellectuals (as well as those from white colonial settler states) are said to share a common family.

Essentially, this is the ethos and imagery of postcolonial discourse generally, and its theoretical support-networks are emphatic and wide-ranging. The wandering soul of the teacher of parables is a Nietzschean figure

1.1 Theory's Nietzsche as Youth Rebel. Reproduced by permission from *Semiotext(e)* 2, no. 3 (1977): back cover.

enshrined in the work of Gilles Deleuze (whose version of Nietzsche has been especially influential among certain postcolonial theorists).[28] In describing Nietzsche's method, Deleuze argues that the philosopher taught us that "what a will wants is not an object, an objective or an end. Ends and objects, even motives, are still symptoms. What a will wants ... is to affirm its difference or to deny what differs."[29] Here is where the philological record (below) would cast doubt on the idea that there was no *goal* in Nietzsche on the colonial question and would in that way challenge the assumption of virtue in the nonteleological as such.

The Deleuzian version of Nietzsche—as much as the Foucauldian and Derridean—helped fashion the left/right amalgam constituting the field. Here the philosopher is portrayed as an ally of youth, an undomesticated radical fighting on a variety of unforeseen fronts ranging across a completely new terrain of corporeal and ethical problems displaced from the vulgar political world. An illustration of this remarkable portrayal can be found in the issue of the journal *Semiotext(e)*, in which Deleuze and Guattari's "Capitalism and Schizophrenia" first appeared. Its frontispiece presents Nietzsche as a comrade in struggle (see Figure 1.1).

This carefully prepared ambiguity and esoteric intent is consonant with the ethos of social escape found in literary modernism itself. Baudelaire reveling (in *Le spleen de Paris*) in his own "craving for disguises and masks, hatred of home and the passion for roaming" is the classic modernist statement of this sort—a statement that, in Baudelaire's original, blends with another and is at one with it. After speaking of "masks," he extols the "founders of colonies, shepherds of peoples, missionary priests exiled to the ends of the earth, [who] probably know something of these mysterious intoxications"—that is, of being alone in a crowd, of hiding one's meanings in parables, and of humiliating the stupid pride of those Baudelaire derisively called the "happy ones."[30] Either dissident theory takes its leads from precursors hostile to its ends, or those ends were never really different at all (which is why they are concealed).

Nietzsche in Time

The political radicalism of the early Marxist Wilhelm Liebknecht was, as Peter Bergmann notes, "a foreign curiosity for Nietzsche."[31] The word *foreign* is the one to concentrate on. Having grasped the "value of having enemies" and the need (for clarity's sake) of having powerful opponents against which he could define himself, Nietzsche learned how to "spiritualiz[e] enmity," and one of his foils was German social democracy.[32] His involuntary immersion in its traditions date from an early period, evident in his polemic in *Untimely Meditations* against the young Hegelian David Friedrich Strauss, whose undoing of the mythical Jesus scandalized Germany after its publication and set the tone for Nietzsche's later (and more radical) assaults on Christianity. Nietzsche's whole intellectual formation took place in the historical-critical method of philology derived from Hegel, which marked him profoundly, although—as "The Uses and Abuses of History for Life" shows—mostly negatively. An enthusiastic supporter of the Prussian royal house in his youth, by the late 1860s and 1870s Nietzsche felt profoundly at odds with his political surroundings. In 1866 he attended a mass rally featuring Ferdinand Lassalle—a member of the Communist League and the founder of the Allgemeiner Deutscher Arbeiterverein (later to become the Social Democratic Party of Germany [SPD]). He was deeply moved by the "powerful words" of the man but recoiled from the "impotent and unreal things" Lassalle advocated, such as a "European workers' state."[33]

Nietzsche was caught up, as many were, in the excitement surrounding the socialist and anarchist challenges during the 1870s and 1880s. In 1868 he rented a flat in the home of Karl Biedermann, the founder of the Leipzig Workers' Educational Society, which August Bebel (the future leader of the SPD) had joined, and who was later to represent the party's Marxist wing. It was in the Leipzig organization, in fact, that Bebel received his training and orientation. Biedermann was more of a moderate but was deeply embroiled nevertheless in the controversies surrounding Marxism in the 1860s, attempting to fend off the influence of Liebknecht, who had been expelled from Prussia earlier for his political activities.[34] The atmosphere was pervasive and could not have escaped Nietzsche. Even Wagner was entranced for a time with the revolutionary ideals of Mikhail Bakunin, whose words he rapturously recited in conversation. Nietzsche, at any rate, was intrigued enough systematically to work through the writings of Eugen Dühring (the target of Engels's famous polemic *Anti-Dühring*, which calls him, among other things, "the Richard Wagner of philosophy"). Dühring had influenced (more than having been influenced by) German Social Democracy, especially in his writings on socialism and the national economy, which Bebel had positively reviewed in the party paper in 1874. When socialism became strong enough under Bismarck to prompt legislation, Nietzsche wrote his friend Franz Overbeck, "requesting the address of a Zurich book dealer from whom he could obtain a catalogue of banned socialist literature."[35] But apart from his hurried look through Bebel's *Woman Under Socialism*, Nietzsche kept abreast of events by way of liberal or conservative writers, reading John Stuart Mill's "Socialism" (1879) and Albert Schäffle's *Quintessence of Socialism*, as well as some of Dühring's works.[36] He knew, however, that he had to define himself in terms of the new movement, and he resolutely did so by adopting its language in order to disable its intent.

Nietzsche saw socialism and anarchism as rivals to his status as the subversive scourge of old Europe.[37] In place of its barricades and congresses he proposed a subterranean politics of immoral redefinition.[38] His attitudes toward the workers movements were indelibly marked by the rumors in 1871 that the Paris Commune had burned down the Louvre (a slander, it turned out, but one that moved Nietzsche to think forever after of the lower classes in terms of a vile cultural barbarism). He recoiled in horror when associates found in his concept of the Dionysian the spirit of revolution, and he was quick to correct them by associating all political conflict of this type with the Apollonian, reserving the Dionysian for a sublime Hellenic affirmation of an older aristocratic agon, part of an aesthetic brotherhood worshipping an apolitical god.[39] Socialism meant "the State" for Nietzsche—the destroyer of great intellects and individuality. Yet he in no way wished to be seen in the costume of the Basel industrialists with whom he politically identified: "The manufacturers and entrepreneurs of business probably have been too deficient so far in all those forms and signs of a *higher race* that alone makes a *person* interesting. If the nobility of birth showed in their eyes and gestures, there might not be any socialism of the masses. For at bottom the masses are willing to submit to slavery of any kind, if only the higher-ups constantly legitimize themselves as higher, as *born* to command—by having noble manners."[40]

He made Switzerland his home in exile because of its reputation as the refuge for all that was dangerous in the late nineteenth century, the place where radicals of all types congregated; and Basel was the very center for a period (1869) of the international socialist movement. Nietzsche recognized the immense appeal of "equality" in the socialist message, and he took this to mean the flattening of differences in Europe generally—the grounds, that is, for superseding nationalist divisions and of creating a unified, cosmopolitan Europe.[41] His pristine vision of Hellenism, and the need for the philosopher to speak in the "vanishing voice of olden times," meant that those (like himself) of the higher cultures would need to establish "the caste of compulsory labor and the caste of free labor"—to embrace an inequality that would ensure the dominion of the arts and the intellect. He implores his fellow poets and savants: "Send your ships into uncharted seas! Live at war with your peers and yourselves! Be robbers and conquerors as long as you cannot be rulers and possessors, you seekers of knowledge!"[42] This goal (*pace* Deleuze) had colonial implications, as he was soon to make clear. To avoid rancor within Europe, and to retain the project of (European) equality that gave socialism its appeal, "backward peoples would have to be imported to undertake society's more menial and unpleasant tasks."[43] According to Waite this was not an isolated comment: "In his early and purloined essay 'The Greek State' (1872), Nietzsche had explicitly promoted at once the modern version of 'slavery' (*Sklaverei*), the necessity for its 'conscious or unconscious' acceptance *by* 'slaves' or 'workers' in their expropriated 'surplus labor' (*Mehrarbeit*), and the concomitant 'anti-Liberal' necessity for an 'esoteric writing' (*Geheimschrift*) appropriate to the 'esoteric doctrine of the relation between the State and genius.'"[44] No German, at any rate, could have been immune to the raging discussions surrounding the German quest for colonies in the years of Nietzsche's most prolific decade of writing.[45]

By 1885 Germany had taken control of four African territories—German Southwest Africa, Togo, Cameroon, and German East Africa—as well as several smaller territories in the Pacific.[46] The large-scale emigration of Germans to the Americas for want of opportunities at home further fueled the colonial impetus and was considered a national scandal already by the 1860s.[47] Nietzsche's frequent phrases "we Europeans" or "we Germans" must be seen in the light of both developments.[48] Hence, Bernhard Förster, who married Nietzsche's sister Elisabeth on May 22, 1885, and moved with her to Paraguay in February of the next year, was one of the promoters of colonial emigration to the Americas and sought Nietzsche as an investor in his enterprise (although Nietzsche in the end declined for financial reasons).[49] Like Nietzsche himself, Förster was not at all interested in the German state's owning colonies for its own national glory or in competition with its European rivals, only that colonies establish Germanness abroad.[50] This is the setting in which we can appreciate Nietzsche's words from *Dawn* (which, like Cacciari above, some leftist circles have misread as a call to proletarian action):

> The workers in Europe should declare that henceforth as a class they are a human impossibility, and not only, as is customary, a harsh and purposeless establishment. They should introduce an era of vast swarming out from the European beehive, the like of which has never been experienced, and with this act of emigration in the grand manner protest against the machine, against capital, and against the choice with which they are now threatened, of becoming of *necessity* either slaves of the state or slaves of a revolutionary party. Let Europe relieve itself of the fourth part of its inhabitants! . . . What at home began to degenerate into dangerous discontent and criminal tendencies will, once outside, gain a wild and beautiful naturalness and be called heroism. . . . Perhaps we shall also bring in numerous *Chinese*: and they will bring with them modes of life and thought suitable to industrious ants. Indeed, they might as a whole contribute to the blood of restless and fretful Europe something of Asiatic calm and contemplativeness and—what is probably needed most—Asiatic *perseverance*.[51]

Not an Aryan supremacist (a weakness based on *ressentiment* that kept Europeans from being "warriors," in Nietzsche's view), not an anti-Semite (since one had better learn from the Jewish genius for transvaluation),[52] Nietzsche was not a colonialist either, if by *colonialist* one means an official supporter of German policies or economic goals in Africa. But this was because the European was "supra-national"—an *Über Rasse* suited to fill the role of the Nietzschean "free spirit."[53] The harsh conditions of workers in Europe in the 1880s led Nietzsche to conclude that the remedy lay in emigration: "Outside of Europe, Europe's virtues will accompany these workers on their wanderings." The workers' "inclination for crime will, once abroad, acquire a wild beautiful naturalness and be called heroism."[54] He does not flinch from the brutality of the operation, and his references to "predatory nature" (*Raubtier-Natur*) in this context is entirely positive. His writing during the last years of sanity just prior to 1890 becomes increasingly biologistic, so although he flatly opposes nationalism and class conflict, he preserves the notions of both domination and difference, advocating a hierarchical order (*Rangordnung*).[55]

His return to the theory of "Great Politics" in this period was a program to institute his philosophical system, founded in part on an elitist Europeanism. What the next two generations of European intellectuals and politicos would make of these prophetic leads is well known. But a good deal of what the insurgents of theory insist are misunderstandings of Nietzsche when confronted by some of his more outrageous utterances is, in the end, stymied by the philological evidence of his role as precursor and enabler. Take, for example, the following passage: "The time for petty politics is past; the next century will bring the struggle for the dominion of the world—the *compulsion* to great politics."[56] Nietzschean ironies (or better, the ironies embedded in the author "Nietzsche") lie at least partly in the degree to which postcolonial theory has been an agent of this compulsion.

The Interwar Interlude

But how *did* the next two generations read Nietzsche, and how did they lay the groundwork for today's portrait of the thinker as the affirmative answer to Eurocentrism on behalf of a canny "difference"? The ascendency of intellectuals of the interwar German right who came of age under Nietzsche's guiding hand—Martin Heidegger, Ernst Jünger, Carl Schmitt—repeats itself today when these writers (along with Nietzsche) become once more

1.2 František Kupka, *The Rhythm of History. Clockwise from top left*: "Work," "Backward Peoples," "Divisions," and "Families, Classes, Tribes." Marie-Pierre Sale, Marketa Theinhardt, and Pierre Brulle. *Vers des temps nouveaux: Kupka—Oeuvres Graphiques, 1894–1912* (Paris: Editions de la Réunion des musées nationaux, 2002). Courtesy of the Musée d'Orsay.

an object of celebration in the circles of cultural theory.[57] Although these three may be the best known, many other protégés have contributed to the contemporary reading of Nietzsche as the premature postcolonial author par excellence.

As early as the beginning of the twentieth century, only a few years after Nietzsche's death, wars and uprisings in the colonies led to a growing mood that alarmed many and found its way into out-of-the-way corners of the European imagination. Working as a popular illustrator in 1904, the Czech émigré to France, František Kupka, for example, captured the sentiments circulating more widely after two deeply traumatic events for the European establishment on the eve of World War I: the stunning defeat of Italy by the

1.3 František Kupka, *The Rhythm of History,* "Barbarians." Marie-Pierre Sale, Marketa Theinhardt, and Pierre Brulle, *Vers des temps nouveaux: Kupka—Oeuvres Graphiques, 1894–1912* (Paris: Editions de la Réunion des musées nationaux, 2002). Courtesy of the Musée d'Orsay.

Abyssinian king Menelek at the Battle of Adwa in 1896 and the victory of Japan in the Russo-Japanese War in 1905.

Kupka's cycle of paintings titled the "rhythms of history" (see Figure 1.2) records the clear connections that he and others detected between the growing socialist movement (with which he sympathized) and challenges to the tired rhetoric of Western "civilization" with all its overtones of approving an implicit hierarchy among peoples. Notice his depiction of "barbarians" in one of these illustrations as prehistoric, blond Europeans (Figure 1.3): a virtual fulfillment of (or perhaps answer to) Nietzsche's "noble races the beast of prey, the splendid *blond beast* prowling about avidly in search of spoil and victory."[58]

With the greatest degree of eloquence, Nietzsche rallied Europe to find again the right to its privileges. He saw very early that socialists, on the one hand, and the insurgents of Asia and Africa, on the other, were related as challenges to the systems of European rank that he fought to redefine. They were not on the same track but, as "slaves," possessed a strong family resemblance, amounting to the same dangerous power of resentment that brought them naturally into each others' camp. He supported the claim that classical antiquity has a patrilineal bond to Europe itself and is the proper source of all political wisdom.

During the interwar era any number of thinkers began to copy, quote, and creatively misapply Nietzsche. Many took his arch-aesthetic loathing to be at one with socialist critiques of a cultural and economic system. Traditional conservatives of the interwar era, many of them frankly racist, considered Nietzsche to be, along with Dostoevsky, a metaphysical sniper giving aid and comfort to the Bolshevist enemy. These conservative defenders of the "West," frightened by the spreading interest in Asian religion and philosophy among European intellectuals drawn to the East by Russia, invoked Nietzsche's repeated phrase "We Europeans" as their rallying cry.

It is in Nietzsche's writing on the "barbarian," in fact, that we find the first hints of a coupling of the image of the socialist and the uncivilized colonial outcast, a strategy that inspired a hugely popular interwar genre of fear-mongering tales of the "death of the white race" in writers such as Maurice Muret, Henri Massis, and (somewhat later) Herbert von Beckenrath. The fact is, also, that the conservatives of the interwar era shared many of Nietzsche's positions, although they expressed them much less skillfully. What was and was not "barbarous" became, as a result of a real colonial insurgency crowding in at the edges of the European family, a question on everyone's mind.

The socialist threat, even more acute in the interwar years than in the 1880s, had made people suddenly conscious of the power of the world outside Europe to *overwhelm* the center by the sheer chaos of its cultural panoply, its strange and ungraspable gradations of self-confidence, and its utter segregation from the problematics of modernity as an intellectual or moral problem. It is here, I am arguing, that the rejection of social democracy took on its sharpest philosophical features and became fused at a conceptual level to a lineage of European writing that sought to represent the left as a new barbarian wave.

In his *Defense of the West*, written in 1927, for example, Henri Massis sets out to attack what he calls the "Asiatic influences on the intellectual life of contemporary Germany." He specifically dedicated a final appendix to

Rabindranath Tagore, who shortly before the appearance of Massis's book had completed a widely publicized speaking tour of Europe and had recently delivered a lecture in Paris that was, according to Massis, "attended by intellectuals, scholars, professors and society people" and was "heard religiously" and with "submissive admiration."[59] For his part, Massis insists, "I was indignant. I recalled our saints, our heroes, our citizens of Europe; I thought of all the work, all the discoveries, all the institutions, which their will had created, and it did not seem to me that we should bow down before the mystical, dreaming, lousy and ever idle East" (247).

Massis was writing when the fear of "Asia rising" was prevalent in Europe among British and czarist military propagandists who had in 1904 and 1905 fought on both sides of the Russo-Japanese War. He does not want to be confused with this merely reactive hammer-pounding sort of rhetoric, so he clarifies his position by stating, "When we speak of an 'Asiatic peril,' we are not accusing the East, in general, but denouncing the philosophic, moral, and social errors and the dubious idealism which Oriental propagandists educated in our schools and served by certain European idea-mongers, set up in the name of the East against the West" (27). The war of ideas, in his mind, centers on Germany, which in these years is "perpetually hesitating between Asiatic mysticism and the Latin spirit, and which seems to be in a state of permanent protest against the Roman idea" (29). Defeated in World War I, it looked with confusion to the East and "began to prophesy, in dark apocalyptic tones, the final bankruptcy of a world, the mastery of which had escaped her" (30). Massis is thinking above all of Spengler's *Decline of the West*.

Conducted, however, on this plane of universal and time-honored nation-bashing in which a loyal Frenchman, fresh from world war, diagnoses the febrile sickness of the German psyche, his discourse does not remain there but becomes more interestingly focused on the unique politics of the moment. The "German mind," he continues, must now seek energies outside itself, and it has done so by turning to "Russia, and, farther still, to India and China. The sympathy shown to Bolshevism by a section of our younger generation is only one of the outward signs of this tendency. The political attitude adopted towards Bolshevism matters little. What is particularly remarkable in its apparition is that it is the expression of a change in the tendencies of the Western mind.... The German mind has ceased to gaze with any interest towards intellectual France" (60–61). It is against "the materialistic West, which is all Machine," that the Asiatic mind compares, "with frantic insistency" its own spirituality; Gandhi and Tagore preach tolerance of all religions "only to reawaken its own beliefs and better to dissolve ours" (135–36). The enablers of this assault? Massis has no trouble locating them. They are Lenin and Zinoviev, who shall overcome the West "by way of the East" (102). Russia is the "Orient of Europe" and has swept into its camp certain "young men of education" who now "invoke the Bolshevist ideal" (102) in the form of Nietzsche and Dostoevsky.

Curiously, the most revered communist intellectual in Europe at the time also singled out the deleterious influence of Tagore's mysticism, not in the name of protecting modernity from the palsied effeminacies of the East, however, but of stanching the poetic subversion of resistance in the colonies that Tagore's pseudo-religious stance of nonviolence and human "understanding" promoted. In a review of Tagore's novel *The Home and the World* in *Die rote Fahne* in 1922, Georg Lukács attacked Germany's "intellectual elite," who he believed had fallen for Tagore's tedious recyclings of scraps from the Upanishads and the Bhagavad-Gita.[60] These intellectuals seek, he said, "an esoteric sanction of profundity and of wisdom from afar." He sees this as a general symptom of the hunger for "intellectual substitutes," where more recent authors (like Spengler) stand in for the earlier classics they are only quoting such that the public can no longer tell the difference. He goes so far as to say that Britain has given Tagore a huge publicity boost, in effect paying him for dampening the energies of the Indian liberation movement. He calls the novel a "pamphlet" that can effectively "combat the freedom struggle in his native country" by appeals to the "universally human."[61] Tagore wants to save the Indians' souls by protecting them from the dangers posed by violence and deceit but ends only by relieving them of the means of fighting. Maurice Muret, whose *Twilight of the White Races*, appeared only two years earlier in 1925, had already set a similar tone.

By singling out Dostoevsky as the mystical goblin who makes spiritualist claptrap and defeatism sexy, and by associating Nietzsche with a "German intoxication" that prepares the gullible intellectuals of Europe for the dance of Siva, Massis seriously misreads his opponents. Yet, despite these departures, the similarities of their positions are striking: both underline the importance of will, appeal to a tribal sense of "our Europe," see their mission as castigating the weakness and effeminacy of the Germans, and exploding German *ressentiment*—the mistake of thinking that whatever one cannot conquer, one should consider worthless.

Literal Foreground, Esoteric Frame

The phrases "we Europeans" and "we Germans" dotting Nietzsche's maxims, letters, and major statements throughout the 1880s come to a head in the "Peoples and Fatherlands" section of *Beyond Good and Evil* (1886). In *A Genealogy of Morals* (1887) he regales the patriots, not so much for their patriotism but for the immaturity of their simple hatred of difference, their simplistic racialism. He offers a more sophisticated, quasi-metaphorical racialism in exchange:

> On the contrary, it is the *pre-Aryan* population that makes itself felt . . . [in] almost all of Europe. . . . The conquered race has there succeeded in getting the upper hand in color, in shortness of skull, perhaps even in intellectual and social instincts. Who will guarantee that modern democracy, and anarchy (which is still more modern), and especially the hankering after *la commune*, the most primitive form of society—which is held in common by all our European socialists—do not represent in the main an immense *atavism*, and that the conquering and *gentleman race*, the race of Aryans, is not among other things physically succumbing?[62]

One can see this intention of learning from the enemy, of not succumbing to ressentiment, even more clearly in a passage from his notebooks in the same year (that is, 1887), later collected in *The Will to Power*:

> Overall view of the future European: the most intelligent slave animals, very industrious, fundamentally very modest, inquisitive to excess, multifarious, pampered, weak of will—a cosmopolitan chaos of affects and intelligence. How could a stronger species raise itself out of him? . . . [With] the will to strengthening . . . the will to be terrible. To fight upward out of that chaos to this form—requires a compulsion: one must be faced with the choice of perishing or prevailing. A dominating race can grow up only out of terrible and violent beginnings. Problem: where are the *barbarians* of the twentieth century? Obviously, they will come into view and consolidate themselves only after tremendous socialist crises—they will be the elements capable of the greatest severity towards themselves and able to guarantee the most enduring will.[63]

The word *barbarian* is another double entendre, a prodding echo, although with a twist of the civilizational rhetoric of the West discussed above, now transformed into an image not of what we seek to conquer or repel but to emulate. As we have seen, Nietzsche had already refashioned the socialists of his day into hordes on the edge of the European encampment; it is a small step to make the jest that the noble must learn a sanctifying barbarism quite unlike the double face of slavish democracy. What might appear ambiguous in the above rendering is clarified in a note from the same year: "What means one has to employ with rude peoples, and that 'barbarous' means are not arbitrary and capricious, becomes palpable in practice as soon as one is placed, with all one's European pampering, in the necessity of keeping control over barbarians, in the Congo or elsewhere."[64]

On the contrary he means to say, as part of the pun, that "socialist crises" will inspire us to act as we know the barbarians of old acted: with terrible violence and furious strength, extinguishing the necessary enemy. Here he approaches the intermeshing of the destinies of the colonies and European socialism from a different angle. He poses the crushing of the weak as the antidote to the "pampered," the "weak," the ones confused by "cosmopolitan chaos." The language of eugenics and colonial control over natives is tightly wed in the late Nietzsche to a vision of European resurgence that entailed for him an assault on social democracy in all its forms; he saw these various strategies as being entirely of a piece: "A doctrine is needed powerful enough to work as a breeding agent: strengthening the strong, paralyzing and destructive for the world-weary. The annihilation of the decaying races. Decay of Europe.—The annihilation of slavish evaluations.—Dominion over the earth as a means of producing a higher type.—... The annihilation of *suffrage universel*, i.e., the system through which the lowest natures prescribe themselves as laws for the higher... to strive for fullness of nature through the pairing of opposites: race mixture to this end."[65]

It is not enough, though, to point out the simple contradiction that lies behind Nietzsche's postcolonial reception. What turn out to be his very literalist, and strangely un-ironic, musings in response to Germany's colonial coming-of-age in the 1880s are nevertheless received as a philosophy of "difference" that escapes the reductive doctrines of European humanism. This is not just a matter of bad research, or symptomatic readings but the political theology of reception itself: the smooth transition from Nietzsche's conservative interwar redactors to the '68ist reception of Nietzsche as a hero of the counterculture.

In the end Germany's colonial significance may have less to do with its experience as a training ground for the policies of Nazism (which is a frequently posed problem) than the global inspiration of German thought—especially its exported philosophical concepts.[66] Arguably, this has been the country's decisive influence from Kant and Hegel through Heidegger. It is above all Nietzsche who arises as an unexpected force in the European (and now American) colonial imagination. He managed a mixed, and stylistically novel, racialist fantasy of conquest, replete with belligerent beckonings to European superiority that have somehow skillfully come down to us unscathed by the liberal criticisms of theory. Fitting in comfortably with a post–cold war discourse, his posture of aristocratic radicalism at war with the socialist idea significantly eased the acceptance of his vision, and this helps explain why he continues to authorize the oddly Eurocentric anti-Eurocentrism that characterizes much of postcolonial studies.

Notes

1. One of Cacciari's claims is that Europe's maritime empires moved it beyond the landlocked consciousness of antiquity when it defined itself as the East's absolute other. It became, in a sense, more "fluid," moving in its imperial phase away from the Asian landmass to the realms of sea and air. Nietzsche for him is the key theorist of the move away from polemical confrontation to a permanent heterogeneity and diversity marked by his undermining of European self-certainty. The "West," as the land of the sun's setting, becomes for Cacciari (and Nietzsche before him, supposedly) the sunset of the will to go beyond. In place of utopia he embraces *atopy* (no place). See Cacciari, *Geofilosofia dell'Europa*, esp. 135–41, 143–49.

2. The epigraph, in German in Cacciari's original, reads: "Ich habe den Geist Europas in mich genommen—nun will ich den Gegenschlag thun!" (8). The English translation used here is my own.

3. Nietzsche, *The Gay Science*, 318 (Nietzsche's emphasis).

4. Quoted in Köhler, *Zarathustra's Secret*, xvi.

5. Nietzsche, *The Gay Science*, 97: "the art of wounding and torturing others with words. . . . Whatever is *said well* is believed."

6. See Waite, "Heidegger, Schmitt, Strauss," esp. 122; see also Nietzsche, *The Gay Science*, 228: "I welcome all signs that a more virile, warlike age is about to begin. . . .

To this end we now need many preparatory courageous human beings... who know how to be silent, lonely, resolute, and content and constant in invisible activities."

7. Waite, *Nietzsche's Corps(e)*, 154.

8. Horkheimer and Adorno, *Dialectic of Enlightenment*, 77. They may have had in mind the following passage: "Who will attain anything great if he does not find in himself the strength and the will to *inflict* great suffering... that belongs to greatness" (Nietzsche, *The Gay Science*, 255).

9. Horkheimer and Adorno, *Dialectic of Enlightenment*, 76.

10. Ibid., 79. Horkheimer and Adorno, of course, recognize Nietzsche's attempt to subvert dominant political culture, and they also describe his project as a "protest against civilization." They go so far as to thank him for betraying the "consoling affirmation" that accompanies official power, as well as the hypocritical utopia of grand philosophies (93). But the realization of Nietzsche's doctrines, they add, "both refutes them and reveals their truth." Against the current assumptions of theory, their view of Nietzsche's link to Nazism is unyielding: German fascism brought Nietzsche's philosophy "to its absurd conclusion" (79), in part because his contempt for reality served the movement's fantasies of dominance, neglecting the positive side of the Enlightenment dialectic, which is reason *as critique.*

11. Quoted in Waite, "Heidegger, Schmitt, Strauss," 122.

12. See Holub, "Nietzsche's Colonialist Imagination."

13. See Bergmann, *Nietzsche, "the Last Antipolitical German."*

14. "In a socialist society life negates itself." Socialists are "harmless lambs of happiness," and their movement signifies "no more than an attack of sickness." "I am opposed to... socialism because it dreams quite naively 'the good, true, and beautiful' and of 'equal rights'—anarchism also desires the same ideal, but in a more brutal fashion" (Nietzsche, *The Will to Power*, 77, 397).

15. See Nietzsche, *The Dawn of Day*, entry no. 189.

16. Nietzsche, *The Gay Science*, 339.

17. Waite, *Nietzsche's Corps(e)*, 139, 142.

18. Nietzsche, *The Gay Science*, 338.

19. Kaufmann, *Basic Writings of Nietzsche*, 472.

20. Gandhi, *Postcolonial Theory*, 37–38. She is referring, presumably, to Edward Said, Homi Bhabha, and Gayatri Spivak. Despite Said's very different, and much earlier, contributions to the field than those of the other two (he takes his leads from Georg Lukács, Noam Chomsky, and Raymond Williams rather than Derrida or Foucault, and he identifies with anticolonial resistance), it is remarkable that his references to Nietzsche throughout *Orientalism* are almost entirely uncritical. For more on Said's relationship to theory see Brennan, "The Illusion of a Future."

21. Gandhi, *Postcolonial Theory*, 38.

22. See Subrahmanyam, "One for the Money, Two for the Show."

23. Ashcroft, *On Postcolonial Futures*, 29.

24. Köhler, *Zarathustra's Secret*, xv.

25. The locus classicus of the move is Foucault's essay "Nietzsche, Genealogy, History." In *States of Injury*, however, Wendy Brown takes this lead in an entirely different direction, arguing that Nietzsche is a thinker who might bring the identitarian focus back from its ethics of ressentiment into a more agonistic and active political orientation: "His thought is useful in understanding the source and consequences of a contemporary tendency to moralize in the place of political argument, and to understand the codification of injury and powerlessness—the marked turn away from freedom's pursuit—that this kind of moralizing politics entails" (27). This view, however, misreads Nietzsche's consistent rejection of all "political argument"—indeed, any discussion at all, which he considered the failing of an incessantly chattering modernity—not to mention his hostility to any "freedom" guaranteed by civic involvement or the political process. On this matter see Pierre-André Taguieff, "The Traditionalist Paradigm—Horror of Modernity and Antiliberalism."

26. Derrida, *Margins of Philosophy*, 17.

27. Césaire, *Discourse on Colonialism*, 33, 35.

28. I am thinking here of Peter Hallward, Paul Gilroy, and Antonio Negri.

29. Deleuze, *Nietzsche and Philosophy*, 78.

30. Baudelaire, *The Parisian Prowler*, 21–22.

31. Bergmann, *Nietzsche, "the Last Antipolitical German,"* 53.

32. Nietzsche, *Twilight of the Idols*, "Morality as Anti-Nature," sec. 3.

33. Bergmann, *Nietzsche, "the Last Antipolitical German,"* 53.

34. Ibid., 52–53.

35. Ibid., 119.

36. Ibid., 121.

37. This view has been repeated since. In *La part maudite* (*The Accursed Share*) (1947), George Bataille invented the current fashion of linking sovereignty to erotics, racial fantasy, and the colonial condition—to remove it, in other words, from the then-prevailing idea of the political sovereignty of newly independent states. His *History of Eroticism* was published thirty years before Foucault's *History of Sexuality*. One gets a strong sense of the force of the phrase "Nietzschean lineage" in postcolonial theory when one recalls Bataille's candid concession in *The Accursed Share* that "today, there are only two admissible positions remaining in the world. Communism . . . and the attitude of Nietzsche. . . . Nietzsche's position is the only one apart from communism" (Bataille, *The Accursed Share*, 3:367).

38. "By which means does a virtue come to power?—By exactly the same means as a political party: the slandering, inculpation, undermining of virtues that oppose it and are already in power, by rebaptizing them, by systematic persecution and mockery. Therefore: through sheer 'immorality'" (Nietzsche, *The Will to Power*, 172).

39. Nietzsche, *The Gay Science*, 329. See also Bergmann, *Nietzsche, "the Last Antipolitical German,"* 87.

40. Nietzsche, *The Gay Science*, 107.

41. A perfect statement of his concept of cosmopolitan Europe—what he meant by "good Europeans" as opposed to the "men of fatherlands" (nationalists)—can be found in *The Will to Power*, where he associates the good European with immoralism, the discipline of the will, and the wearing of masks. This amounts, he says, to thinking in a "supra-European" way (80–81).

42. Bergmann, *Nietzsche, "the Last Antipolitical German,"* 123; Nietzsche, *The Gay Science*, 228.

43. Bergmann, *Nietzsche, "the Last Antipolitical German,"* 122.

44. Waite, "Heidegger, Schmitt, Strauss," 120–21.

45. In a single decade, the 1880s, Nietzsche published the largest part of his total oeuvre and all of the most important work with the exception of *The Birth of Tragedy* (1872) and *Untimely Meditations* (1873–76). This includes the notes that were later published posthumously as *The Will to Power* (1901).

46. Friedrichsmeyer, Lennox, and Zantop, "Introduction," 10.

47. For more on this see Naranch, "Inventing the *Auslandsdeutsche*."

48. "It is not too late for the Germans to turn their abusive name into a name of honor by becoming the first un-Christian nation in Europe" (Nietzsche, *The Gay Science*, 194).

49. In *Empire* Michael Hardt and Antonio Negri exemplify the confusion by ignoring context. They celebrate what they call Nietzsche's embrace of a "new nomad horde, a new race of barbarians, [that] will arise to invade or evacuate Empire." They then quote Nietzsche directly: "'Problem: where are the *barbarians* of the twentieth century? Obviously they will come into view and consolidate themselves only after tremendous socialist crises'" (Hardt and Negri, *Empire*, 213). As noted above, cultural "barbarism" is what Nietzsche considered to be the downfall of the worker in his or her militant mode (the Communards are his nightmare vision); it was not a positive connotation. He is saying that the workers can nevertheless redeem themselves on behalf of Europe by participating in an emigration wave to colonize distant climes.

50. Holub, "Nietzsche's Colonialist Imagination," 36–37.

51. Nietzsche, *The Dawn of Day*, 206. Sylvère Lotringer and Christian Marazzi quote from this passage in *Autonomia*, 8.

52. Kaufmann, *Basic Writings of Nietzsche*, 470.

53. Holub, "Nietzsche's Colonialist Imagination," 41.

54. Ibid., 42. See also A. Dirk Moses's essay in the present volume. What I am arguing that Nietzsche embraced—the removal of social constraints in the colonies—is precisely what Moses observes moved Arendt to oppose imperialism in *The Origins of Totalitarianism*.

55. Holub, "Nietzsche's Colonialist Imagination," 43, 47.

56. Ibid., 48.

57. See Hohendahl, "Radical Conservative Thought in Transition." The special issue examines the postwar careers of writers seeking to retain, while refashioning, their discredited interwar period views.

58. Kaufmann, *Basic Writings of Nietzsche*, 476–77. With almost comical disregard for the text, Walter Kaufmann tries to argue that "the 'blond beast' is not a racial concept and does not refer to the 'Nordic race'" (477). Only a few pages earlier, though, Nietzsche has declared that Germans must submit to "blood-poisoning (it has mixed the races together)" in order to fulfill its "world-historic mission" (472). He has spent long passages associating the Greek terms for *ugly*, *ill-born*, and *vile* with the slippage (in Latin) between "bad" (*malus*) and "dark" (*melus*), declaring that the "common man [is designated] as the dark-colored, above all as the black-haired man . . . as the pre-Aryan occupant of the soil of Italy was distinguished most obviously from the blond, that is Aryan, conqueror race by his color" (466). Nietzsche's point may not be racist in the sense of Gobineau, perhaps, since for him the earlier suppressed races were gradually recovering the upper hand (and because a blending, rather than racial purity, was his key to creating the master race). But it is absurd to say the "blond beast" is not a racial concept.

59. Massis, *Defense of the West*, 247–48; subsequent references are cited parenthetically in the text.

60. See Lukács, "Tagore's Gandhi Novel."

61. Ibid., pars. 2–4.

62. Quoted in Kaufmann, *Basic Writings of Nietzsche*, 466–67.

63. Nietzsche, *The Will to Power*, 465.

64. Ibid., 487.

65. Ibid., 459.

66. See, e.g., essays in the present volume by Kitty Millett, A. Dirk Moses, and Russell A. Berman, which partake of this debate in German studies about whether there is a historical continuity between colonialism and later fascism.

Bibliography

Arendt, Hannah. *The Origins of Totalitarianism*. 1948. New York: Harcourt Brace, 1973.

Ashcroft, Bill. *On Postcolonial Futures: Transformations of Colonial Culture*. London: Continuum, 2001.

Bataille, Georges. *The Accursed Share*. Vols. 2 and 3, *"The History of Eroticism"* and *"Sovereignty."* New York: Zone Books, 1993.

Baudelaire, Charles. *The Parisian Prowler (Le spleen de Paris: Petits poèmes en prose)*. Translated by Edward K. Kaplan. Athens: University of Georgia Press, 1989.

Becker, Wilhelm Carl. *Der Nietzschekultus: Ein Kapitel aus der Geschichte der Verirrungen des menschlichen Geistes.* Leipzig: Verlag von Richard Lipinski, 1908.

Bergmann, Peter. *Nietzsche, "the Last Antipolitical German."* Bloomington: Indiana University Press, 1987.

Brennan, Timothy. "The Illusion of a Future: *Orientalism* as Traveling Theory." *Critical Inquiry* 26 (spring 2000): 558–83.

Brown, Wendy. *States of Injury: Power and Freedom in Late Modernity.* Princeton, NJ: Princeton University Press, 1995.

Cacciari, Massimo. *Geofilosofia dell'Europa.* Milano: Adelphi Edizioni, 1994.

Césaire, Aimé. *Discourse on Colonialism.* New York: Monthly Review Press, 1972.

Deleuze, Gilles. *Nietzsche and Philosophy.* New York: Columbia University Press, 1983.

Derrida, Jacques. *Margins of Philosophy.* Translated by Alan Bass. Chicago: University of Chicago Press, 1982.

Foucault, Michel. "Nietzsche, Genealogy, History." In *Language, Counter-Memory, Practice*, edited by Donald F. Bouchard, 139–64. New York: Cornell University Press, 1977.

Friedrichsmeyer, Sara, Sara Lennox, and Susanne Zantop, eds. *The Imperialist Imagination: German Colonialism and Its Legacy.* Ann Arbor: University of Michigan Press, 1998.

Friedrichsmeyer, Sara, Sara Lennox, and Susanne Zantop. Introduction. In Friedrichsmeyer, Lennox, and Zantop, *The Imperialist Imagination*, 1–29.

Gandhi, Leela. *Postcolonial Theory: A Critical Introduction.* New York: Columbia University Press, 1998.

Hardt, Michael, and Antonio Negri. *Empire.* Cambridge, MA: Harvard University Press, 2000.

Hohendahl, Peter Uwe, ed. "Radical Conservative Thought in Transition: Martin Heidegger, Ernst Jünger, Carl Schmitt, 1940–1960." Special issue, *Cultural Critique* 69 (spring 2008).

Holub, Robert C. "Nietzsche's Colonialist Imagination: Nueva Germania, Good Europeanism, and Great Politics." In Friedrichsmeyer, Lennox, and Zantop, *The Imperialist Imagination*, 33–50.

Horkheimer, Max, and Theodor W. Adorno. *Dialectic of Enlightenment.* Translated by Edmund Jephcott. Palo Alto, CA: Stanford University Press, 2002.

Kaufmann, Walter, trans. and ed. *Basic Writings of Nietzsche.* New York: Modern Library, 1992.

Köhler, Joachim. *Zarathustra's Secret: The Interior Life of Friedrich Nietzsche.* Translated by Ronald Taylor. New Haven, CT: Yale University Press, 2002.

Kupka, František. *Vers des temps nouveaux: Kupka, œuvres graphiques, 1894–1912*. Musée d'Orsay, Paris, June 25–Oct. 6, 2002. Paris: Réunion des musées nationaux, 2002.

Lotringer, Sylvère, and Christian Marazzi. *Autonomia: Post-political Politics*. Los Angeles: Semiotext(e), 2007.

Lukács, Georg. "Tagore's Gandhi Novel: Review of Rabindranath Tagore: *The Home and the World*." www.mukto-mona.com/Articles/rabindra_probondho/lukacs_on_tagore.htm (accessed April 27, 2009). Originally published in *Die rote Fahne* (1922). Reprinted in *Mukto-Mona*, Feb. 13, 2007, 1–2.

Massis, Henri. *Defense of the West*. New York: Harcourt, Brace, 1928.

Muret, Maurice. *The Twilight of the White Races*. Translated by Mrs. Touzalin. New York: Charles Scribner's Sons, 1926.

Naranch, Bradley D. "Inventing the *Auslandsdeutsche*: Emigration, Colonial Fantasy, and German National Identity, 1848–71." In *Germany's Colonial Pasts*, edited by Eric Ames, Marcia Klotz, and Lora Wildenthal, 21–40. Lincoln: University of Nebraska Press, 2005.

Nietzsche, Friedrich. *The Dawn of Day*. Translated by J. M. Kennedy. New York: Dover, 2007.

——. *The Gay Science*. Translated by Walter Kaufmann. New York: Vintage, 1974.

——. *"Twilight of the Idols" and "The Anti-Christ."* Translated by R. J. Hollingdale. Harmondsworth: Penguin, 1968.

——. *The Will to Power*. Translated by Walter Kaufmann and R. J. Hollingdale. New York: Vintage, 1968.

Subrahmanyam, Sanjay. "One for the Money, Two for the Show: On Postcolonial Studies and South Asian History," *L'Homme* 187–88 (2008): 93–104.

Taguieff, Pierre-André. "The Traditionalist Paradigm—Horror of Modernity and Antiliberalism: Nietzsche in Reactionary Rhetoric." In *Why We Are Not Nietzscheans*, edited by Luc Ferry and Alain Renaut, 158–223. Chicago: University of Chicago Press, 1997.

Waite, Geoff. "Heidegger, Schmitt, Strauss: The Hidden Monologue, or, Conserving Esotericism to Justify the High Hand of Violence." In Hohendahl, "Radical Conservative Thought in Transition," 113–44.

——. *Nietzsche's Corps(e): Aesthetics, Politics, Prophecy, or, The Spectacular Technoculture of Everyday Life*. Durham, NC: Duke University Press, 1996.

2

German Colonialism

Some Reflections on Reassessments, Specificities, and Constellations

Birthe Kundrus

In late October 2006 former chancellor Gerhard Schröder publicly praised Vladimir Putin (and not for the first time). Asked by representatives of the media why businessmen are thrown into prison in Russia, Schröder replied: "We send tax evaders to prison, too. But we don't have Siberia at our disposal."[1]

Leaving aside the political and legal scandal of this statement, as well as Schröder's presumably rather cool yearnings for Siberia, one might read his witticism as an involuntary expression of the German imperial dilemma of the nineteenth and twentieth centuries: discussions always revolved around something that Germany didn't have. This is one trait characteristic of German imperial efforts. The second trait I would like to highlight is the fact that German imperialism set its sights not only on overseas territories—in Africa, Oceania, the Far East, the Near East, and South America—but also on the European continent.

Current reflection on German colonial history is most interesting when it focuses on these two themes: first, the almost complete lack of an actual practice of colonial or imperial rule, and, second, the search for targets for colonization between overseas territories and central and eastern Europe. What is the significance of this unique German constellation—a fleeting national imperial phase in the long global era of imperialism—in the context of the country's history? What tensions result from a transient "real" imperial history and a much longer and more intensive history of imperial intentions? Moreover, can we trace back to a common source Germany's various attempts to seize new parts of the world?

Although I would hold that the events of 1884, 1918, and 1945 are highly relevant for those seeking answers to these and similar questions, debates among scholars have tended to overstep the bounds these watersheds suggest. Thus, one issue that has attracted considerable attention is the relationship between colonial expansionism and Nazi expansionism. Can we subsume both phenomena under the concept of imperialism? Or are these, in fact, two very different developments?[2] In addition to these questions of possible relations between colonialism and Nazism, research has focused on the phase of formal German colonial rule between 1884 and 1918. One question of special interest in this context is whether and to what extent German colonialism differed from the hegemonic modes of other imperial powers. In recent years we have witnessed an at times lively debate about the significance of colonialism for the German Kaiserreich and for contemporary German history. I would like to review these discussions and offer a few observations and remarks on them.

A New Colonial Historiography?

As central reasons for the current interest in colonial studies, I would point to the changes in some fields of research and the reconstitution of others. These changes are an effect of the rise of cultural studies and colonial and postcolonial studies, which for the most part arrived in Germany, in a manner of speaking, via the United States. Moreover, incorporation of transnational and global perspectives in the study of national history has led to heightened awareness and increased consideration of the colonial past.

A shift in perceptions of colonialism and its significance has accompanied this surge of interest.[3] Earlier analyses—and to an even greater extent the responses to them—were limited to studies of policies aimed at acquiring and exploiting overseas territories. Thus, they referred to occurrences that took place "over there" and interpreted them for the most part in terms of power politics and economic aspects. Newer approaches to colonial history cannot and, indeed, should not replace or ignore older approaches based in the sociology of hegemony, as Jürgen Osterhammel and Sebastian Conrad have quite rightly pointed out.[4] But as imperialism was, in its heyday, a phenomenon of global and overarching temporal significance, colonialism is today also viewed as a part of European history and as a history of entanglement. These interactions not only affected the colonies—in ways that varied from country to country and that were at times contradictory—but also influenced the metropolises.[5] Moreover, new approaches to the study of colonialism help to elucidate just how relevant non-European cultures were for Western European civilization's perception of itself as a culture.[6] This denotes a further characteristic of newer modes of research: their attempts to grasp colonialism as a phenomenon that is always simultaneously global, European, national, and local.

Within the German Reich, colonial subjects (and former colonial subjects) began to migrate—albeit in small numbers—especially from Africa.[7] Colonialism also left its mark on such diverse spheres as literature, film, the academic world, medicine, advertising, urban topography, legislation, infrastructural planning, small businesses referred to as *Kolonialwarenläden* (shops selling colonial wares), the world of scandals, warfare, leisure-time activities such as parlor games, and political-administrative planning programs and demands for participation by political parties and associations of all kinds.[8] In other words, colonialism found its way into the thoughts and experience of German society.

For the most part, members of the educated bourgeoisie dominated German debates about colonialism and reflected collective and individual projections, hopes, and fears, thus paralleling German concerns of the period. The tendency of the colonial movement to essentialize difference occurred at a time when women, social democrats, and others were enunciating with increasing vehemence socialist and liberal democratic demands for individual freedoms, equality, and more political participation.[9] Thus, the relatively new sphere of formal colonial rule contributed to the upsurge of hierarchical and racially defined models of social order that emerged around 1900.[10]

Recent shifts in historical perspective that have led to a focus not only on the actual experience of colonialism but also on the discursive practices, fantasies, and plans conjure up a picture of Germany between 1871 and 1914 that is in part rather unfamiliar. On the one hand, an increasingly essentialist understanding of identity developed, with concomitant effects in the political arena, such as arbitrary rule and the excessive use of force.[11] Media and politicians essentialized race and culture in biological terms and consolidated exclusive, dual-structured views of whites and blacks, civilized and barbarians, modernity and despotism. On the other hand, there were signs of a remarkable and dubious curiosity about what was considered foreign. Emperor Wilhelm II, for example, and with him several of the many Germans who traveled through the Near East at that time, loved to wear "oriental" uniforms. Paintings of August Macke or Paul Klee show a different variation of this impressionableness.[12]

Long before 1884, German merchants, missionaries, voyagers, scholars, and traders traveled beyond the borders of Europe, and an active lobby campaigned for German imperial engagement.[13] By 1900, supporters, as well as opponents, of German colonial involvement could be found in all political camps, including the ranks of the Social Democrats. This heightened interest in the colonial enterprise was potentially disruptive because colonies became a realm in which controversies over competing social designs and solutions for domestic problems played out—at the expense of the colonized peoples. Officials in Berlin and Windhoek, for example, decided to settle Germans in southwest Africa to solve the "problem" of overpopulation and to redirect migration from the United States to German territories. But to a great extent this remained wishful thinking. Neither a sufficient number of settlers were interested, nor did their financial and personal background satisfy colonial bureaucracy. Yet officials in Germany and Africa (as well as the settlers) maintained the fiction of a settler colony. They treated the colonized either as exploitable laborers or as obstacles that they had to "put away" in order to occupy their land.[14]

As in earlier periods, the German public's fascination with the colonies could be associated with quite diverse topics and issues for each region and its inhabitants. Consequently, German colonial rule varied considerably from one overseas possession to the next, with respect both to fundamental concepts and to practical policies. Whereas the Germans under the command of Lothar von Trotha in southwest Africa perpetrated mass violence, with catastrophic consequences for the Herero and Nama, Governor Wilhelm Solf and his successors in Samoa pursued a course of nonviolent, paternalistic defense of local traditions, which often even ran counter to the interests of the European settlers. And in the course of seventeen years of colonial rule in Qingdao, German officials shifted from Sinophobic segregation in legal and administrative structures and urban space to new policies of "rapprochement, syncretism, and exchange between two civilizations conceptualized as different but relatively equal in value."[15]

This preoccupation with Germany's "Going Abroad" was not limited to the country's overseas possessions, nor was it always about political and military mastery: one need only recall German orientalism and the plans for colonies in the Orient, the trips made there by Kaiser Wilhelm II, and the construction of the Baghdad Railway.[16] Also in the nineteenth century, similar phases of popular projection focused on Rome and Greece in antiquity, as well as on China and Egypt.

The same period saw an upsurge of interest in central and eastern Europe, areas in which Germans had formerly settled. Annexation of these territories was a political demand championed by *völkisch* extremists. Whether and how these very diverse expansions, these "moral"[17] and military conquests, were related to (or competed with) one another are questions that research has not yet explored in detail. Were, for example, the *völkisch* dreams of a "German East" that emerged around 1900 a response to the frustrating political fruits of German colonial endeavors? To what extent can we support Philipp Ther's suggestion that we must explore the imperial dimension of the Kaiserreich not only in the overseas possessions but also in the sphere of German rule over the Polish population of Prussia's eastern provinces?[18] Did Germany perceive Poland more and more as a "substitute colony,"[19] indeed perhaps even as the only real colony of the German Reich? Bringing together these separate strands of inquiry to a greater extent than has been the case so far would seem to be a productive approach for further studies. In this respect the work of David Blackbourn is quite stimulating. He views the affective tension associated with eastern Europe as an element of a specific German colonial history. As early as the Wilhelminian period, as Blackbourn notes, there were indications that the true parallel to India or Algeria was not Cameroon but central Europe. Blackbourn concludes that the country's formal loss of the colonies in 1919 did not mark the colonial caesura for the German Reich but rather it was the end of the German settlements in Eastern and Central Europe in 1945. This still leaves unanswered the question of whether and, if so, how overseas colonialism and the German "drive" toward eastern Europe influenced each other. Moreover, there is still the task of differentiating among all these expansionist aims and practices.[20] Was Nazi expansionism indeed merely a radicalized continuation of imperial ambitions of the nineteenth century, a kind of worst empire ever? Or did it instead break with key elements of imperial rule? Continuity is one of the most difficult theoretical and methodological problems in historiography.[21] There is very little agreement about what the term actually means. Since linear relationships and causal chains are rarely evident in history, especially over long periods and distances, one solution to the dilemma of continuity might be a strategy that examines the productive adaptation of ideas, structures, images, knowledge, experience, or practices. Further research might thus consider how the Nazis adapted their expansionist plans and practices to British or U.S. (rather than German overseas) imperialism and assess what conceptual modifications emerged in the course of such transfer processes. In what way did empires—be they Rome, the United States, or Britain—function as a kind of sounding board for Nazi attitudes and practices?

A Specific Kind of German Colonialism?

Thus we can conclude that colonialism was and is an integral element of Western societies. But what distinguished German colonialism from the colonial systems of other European nations? Looking at the brief phase of colonial rule overseas, we see that most findings accrued thus far for European imperialism also apply to the German Reich:[22] the considerable significance of prestige, a constant vacillation between self-affirmation and perceived threat by the foreign Other, the "white woman" as a guarantor of culture, the sexualized metaphor of the conquest, the pronounced de facto caste system in the colonies, the cultures of difference in colonial policies, and the considerable significance of local factors for social and political practices of colonial rule and the concomitant limited influence of policies formulated in Berlin. Just as in France, Great Britain, or the United States, German colonialism demonstrated and documented hegemony by exhibiting the subjugated "Others"; colonizers viewed the way of life of the colonized with a mixture of idealization and aloofness. As elsewhere, the creed of inequality, segregation, paternalism, and condescension, as well as systematic exploitation and slave labor, were the trademarks of dealings with indigenous cultures. And as elsewhere, German colonies manifested the contradictions inherent in claims that Europeans represented a "master race": the structural instability of colonial domination, as well as a hegemonic order that unfailingly demonstrated outward strength and yet was marked internally by fragility and disintegration. This conglomerate of phantasmagoric desires, absolute pretensions to power, and the unrestrained pursuit of hegemony led regularly to conflicts with the indigenous societies that all too often ended in extreme forms of violence. As all forms of colonial rule damaged and injured minds, souls, and bodies of the colonized, so did German colonialism.

Brutality, domination, and exploitation were the basal structures of every kind of imperialism. Nevertheless, new research on colonial systems stresses the point that to interpret colonizers and colonized only in terms of perpetrators and victims or to understand the concrete lives of the "natives" only in terms of force and compulsion oversimplifies the complex realities of imperial experiences, reduces the diverse strategies of agency by the colonized, and succumbs to the fantasies of omnipotence created by the colonizers.[23] We can reconstruct this "middle ground,"[24] this more nuanced picture of imperial rule, in German colonialism as well. Frequently—though by no means always—German interpretations of Africa, Asia, or Oceania or their inhabitants were not off the mark. At times there were also perceptive observations about mutual insecurities, misunderstandings, and deceptions. The reverse is also true: the colonized peoples had learned to play their own games of imperialism and produced their own knowledge about the "foreigners."[25] Furthermore, colonial domination was initially limited to a thin network of stations, most of them located along the coastlines, with a few outposts in the interior. Just as the colonizers achieved control of the territories in stages and never secured them at all in some regions—the Caprivi Strip and Ovamboland in German Southwest Africa are examples—so were attempts to subjugate the population only gradually successful.[26] This suggests a further desideratum in research on the German colonies, namely, comparative or transfer studies. On the one hand, these studies might compare the individual German colonies. Especially in Africa—the situation in the South Pacific was different[27]—it would appear that the colonial state was far from representing a reliable political order. But this, too, is a characteristic that German colonialism shares with other European powers. On the other hand, transfer studies should consider other European "cultures of colonialism," as Bradley Naranch and Geoff Eley have termed them. High imperialism was a European project, so how did cooperation and exchange of knowledge influence colonial rule?[28] We already know that many German colonial concepts—such as the German equivalent of "bride ships," which sent potential wives to the colonists, or the prohibitions on emigration to the colonies for those deemed undesirable—were patterned after the practices of other imperial powers and were thus in effect "hybrid" phenomena.

What might have been special were Germany's attempts to catch up with the Great Powers, with France and Great Britain. The result of these attempts was a certain lack of planning on the part of the German bureaucracy and a constant tendency to improvise, which did not end when Bernhard Dernburg became state secretary for colonial affairs in 1907.[29] Owing to this feeling of being a straggler, and in an attempt to bridge the gap, developments in the German protectorates were at times more exaggerated, more intense, and only rarely more low-key than in the other European colonies.

A telling example for this kind of extreme is the discussion about so-called mixed marriages between white German men and indigenous women in the colonies. Around 1900 many colonial powers raised the issue of whether it was possible or desirable to thwart such unions. In southern Rhodesia a law prohibiting sexual relations between European women and black men, but not between European men and African women, went into force in 1903. In Capeland, Natal, and Oranjeland, as well, extramarital sexual relations between black men and white women were declared illegal from 1902/3 on, as part of a campaign against prostitution. In Transvaal such marriages had already been outlawed in 1897. Great Britain forbade marriages between civil servants in the colonies and indigenous partners in 1909. The German Reich attempted to hinder such relationships by enacting territorial "marriage bans." On the one hand, all colonial powers chose similar strategies; mobbing and social discrimination were to "take care of" the problem. Prohibitions of sexual relations and marriages were common but were aimed almost completely at white women and black men. On the other hand, high-ranking colonial officials in the Reich decided to turn the screw a bit further than the other European imperial powers, as their target was the male German settler and his mixed offspring. At the same time, however, the Reichstag called on the *Bundesrat* (Federal Council) to submit legislation that would ensure the validity of all marriages between "whites" and "natives" in all German colonies. Race was not to pose an obstacle to marriage. Thus, German policy on mixed marriages and miscegenation reflected two diametrically opposed objectives—a constellation that was presumably unique within European colonialism, with some advocating that difference be upheld at all costs, while others emphasized that securing legal equality was imperative. This marked ambivalence seems to suggest one answer to the question about the specific characteristics of German colonialism: despite being, in general, similar to the structures and actions of other colonial powers, German policies were nonetheless radical in a way that presumably was not limited to the colonial realm.

A second answer to the question about specific characteristics of German colonialism would involve pointing to its near nonexistence. Thus, research in the coming years will face the challenge of examining whether this special constellation—a long period of colonialism without colonies and a brief imperial phase—had effects on German history and, if so, what those effects were.[30] Did this constellation generate mercantile, academic, and political energies? Did it exacerbate colonial discourses?[31] Was the shock effect of "disappropriation" in 1919, this sudden shift from power to powerlessness, a key element?[32] How did the lack of a decolonization phase, the lack of confrontation with the formerly colonized nations, the almost complete lack of migration from the colonies to metropolitan society affect German society and its politics? Did all of this heighten German "provincialism," as Erich Kästner's ironic parody on Bertolt Brecht's song "Surabaya Johnny," written in 1930, suggested?

> Du sprachst von Kolonien,
> Johnny, sunny Johnny,
> und kanntest nur Berlin.[33]

Or did most people, like Kästner, come to terms with the situation? Indeed, did some among the German elite even feel "relieved of a burden"? Asked in a survey of two hundred prominent people from public life whether the German Reich needed colonies, Thomas Mann responded: "The idea of freedom and self-determination has awakened everywhere and will never again be laid to rest. I believe that events have taught us to perceive our freedom from colonial baggage as an advantage."[34] For those interested in the significance of colonialism, the fact that there has been relatively little research on the critique of it is indeed unfortunate.[35] Finally, there is the question of what the effect of colonial amnesia in the post-1945 phase was. For example, how did the legend according to which Germany had never been active in the usual sense of colonialism influence the relations of both German states to the "Third World"?[36]

(German) Colonialism: Contexts and Constellations, Links and Limits

Even though the epoch of colonial rule was short, colonial topics and mentalities continue to have a lasting effect up to the present day. Explicit positive references to the colonial period were a persistent feature of post-

1945 German society, as evidenced, for example, in the names given to *Bundeswehr* (federal army) garrisons. More widespread are implicit patterns in popular culture or in perceptions of "foreigners" and "the foreign." But it is important to note that these were often drawn not from a specific German but rather European reservoir of colonial knowledge. During the Kaiserreich, as well as during the Weimar Republic, Germany's cultural avant-garde generally refrained from any involvement in national colonialism: it was "Surabaya Johnny" rather than "Kiaochow Johnny." If German cultural elites were engaged with colonial issues, then their inspiration came mainly from French and British literature—or even Dutch colonialism.[37] Besides the need to contextualize German colonialism within the larger framework of European colonialism, a further issue warrants closer consideration: how influential was firsthand and secondhand experience with colonies? Some scholars concerned with these research questions in the United States emphasize with considerable verve the great significance of colonialism for German history. There is a tendency to label nearly every illegitimate form of rule, every exotic phenomenon, as "colonial."[38] As a result, Germany has a rich—perhaps the term *catastrophic* would be more fitting—colonial heritage. From my point of view this is a problematic overextension, as it underestimates the different contexts in which these colonial effects were just one factor among others. More telling would be an analysis of the interplay of all these factors to determine in what constellations colonial topics were activated, by what actors, and for what purposes. For example, during the Weimar Republic blacks appeared in new roles that transcended colonial stereotypes. As jazz became more popular in Germany in the second half of the 1920s, not only Afro-Americans but also Afro-Germans performed in public as jazz musicians and as dancers. Although they still served as a surface onto which the political right could project social-Darwinist scenarios of degeneration, the coordinates of those visions changed, with blacks now also decried by the right—or lauded by others—as embodiments of the dynamics of modernity.

Contextualizing colonialism might at times reveal that colonial topics played a minor role or even no role at all. As Sonja Levsen discovered in her study on students at Cambridge and Tübingen in the period from 1900 to 1929,[39] students at Cambridge based their self-definition on Great Britain's role as an empire and, despite the fact that some one hundred Indian students were registered there in 1909, an "Indian problem" and the increasing discrimination of Indian students developed. For their German counterparts, in contrast, imperial "pride and prejudice" was not an issue. Colonies were not a factor in shaping identity, there were no "colored students," and racist resentment manifested itself as anti-Semitism against Jewish fellow students. In this elite milieu German colonialism apparently played only a minor role in shaping racist consciousness in everyday life. The colonies did play an important role in the discussions about the reform of German citizenship laws that took place around 1913, as Dieter Gosewinkel has shown. But the decisive issue involved in this reform was achieving closure with respect to the Poles and the Jews.[40] Another aspect that warrants closer scrutiny is the question of how persistent racist patterns of interpretation, stereotypes, and references really were. For example, how did the rules about what people could say in public or in private about "race" change between 1871 and 1990—or after "reunification"?[41] Germans came to know "foreigners" in the course of the twentieth century, not in the least because of the Nazis, in a manner that has hardly been studied to date.[42] It is to be hoped that future research will reflect to a greater extent the multifaceted background of developments that accelerated and intensified beginning in the second half of the nineteenth century.

A tendency to exaggerate the effects of colonialism is also due in part to the poststructuralist turn in colonial studies, as Frederick Cooper recently warned: "Looking for a 'textual colonization' or a 'metaphoric constellation' distinct from the institutions through which colonial power is exercised risks making colonialism appear everywhere—and hence nowhere."[43] His message is a more nuanced and constructive call for greater conceptual clarity among all those interested in colonial issues. Similar tendencies of conceptual confusion are also apparent in some parts of German education studies. They no longer see the challenges to pedagogical efforts as resulting from a "multicultural" society of immigrants but from a "postcolonial" society of immigrants.[44] Portraying globalization only as an aftereffect of colonial relations is clearly a reduction of complexity and ignores the specific nature of immigration to Germany. It also compounds the problem by missing the salient point of Germany's colonial past—a very short phase of formal colonial rule, including very limited migration, and a much longer phase of imperial longings undisturbed by any challenge from decolonization. Presumably, such exaggerated accounts are a reaction to decades in which German society neglected colonial themes.[45]

For the moment it is obviously essential that we explore the colonial or imperial dimension that shaped the German experience of modernity, probe the mechanisms of perception or nonperception of German or European colonialism in Germany, and seek to understand how deeply such mechanisms influenced political thought, political and social practices, and the cultural identity of the Germans. Among the challenges that will have to be dealt with is also the issue of how to better relate the conflicting histories of colonizers and colonized and how to move beyond accounts that characterize non-Europeans as merely an exotic element of the scenery.

Notes

1. Hanauer, "Gerhard Schröders staatsmännischer und doch salopper Blick zurück."
2. See Zimmerer, "The Birth of the *Ostland* Out of the Spirit of Colonialism"; Kundrus, "Continuities, Parallels, Receptions" (an abridged version of Kundrus, "Kontinuitäten, Parallelen, Rezeptionen"); as well as the contributions by Shelley Baranowski, Kitty Millet, and A. Dirk Moses in this volume.
3. See Lindner, "Plätze an der Sonne?"
4. See Conrad and Osterhammel, "Einleitung," 16.
5. Uerlings, "Kolonialer Diskurs, Globalisierung und postkoloniale Analyse," 17.
6. See Honold and Simons, *Kolonialismus als Kultur*; Honold and Scherpe, *Mit Deutschland um die Welt*; Kundrus, *Phantasiereiche*; Friedrichsmeyer, Lennox, and Zantop, *The Imperialist Imagination*.
7. See, e.g., Mazón and Steingröver, *Not So Plain as Black and White*; Kundrus, "Section: Germany."
8. On literature see, e.g., Zantop, *Colonial Fantasies*; on film: Schöning, *Triviale Tropen*; on academia: Grosse, *Kolonialismus, Eugenik und bürgerliche Gesellschaft in Deutschland, 1850–1918*; Penny and Bunzl, *Worldly Provincialism*; and Zimmerman, *Anthropology and Antihumanism in Imperial Germany*; on medicine: Eckart, *Medizin und Kolonialimperialismus*; on advertising: Ciarlo, *Advertising Empire, Consuming Race*; on urban topography: Heyden and Zeller, *Kolonialmetropole Berlin*; and Heyden and Zeller, *Macht und Anteil an der Weltherrschaft*; on legislative issues: Fischer, *Die deutschen Kolonien*; on infrastructural planning: Laak, *Imperiale Infrastruktur*; astonishingly enough, no systematic study of colonialism's impact on small retail businesses has been published to date, but see the essays in Epple and Wierling, "Globale Waren"; on the world of scandal: Bösch, "'Are We a Cruel Nation?'"; on warfare: Hull, *Absolute Destruction*; on leisure-time activities: Badenberg, "Spiel um Kamerun"; and on administrative and organizational issues: Wildenthal, *German Women for Empire, 1884–1945*.
9. Sebastian Conrad labels "this shaping of national self-interpretation by race discourse as the central characteristic of the radicalization of nationalism

around 1900" (Conrad, *Globalisierung und Nation im Deutschen Kaiserreich,* 22–23; my translation).

10. See Geulen, "The Common Grounds of Conflict."
11. See Perraudin and Zimmerer, *German Colonialism and National Identity.*
12. See Conrad and Osterhammel, "Einleitung," 19.
13. On colonialism before 1884 see Fitzpatrick, *Liberal Imperialism in Germany*; Fenske, "Ungeduldige Zuschauer"; and Müller, "Imperialist Ambitions in *Vormärz* and Revolutionary Germany."
14. See Kundrus, *Moderne Imperialisten.*
15. Steinmetz, *The Devil's Handwriting*, 470.
16. See Fuhrmann in this volume; as well as McMurray, *Distant Ties.*
17. Pöppinghaus, "*Moralische Eroberungen?*
18. See Ther, "Imperial Instead of National History."
19. Conrad, *Globalisierung und Nation im Deutschen Kaiserreich*, 29. See also Nelson, *Germans, Poland, and Colonial Expansion to the East*; as well as Kopp in this volume.
20. For an outstanding survey see Osterhammel, *Die Verwandlung der Welt*, esp. chap. 8, "Empires and Nation States."
21. See Kundrus, *Kontinuitäten*; see also Smith, *The Continuities of German History*; as well as the reviews of Smith's book at www.sehepunkte.de/2009/01/forum/mehrfachbesprechung-brhelmut-walser-smith-the-continuities-of-german-history-61/ (accessed April 22, 2009), esp. the critique by Langewiesche: "Wie Helmut Walser Smith Kontinuitätslinien in der deutschen Geschichte erzeugt und was dabei verloren geht."
22. On European imperialism in general see Osterhammel, *Die Verwandlung der Welt*; Albertini, *Europäische Kolonialherrschaft, 1880–1940*; Reinhard, *Geschichte der europäischen Expansion*; and Fieldhouse, *The Colonial Empires*. On colonialism and the German Reich see Speitkamp, *Deutsche Kolonialgeschichte*; Gründer, *Geschichte der deutschen Kolonien*; Laak, *Über alles in der Welt*; Conrad, *Deutsche Kolonialgeschichte*. Obviously, forms of colonial rule varied considerably across different colonies, even when they were governed by the same power. Moreover, different and often competing national concepts of colonial governance and modes of administration existed, and they changed over time. Furthermore, practices were adjusted to fit local circumstances. See Lindner, "Colonialism as a European Project in Africa Before 1914?" The summary that follows here is thus of necessity simplified and merely outlines tendencies in the period up to World War I.
23. See, e.g., Osterhammel, *Die Verwandlung der Welt*, 662–72; see also Trotha, "Was war Kolonialismus?"
24. See White, *The Middle Ground.*
25. See Eckert, *Herrschen und Verwalten.*
26. Pesek, *Koloniale Herrschaft in Deutsch-Ostafrika.*

27. See Steinmetz, *The Devil's Handwriting*.

28. See Ulrike Lindner und Luís Madureira in this volume.

29. An explicitly scientific approach toward colonies and colonialism was perhaps more developed in Germany than in other empires. See, e.g., Ruppenthal, *Kolonialismus als "Wissenschaft und Technik."*

30. See Grosse, "What Does German Colonialism Have to Do with National Socialism?" Readers should recall the extent to which the world was shaped by empires in the period between 1880 and 1940. The British, French, Belgians, Dutch, Danes, Spanish, Portuguese, Italians, Germans, Russians, Japanese, and Americans ruled, at least formally, nearly two-thirds of humanity; see Trotha, *Kolonialismus*, 51. See also Eley, *Empire by Land or Sea?*: "By the colonial effect, I mean the sum of transference and translation of complex and heterogeneous knowledge, idioms of thought, direct and vicarious experiences, spectacular events, arresting and seductive images, compelling arguments about economics, prosperity, and global survival, a visual repertoire of fantasy and desire, manifold forms of everyday consumption and all the relevant registers of governmentality" (12).

31. Dunker, "Einleitung," 14.

32. Struck, "Ein renegatisches Machtabenteuer unter den Negern," 195–96.

33. "You spoke of colonies, / Johnny, sunny Johnny, / and only knew Berlin" (Kästner, "Surabaya-Johnny II," 334–35).

34. Quoted in Bartholdy, "Soll Deutschland Kolonialpolitik treiben? 624.

35. See Schwarz, *"Je weniger Afrika, desto besser."* See, by contrast, the eight-volume series edited by Peter J. Cain, *The Empire and Its Critics, 1899–1939*.

36. See the essays in Kruke, "Dekolonisation"; and Luis Madureira in this volume.

37. Struck, "Ein renegatisches Machtabenteuer unter den Negern," 179–80.

38. See Poiger, "Imperialism as Paradigm for Modern German History." Astutely argued is Gilroy, *After Empire*.

39. See Levsen, *Elite, Männlichkeit und Krieg*, 150–71.

40. Gosewinkel, *Einbürgern und Ausschließen*.

41. See, e.g., Fehrenbach, *Race After Hitler*.

42. On the Nazis see Patel, "Analysen und Alternativen." Meanwhile, studies have been published that deal with specific groups at specific times, for example Africans in Nazi Germany or the GDR, or the *Gastarbeiter* in the Federal Republic or on problems of integration of the *Russlanddeutsche* (Russian Germans). See, e.g., Campt, *Other Germans*; Chin, *The Guest Worker Question in Postwar Germany*; and Wierling, *Heimat finden*. A more conceptual access is chosen by studies on racism. See Grosse, *Kolonialismus, Eugenik und bürgerliche Gesellschaft in Deutschland, 1850–1918*; or Geulen, *Geschichte des Rassismus*. Yet still missing are syntheses that take into consideration the social and political interactions between Germans and "foreigners" in the twentieth century, thereby also reconstructing the zigzagging of attitudes and mentalities on both sides. See, as an exception, Bade, *Deutsche im Ausland*.

43. Cooper, *Colonialism in Question*, 47.
44. See the essays in Deutsche Vereinigung für politische Bildung e.V., "Kolonialismus bis heute?"
45. The question has also been raised about whether the British Empire, even at the height of its power, was as constitutive for British culture and the lives of most British citizens as has often been asserted. See Porter, *The Absent-Minded Imperialists*.

Bibliography

Albertini, Rudolf von. *Europäische Kolonialherrschaft, 1880–1940*. Zürich: Steiner, 1976.
Bade, Klaus J., ed. *Deutsche im Ausland—Fremde in Deutschland: Migration in Geschichte und Gegenwart*. Munich: Beck, 1992.
Badenberg, Nana. "Spiel um Kamerun: Kolonialismus in Brett- und Gesellschaftsspielen." In Honold and Scherpe, *Mit Deutschland um die Welt*, 86–94.
Bartholdy, A. Mendelsohn, ed. "Soll Deutschland Kolonialpolitik treiben? Eine Umfrage aus dem Jahr 1927." Special issue, *Europäische Gespräche, Hamburger Monatshefte für Auswärtige Politik* 5 (1927): 610-656.
Bösch, Frank. " 'Are We a Cruel Nation?' Colonial Practices, Perceptions and Scandals." In *Wilhelmine Germany and Edwardian Britain: Essays on Cultural Affinity*, edited by Dominik Geppert and Robert Gerwarth, 115–42. Oxford: Oxford University Press, 2008.
Cain, Peter J., ed. *The Empire and Its Critics, 1899–1939: The Classics of Imperialism*. 8 vols. London: Routledge, 1998.
Campt, Tina. *Other Germans: Black Germans and the Politics of Race, Gender, and Memory in the Third Reich*. Ann Arbor: University of Michigan Press, 2004.
Chin, Rita C.-K. *The Guest Worker Question in Postwar Germany*. Cambridge, UK: Cambridge University Press, 2007.
Ciarlo, David. *Advertising Empire, Consuming Race: Colonialism and Visual Culture in Germany, 1887–1914*. Cambridge, MA: Harvard University Press, forthcoming.
Conrad, Sebastian. *Deutsche Kolonialgeschichte*. Munich: Beck, 2008.
———. *Globalisierung und Nation im Deutschen Kaiserreich*. Munich: Beck, 2006.
Conrad, Sebastian, and Jürgen Osterhammel. "Einleitung." In *Das Kaiserreich transnational: Deutschland in der Welt, 1871–1914*, edited by Sebastian Conrad and Jürgen Osterhammel, 7–27. Göttingen: Vandenhoeck und Ruprecht, 2004.
Cooper, Frederick. *Colonialism in Question: Theory, Knowledge, History*. Berkeley: University of California Press, 2005.
Deutsche Vereinigung für politische Bildung e.V., ed. "Kolonialismus bis heute?" Special issue, *Politisches Lernen* 24, no. 1–2 (2006).

Dunker, Axel. "Einleitung." In Dunker, *(Post-)Kolonialismus und deutsche Literatur*, 7-16.

———, ed. *(Post-)Kolonialismus und deutsche Literatur: Impulse der angloamerikanischen Literatur- und Kulturtheorie*. Bielefeld: Aisthesis, 2005.

Eckart, Wolfgang U. *Medizin und Kolonialimperialismus: Deutschland, 1884–1945*. Paderborn: Schöningh, 1997.

Eckert, Andreas. *Herrschen und Verwalten: Afrikanische Bürokratien, staatliche Ordnung und Politik in Tanzania, 1920–1970*. Munich: Oldenbourg, 2007.

Eley, Geoff. *Empire by Land or Sea? Germany's Imperial Imaginary, 1871–1945*. Speech delivered at the German Historical Institute in Washington, DC, March 28, 2007.

Epple, Angelika, and Dorothee Wierling, eds. "Globale Waren." Special issue, *Werkstattgeschichte* 45 (2007).

Fehrenbach, Heide. *Race After Hitler: Black Occupation Children in Postwar Germany and America*. Princeton, NJ: Princeton University Press, 2005.

Fenske, Hans. "Ungeduldige Zuschauer: Die Deutschen und die europäische Expansion, 1815–1880." In *Imperialistische Kontinuität und nationale Ungeduld im 19. Jahrhundert*, edited by Wolfgang Reinhard, 87–123. Frankfurt: Fischer, 1991.

Fieldhouse, David K. *The Colonial Empires: A Comparative Survey from the Eighteenth Century*. 2nd ed. London: Macmillan, 1982.

Fischer, Hans-Jörg. *Die deutschen Kolonien: Die koloniale Rechtsordnung und ihre Entwicklung nach dem Ersten Weltkrieg*. Berlin: Dunker und Humblot, 2001.

Fitzpatrick, Matthew. *Liberal Imperialism in Germany: Expansionism and Nationalism, 1848–1884*. New York: Berghahn, 2008.

Friedrichsmeyer, Sara, Sara Lennox, and Susanne Zantop, eds. *The Imperialist Imagination: German Colonialism and Its Legacy*. Ann Arbor: University of Michigan Press, 1998.

Fuhrmann, Malte. *Der Traum vom deutschen Orient: Zwei deutsche Kolonien im Osmanischen Reich, 1851–1918*. Frankfurt: Campus, 2006.

Geulen, Christian. "The Common Grounds of Conflict: Racial Visions of World Order, 1880–1940." In *Competing Visions of World Order: Global Moments and Movements, 1880s–1930s*, edited by Sebastian Conrad and Dominic Sachsenmaier, 29–68. New York: Palgrave Macmillan, 2007.

———. *Geschichte des Rassismus*. Munich: Beck, 2007.

Gilroy, Paul. *After Empire: Melancholia or Convivial Culture*. Oxford: Routledge, 2004.

Gosewinkel, Dieter. *Einbürgern und Ausschließen: Die Nationalisierung der Staatsangehörigkeit vom Deutschen Bund bis zur Bundesrepublik Deutschland*. Göttingen: Vandenhoeck und Ruprecht, 2001.

Grosse, Pascal. *Kolonialismus, Eugenik und bürgerliche Gesellschaft in Deutschland, 1850–1918*. Frankfurt: Campus, 2000.

———. "What Does German Colonialism Have to Do with National Socialism? A Conceptual Framework." In *Germany's Colonial Pasts*, edited by Eric Ames, Marcia Klotz, and Lora Wildenthal, 115–34. Lincoln: University of Nebraska Press, 2005.

Gründer, Horst. *Geschichte der deutschen Kolonien*. Paderborn: Schöningh, 2000.

Hanauer, Florian. "Gerhard Schröders staatsmännischer und doch salopper Blick zurück." *Die Welt*, Oct. 30, 2006.

Heyden, Ulrich van der, and Joachim Zeller, eds. *Kolonialmetropole Berlin: Eine Spurensuche*. Berlin: Berlin-Ed., 2002.

———. *Macht und Anteil an der Weltherrschaft: Berlin und der deutsche Kolonialismus*. Münster: Unrast, 2005.

Honold, Alexander, and Klaus R. Scherpe, eds. *Mit Deutschland um die Welt: Eine Kulturgeschichte des Fremden in der Kolonialzeit*. Stuttgart: Metzler, 2004.

Honold, Alexander, and Oliver Simons, eds. *Kolonialismus als Kultur: Literatur, Medien, Wissenschaft in der deutschen Gründerzeit des Fremden*. Tübingen: Francke, 2002.

Hull, Isabel V. *Absolute Destruction: Military Culture and the Practices of War in Imperial Germany*. Ithaca, NY: Cornell University Press, 2004.

Kästner, Erich. "Surabaya-Johnny II: Frei nach Kipling und Brecht." In *Wir sind so frei: Chansons, Kabarett, Kleine Prosa*, 334–35. Munich: Büchergilde Gutenberg, 1998.

Kruke, Anja, ed. "Dekolonisation: Prozesse und Verflechtungen (1945–1990)." Special issue, *Archiv für Sozialgeschichte* 48 (2008).

Kundrus, Birthe. "Continuities, Parallels, Receptions: Reflections on the 'Colonization' of National Socialism." *Journal of Namibian Studies* 1, no. 4 (2008): 25–46.

———. "Kontinuitäten, Parallelen, Rezeptionen: Überlegungen zur Kolonialisierung des Nationalsozialismus." *WerkstattGeschichte* 43 (2006): 45–62.

———. *Moderne Imperialisten: Das Kaiserreich im Spiegel seiner Kolonien*. Cologne: Böhlau, 2003.

———, ed. *Phantasiereiche: Zur Kulturgeschichte des deutschen Kolonialismus*. Frankfurt: Campus, 2003.

———, regional ed. "Section: Germany." In *A Historical Companion to Postcolonial Literatures—Continental Europe and Its Empires*, edited by Prem Poddar, Rajeev S. Patke, and Lars Jensen, 198–251. Edinburgh: University of Edinburgh Press, 2008.

Laak, Dirk van. *Imperiale Infrastruktur: Deutsche Planungen für eine Erschließung Afrikas, 1880 bis 1960*. Paderborn: Schöningh, 2004.

———. *Über alles in der Welt: Deutscher Imperialismus im 19. und 20. Jahrhundert*. Munich: Beck, 2005.

Langewiesche, Dieter. "Wie Helmut Walser Smith Kontinuitätslinien in der deutschen Geschichte erzeugt und was dabei verloren geht." Review of *The Continuities of German History*, by Helmut Walser Smith, *Sehepunkte* 9, no. 1 (2009): www.sehepunkte.de/2009/01/15041.html (accessed March 19, 2010).

Levsen, Sonja. *Elite, Männlichkeit und Krieg: Tübinger und Cambridger Studenten, 1900–1929*. Göttingen: Vandenhoeck und Ruprecht, 2006.

Lindner, Ulrike. "Colonialism as a European Project in Africa Before 1914? British and German Concepts of Colonial Rule in Sub-Saharan Africa." In "Ordering the Colonial World Around the 20th Century: Global and Comparative Perspectives," edited by Sebastian Conrad, Nadin Heé, and Ulrike Schaper. Special issue, *Comparativ* 19, no. 1 (2009): 88–106.

———. "Plätze an der Sonne? Die Geschichtsschreibung auf dem Weg in die Deutschen Kolonien." *Archiv für Sozialgeschichte* 48 (2008): 487–510.

Mazón, Patricia, and Reinhild Steingröver, eds. *Not So Plain as Black and White: Afro-German Culture and History, 1890–2000*. Rochester, NY: University of Rochester Press, 2005.

McMurray, Jonathan S. *Distant Ties: Germany, the Ottoman Empire, and the Construction of the Baghdad Railway*. Westport, CT: Greenwood, 2001.

Müller, F. L. "Imperialist Ambitions in *Vormärz* and Revolutionary Germany: The Agitation for German Settlement Colonies Overseas, 1840–1849." *German History* 17, no. 3 (1999): 346–68.

Nelson, Robert L., ed. *Germans, Poland, and Colonial Expansion to the East: 1850 Through the Present*. Basingstoke, UK: Palgrave Macmillan, 2009.

Osterhammel, Jürgen. *Die Verwandlung der Welt: Eine Geschichte des 19. Jahrhunderts*. Munich: Beck, 2009.

Patel, Kiran Klaus. "Analysen und Alternativen—Der Nationalsozialismus in transnationaler Perspektive." *Blätter für deutsche und internationale Politik* 49, no. 9 (2004): 1123–34.

Penny, H. Glenn, and Matti Bunzl, eds. *Worldly Provincialism: German Anthropology in the Age of Empire*. Ann Arbor: University of Michigan Press, 2003.

Perraudin, Michael, and Jürgen Zimmerer, eds. *German Colonialism and National Identity*. London: Routledge, 2010.

Pesek, Michael. *Koloniale Herrschaft in Deutsch-Ostafrika: Expeditionen, Militär und Verwaltung seit 1880*. Frankfurt: Campus, 2005.

Poiger, Uta G. "Imperialism as Paradigm for Modern German History." In *Conflict, Catastrophe, and Continuity: Essays on Modern German History*, edited by Frank Biess, Mark Roseman, and Hanna Schissler, 177–99. New York: Berghahn, 2007.

Pöppinghaus, Ernst-Wolfgang. *"Moralische Eroberungen?" Kultur und Politik in den deutsch-spanischen Beziehungen der Jahre 1919 bis 1933*. Frankfurt: Vervuert, 1999.

Porter, Bernard. *The Absent-Minded Imperialists: Empire, Society, and Culture in Britain*. Oxford: Oxford University Press, 2004.

Reinhard, Wolfgang. *Geschichte der europäischen Expansion*. 4 vols. Stuttgart: Kohlhammer, 1983–1990.

Ruppenthal, Jens. *Kolonialismus als "Wissenschaft und Technik": Das Hamburgische Kolonialinstitut, 1908–1919.* Stuttgart: Steiner, 2007.
Schöning, Jörg, ed. *Triviale Tropen: Exotische Reise- und Abenteuerfilme aus Deutschland, 1919–1933.* München: Ed. Text + Kritik, 1997.
Schwarz, Maria-Theresia. *"Je weniger Afrika, desto besser": Die deutsche Kolonialkritik am Ende des 19. Jahrhunderts; Eine Untersuchung zur kolonialen Haltung von Linksliberalismus und Sozialdemokratie.* Frankfurt: Lang, 1999.
Smith, Helmut Walser. *The Continuities of German History: Nation, Religion, and Race Across the Long Nineteenth Century.* Cambridge, UK: Cambridge University Press, 2008.
Speitkamp, Winfried. *Deutsche Kolonialgeschichte.* Stuttgart: Reclam, 2005.
Steinmetz, George. *The Devil's Handwriting: Precoloniality and the German Colonial State in Qingdao, Samoa, and Southwest Africa.* Chicago: University of Chicago Press, 2007.
Struck, Wolfgang. "Ein renegatisches Machtabenteuer unter den Negern: Der phantasierte Kolonialismus der literarischen Moderne in Deutschland." In Dunker, *(Post-)Kolonialismus und deutsche Literatur,* 179–202.
Ther, Philipp. "Imperial Instead of National History: Positioning Modern German History on the Map of European Empires." In *Imperial Rule,* edited by Alexei Miller and Alfred Rieber, 47–68. Budapest: Central European University Press, 2004.
Trotha, Trutz von. "Was war Kolonialismus? Einige zusammenfassende Befunde zur Soziologie und Geschichte des Kolonialismus und der Kolonialherrschaft." *Saeculum* 55, no. 1 (2004): 49–96.
Uerlings, Herbert. "Kolonialer Diskurs, Globalisierung und postkoloniale Analyse." In Dunker, *(Post-)Kolonialismus und deutsche Literatur,* 17–44. Bielefeld: Aisthesis, 2005.
White, Richard. *The Middle Ground: Indians, Empires, and Republics in the Great Lakes Region, 1650–1815.* Cambridge, UK: Cambridge University Press, 1991.
Wierling, Dorothee. *Heimat finden: Lebenswege von Deutschen, die aus Russland kommen.* Hamburg: Körber-Stiftung, 2004.
Wildenthal, Lora. *German Women for Empire, 1884–1945.* Durham, NC: Duke University Press, 2001.
Zantop, Susanne. *Colonial Fantasies: Conquest, Family, and Nation in Precolonial Germany, 1770–1870.* Durham, NC: Duke University Press, 1997.
Zimmerer, Jürgen. "The Birth of the *Ostland* Out of the Spirit of Colonialism: A Postcolonial Perspective on Nazi Policy of Conquest and Extermination." *Patterns of Prejudice* 39, no. 2 (2005): 197–219.
Zimmerman, Andrew. *Anthropology and Antihumanism in Imperial Germany.* Chicago: University of Chicago Press, 2001.

PART II
Lebensraum *and Genocide*

3

Against "Human Diversity as Such"
Lebensraum *and Genocide in the Third Reich*

Shelley Baranowski

Much of the debate on colonialism and the imperial imagination in German history focuses on the links between Imperial Germany's colonial experience overseas, especially in Africa, and the Nazi regime's campaigns to acquire "living space" (*Lebensraum*), remove or eliminate racial inferiors, and exterminate the Jews. To be sure, scholars are reluctant to impose simplistic continuities between the Holocaust and the most notorious event in pre-1918 German colonial history, the Herero and Nama genocides in Southwest Africa between 1904 and 1908. Nevertheless, historians of Imperial German colonialism have identified concepts and practices that laid the foundation for the murderous fantasies of the Third Reich. They include bureaucratized violence, the bourgeois obsession with racial hierarchies, the compulsion to territorial expansion (or "race and space"), the appeal of eugenics as the key to improving the "quality" of the German *Volk* (people), as well as the fear of miscegenation and the ban on "race mixing," intermarriage between German colonists and colonial subjects. All contributed to a reservoir of ideas and experiences that National Socialism adapted and radicalized.[1] By widening the lens through which to study the Third Reich, the attention to Germany's maritime colonialism before World War I has encouraged fresh debate about the origins of the Holocaust. At the same time, it forces a broader public to confront the colonial roots of German racism and its implications for the Nazi Judeocide. Yet the debate has evolved to the point that historians increasingly question the assumptions of the "new continuity thesis." Some examine specific issues, such as the connection between colonial prohibitions on intermarriage under the Kaiserreich and the Nuremberg Laws of the Third Reich. These critics argue that the Jews, as the primary target of Nazi racial policy, assume a different status from that of the African spouses of German settlers or their mixed-race offspring. Furthermore, they state, the racial foundations of citizenship that the Nuremberg Laws expressed drew from the obsession with blood pollution that grew acute only during and after World War I, when the external markers of European or German colonial domination had lost their potency.[2] Other critics are more comprehensive. They point to numerous dissimilarities between the colonial practices of Imperial Germany and the Third Reich and see as more relevant the interwar European crisis that ensued from the dissolution of the Habsburg and Ottoman empires and the reductions of German and Soviet territory.[3] Still other scholars, including Russell A. Berman in this volume, recognize Germany as a European empire with beginnings in the legacies of ancient Rome and in the Holy Roman Empire. In its post-1871 incarnation Germany was a multiethnic and religiously diverse entity that included Polish lands annexed by Prussia in the eighteenth century, as well as the Danish-speaking parts of Schleswig-Holstein, and Alsace and Lorraine, which Germany acquired in the wars of unification.[4] Thus, the European setting of the Nazi Lebensraum project, wherein the East, according to Nazi leadership, was to be the foundation of Germany's economic resurgence and racial revitalization, did not arise from a vacuum. The centrality of European living space to Nazism demands that we examine the contributions of German continental aspirations before and after the Great War to the murderous extremes of the Third Reich that scholars of colonialism and genocide have acknowledged.[5]

By focusing on Germany as a European empire, this essay identifies four elements that defined the Nazi Lebensraum project. The first element evolves out of the colonial history of Prussia and subsequently the German Reich. This includes the tensions along the eastern Prussian frontier that the post-1918 territorial settlements in east-central Europe ironically exacerbated and promised to resolve. The second element is the Nazi regime's pursuit of a homogeneous "racial community." Through various means that it deemed essential to waging war, namely police repression, measures to "honor" wage earners to assure their integration, institutionalized racism, and unprecedented biological interventionism, the Third Reich sought to homogenize its population. The third element is Nazism's attempt to reshape Europe as a racial polity by subordinating or destroying the existing mix of nation-states. The final element is Nazism's hatred of the Jews, who personified Germany's imperial rivals. Taken together, these elements produced what Hannah Arendt identified as the most pronounced characteristic of the Third Reich, its "attack on human diversity as such," an assault against "the 'human status' without which the very words 'mankind' or 'humanity' would be devoid of meaning."[6] Launched at a time when most European states struggled to preserve their empires and maintain their internal cohesion, Nazi expansionism promised a new order, in which racial purification and the removal or elimination of *Untermenschen* would inoculate the Volk against "degeneration" in a new kind of empire defined by homogeneity.

The Lure of the East:
Lebensraum and Its Antecedents

Ethnic tensions that accompanied the unification of Germany exposed the Prussian eastern borderlands as a site of contestation, in which Germans routinely cast Poles as colonial subjects, as Kristin Kopp's chapter in this volume makes clear. Distrusting the Poles who resided along the eastern frontier, German liberal nationalists backed the semiauthoritarian constitution of the new Germany, in part because it would contain the nationalist aspirations of the new Reich's Polish citizens.[7] In the 1870s the "battle for culture" (*Kulturkampf*), which Otto von Bismarck, goaded by his liberal supporters, launched against the Catholic Church, affected subject nationalities most intensely, particularly Alsatians, Lorrainers, and Prussian Poles. Bismarck's efforts to contain and marginalize "enemies of the Reich" in the 1880s extended to his failure, and that of his successors, to repopulate the border regions with Germans to be settled on the purchased or confiscated estates of Polish landowners. Cross-border mobility presented another challenge. The influx of Jews from the Russian and Austro-Hungarian empires and the Polish seasonal laborers, who toiled on Prussian and Saxon landed estates, prompted radical nationalists to advocate drastic solutions to the "ethnic struggle" that pitted Germans against Slavs and Jews. They sought the disenfranchisement of the Jews, expanded "living space" at the expense of the

Russian Empire, the accelerated settlement of German "overpopulation" in eastern Europe, and the expulsion of Slavs.[8]

Yet during the Wilhelminian era, the push for a powerful navy and an overseas empire competed with the aspiration to continental Lebensraum, such that Germany distinguished itself among the European great powers and the emerging world power, the United States.[9] Although the United States and Italy entertained similar ambitions, German objectives held greater potential for undermining the European state system put in place after the Napoleonic Wars. The dual foci of German imperialism rivaled and reinforced each other, producing a strategic incoherence that contributed to Germany's encirclement by its continental enemies and the imperial government's gamble at a preventive war in 1914.[10] Nevertheless, the loss of most of the German holdings overseas, the stalemate on the western front, and the success of the Central Powers against Russia elevated the significance of the East in present and future German colonialist calculations. The German occupation of the Courland, Lithuania, and parts of White Russia under Erich Ludendorff's Supreme Command of the East (*Ober Ost*) was not as extreme as the "drive to the East" (*Drang nach Osten*) of the Third Reich. The Germans pragmatically encouraged ethnic distinctiveness by constructing schools and staging culture productions with local actors, composers, and playwrights. Allowing the expression of local cultures and languages would make the "natives" appreciate their "liberation" from czarism and make them amenable to German rule. Otherwise, Ludendorff's policies resembled colonialism at its harshest: the requisitioning of food and draft animals, the dragooning of local labor for road building and other infrastructural modernization projects, and an intrusive system of identification and mobility control. In March 1918 the Soviet Union's withdrawal from the war to preserve the revolution promised to transform the German occupation into permanent territorial gains. The Treaty of Brest-Litovsk, concluded between Germany and the Bolshevik government, would enable future German settlements and abundant resources that would sustain Germany as a global power.

Although *Freikorps* units sought to colonize land of their own while fighting Bolshevism in the Baltic regions after World War I, annexationism in the East came to naught.[11] The Treaty of Versailles subjected the Rhineland to French occupation, stipulated the return of Alsace and Lorraine to France, deprived Germany of its eastern conquests, and forced the "decolonization" of frontier regions that had belonged to Prussia since the eighteenth century. The economic impact of the loss of prewar territory and the ethnic clashes in the borderlands during the republic more consistently agitated the German public than the loss of the maritime empire, especially because the precarious position of Germans outside Germany heightened the vulnerability of Germans inside. Prior to World War I, ethnic Germans who resided in the Russian and Austro-Hungarian empires could retain their cultural identity despite mounting ethnic conflict or nationalizing pressures from within.[12] Yet the "stranding" of millions of ethnic Germans in postwar successor states where they faced pressure to assimilate spawned numerous Weimar organizations to lobby on their behalf. Although Weimar governments used the League of Nations to press the claims of German minorities, the conflict-ridden outcomes of the territorial settlement in central and east-central Europe increased the attraction to war and ethnic cleansing to undermine the new nation states.[13]

The weakness of agriculture under the republic, which affected especially what remained of the Prussian East, heightened fears of the Slavic "threat," a crisis of ethnicity magnified by resentment toward high interest rates, price scissors, and government policies that putatively favored urban consumers. The dissatisfaction of peasants and large estate owners had been a chronic feature of Weimar politics, and these sentiments intensified with the collapse of the global commodities market even before the Depression. Many among the Junker nobility, who had long dominated the economy and politics east of the Elbe River, fueled antirepublicanism, anti-Slavism, anti-Semitism, and expansionism. Impoverished younger nobles with few prospects for earning a living suitable to their rank abandoned monarchism and gravitated to the Nazis, whose promise of a new elite seemingly conformed to their own perception of their place in society. In addition to restoring military careers curtailed by the Versailles limitations on the size of the officer corps, living space in the East promised new estates to sustain them.[14] The radicalization of estate owners, including the declining number of Junkers who remained on the land, facilitated the growth of the Nazi electorate after 1928 and led to the negotiations that brought Hitler to power.

Agrarian economic weakness and ethnic insecurity did not end in 1933. Despite the Nazi regime's attempts to prevent farm foreclosure, especially among peasants, limit the ownership of land to those who were racially fit, and boost food production, the regime's inability to make Germany self-sufficient in food fueled its determination to exploit the weak successor states of east-central Europe either through bilateral trade agreements or through occupation and colonization.[15] Unlike the Second Empire, the Nazi regime prioritized eastward expansion, haunted by the domestically divisive impact of the British wartime blockade, a humiliating peace settlement, the insufficiencies of German agriculture, and the failure to defeat the "Slavic threat" through settlement. Having rejected what it termed the "bourgeois nationalist" colonial policy of the Kaiserreich for privileging commercial interests over the survival of the Volk, Hitler and the Nazi elite gave pride of place to the acquisition of living space as the foundation of Germany's economic and racial vitality.[16] As a German from outside the Reich, Hitler was to be the agent of an enlarged German Reich, purified of "Others."

To be sure, the Third Reich did not rule out overseas acquisitions. The ambitions of the colonial office under Franz Xaver Ritter von Epp and the German Labor Front's Institute of Labor Science (*Arbeitswissenschaftliches Institut*) included a large central African economic space that would provide labor and resources for exploitation. In addition to organizing the instruments of colonialism, including a colonial army, the regime used the media to promote a more pervasive overseas colonial imaginary than had existed under the Weimar Republic. Much of it catered to popular images of the World War I hero Paul von Lettow-Vorbeck, who with his Askaris fought the Entente over the length of East Africa. The Third Reich rehabilitated the colonial pioneer of the Kaiserreich, Carl Peters, whose masculine brutality accorded with the Nazi ideal of leadership, and it celebrated the "Desert Fox," Erwin Rommel, whose victories in North Africa seemed to reconcile industrialized warfare and paternalism. After the Germans defeated France, Belgium, and the Netherlands in the spring of 1940, the control of its enemies' colonial empires lay open to the Reich until Rommel's defeat and the disaster at Stalingrad put an end to the regime's plans.[17]

Nevertheless, building on the geopolitical theory that flowered during the Weimar era, the Nazi regime redirected previous geopolitical imaginings of space, which, in addition to straddling overseas and continental locations, had accorded secondary importance to racial revitalization. Unlike the projected African empire, which the regime envisioned primarily as a source of labor managed by relatively few German overseers and administrators, large-scale German settlements in the East and the expulsion or elimination of racial inferiors were essential to recovering the biological integrity of the Volk and assuring its material prosperity.[18] The regime eagerly sought former settlers from the African colonies for their pioneering spirit and practical experience, and even if they were few in number, the pervasiveness of colonial knowledge during the Kaiserreich and after undoubtedly influenced the many others who went to the East.[19] Yet Michael Mann's survey of more than fifteen hundred perpetrators of Nazi genocide, which underscores the overrepresentation of ethnic Germans from borderlands lost after World War I, suggests that the postwar continental upheavals and the opportunity they provided for expansion and ethnic revitalization counted more than the legacies of Imperial German maritime colonialism.[20] Moreover, the racism of Imperial German colonial administrators, settlers, and advocates of colonialism at home very likely preceded the acquisition of an overseas empire and drew sustenance from the hostile stereotypes of Slavs and Jews. At least the "otherness" imposed on Africans and Pacific Islanders reinforced the parallels or reinforced the "otherness" of Prussian Poles.[21]

Volksgemeinschaft and *Volkskörper*: Social and Biological Antecedents of War

Germany's diminished continental position after World War I profoundly influenced the Nazi regime's social and racial policies. To prevent the internal divisions that, in its view, brought defeat, revolution, and subjugation to the Entente, the Nazi regime deemed a militarized and self-sacrificing "racial community" (*Volksgemeinschaft*) essential to its future war for Lebensraum. Thus it undertook two missions, the first political and social, and the second biopolitical, both as necessary to living space as rearmament and an expanded armed forces. For its first task the Third Reich assaulted its most formidable opposition, the Social Democratic and Communist parties, which, despite the bitter divisions between them, composed Europe's largest and best-organized labor movement. In contrast to previous European practice, in which colonial hierarchies of race blended with bourgeois hierarchies of class,[22] Nazism claimed to "raise" the status of German workers by suppressing bourgeois "snobbery" and integrating wage earners, liberated from the left, into its new racially defined polity. To be sure, the German Labor Front (Deutsche Arbeitsfront, or DAF), the regime's megaunion, which claimed to mediate between wage earners and employers, eliminated collective bargaining and other constraints that Weimar labor laws had imposed on employers. Yet rapid rearmament ended the Depression-era unemployment and created labor shortages that allowed workers some room for negotiation. The cultural, sport, and tourism programs delivered by the Labor Front's subsidiary, Strength through Joy, which would provide workers with a foretaste of the high standard of living that Lebensraum would offer, strove to eliminate the class barriers that governed leisure activities, bestow "honor" on workers, and dissolve class parochialism. Although the number of workers who participated fell below the DAF's targets, the impression of wage earners who did participate was generally favorable. Despite long working hours, frozen wages, the lack of consumer goods, a higher cost of living, and the restiveness they generated, the Nazi regime succeeded in assuring wage earners' compliance.[23]

Second, the regime imposed "racial hygiene" to remedy the "degeneration" of the Volk. The sterilization of the "unfit" began within six months of Hitler's taking power, facilitated by the "synchronization" of social welfare and health care and the elimination of "unreliable" social welfare and healthcare professionals, many of them leftists.[24] Under the Kaiserreich and the Weimar Republic, environmental solutions to population decline, which emphasized improved public health and welfare to mitigate poverty, competed with proposals to prevent the genetically defective from reproducing.[25] The multiple vulnerabilities of Weimar, however, worked to the advantage of eugenicists, who wanted to "weed out" the genetically and racially inferior. The republic's liabilities began with the French occupation of the Rhineland, which, by deploying colonial troops, inverted the racial hierarchies of imperialism and spawned fantasies of a "race war" in Europe to recover and expand German supremacy. Prior to World War I, "miscegenation" between German colonial settlers and indigenous women already threatened the social and political dominance of whites by raising the prospect of legal equality for nonwhite spouses and their mixed-race offspring. In the aftermath of defeat and occupation, however, lurid tales of sexual contact between German women and French African soldiers contributed to fears of "blood poisoning" that threatened the survival of the Volk. Weimar weaknesses culminated in the Depression. Plummeting tax revenues and declining resources to support public health and welfare only strengthened the hand of those who advocated ruthless biological interventionism.[26]

The perceived "colonial" occupation of Germany fueled an even more lethal component of the biopolitics of fear, anti-Semitism. For the Nazi movement, "Jewry" personified the depredations of Versailles, the penetration of American economic power, and the threat of Bolshevism. Yet the Third Reich succeeded where earlier anti-Semites had failed, for it engineered the civic disenfranchisement and progressive economic impoverishment of Jewish Germans. The Civil Service Law and the anti-Jewish boycott began the fitful but devastating "social death" of Jews, which later included the denial of intermarriage and citizenship, the "aryanization" of Jewish property, and repeated acts of violence initiated by party rowdies, which ordinary bystanders tolerated or condoned.[27] The decisive contribution of the Third Reich resided not only in the ruthless and centralized implementation of its policies but also in how its eugenic and anti-Semitic measures presupposed another war. During the interwar period eugenicists elsewhere in the industrialized world commonly opposed war because of its potentially devastating consequences for populations. Nazi eugenicists, however, accepted the likelihood of another war and the killing of the "incurable" as a necessary sacrifice comparable to that of soldiers who would lay down their lives for the Volk.[28] As the violence of Kristallnacht in November 1938 revealed, the approach of war radicalized Nazi Jewish policy, while hostile foreign reactions to the pogrom rendered "Jewry" even more dangerous for its presumed sponsorship of Germany's enemies abroad.[29] In all its breadth and depth the regime's racial policy amounted to biological rearmament.

The Nazi "Place in the Sun": Forced Settlements and the Elimination of "Redskins"

Had the Third Reich succeeded, Lebensraum would have fulfilled Hitler's and Himmler's goal of a new racial order in Europe, which would have united ethnic Germans at the expense of Germany's neighbors. In addition to undermining the liberal premises of the postwar peace settlement that guaranteed the rights of minorities—indeed eschewing classical European diplomacy as the means to maintaining the balance of power—Nazism would solve the plight that had long informed the fearful imaginings of German nationalists: Germany's devastating history of internal division and weakness, foreign intervention, and the loss of ethnic identity through emigration to the Americas. Now Germans would be protected from division and degeneration for all time.[30] Nazi expansionist ambitions exceeded previous conquests that the Nazi hierarchy often evoked as models to imagine a replication of the North American frontier, which, in Hitler's view, had absorbed the finest European racial stock and eliminated millions of Indians to make room for them. "One thing the Americans have, and which we lack," Hitler remarked in June 1943, "is the sense of the vast open spaces."[31] The American conquest of the West to the Pacific Ocean merged with the more distant model of the German colonization of the East during the late Middle Ages.

The Nazi war in the East, however, was a renovation, rather than a replication, of multiple colonialisms, including the Prussian policies of settlement and forced assimilation. Rather than compete with Prussian Poles for demographic space and occupy Polish land purchased by the Prussian Settlement Commission, ethnic German settlers would replace expelled or murdered "natives," except the relative few whose fluidly defined attributes rendered them capable of Germanization and others whose labor simply could not be dispensed with. Starting with the territories annexed from Poland in 1939, and developed further in the General Plan East first sketched out in July 1941, the removal of Slavs and Jews would make room for Germans and compensate for Germany's inadequate supplies of food and raw materials. The Hunger Plan that was put together during the months leading up to the German attack on the Soviet Union presupposed the deaths of twenty to thirty million Slavs by starvation and exposure, and the deurbanization of Russia west of the Urals. Unlike America, where westward expansion enlarged the union that the Civil War had preserved, the Nazi regime sought to eliminate the new nation-states and the remainder of the Russian Empire that the Bolsheviks had managed to salvage during their civil war against the Whites.

Moreover, the character of settlement differed. Because the transfer of prospective settlers was engineered from on high, the Nazi campaign to populate large swaths of the "wild East" relied less on the autonomous decisions of ethnic Germans who lived outside the Reich, the *Volksdeutschen* (many of them coerced into moving by transfer agreements between Germany and the Soviet Union and bilateral agreements with other states), and more on the direction of the SS and the civil administrations of the East. Unlike previous European settlements, in which land-hungry transplants provoked conflict with indigenous peoples that sometimes threatened the metropole's peacekeeping efforts,[32] the Nazi metropole's objective in the East was to eliminate "native" leaderships outright. Over the long term the Nazi leadership expected that settlement would prove sufficiently attractive to Germans from the Old Reich and the Americas to encourage their voluntary migration. Yet few would accept the offer before German military setbacks terminated settlement projects altogether. As a consequence the Nazi project assumed a level of centralized orchestration that Jürgen Zimmerer rightly stresses as the distinctiveness of bureaucratized violence in the Third Reich. It enabled the

Nazi state to prosecute its genocide with a thoroughness that exceeded that of premodern colonial regimes.[33]

It is incorrect to see Nazi epigones marching in lockstep to dictates from the top, for the Third Reich was indeed "social Darwinian" in its polycratic infighting among multiple fiefdoms. Internecine competition, however, did nothing to impede the principal goals of the regime.[34] A common ideological vision united the SS, the military and civil administrations, and Göring's economic apparatus, which spurred the regime's agents to unleash their own ambitions while conforming to the goals of the leadership. The result was a departure from previous imperialist or colonialist practices. For German colonizers during the Kaiserreich, settlements overseas were to encourage the formation of a new elite of independent farmers as an alternative to "socialist leveling" and urbanization at home. "Germanness" would be preserved if uncontaminated by metropolitan problems.[35] The Nazi New Order envisioned no such distinction. In those regions designated for settlement—the annexed territories of Danzig-West Prussia, Upper Silesia, the Warthegau, the Baltic states of Lithuania, Latvia, and Estonia, as well as portions of Ukraine—the metropole and its colonies would merge into a racially homogenous empire in which the elimination of racial enemies assured the biological and material prosperity of the Volk.[36] Unlike previous empires that ruled over religiously or ethnically diverse populations, using strategies ranging from repression to cooptation to manage them, the Nazi empire would eliminate diversity altogether.[37]

To be sure, the regime's intentions should not be confused with their implementation on the ground. The German occupation of most of Scandinavia and western Europe followed different rules. Except for Alsace and Lorraine, northern and western Europe were not slated for German settlement. The efforts of Werner Best, the SS Reich Security Main Office's emissary to the military occupation in Paris, to redraw the western map according to race came to naught.[38] His ambition to merge the Netherlands, Flanders, and French territory north of the Loire River into the Reich, transform Wallonia and Brittany into protectorates, merge Northern Ireland with the Irish Republic, create a decentralized British federation, and declare independence for the Basques, Catalonians, and Galicians from Spain foundered on the resistance of the military and the foreign office, which preferred the existing national states, albeit under German domination. Despite the exactions that the Third Reich imposed on the defeated nations in "occupation costs," "accommodation services," and exchange rates favorable enough to allow German soldiers to strip store shelves of consumer goods intended for local populations,[39] German entrepreneurs and managers were less successful in taking control of foreign companies than they were in the East. In fact, corporate boards often preferred to collaborate with companies rather than absorb them, as long as the arrangement was profitable.[40] Even in the East, implementing the settlement plan proved messier than the Nazi imperial imagination had anticipated. Bottlenecks, especially in the annexed territories of Danzig-West Prussia and the Warthegau, arose as the number of settlers exceeded the homesteads available to them. When the invasion of the Soviet Union stalled in late 1941, the spiraling demand for workers afterward forced the curtailment of the profligate destruction of human life. Even Soviet prisoners of war, who perished by the millions from hunger and exposure in the months immediately following the launch of Barbarossa, became less disposable. The regime's increasing need for labor created another problem. Putting millions of foreign workers in close proximity to German civilians compromised the drive for racial purification, despite the regime's draconian punishments for "racial defilement."[41] Nevertheless, the Nazi *Drang nach Osten* proved extraordinarily destructive. The racially infused invasion and occupation of Poland provided a foretaste of the horror to come. And the cataclysmic violence of the war between the Reich and the Soviet Union, in which the numbers of dead only increased as the outcome became less in doubt, became the context for something even more catastrophic: the extermination of the Jews.

"Who, after all, speaks today of the annihilation of the Armenians?"

This statement, which Hitler reportedly uttered on the eve of the invasion of Poland, ensued from the Führer's orders to the Wehrmacht to wage war ruthlessly. Whether apocryphal or not, the comment suggests commonalities between the Ottoman Empire's treatment of Armenians during World War I and the Nazi regime's genocide against the Jews later: both were campaigns for ethnic purity as the solution to foreign imperial depredations. Occurring in the midst of the twentieth century's first global war, in which the Armenians were linked to the Ottoman Empire's external enemies, especially Russia, the ruling Committee of Union and Progress initiated ethnic cleansing and murder as integral to its war aim, a new Turkic empire in Anatolia, the Caucasus, and central Asia.[42] This new homogeneous polity would dissolve existing political boundaries and eliminate those who could not be nationalized. It would compensate for the humiliations suffered by the empire at the hands of the European great powers over the previous century, particularly their support for the autonomy or independence of non-Muslim minorities.

The Nazi regime launched its own campaign to make the Jews "disappear from the face of the earth"[43] during the twentieth century's second global war, albeit in a more systematic and centralized way. Beginning with the liquidation of Soviet Jews, which was under way by the fall of 1941, and of ghettoized Polish Jews after late 1941, the Wannsee Conference in January 1942 signified the determination to exterminate all Jews across the continent. Had Rommel's Afrika Korps conquered North Africa, Middle Eastern Jews would no doubt have been at risk. Similar to its reliance in the occupied East on anti-Soviet and anti-Semitic local forces to round up and execute Jews, the regime expected to exploit Arab anti-Semitism and anti-imperialism against the British, who had encouraged Zionist settlements in Palestine.[44] At first, the "final solution" to the "Jewish question" did not mean the total elimination of the Jews, despite the regime's barbarous rhetoric that rendered the boundaries between propaganda and action increasingly porous. Rather, the term referred to the deportation of Jews to "reservations" such as the Nisko project near Lublin in the General Government, to Madagascar in the Indian Ocean, or to the interior of the Soviet Union beyond the regions slated for settlement. During the first two years of the war the regime's actions against Jews arguably followed historical precedent: ghettos and camps, expulsions and relocations, and massacres that arose from the tasks of extracting resources or making space for German settlers. Moreover, during the same period the regime pressed Jews into labor gangs for tasks such as road construction and garbage collection in the employ of the military, private companies, and municipalities.[45] Finally, the timing of mass killings of Jews often followed the economic imperatives of colonialism, namely the need to remedy food shortages to provision the Wehrmacht and workers, whose labor, forced or otherwise, was essential to the Nazi war machine.[46] Yet similar to the Ottoman Turkish view of the Armenians, the Nazis' identification of Jews with Germany's wartime enemies accelerated the regime's attempt at the total elimination of the former. Fusing racial and political "otherness," the Jew personified Germany's victimization by the empires that threatened it, be they the United States and Great Britain, and the Jewish bankers who financed them, or the Jews in the Soviet *politburo* who threatened Germany with extinction. With roots in the Pan-German movement in the Kaiserreich and cast within the frame provided by the "Protocols of the Elders of Zion," to which Hitler was first exposed by anti-Bolshevik refugees in the apocalyptic climate of post–World War I Munich, Jews embodied the global menaces of international capitalism and Bolshevism and the states that sought to extend them. Although going back to the Kaiserreich, many Germans believed that Jews possessed traits similar to those of Africans, such as rootlessness and deviousness, Germany's enemies were not simply distant "savages," who would disappear as the "natural" consequence of the incursions of a "superior" European "civilization."[47] Rather, because they personified Germany's imperial rivals, they were its potential colonizers and destroyers.

Because it opens the way to less Eurocentric treatments of German genocide, the recent focus on German imperialism adheres to a broader effort to place mass killing in a global context. Accordingly, Mark Mazower has challenged the inclination of historians to reduce episodes of mass violence to a "small number of decontextualized European exemplars—notably, the Holocaust and Stalin's USSR." He concludes that research should place the German and Soviet examples of mass killing in "a historical context that stretches back to the age of empire and forward to encompass the spread of independent, more or less violent, states across the globe."[48] Ben Kiernan's history of genocide reaches even further back to include the ancient world and forward to incorporate Cambodia and Rwanda.[49] Mark Levene's massive study of genocide, which he defines as "the state organized partial or total extermination of perceived or actual communal groups," attributes twentieth-century genocides to the dynamics of uneven development in a global system of existing and emerging nation-states. Emerging states in the process of nation building and obsessed with "catching up" to the leading states, or even circumventing the rules of the global economy that the leaders have established, have sought to eliminate communities whose putatively foreign ties made them a danger to the nation's existence.[50] In short, National Socialism belongs to a longer history of violence associated with the rise and disintegration of empires. The Holocaust as a specifically German crime, to pose the problem more narrowly, belongs to a longer history of German colonialism.

Yet it is not Eurocentric to recognize that National Socialism amounted to more than the boomerang effect of Imperial Germany's maritime colonialism. Nor does it deny the value of comparison synchronically and diachronically to suggest the distinctiveness of the Nazi enterprise and the European context for its emergence and execution. The roots of its vicious and unparalleled campaign to eliminate the problem of nationalizing diverse populations lay in Germany's contested eastern frontiers, which combined economic weakness and ethnic conflict. They also resided in the Nazi regime's determination even before 1939 to racialize its population by imposing "racial hygiene" and institutionalizing radical anti-Semitism, and in its campaign to create a novelty, a homogeneous empire that attacked "human diversity as such."

Notes

1. See Grosse, "From Colonialism to National Socialism to Postcolonialism"; Grosse, "What Does German Colonialism Have to Do with National Socialism?"; Zimmerer, "Colonialism and the Holocaust"; Zimmerer, "Holocaust und Kolonialismus"; Zimmerer, "Die Geburt des 'Ostlandes' aus dem Geiste des Kolonialismus"; and Madley, "From Africa to Auschwitz."

2. Kundrus, "Von Windhoek nach Nürnberg?"; Essner, "'Border-line' im Menschenblut und Struktur rassistischer Rechtsspaltung," esp. 39, 60; and Fitzpatrick, "The Pre-History of the Holocaust?"

3. See Gerwarth and Malinowski, "Der Holocaust als 'kolonialer Genozid'?"; and Gerwarth, "The Central European Counter-Revolution."

4. See Ther, "Beyond the Nation"; Ther, "Deutsche Geschichte als imperiale Geschichte"; and Dickinson, "The German Empire."

5. See Kiernan, *Blood and Soil*, 454.

6. Arendt, *Eichmann in Jerusalem*, 268–69.

7. Ther, "Deutsche Geschichte als imperiale Geschichte"; and Ther, "Beyond the Nation."

8. Conrad, *Globalisierung und Nation im Deutschen Kaiserreich*, 124–67; Chickering, *We Men Who Feel Most German*.

9. Grosse, "Colonialism to National Socialism," 46; Grosse, "What Does German Colonialism Have to Do with National Socialism?" 120.

10. Hewitson, *Germany and the Causes of the First World War*, 145–69; Blackbourn, *History of Germany, 1780–1918*, 339–40.

11. Liulevicius, *War Land on the Eastern Front*, 227–46.

12. Dickinson, "The German Empire," 150–54.

13. Luther, *Volkstumspolitik des Deutsche Reiches, 1933–1938*, 25–55.

14. Malinowski, *Vom König zum Führer*, 500–503.

15. Corni, *Hitler and the Peasants*; Mai, "Rasse und Raum," 16–76.
16. Hitler, *Hitler's Second Book*, 76–90.
17. Maß, *Weiße Helden, schwarze Krieger*, 217–96.
18. Madley, "Africa to Auschwitz," 432–36; Murphy, *The Heroic Earth*, 241–52; Smith, *The Continuities of German History*, 182–88.
19. Zimmerer, "Geburt des 'Ostlandes,'" 36; Furber, "Going East," chaps. 3, 4; Laak, *Über alles in der Welt*, 118–19.
20. See Mann, *The Dark Side of Democracy*, 225–78.
21. Davis, "Colonialism, Antisemitism, and Germans of Jewish Descent in Imperial Germany"; Kopp, "Constructing Racial Difference in Colonial Poland."
22. McClintock, *Imperial Leather*, 4–9; Conrad, "'Eingeborenenpolitik' in Kolonie und Metropole."
23. Baranowski, *Strength Through Joy*.
24. Grossmann, *Reforming Sex*, 136–65.
25. Hoffmann and Timme, "Reproductive Biopolitics, Gender Roles, and Sexuality in Nazi Germany and the Soviet Union," 95, 98–101.
26. Grosse, "What Does German Colonialism Have to Do with National Socialism?" 128–29.
27. Longerich, *"Davon haben wir nichts gewusst!"* 55–73; Wildt, *Volksgemeinschaft als Selbstermächtigung*, 101–218.
28. Kühl, "The Relationship Between Eugenics and the So-called 'Euthanasia Action' in Nazi Germany," 202.
29. Tooze, *The Wages of Destruction*, 281–83.
30. Wildt, "'Eine neue Ordnung der ethnographischen Verhältnisse.'"
31. Trevor-Roper, *Hitler's Table Talk, 1941–1944*, 707.
32. See Reynolds, "Genocide in Tasmania?"; Lumans, *Himmler's Auxiliaries*, 151–83.
33. Zimmerer, "Holocaust und Kolonialismus," 1118; Zimmerer, "Colonialism and the Holocaust," 68.
34. See Gerlach, *Kalkulierte Mord*.
35. See Kundrus, *Moderne Imperialisten*.
36. Heinemann, *Rasse, Siedlung, deutsches Blut*, 357–76; Longerich, *Heinrich Himmler*, 531–663.
37. Maier, *Among Empires*, 24–36.
38. Herbert, *Best*, 295–98.
39. Aly, *Hitlers Volksstaat*.
40. Tooze, *The Wages of Destruction*, 380–93; Overy, "The 'Reichswerke Hermann Göring'"; Mazower, *Hitler's Empire*, 268–69.
41. See Mazower, *Hitler's Empire*, 223–56.
42. Akçam, *A Shameful Act*, 92–93.
43. Arendt, *Eichmann in Jerusalem*, 268.

44. See Mallmann and Cüppers, *Halbmond und Hakenkreuz.*
45. See Grüner, *Jewish Forced Labor Under the Nazis.*
46. Gerlach, *Kalkulierte Mord,* 502–775; Tooze, *The Wages of Destruction,* 513–51.
47. Traverso, *The Origins of Nazi Violence,* 54–63.
48. Mazower, "Violence and the State in the Twentieth Century," 1176.
49. See Kiernan, *Blood and Soil.*
50. Levene, *The Meaning of Genocide,* 203; Levene, "Why Is the Twentieth Century the Century of Genocide?" 319.

Bibliography

Akçam, Taner. *A Shameful Act: The Armenian Genocide and the Question of Turkish Responsibility.* Translated by Paul Bessemer. New York: Metropolitan Books, 2006.
Aly, Götz. *Hitlers Volksstaat: Raub, Rassenkrieg und nationaler Sozialismus.* Frankfurt: Fischer, 2005.
Ames, Eric, Marcia Klotz, and Lora Wildenthal, eds. *Germany's Colonial Pasts.* Lincoln: University of Nebraska Press, 2005.
Arendt, Hannah. *Eichmann in Jerusalem: A Study in the Banality of Evil.* Harmondsworth: Penguin, 1984.
Baranowski, Shelley. *Strength Through Joy: Consumerism and Mass Tourism in the Third Reich.* Cambridge, UK: Cambridge University Press, 2004.
Blackbourn, David. *History of Germany, 1780–1918: The Long Nineteenth Century.* 2nd ed. Oxford: Blackwell, 2003.
Chickering, Roger. *We Men Who Feel Most German: A Cultural Study of the Pan-German League, 1886–1914.* Boston: George Allen and Unwin, 1984.
Conrad, Sebastian. "'Eingeborenenpolitik' in Kolonie und Metropole: 'Erziehung zur Arbeit' in Ostafrika und Ostwestfalen." In Conrad and Osterhammel, *Das Kaiserreich transnational,* 107–28.
———. *Globalisierung und Nation im Deutschen Kaiserreich.* Munich: C. H. Beck, 2006.
Conrad, Sebastian, and Jürgen Osterhammel, eds. *Das Kaiserreich transnational: Deutschland in der Welt, 1871–1914.* Göttingen: Vandenhoeck und Ruprecht, 2004.
Corni, Gustavo. *Hitler and the Peasants: Agrarian Policy of the Third Reich, 1930–1939.* Translated by David Kerr. New York: Berg, 1990.
Davis, Christian. "Colonialism, Antisemitism, and Germans of Jewish Descent in Imperial Germany." PhD diss., Rutgers University, 2005.
Dickinson, Edward Ross. "The German Empire: An Empire?" *History Workshop Journal,* no. 66 (2008): 129–62.

Essner, Cornelia. "'Border-line' im Menschenblut und Struktur rassistischer Rechtsspaltung: Koloniales Kaiserreich und 'Drittes Reich.'" In *Gesetzliches Unrecht: Rassistisches Recht im 20. Jahrhundert*, edited by Michael Brumlik, Suzanne Meid, and Werner Renz, 27–64. Frankfurt: Campus, 2005.

Fitzpatrick, Matthew P. "The Pre-History of the Holocaust? The *Sonderweg* and *Historikerstreit* Debates and the Abject Colonial Past." *Central European History* 41, no. 3 (2008): 477–503.

Furber, David. "Going East: Colonialism and German Life in Nazi-Occupied Poland." PhD diss., State University of New York at Buffalo, 2003.

Gerlach, Christian. *Kalkulierte Mord: Die deutsche Wirtschafts- und Vernichtungspolitik in Weißrussland, 1941 bis 1944*. Hamburg: Hamburger Edition, 1998.

Gerwarth, Robert. "The Central European Counter-Revolution: Paramilitary Violence in Germany, Austria, and Hungary After the 'Great War.'" *Past and Present*, no. 200 (Aug. 2008): 175–209.

Gerwarth, Robert, and Stephan Malinowski. "Der Holocaust als 'kolonialer Genozid'? Europäische Kolonialgewalt und nationalsozialistischer Vernichtungskrieg." *Geschichte und Gesellschaft* 33, no. 3 (2007): 439–66.

Grosse, Pascal. "From Colonialism to National Socialism to Postcolonialism: Hannah Arendt's *Origins of Totalitarianism*." *Postcolonial Studies* 9, no. 1 (2006): 35–52.

———. "What Does German Colonialism Have to Do with National Socialism? A Conceptual Framework." In Ames, Klotz, and Wildenthal, *Germany's Colonial Pasts*, 115–36.

Grossmann, Atina. *Reforming Sex: The German Movement for Birth Control and Abortion Reform, 1920–1950*. New York: Oxford University Press, 1995.

Grüner, Wolf. *Jewish Forced Labor Under the Nazis: Economic Needs and Racial Aims, 1938–1944*. Translated by Kathleen M. Dell'Orto. Cambridge, UK: Cambridge University Press, 2006.

Heinemann, Isabel. *Rasse, Siedlung, deutsches Blut: Das Rasse- und Siedlungshauptamt der SS und die rassenpolitische Neuordnung Europas*. Göttingen: Wallstein, 2003.

Herbert, Ulrich. *Best: Biographische Studien über Radikalismus, Weltanschauung, und Vernunft, 1903–1989*. Bonn: Verlag J. H. W. Dietz Nachf., 2001.

Hewitson, Mark. *Germany and the Causes of the First World War*. Oxford: Berg, 2004.

Hitler, Adolf. *Hitler's Second Book: The Unpublished Sequel to "Mein Kampf."* Edited by Gerhard L. Weinberg. Translated by Krista Smith. New York: Enigma, 2003.

Hoffmann, David L., and Annette F. Timme. "Utopian Biopolitics: Reproductive Biopolitics, Gender Roles, and Sexuality in Nazi Germany and the Soviet Union." In *Beyond Totalitarianism: Stalinism and Nazism Compared*, edited by Michael Geyer and Sheila Fitzpatrick, 87–129. Cambridge, UK: Cambridge University Press, 2009.

Kiernan, Ben. *Blood and Soil: A World History of Genocide and Extermination from Sparta to Darfur*. New Haven, CT: Yale University Press, 2007.
Kopp, Kristin. "Constructing Racial Difference in Colonial Poland." In Ames, Klotz, and Wildenthal, *Germany's Colonial Pasts*, 76–96.
Kühl, Stephan. "The Relationship Between Eugenics and the So-called 'Euthanasia Action' in Nazi Germany: A Eugenically Motivated Peace Policy and the Killing of the Mentally Handicapped During the Second World War." In *Science in the Third Reich*, edited by Margit Szöllösi-Janze, 185–210. Oxford: Berg, 2001.
Kundrus, Birthe. *Moderne Imperialisten: Das Kaiserreich im Spiegel seiner Kolonien*. Vienna: Böhlau, 2003.
———. "Von Windhoek nach Nürnberg? Koloniale 'Mischehenverbote' und die nationalsozialistische Rassengesetzgebung." In *Phantasiereiche: Zur Kulturgeschichte des deutschen Kolonialismus*, edited by Birthe Kundrus, 110–31. Frankfurt: Campus, 2003.
Laak, Dirk van. *Über alles in der Welt: Deutscher Imperialismus im 19. und 20. Jahrhundert*. Munich: C. H. Beck, 2005.
Levene, Mark. *The Meaning of Genocide*. Vol. 1 of *Genocide in the Age of the Nation State*. London: I. B. Tauris, 2005.
———. *The Rise of the West and the Coming of Genocide*. Vol. 2 of *Genocide in the Age of the Nation State*. London: I. B. Tauris, 2005.
———. "Why Is the Twentieth Century the Century of Genocide?" *Journal of World History* 11, no. 2 (2000): 305–36.
Liulevicius, Vejas Gabriel. *War Land on the Eastern Front: Culture, National Identity, and German Occupation in World War I*. Cambridge, UK: Cambridge University Press, 2000.
Longerich, Peter. *"Davon haben wir nichts gewusst!" Die Deutschen und die Judenverfolgung, 1933–1945*. Munich: Siedler, 2006.
———. *Heinrich Himmler: Biographie*. Hamburg: Siedler, 2008.
Lumans, Vladis. *Himmler's Auxiliaries: The "Volksdeutsche" Mittelstelle and the German National Minorities of Europe, 1933–1945*. Chapel Hill: University of North Carolina Press, 1993.
Luther, Tammo. *Volkstumspolitik des Deutsche Reiches, 1933–1938: Die Auslandsdeutschen im Spannungsfeld zwischen Traditionalisten und Nationalsozialisten*. Stuttgart: Franz Steiner, 2004.
Madley, Benjamin. "From Africa to Auschwitz: How German South West Africa Incubated Ideas and Methods Adopted and Developed by the Nazis in Eastern Europe." *European History Quarterly* 35, no. 3 (2005): 429–64.
Mai, Uwe. *"Rasse und Raum": Agrarpolitik. Sozial- und Raumplanung im NS-Staat*. Paderborn: Schöningh, 2002.
Maier, Charles S. *Among Empires: American Ascendency and Its Predecessors*. Cambridge, MA: Harvard University Press, 2006.

Malinowski, Stephan. *Vom König zum Führer: Deutscher Adel und Nationalsozialismus.* Frankfurt: Fischer, 2004.

Mallmann, Klaus, and Martin Cüppers. *Halbmond und Hakenkreuz: Das Dritte Reich, die Araber und Palästina.* Darmstadt: Wissenschaftliche Buchgesellschaft, 2006.

Mann, Michael. *The Dark Side of Democracy: Explaining Ethnic Cleansing.* Cambridge, UK: Cambridge University Press, 2005.

Maß, Sandra. *Weiße Helden, schwarze Krieger: Zur Geschichte kolonialer Männlichkeit in Deutschland, 1918–1964.* Cologne: Böhlau, 2006.

Mazower, Mark. *Hitler's Empire: Nazi Rule in Occupied Europe.* London: Allen Lane, 2008.

———. "Violence and the State in the Twentieth Century." *American Historical Review* 107, no. 5 (2002): 1158–78.

McClintock, Anne. *Imperial Leather: Race, Gender, and Sexuality in the Colonial Context.* New York: Routledge, 1995.

Moses, A. Dirk, ed. *Genocide and Settler Society: Frontier Violence and Stolen Indigenous Children in Australian History.* New York: Berg, 2004.

Murphy, David Thomas. *The Heroic Earth: Geopolitical Thought in Weimar Germany, 1918–1933.* Kent, OH: Kent State University Press, 1997.

Overy, R. J. "The 'Reichswerke Hermann Göring': A Study in German Economic Imperialism." In *War and Economy in the Third Reich*, 144–74. Oxford: Clarendon, 1994.

Reynolds, Henry. "Genocide in Tasmania?" In Moses, *Genocide and Settler Society*, 127–49.

Smith, Helmut Walser. *The Continuities of German History: Nation, Religion, and Race Across the Long Nineteenth Century.* Cambridge, UK: Cambridge University Press, 2008.

Ther, Philipp. "Beyond the Nation: The Relational Basis of a Comparative History of Germany and Europe." *Central European History* 36, no. 1 (2003): 45–73.

———. "Deutsche Geschichte als imperiale Geschichte: Polen, slawophone Minderheiten und das Kaiserreich als kontinentales Empire." In Conrad and Osterhammel, *Das Kaiserreich transnational*, 129–48.

Tooze, Adam. *The Wages of Destruction: The Making and Breaking of the Nazi Economy.* London: Allen Lane, 2006.

Traverso, Enzo. *The Origins of Nazi Violence.* Translated by Janet Lloyd. New York: New Press, 2003.

Trevor-Roper, Hugh, ed. *Hitler's Table Talk, 1941–1944: His Private Conversations.* Translated by Norman Cameron and R. H. Stevens. New York: Enigma, 2000.

Wildt, Michael. "'Eine neue Ordnung der ethnographischen Verhältnisse': Hitlers Reichstagsrede vom 6. Oktober 1939." *Zeitgeschichte online-Fachportal für die Zeitgeschichte.* www.zeithistorische-forschungen.de (accessed Oct. 13, 2006).

——. *Volksgemeinschaft als Selbstermächtigung: Gewalt gegen Juden in der deutschen Provinz, 1919 bis 1939*. Hamburg: Hamburger Edition, 2007.

Zimmerer, Jürgen. "Colonialism and the Holocaust: Towards an Archeology of Genocide." In Moses, *Genocide and Settler Society*, 49–76.

——. "Die Geburt des 'Ostlandes' aus dem Geiste des Kolonialismus: Die nationalsozialistische Eroberungs- und Beherrschungspolitik in (post-)kolonialer Perspektive." *Sozial.Geschichte: Zeitschrift für historische Analyse des 20. Und 21. Jahrhunderts* 19, no. 1 (2004): 10–43.

——. "Holocaust und Kolonialismus: Beitrag zu einer Archäologie des genozidalen Gedenkens." *Zeitschrift für Geschichtswissenschaft* 51, no. 12 (2003): 1098–1119.

4

Hannah Arendt, Imperialisms, and the Holocaust

A. Dirk Moses

Hannah Arendt has made a comeback with scholars of German colonialism and mass violence via renewed attention to her book *The Origins of Totalitarianism* (1951). Routinely cited in the 1970s, she was subsequently forgotten as Holocaust researchers focused on anti-Semitism or conducted regional case studies and as German historiography studied the postwar legacies of the dictatorships and the cultural history of German modernities.[1] The revival of colonial and imperial questions with the transnational paradigm and the exhaustion of the internationalist and structuralist frameworks in Holocaust research have driven some scholars to revisit "grand" historical theory.[2] In this context Arendt's argument that Nazi totalitarianism and the Holocaust were prefigured by, or had their roots in, European imperialism offers orientation because it embeds these German and European formations in a world-historical framework. A new, and heated, "continuity thesis" debate has broken out in German historiography over this question, more than forty years after the Fischer controversy about German aims in the First World War and their relationship to Hitler's expansionism.[3] Jürgen Zimmerer, to name the most prominent advocate of the continuity thesis, invokes Arendt to authorize the contention that the Holocaust had colonial roots or was even an extreme form of colonial violence. And he is not alone. German atrocities in Southwest Africa between 1904 and 1907, notes Trutz von Trotha, citing the earlier work of Horst Gründer, is the "only proof of Hannah Arendt's thesis that the foundations of totalitarianism could be seen to be emergent in the colonial policy of Africa."[4]

I will show that this invocation of Arendt is based on a mistaken understanding of her position. Far from proposing a "boomerang" thesis about the corrosive effect of colonialism in Africa on the German and European metropole, Arendt was advancing an alternative continuity argument in service of a broader agenda about the *discontinuity* between what she called "the Western tradition" and totalitarian crimes. The relevance of her invocation of British colonialism in Africa was not to demonstrate their infection of Germany, let alone Russia. It was to redeem British rule, which she admired. The German colonialism and imperialism relevant to Nazism and the Holocaust was not to be found in Africa, as commonly supposed, but in the Pan-Germanism and Pan-Slavism of central Europe. "Continental imperialism," as she called Pan-Germanism and Pan-Slavism, fed into totalitarianism and its unique crimes, while any abuses of "Western imperialism" were rationally limited.[5]

I will question Arendt's distinction between these types of imperialism and her justification for the Holocaust's uniqueness. Arendt's argument, which scholars such as Dan Diner and Russell A. Berman have taken up, ascribes the origins of totalitarian ideologies to non-Western sources, such as Islamism. A postcolonial approach to the relationship between imperialism and genocide places the German experience in a transnational context. This context challenges the comforting exculpations of Western imperialism by the invocation of totalitarian ideologies, without, however, crudely reducing Nazism and the Holocaust to a mere instance or function of European colonial expansion, as the boomerang thesis implies.

The Other German Imperialism

Let us recall that for Arendt the problem with late-nineteenth-century European imperialism was that it undermined the nation-state that she thought continued the Western tradition of politics rooted in Greek and Roman sources. The global economic expansionism of excess, parasitic capital, and the "human detritus" produced by industrialization meant that national politics became corrupted by annexation and rule over distant peoples, using racism as an ideology of justification. Rule over foreign peoples in the colonies corrupted Europeans because they were far removed from the "healthy restraint of ordinary European society."[6] But Arendt was also quite explicit that the roots of Nazism did *not* lie in African colonialism or imperialism:

> The immediate predecessor of totalitarian imperialism is not the British, Dutch or French version of overseas colonial rule, but the German, Austrian, and Russian version of a *continental imperialism* which never actually succeeded, therefore is neglected by students of imperialism, but which in the form of the so-called pan-movements—pan-Germanism and pan-Slavism—was a very potent political force in Central and Eastern Europe.... and since continental imperialism intended to found its "empire" in Europe itself, it did not depend upon a color line to distinguish between "higher and lower" breeds; instead it proposed to treat European peoples as colonials under the rule of a master race of Germanic or Slavic origin.[7]

With this statement Arendt anticipated, by many decades, the current trend to regard east-central Europe as Germany's colonial space.[8] Her suggestion that Europe was the functional equivalent of extra-European possessions of other empires echoed Hitler's well-known statement that the Ukraine would be for Germany what India was for the British.[9] The common denominator was the aspiration for German expansion in the interests of power, prosperity, and security. *Weltpolitik* (the acquisitions of extra-European colonies with a strong navy) and *Ostpolitik* (eastern Europe as Germany's imperial space: *Mitteleuropa*) represented flip sides of the same coin.[10] Colonialism is an analytical category that can apply in both maritime and contiguous contexts. "Modern colonialism," as one scholar put it recently, "can be defined as the annexation of a territory by people with ties to a foreign state who perceive the conquered population as culturally distant and inferior. Annexation is followed by efforts to appropriate the resources of the colony and to dominate its inhabitants in an ongoing way, that is, by a state apparatus."[11] For this reason restricting colonialism to maritime empires is misleading.

Arendt went to great lengths to distinguish what she called "the more respectable imperialism of the Western nations" from the continental imperialism of Pan-Germanism and Pan-Slavism that she thought led to Hitler and Stalin respectively.[12] The point of her British example is to show how that empire avoided the boomerang effect by resisting the temptation to crush Indian resistance with "administrative massacres" and by relinquishing "government over subject races." The French, far from being driven out of North Africa, had "*dared* to give up Algeria."[13] The success of European decolonization was a major story for her. "It is one of the *glories* of Europe, and especially of Great Britain, that she preferred to liquidate the empire."[14] For Arendt this development marked the victory of the nation-state over the transnational movements of racism and imperialism that overwhelmed Germany and Russia. The Western empire-states represented the survival of the Western political tradition that she wished to redeem.

The distinction between East and West obtained during the life of the Western empires, as well. Oceans insulated the maritime empires of Britain and France from the brutal realities of their faraway colonies. But continental empire, by virtue of its contiguous territory, "does not allow for any geographic distance between the methods and institutions of colony and of nation, so that it did not require boomerang effects in order to make itself and all its consequences felt in Europe." As a consequence, this sort of "imperialism truly begins at home."[15] Why the domestic origins of this imperialism proved so pernicious, Arendt continued, was that the German version was an expression of Pan-German tribalism, whereas "Western imperialism" retained the salutary traditions of the Roman Empire, above all the rule of law and integrity of state institutions. Indeed, Western imperialism, notwithstanding "its antinational tendencies," had been given "a new lease on life to the antiquated institutions of the nation-state" (*OT* 225). Britain's two-party system contained the imperialist impulse, and no radical expansionist or chauvinist movements were able to establish themselves outside it. The party system also oriented the political class to the common good rather than simply advocating sectional interests (*OT* 250). Parliament and public opinion also ensured that minimum human rights were respected in the colonies, violent pacification and oppression notwithstanding: "It is to the salutary restraining of these institutions that we owe those benefits which, after all and despite everything, the non-European peoples have been able to derive from Western domination."[16]

Political cultural differences between East and West were salient. If in Britain the citizens acting through the parties could become proprietors of the state at the next election, for racist Pan-Germans the state was an alien institution above the citizenry. It thus sought to subvert the state and enthrone its "movement" to rule exclusively for its tribal members rather than for all citizens of the state (*OT* 255). Moreover, because central and eastern European leaders had little or no experience of constitutional government, they were all too inclined to resort to authoritarianism, that is, rule by decree.

Now Arendt knew that rule by decree, which was the classic mode of unlimited bureaucratic rather than limited constitutional government, obtained in the Western (or what she called also "overseas") empires; but, yet again, she distinguished between the imperialisms, mitigating the worst of Western imperial rule. Whereas in continental imperialism, however secretive and arbitrary, "native rules and a native bureaucracy were accepted as legitimate government," in overseas colonialism "the very fact that the administrators over native populations were imported and felt to be usurpers, mitigated its influence on the subject peoples" (*OT* 243–44). And, as Marx had observed, while domination was naked in the colonies, it was less apparent on the continent, thus preventing the "political reasoning by the people through the withholding of information" (*OT* 246).

Pan-German racism was also different from that of Western imperialism. While the prejudices of the French and British could "claim a certain basis in authentic experience" (presumably she means ruling over "racially" different people), German discrimination against Slavs and the Aryan/non-Aryan distinction was "completely ideological in basis." The racism was therefore all the more fanatical. Capitalist expansion drove "overseas imperialism," but the continental variant was animated by chiliastic dreams of fulfilling the German people's fantasized destiny removed from any reality check. Arendt attributed this distinction to the great influence of intellectuals and "the mob" in the latter, unlike the business elites who directed British and French capital (*OT* 224–26).

But why did this tribal nationalism of "the mob" exist at all? We know that Arendt drew on the liberal historiography of scholars like Hans Kohn to posit the traditional distinction between the (negative) integral nationalism of the East and (positive) civic nationalism of the West. The reason for the difference, she argued, was that the populations of Western countries had "achieved the sovereignty of a nation-state" (*OT* 227) in revolutions against absolutism, while the mixed ethnic borderlands of the Austro-Hungarian Empire could only be ruled by a neutral state standing above the national fray. A region with changing frontiers and experiencing "continuous migration," it was populated by rootless people, "masses who had not the slightest idea of the meaning of *patria* and patriotism, not the vaguest notion of responsibility for a common, limited community" (*OT* 232). The peoples of these mixed-population areas on the edge of empires did not recognize the shared humanity of one another because they were all too aware of cultural difference. Instead, they equated consanguinity with politics, envisaging borders wherever their conationals resided. Tribal nationalism was thereby expansionist. If in the West the state of emancipated citizenry inherited the function to regard all citizens equally under the law, in central and eastern Europe the state and law became an instrument of the ethnically exclusive body politic.

Arendt posited two reasons for the anti-Semitism of the German and Slavic nationalist movements. One was the identification of Jews with the alien Habsburg state; that is, they were colluders with foreign oppressors, a supranational people, and scapegoats against which to mobilize their masses. The other was the religious dimension that suffused German continental imperialism, which displayed messianic tendencies—above all, the myth of "chosen people"—imported from Judaism into Western culture by Christianity. Focusing on this mythic dimension allowed Arendt, once again, to distinguish German and Western imperialism: "In contrast to overseas imperialism, which was content with relative superiority, a national mission, or a white man's burden, the pan-movements started with absolute claims to chosenness" (*OT* 232–33).

The links between the Pan-Germans and National Socialism are not empirically fleshed out in *The Origins of Totalitarianism*. Arendt's basic point was to demonstrate that the Pan-Germans nurtured a culture of racist imperialism and that Hitler was a product of this culture. The Austrian Pan-German Georg von Schoenerer was his "spiritual father" (*OT* 241). It is no accident that Arendt originally wanted to call Nazism "race imperialism" rather than a type of totalitarianism.[17] Her other basic point was that this culture was limited in the British and other Western cases in two ways: within its colonies and in the metropole.

Making this distinction led Arendt to make some problematic arguments. To begin with, her intention in the analysis of Boer rule in southern Africa was to show that the Boers had not developed a polity along Western lines either. In fact, she mounted her case for this problem in terms of the Europeans' reversion to the "savages" they were governing and exploiting.[18] Thus the Boers had degenerated—in a memorable phrase, she wrote that they "had sunk back to the level of savage tribes," again echoing British propaganda, as George Steinmetz has pointed out[19]—because they lived parasitically on the labor of the Africans, thereby forsaking the fabrication of a human polis.[20]

Arendt appreciated that the "African savages ... had frightened Europeans literally out of their wits" (*OT* 206). It was understandable, if not admirable, that the Boers became racists, though less so with the imported Indian and Chinese laborers because they were closer to the human world than the natural world.

Second, this blind spot regarding Africans was evident in her touching faith in the power of civilization to inhibit genocide. Thus, she praised the Italian reluctance to join in the Nazi persecution of Jews by ascribing it to "the almost automatic general humanity of an old and civilized people," although she was also aware that Italian troops at the time were butchering citizens of Ethiopia by aerial bombing.[21] Arendt was able to make such claims by literally consigning to a footnote the apparently atypical case of the Belgian Congo, which she knew cost tens of millions of lives, and excusing the large-scale massacres as instrumentally limited actions.[22] Far from trying to link European colonialism in Africa to Nazism and the Holocaust, then, the purpose of *The Origins of Totalitarianism* and her oeuvre in this respect was to disentangle them and distinguish the Holocaust from previous genocides.

Arendt's Uniqueness of the Holocaust

What, then, according to Arendt, was unprecedented about the Holocaust? Arendt's only extensive discussion of this question in relation to the new genocide concept appears in *Eichmann in Jerusalem*. She criticized the indictment of Eichmann by the Jerusalem court for interpreting the Holocaust as "not much more than the most horrible pogrom in Jewish history," instead of recognizing its unprecedented nature. Unprecedented was the Nazi regime's determination that "the entire Jewish people disappear from the face of the earth." This was a "new crime," a crime "against the human status." "Expulsion" (by which she seemingly meant forced emigration, deportation, and what today is often called "ethnic cleansing"), by contrast, was "an offense against fellow-nations." Genocide, she continued, was "an attack on human diversity as such," a statement that echoed the United Nations Declaration on Genocide in 1946, which was heavily influenced by Raphael Lemkin's philosophy that the "human cosmos" was violated by the destruction of its constituent nations.[23] But why did she insist that genocide was unprecedented when elsewhere she suggested it was not? Even if she qualified this statement by confining it to the modern era, was she suggesting that no genocides had taken place, for instance, in the colonial world since 1500?

The answer is that she distinguished between the Holocaust and previous genocides. The former was purely ideological while the latter were pragmatic. Whereas conventional genocides, so to speak, were limited by utilitarian aims, such as pacification or domination, and were to that extent rational, the extermination of Jews was unlimited, running counter to the war effort by the diversion of resources; it was therefore irrational (*OT* 445). The posited homology was the limitless expansionism of imperialism with the limitless, ideologically motivated intention to exterminate all Jews. The Holocaust, she argued, "could not be explained by any utilitarian purpose; Jews had been murdered all over Europe, not only in the East, and their annihilation was not due to any desire to gain territory that 'could be used for colonization by Germans.'"[24] This distinction has become a commonplace among proponents of the uniqueness thesis, who set off the Holocaust from other mass crimes.

What Arendt intended by "pragmatic" considerations was made clear by her references to territorial gain and colonization but also when she praised the Jerusalem court for making distinctions between suppressing opposition. Such suppression amounted to "war crimes, such as shooting of partisans and killing of hostages," and even ethnic cleansing and destruction "of native populations to permit colonization by an invader." These were a "known, though criminal, purpose," a telling slippage about the criminal nature of imperial expansion through the ages that she did not explore. The extermination of the Jews, however, was a "'crime against humanity,' whose intent and purpose were unprecedented."[25]

What precisely is the content of this "unprecedentedness"? She implied that the nature of the regime prevented Eichmann from judging his own actions by civilized standards. Eichmann and other Nazi criminals were committing crimes "under circumstances that make it well-nigh impossible for him to know or to feel that he is doing wrong."[26] The context was unique and the motives for the Holocaust incomprehensible, that is, irrational. The Nazis could not see that they were embarking on a criminal enterprise. For Arendt "the unprecedented crime of genocide in the midst of Occidental civilization" applied only to the Holocaust (*OT* xiv).

To make her point, Arendt entertained Eichmann's claim that German actions could be understood in terms of a *realpolitische* state of emergency, the rule of raison d'état. In keeping with the Western tradition, she noted that "concessions [can be] made to the stringencies of *Realpolitik*, in order to preserve power and thus assure the continuance of the existing legal order as a whole." Usually, such crimes were exempt from legal redress "because the existence of the state itself is at stake, and no outside political entity has the right to deny a state its existence or prescribe how it is to preserve it." This argument did not apply to Eichmann, she concluded, when the state concerned, like the Nazi regime, "is founded on criminal principles." She left the analysis at that, posing only a series of rhetorical questions: "Can we apply the same principle that is applied to a governmental apparatus in which crime and violence are exceptions and borderline cases to a political order in which crime is legal and the rule"?[27]

The Holocaust and the "Western Tradition"

Perhaps we can. Arendt may not have pursued this line of reasoning because it may have revealed that the Nazi persecution of Jews and communists was a radical manifestation of a venerable Western tradition of legitimately liquidating internal enemies, real or imagined. Far from being a "restraint" (her term) on mass violence, the "Western tradition" can license it in its own defense because the state need not abide by the rules of war when suppressing rebellion and insurgency, which is necessarily criminalized.[28] Counterinsurgency served the same function in the Nazi empire in which Jews were murdered preemptively as potential rebels or partisans. Consider Himmler's infamous Posen speech, with its well-known reference to "the unwritten and never-to-be-written page of glory [*Ruhmesblatt*]," a statement often interpreted as the euphoric *Rausch* of victorious psychopaths: "For we know how difficult we would have made it for ourselves if today—amid the bombing raids, the hardships and the deprivations of war—we still had the Jews in every city as secret saboteurs, agitators, and demagogues. If the Jews were still ensconced in the body of the German nation, we probably would have reached the 1916–17 stage by now."[29]

Jews were particularly suspect, above all Soviet Jews, because Nazism defined them as congenitally hostile to Germans. The Nazis had convinced themselves that Jews were responsible for the traumatic collapse of the German home front and military morale in 1917 and 1918, as well as the short-lived postwar socialist government in Munich and for other Bolshevik uprisings.[30] As the supposed bearers of Bolshevism, Jews were perceived by many Germans as linked both to insurrection at home and to the terrorist regime in the USSR that had exterminated classes and peoples in an "Asiatic" manner. There could be no place for such a dangerous people in the German Empire.

Moreover, by criminalizing Soviet and Jewish enemies, the German state authorized its military to conduct the eastern campaign as a colonial or civil conflict in which the laws of war regarding the treatment of combatants and civilians did not apply. The German state regarded all resistance as illegitimate and targeted civilians *preemptively* and often *collectively* to forestall future resistance, just as in colonial wars of "pacification" against unruly tribes. Hitler rejected the application of the laws of war in the Soviet campaign with the infamous "commissar order" of June 6, 1941, which permitted the summary execution of Bolshevik functionaries. The Wehrmacht subsequently allowed three million Russian POWs to perish. *Einsatzgruppen* acting according to the formula "Jew equals Bolshevik equals partisan"[31] murdered Soviet Jewish men and eventually women and children.

Fantastical as these beliefs may have been, are they qualitatively different from other genocidal conjunctures in which innocent civilians are also targeted as putative security threats? Contrary to Arendt's claim that the camps served no utilitarian purpose and were therefore historically unprecedented, it could be argued that, for the Nazis, they served a purpose of existential significance, ensuring that a perceived mortal enemy would never again represent a threat. Arendt may respond by pointing out, accurately, that the threat was a fantasy, but so they usually are in genocides. Genocidal elites are always gripped by paranoia, often in moments of military crisis, such as in Ottoman Turkey in 1915 and Rwanda in 1994.

Military crisis is not always necessary to precipitate genocide, however. Demographic anxieties may suffice. Serbian intellectuals and national elites thought that the Albanian majority in Kosovo threatened the existence of Serbia itself. In the manner of genocidal propaganda generally, the Serbian media portrayed ethnic Serbs as hapless victims of Croatians and Bosnian Muslims who were intent on destroying Serbia—like during the Second World War. It constructed a nationalist "unconscious" and a "new reality" in which the destruction of their "enemies" was an act of self-defense.[32] What is more, the crushing of rebellion all too often leads to collective punishment of entire groups, such as the Bolshevik genocidal attack, in 1919 and 1920, on the Don and Kuban Cossacks, who were targeted for "mass terror" and "extermination." Of three million, up to half a million Cossacks were killed or deported before the Bolsheviks stopped the campaign. The trauma of having to establish the revolutionary regime against inner and outer enemies led to a hypervigilant countenance toward perceived "socially harmful" elements in the populations, who were murdered or jailed preemptively as a prophylaxis—that is, not because of what they had done but because of who they were and what they *might* do.[33] Genocide and "ethnic cleansing" are ultimately as much about security, including future security, as they are exercises in racial purity. Students of comparative genocide can identify common logics and patterns in an astonishing number of cases while also acknowledging differences between them.[34]

Arendt would reply by saying such a method was mistaken. The "hallmark of the modern historical and political sciences," she wrote, was the confusion in which "everything distinct disappears and everything that is new and shocking is (not explained but) explained away either through drawing some analogies or reducing it to a previously known chain of causes and influence."[35] Moreover, she would say that I have not understood that humanity was confronted with a "radical evil" that cannot "be explained by comprehensible motives" (*OT* 459). What I need to appreciate, she would say, is that totalitarian crimes had shattered the received categories of political thought. The burden of our time was to recognize this fact and imagine a new political science in which action, in her sense of the word, would rupture the automism of events and totalitarian ideologies unleashed by modernity.[36]

What is this radical evil if it is incomprehensible in human terms? "There is only one thing that seems to be discernible," she wrote: "we may say that radical evil has emerged in connection with a system in which all means have become equally superfluous" (*OT* 459). A suprahuman historical process of limitless expansion, which began shattering the stable limits of the nation-state, had, in the form of totalitarianism, overwhelmed Germany and Russia, which were "caught in the process of nature or history for the sake of accelerating its movement; as such, they can only be executioners or victims of its inherent law" (*OT* 468).[37] She made equally speculative and opaque comments about the camps, whose goal was to "liquidate all [human] spontaneity" (*OT* 456). Her point was that the evil that Eichmann and his ilk perpetrated was banal because the significance of the Holocaust cannot be read from their limited subjective intentions or conscience. They were manifestations of a broader, world-historical process that they did not understand, whose contours Arendt was outlining and against whose radical evil she was warning her contemporaries. Her sketch of Lawrence of Arabia in *The Ori-*

gins of Totalitarianism, for instance, made this point about imperialism in general; Lawrence, as a man who gave himself over to blind historical forces, "took great delight in a role that demanded reconditioning of his whole personality until he fitted into the Great Game, until he became the incarnation of the force of the Arab national movement, until he lost all natural vanity in his mysterious alliance with forces necessarily bigger than himself no matter how big he could have been, until he acquired a deadly 'contempt, not for other men, but for all they do' on their own initiative and not in alliance with the forces of history" (*OT* 317–18).

Historians of the Holocaust might wonder whether Arendt's philosophical approach can be applied in empirical research. However distasteful and difficult a serious consideration of their motives may be, the genocidal killers are comprehensible because they are human—and closer to commonplace thinking about security and legitimate violence than many are prepared to countenance. The burden that the twentieth century placed on us is actually to confront the proposition that sources within "Western civilization" may be the culprit rather than resorting to speculative historical philosophies that are empirically impossible to demonstrate.[38]

The signs are strong enough to warrant asking whether Arendt obsessed about this "system," its independent power, and its radical novelty to obscure the fact that the Western tradition found an application in the Nazi paranoia about a Jewish security threat and consequent extermination policies. This was no subterranean tradition that rose to the surface, as she supposed. There was, rather, an explicitly articulated doctrine of total war against inner rebels and colonial others that philosophers, international lawyers, and military thinkers had repeated and handed down for hundreds of years. What is more, notwithstanding obvious differences between Nazis and (other) Western powers, they shared a discursive terrain in which Europe (or the Occident) was counterposed to a degenerate "Asiatic" influence, against which Western culture, however defined, was to be defended. Hitler's writings are littered with such justifications of Nazi expansionism; as the *Völkische Beobachter* put it, "Without Germany, the West would be lost" to Soviet barbarism.[39]

Colonial Memory and the Holocaust

Non-European intellectuals and their European supporters challenged this perspective for most of the twentieth century. As might be expected, asking them what "shocks the conscience of mankind," as the preamble to the Universal Declaration of Human Rights expresses the threshold of humanitarian consciousness, yields different answers from Arendt's. Suffice it for our purposes to recall the answers of W. E. B. Du Bois, Aimé Césaire, and Frantz Fanon about the fascist nature of colonial rule. Du Bois, for instance, wrote in *The World and Africa* in 1947 that "there was no Nazi atrocity—concentration camps, wholesale maiming and murder, defilement of women or ghastly blasphemy of children—which the Christian civilization of Europe had not long been practicing against colored folks in all parts of the world in the name of and for the defense of a Superior Race born to rule the world."[40]

In response to such a flattening out of events and memory, the German-Israeli historian Dan Diner has reiterated the status of the Holocaust as a civilizational rupture (*Zivilisationsbruch*) by distinguishing it from colonial genocides. His book *Gegenläufige Gedächtnisse* is worth considering briefly because it is a conscious defense of the Arendtian thesis against a comparative genocide studies and postcolonial memory. Following Arendt, Diner contends that colonial violence, even when genocidal, was pragmatically limited in scope, whereas the Holocaust was perpetrated for purely ideological reasons as demonstrated by the murder of valuable Jewish workers. Murder for the sake of murder, the Holocaust transgressed all hitherto "observed ethical and instrumental limitations of action" and thereby "destroyed ontological security."[41] Citizens of postcolonial countries, especially Muslim ones, are blind to this distinction, he thinks, because the European powers that had resisted Nazis inflicted violence on them, such as in the French massacre in Setif on May 8, 1945, the day of Europe's liberation from Nazi rule. For many colonized people, then, all Europeans tend to be the same, and some even thought that Nazi Germany could be a possible ally in the anti-imperial struggle.

To make his case, Diner resorts to an ontological argument, much like Arendt. The Holocaust as *Zivilisationsbruch* is only recognizable against the background of the Enlightenment's premises because it negates them, he thinks. Those still in thrall to a religious worldview—Diner refers to Muslims—cannot appreciate the profane role in Western consciousness played by the Holocaust as a surrogate source for ethical norms and identity. Likewise, a "trans-historical and simultaneously anthropological-oriented notion of violence," which he fears is beginning to move to the "centre of discourse," loses the ability to make the necessary historical distinctions. Only a sense of historical judgment that is prepared to make distinctions can recognize

Auschwitz's special significance as the "ultimate genocide," he states in a circular argument.[42] Whether you can see what he wants you to see depends, ultimately, on who you are.

Diner ends up sacralizing the Holocaust against his own intentions and in contradiction to his secularization thesis. "While the Enlightenment placed itself in the position of God and was, in turn, negated by the Holocaust, now the Holocaust, with its nullification of belief in the Enlightenment, takes the place that was formerly occupied by God."[43] Diner makes explicit what is implicit in this discourse, namely that attempts to draw radical distinctions between the Holocaust and other genocides end up reproducing the binary of sacred and profane.[44]

The corner into which authors paint themselves in trying to make points like this is all too evident here. The unprecedentedness of the Holocaust is asserted based on contestable assertions and then made a cornerstone of Western civilization. Those who will not or cannot recognize Diner's position are at best lacking in historical judgment; at worst they are relativizing the Holocaust.[45] Unlike Arendt, then, Diner, who is concerned by denial and relativization of the Holocaust in the Muslim and Arab worlds, admits that his understanding of the Holocaust is necessarily Western-centric. His answer is that the rest of the world needs to learn from the West.[46]

Diner's choices of either recognizing the Holocaust as the "ultimate genocide" or being a "denier" are as unnecessarily stark as the sacred/profane binary is reductive. There are alternatives. One is to narrate or situate the Holocaust into the broader history of empire, showing how the Nazi project was intended at once as a compensation for the colonies lost at Versailles and as an invulnerable rival to the British, French, and ever-more-powerful U.S. empires.[47] Another is discernible in the work of the literature scholar Michael Rothberg, who shows how a transnational perspective can make links between Holocaust memory and memories of colonialism and decolonization without entering into identity politics. Rothberg identifies a tradition that he calls "multidirectional memory," in which Jewish and non-Jewish intellectuals remember and relate different forms of racism and extreme violence without lapsing into facile equation or producing crude hierarchies of suffering. As it happens, Rothberg can show that Holocaust memory developed in the 1960s, at the height of decolonization, and that the different traumas were always refracted through the other in complex ways.[48] Recourse need not be made to ontologically based arguments that claim the privileges of insight. *Pace* Arendt and Diner, just as the conventional tools of historical analysis can map out the common logics and patterns of genocide, they can also reconstruct the cogeneration of different traumatic memories and show thereby that the differences and similarities between the Holocaust and colonial violence were apparent to many intellectuals at the time.

Notes

1. To be sure, political theorists continued to work on Arendt, but genocide and Holocaust historiography was not their focus; see, e.g., Canovan, *Hannah Arendt*; Benhabib, *The Reluctant Modernism of Hannah Arendt*; and Pitkin, *The Attack of the Blob*.
2. See Levene, *Genocide in the Age of the Nation State*; Traverso, *The Origins of Nazi Violence*; King and Stone, *Hannah Arendt and the Uses of History*; Kiernan, *Blood and Soil*; and Smith, *The Continuities of German History*.
3. See Fitzpatrick, "The Pre-History of the Holocaust?" On the Fischer controversy see Moses, *The Politics of Illusion*.
4. Trotha, "'The Fellows Can Just Starve,'" 434. See also Zimmerer, "Colonialism and the Holocaust"; Zimmerer, "The Birth of the *Ostland* Out of the Spirit of Colonialism"; and Chickering, "Total War."
5. Arendt's argument is largely repeated by Shelley Baranowski and Kitty Millet in this volume.
6. Arendt, "Imperialism, Nationalism, Chauvinism," 460.
7. Arendt, "Totalitarian Imperialism," 37–38 (my emphasis).
8. See Kristin Kopp's and Shelley Baranowski's chapters in this volume. See also Nelson, *Germans, Poland, and Colonial Expansion to the East*; Dickinson, "The German Empire"; Blackbourn, *The Conquest of Nature*; and Ther, "Deutsche Geschichte als imperiale Geschichte."
9. See Stone, *History, Memory and Mass Atrocity*, 174–95.
10. Geoff Eley has made this point in a number of conference and workshop commentaries. See Liulevicius, *War Land on the Eastern Front*, 166–67.
11. Steinmetz, "'The Devil's Handwriting,'" 42.
12. Arendt, *The Origins of Totalitarianism*, 222–24.
13. Ibid., xvii (my emphasis).
14. Arendt, "Totalitarian Imperialism," 35 (my emphasis); Arendt, *The Origins of Totalitarianism*, xviii.
15. Arendt, *The Origins of Totalitarianism*, 223; subsequent references are cited parenthetically in the text, using the abbreviation *OT*.
16. Arendt, "Imperialism, Nationalism, Chauvinism," 447.
17. Canovan, *Hannah Arendt*, 18.

18. To be sure, a handful of scholars have noted this racist strain in Arendt's argument. See, e.g., Dossa, "Human Status and Politics"; Norton, "Heart of Darkness"; Presbey, "Critic of Boers or Africans?"; James, "All Power to the People!"; Gines, "Race Thinking and Racism in Hannah Arendt's *The Origins of Totalitarianism*"; and Bernasconi, "When the Real Crime Began."

19. Steinmetz, "Decolonizing German Theory," 8.

20. Arendt, *The Origins of Totalitarianism*, 207. "The Boers were the first European group to become completely alienated from the pride which Western man felt in living in a world created and fabricated by himself" (194).

21. Arendt, *Eichmann in Jerusalem*, 179; see also Arendt, *The Jewish Writings*, 168.

22. Arendt, "Imperialism, Nationalism, Chauvinism," 444n8; Arendt, *The Origins of Totalitarianism*, 185.

23. Arendt, *Eichmann in Jerusalem*, 267–69; see also Moses, "Raphael Lemkin, Culture, and the Concept of Genocide."

24. Arendt, *Eichmann in Jerusalem*, 275. See also Bauer, *Rethinking the Holocaust*, chap. 3; and Katz, *The Holocaust in Historical Context*.

25. Arendt, *Eichmann in Jerusalem*, 275.

26. Ibid., 276.

27. Ibid., 291–92.

28. Arendt, *The Origins of Totalitarianism*, 157. On this doctrine see Neff, *War and the Law of Nations*, chap. 6.

29. Quoted in Dawidowicz, *A Holocaust Reader*, 132–33.

30. Hitler, *Hitler's Words*, 246; Förster, "Operation Barbarossa as a War of Conquest and Annihilation," 491–92, 498.

31. Shepherd, *War in the Wild East*, 93.

32. See Parin, "Open Wounds."

33. See Holquist, "'Conduct Merciless, Mass Terror.'"

34. Bloxham and Moses, *The Oxford Handbook on Genocide Studies*; Stone, *The Historiography of Genocide*.

35. Arendt, "A Reply to Eric Voegelin," 405.

36. Ibid.

37. See also Mayer, "Hannah Arendt, National Socialism, and the Project of Foundation."

38. See *The Origins of Totalitarianism*, viii. I explore the relationship between modernity and genocide in Moses, "Genocide and Modernity."

39. Quoted in Herf, *The Jewish Enemy*, 351n88.

40. Du Bois, *The World and Africa*, 23. See also Césaire, *Discourse on Colonialism*; and Fanon, *The Wretched of the Earth*, 101. Du Bois's views on this matter changed after his visit to the ruins of the Warsaw Ghetto in 1949. On his development see Rothberg, "W. E. B. Du Bois in Warsaw."

41. Diner, *Gegenläufige Gedächtnisse*, 13–14, 35, 81.
42. Ibid., 104–7.
43. Ibid., 106.
44. See Moses, "Conceptual Blockages and Definitional Dilemmas in the 'Racial Century.'"
45. I am not disputing that there is, in fact, much Holocaust denial in the Muslim world. See, e.g., Litvak and Webman, "Perceptions of the Holocaust in Palestinian Public Discourse."
46. On Holocaust memory as part of a Western civilizing mission see Stone, *Constructing the Holocaust*.
47. See Moses, *Empire, Colony, Genocide*; and Mazower, *Hitler's Empire*.
48. See Rothberg, *Multidirectional Memory*; Rothberg, "W. E. B. Du Bois in Warsaw"; Rothberg, "The Work of Testimony in the Age of Decolonization"; and Rothberg, "Between Auschwitz and Algeria." Diner's title, *Gegenläufige Gedächtnisse*, bears a striking resemblance to Rothberg's "multidirectional memory" that was first articulated in his 2004 article cited above, but it is not cited in Diner's book.

Bibliography

Arendt, Hannah. *Eichmann in Jerusalem: A Report on the Banality of Evil*. Rev. enl. ed. New York: Viking, 1964.
———. *Essays in Understanding, 1930–1954*. Edited by Jerome Kohn. New York: Harcourt and Brace, 1994.
———. "Imperialism, Nationalism, Chauvinism." *Review of Politics* 7, no. 4 (Oct. 1945): 441–63.
———. *The Origins of Totalitarianism*. 1951. Rev. ed. New York: Andre Deutsch, 1986.
———. "A Reply to Eric Voegelin." 1953. In Arendt, *Essays in Understanding, 1930–1954*, 401–8.
———. "Totalitarian Imperialism: Reflections on the Hungarian Revolution." *Journal of Politics* 20, no. 1 (1958): 5–43.
Bauer, Yehuda. *Rethinking the Holocaust*. New Haven, CT: Yale University Press, 2001.
Benhabib, Seyla. *The Reluctant Modernism of Hannah Arendt*. Thousand Oaks, CA: Sage, 1996.
Bernasconi, Robert. "When the Real Crime Began: Hannah Arendt's *The Origins of Totalitarianism* and the Dignity of the Western Philosophical Tradition." In King and Stone, *Hannah Arendt and the Uses of History*, 54–67.
Blackbourn, David. *The Conquest of Nature: Water, Landscape, and the Making of Modern Germany*. New York: Norton, 2006.

Bloxham, Donald, and A. Dirk Moses, eds. *The Oxford Handbook of Genocide Studies*. Oxford: Oxford University Press, 2010.

Boemeke, Manfred F., Roger Chickering, and Stig Förster, eds. *Anticipating Total War: The German and American Experiences, 1871–1914*. New York: Cambridge University Press, 1999.

Canovan, Margaret. *Hannah Arendt: A Reinterpretation of Her Political Thought*. Cambridge, UK: Cambridge University Press, 1992.

Césaire, Aimé. *Discourse on Colonialism*. 1955. New York: Monthly Review Press, 1972.

Chickering, Roger. "Total War: The Use and Abuse of a Concept." In Boemeke, Chickering, and Förster, *Anticipating Total War*, 13–28.

Dawidowicz, Lucy, ed. and trans. *A Holocaust Reader*. West Orange, NJ: Behrman House, 1976.

Dickinson, Edward Ross. "The German Empire: An Empire?" *History Workshop Journal*, no. 66 (2008): 129–62.

Diner, Dan. *Gegenläufige Gedächtnisse: Über Geltung und Wirkung des Holocaust*. Göttingen: Wallstein, 2007.

Dossa, Shiraz. "Human Status and Politics: Hannah Arendt on the Holocaust." *Canadian Journal of Political Science* 13, no. 2 (June 1980): 309–23.

Du Bois, W. E. B. *The World and Africa*. Millwood, NY: Kraus-Thomson Organization, 1967.

Fanon, Frantz. *The Wretched of the Earth*. New York: Grove, 1963.

Fitzpatrick, Matthew. "The Pre-History of the Holocaust? The *Sonderweg* and *Historikerstreit* Debates and the Abject Colonial Past." *Central European History* 41, no. 3 (2008): 477–503.

Förster, Jürgen. "Operation Barbarossa as a War of Conquest and Annihilation." In *The Attack on the Soviet Union*. Vol. 4 of *Germany and the Second World War*, edited by Horst Boog et al., 481–521. Oxford: Clarendon, 1998.

Gines, Kathryn T. "Race Thinking and Racism in Hannah Arendt's *The Origins of Totalitarianism*." In King and Stone, *Hannah Arendt and the Uses of History*, 38–53.

Herf, Jeffrey. *The Jewish Enemy: Nazi Propaganda During World War II and the Holocaust*. Cambridge, MA: Harvard University Press, 2006.

Hitler, Adolf. *Hitler's Words: Two Decades of National Socialism, 1923–1943*. Edited by George W. Prange. Washington: American Council on Public Affairs, 1944.

Holquist, Peter. "'Conduct Merciless, Mass Terror': Decossackization on the Don, 1919." *Cahiers due Monde russe* 38, nos. 1–2 (1997): 127–62.

James, Joy. "All Power to the People! Hannah Arendt's Theory of Communicative Power in a Racialized Democracy." In *Race and Racism in Continental Philoso-*

phy, edited by Robert Bernasconi, with Sybol Cook, 249–67. Bloomington: Indiana University Press, 2003.

Katz, Steven T. *The Holocaust in Historical Context*. New York: Oxford University Press, 1994.

Kiernan, Ben. *Blood and Soil: A World History of Genocide and Extermination from Sparta to Darfur*. New Haven, CT: Yale University Press, 2008.

King, Richard H., and Dan Stone, eds. *Hannah Arendt and the Uses of History: Imperialism, Nation, Race, and Genocide*. New York: Berghahn, 2007.

Levene, Mark. *Genocide in the Age of the Nation State*. 2 vols. London: I. B. Tauris, 2005.

Litvak, Meir, and Esther Webman. "Perceptions of the Holocaust in Palestinian Public Discourse." *Israel Studies* 8, no. 3 (2003): 123–40.

Liulevicius, Vejas G. *War Land on the Eastern Front: Culture, National Identity and German Occupation in World War I*. Cambridge, UK: Cambridge University Press, 2000.

Mayer, Robert. "Hannah Arendt, National Socialism, and the Project of Foundation." *Review of Politics* 53, no. 3 (1991): 469–87.

Mazower, Mark. *Hitler's Empire: Nazi Rule in Occupied Europe*. London: Allen Lane, 2008.

Moses, A. Dirk. "Conceptual Blockages and Definitional Dilemmas in the 'Racial Century': Genocides of Indigenous People and the Holocaust." In Moses and Stone, *Colonialism and Genocide*, 148–80.

———, ed. *Empire, Colony, Genocide: Conquest, Occupation, and Subaltern Resistance in World History*. New York: Berghahn, 2008.

———. "Genocide and Modernity." In Stone, *The Historiography of Genocide*, 156–93.

———. "Raphael Lemkin, Culture, and the Concept of Genocide." In Bloxham and Moses, *The Oxford Handbook of Genocide Studies*, 19–41.

Moses, A. Dirk, and Dan Stone, eds. *Colonialism and Genocide*. London: Routledge, 2007.

Moses, John A. *The Politics of Illusion: The Fischer Controversy in German Historiography*. London: Prior, 1975.

Neff, Stephen C. *War and the Law of Nations*. Cambridge, UK: Cambridge University Press, 2005.

Nelson, Robert L., ed. *Germans, Poland, and Colonial Expansion to the East: 1850 to the Present*. New York: Palgrave MacMillan, 2009.

Norton, Anne. "Heart of Darkness: African and African Americans in the Writings of Hannah Arendt." In *Feminist Interpretations of Hannah Arendt*, edited by Bonnie Honig, 247–61. University Park: Pennsylvania State University Press, 1995.

Parin, Paul. "Open Wounds: Ethnopsychoanalytical Reflections on the Wars in the Former Yugoslavia." In *Mass Rape: The War Against Women in Bosnia-Herze-*

govina, edited by Alexandra Stiglmayer, 35–53. Lincoln: University of Nebraska Press, 1993.

Pitkin, Hannah F. *The Attack of the Blob: Hannah Arendt's Concept of the Social*. Chicago: University of Chicago Press, 1998.

Presbey, Gail. "Critic of Boers or Africans? Arendt's Treatment of South Africa in *The Origins of Totalitarianism*." In *Postcolonial African Philosophy: A Critical Reader*, edited by Emmanuel Chukwudi Eze, 162–80. Cambridge: Blackwell, 1997.

Rothberg, Michael. "Between Auschwitz and Algeria: Multidirectional Memory and the Counterpublic Witness." *Critical Inquiry* 33, no. 1 (2006): 158–84.

———. *Multidirectional Memory: Remembering the Holocaust in the Age of Decolonization*. Stanford: Stanford University Press, 2009.

———. "W. E. B. Du Bois in Warsaw: Holocaust Memory and the Color Line, 1949–1952." *Yale Journal of Criticism* 14, no. 1 (2001): 169–89.

———. "The Work of Testimony in the Age of Decolonization: *Chronicle of a Summer*, Cinema Verité, and the Emergence of the Holocaust Survivor." *PMLA* 119, no. 5 (2004): 1231–46.

Shepherd, Ben. *War in the Wild East: The German Army and Soviet Partisans*. Cambridge, MA: Harvard University Press, 2004.

Smith, Helmut Walser. *The Continuities of German History: Nation, Religion, and Race Across the Long Nineteenth Century*. Cambridge, UK: Cambridge University Press, 2008.

Steinmetz, George. "Decolonizing German Theory: An Introduction." *Postcolonial Theory* 9, no. 1 (2006): 3–13.

———. "'The Devil's Handwriting': Precolonial Discourse, Ethnographic Acuity, and Cross-Identification in German Colonialism." *Comparative Study of Society and History* 45, no. 1 (2003): 41–95.

Stone, Dan. *Constructing the Holocaust: A Study in Historiography*. London: Vallentine Mitchell, 2003.

———, ed. *The Historiography of Genocide*. Basingstoke, UK: Palgrave MacMillan, 2008.

———. *History, Memory and Mass Atrocity: Essays on the Holocaust and Genocide*. London: Vallentine Mitchell, 2006.

Ther, Philipp. "Deutsche Geschichte als imperiale Geschichte: Polen, slawophone Minderheiten und das Kaiserreich als kontinentale Empire." In *Das Kaiserreich transnational: Deutschland in der Welt, 1871–1914*, edited by Sebastian Conrad and Jürgen Osterhammel, 129–48. Göttingen: Vandenhoeck und Ruprecht, 2004.

Traverso, Enzo. *The Origins of Nazi Violence*. New York: Free Press, 2005.

Trotha, Trutz von. "'The Fellows Can Just Starve': On Wars of 'Pacification' in the African Colonies of Imperial Germany and the Concept of 'Total War.'" In Boemeke, Chickering, and Förster, *Anticipating Total War*, 415–35.

Zimmerer, Jürgen, "The Birth of the *Ostland* Out of the Spirit of Colonialism: A Postcolonial Perspective on the Nazi Policy of Conquest and Extermination." In Moses and Stone, *Colonialism and Genocide*, 101–23.

———. "Colonialism and the Holocaust: Towards an Archeology of Genocide." In *Genocide and Settler Society: Frontier Violence and Stolen Indigenous Children in Australian History*, edited by A. Dirk Moses, 49–76. New York: Berghahn, 2004.

5

Caesura, Continuity, and Myth
The Stakes of Tethering the Holocaust to German Colonial Theory

Kitty Millet

In *Landscape and Memory* Simon Schama describes Białowieża, a primeval forest at the border of Poland and Belarus, in relation to the German concept of the *Urwald*. Quoting Adam Mickiewicz's *Pan Tadeusz* to get at the underpinnings of Białowieża as *Urwald*, Schama demonstrates the forest's imagined significance to the Poles and then, by extension, to the Germans, Lithuanians, and Russians: "—in a dense fog beyond which, 'fables so declare,' is a kind of primitive paradise: an ark of species, animal and vegetable; some of every kind.... Their progeny are sent beyond the secret cradle-world, called 'Motherland' by the huntsmen, but the archetypal animals remain in zoological utopia."[1]

Associating Białowieża with Eden, the huntsman who enters this place has an opportunity to regain access to "an ark of species," in which the depths of the forest signify a life-giving center. It is salvific and redemptive, preserving species by virtue of sequestering them away from "civilizing human custom" so that "the wild beast with the tame lives as a brother" and the unarmed man "would pass through the midst of them unharmed" (*LM* 60). Tellingly, this subjunctive construction suggests an imagined place that could be realized but is not. In this respect Mickiewicz's archetypal beginning of nature proposes "the secret cradle-world" as home both to the hunter and to the beast. In this cradle-world nature protects the hunter as one of its own by keeping him safe from civilization. The subjunctive element also inscribes the place as an imagined possibility but without real purchase on the empirical world. An aesthetic terrain, eliciting the imagination, it is not a political entity.

The Polish nobility's desire to link themselves with "the sylvan arcadia" (*LM* 48), "the sylvan world of Lithuanian warrior aristocracy" (41), motivated many of them to imagine that "Sarmatian blood coursed through their veins, that they remained the worthy heirs of warriors who had vanquished Teutonic knights, the Tatar hordes, and the Turkish janissaries" (43). Schama reminds us, however, that this aesthetic imagining is not limited to Mickiewicz and Poles, since Lithuanians, Russians, and Germans ascribe similar beliefs to the mystical recesses of Białowieża in their national folklores. For Germans Białowieża exemplified the quintessential *Urwald*, and, as such, it resonated with the mythical places well known from German folktales. Sent to Białowieża in 1820, Julius von Brinken, a German forester, described the forest as "*Urwald* . . . a thing of glory and terror" (50), adding to its mythical notoriety an aesthetic and sublime connotation.

In 1915, when the German army took possession of Białowieża during the First World War, the Kaiser's Military Forest Administration viewed the *Urwald* as an exploitable resource. They conscripted Poles and Jews, men and women, boys and girls, to work the mills, cut the trees, and haul lumber. Although the Germans determined each group's value according to "racialized" abilities,[2] the Jews presented no real resistance to their conscription into the German forest exploitation project; thus, the Germans forcibly enlisted the Jews—as well as their neighbors—in the harsh and dangerous working of the forest for the Kaiser's Forest Administration.

Since the Nazis believed the Jews to have actual capabilities predisposing them for some elements of this work, they had a value to the Forest Administration's aim of exploiting Białowieża's stands of hardwood. In this respect the Jews of Białowieża were imagined, like their Polish neighbors, as subalterns, who could be pressed into service for German purposes, notably because the Jews living in Białowieża were "people of the forest, of the wilderness *puszcza*."[3] They knew how to harvest wood. Furthermore, as *puszcza*, they were known as indigenous inhabitants of the forest, similar in status to the other groups living in villages, the small outposts within Białowieża.

When the Nazis imagined Białowieża as *Urwald*, however, they imagined it as if it were a real repository not only for the "ark of species" but also as "an unbroken extension of East Prussia" (*LM* 70), the soil that gave birth to Aryan essence. In this way Białowieża already existed as a natural and ancestral *Heimat* or mythical home of the Aryan people from which they had been displaced. In other words, it was an imagined "archive" of evidence proving their lineage, recuperating Mickiewicz's "ark of species" to signify that they, the Nazis, were returning to their own lands and not "merely" stealing the forest from its inhabitants, appropriating its use value.

By 1941 the Nazis had recast Białowieża's Jews, like all other Jews, as signifiers of contagion,[4] who, if left to their own devices, would exterminate German bloodlines by their simple existence. At the same time, the Nazis identified themselves as "a sylvan people." Göring became the real exemplar of "a man of the forest." When the Nazis invaded Białowieża in 1941, then, Jews were rounded up in front of "the forecourt of the hunting palace, the women and children separated from the men and boys over sixteen" (*LM* 70). The next day the Nazis took the men far into the forest, shot them, and left them in a pit; the women and children ended up in Treblinka. They relocated the Poles.

Consequently, we have to ask why the Jews' status changes from potential slave laborers in 1915 to stock to be slaughtered, and eventually to the discarded material, *Stücke*, of the camps in twenty-five years' time? How do they shift from subalterns to "useless" phenomena by 1941?[5] Is this shift a progression of the colonial project advanced earlier by the Kaiserreich, or was it something radically different from colonialism?

Schama's account maps an aspect of the Jews' transformation by highlighting how the forest's use value receded as its mythical desirability rose. Although the Nazis still considered the forest "an unbroken extension of East Prussia," potentially *Lebensraum*,[6] it was an extension imagined as Aryan Heimat, its symbolic place contaminated by Jews, pollutants of both "blood and soil," and occupied by Poles, who were to be relocated. In this instance the transformation of the Jews from subalterns in Białowieża to *Stücke* at Auschwitz derives from the coupling of Nazi myth to Nazi race theory, an imagined narrative to justify a "scientific" and "political" set of theories. In other words, when the forest shifted from exploitable resource to mythical component in the Nazi imaginary, the Jews found themselves forcibly elided from even the subaltern ranks of their neighbors. But how did this shift take place? Could the coupling of political ideology and science really produce this outcome?

In 1931 Lutz Heck became the director of Berlin's zoo. In 1936, under the Nazis, Heck was charged with the "reinvention of Nature," a project that comprised three steps: the eugenics project known as his "back-breeding" program, the looting of prized and almost "mythical" animals from Warsaw's zoo to be sent to his own zoo in Berlin, and the securing of Poland's primeval forest, Białowieża, as a gift to Hermann Göring, his patron.[7] From these three examples, Heck's science projects appear to depend explicitly on Poland as a place of potential resources, as "a colonial space." To some degree, all of these actions appear to reflect a long-standing colonial attitude toward Poland.

In 1941 Heck went to Warsaw ostensibly to restructure the Warsaw zoo, a restructuring that entitled him to loot the zoo of its exotic animals. He was motivated for many reasons, not least of which was the "Blood and Soil" ideology, whose adherents imagined the erasing or "cleansing" of "impurities" from German biology and territory. This ideology provided Nazism with the necessary components for a new aesthetic of identity, a myth to impose on Nature itself, through political and scientific arenas.

A minor event in Nazi history, Heck's liquidation of the Warsaw zoo's holdings suggests a simple process of resource allocation during wartime. He identified a resource for Nazi exploitation that happened to be the property of a subaltern people, the Poles. We could conceivably view this action as an adjunct action executed under the *Generalplan Ost* (GPO),[8] in which the Nazis sought to gain control over eastern territory, reordering it and redefining it as they desired. But Heck's actions did not end with the reappropriation of the zoo's animals and resources.

After sending the best examples of the zoo's collections of exotic animals to his own Berlin zoo, Heck determined that some of the zoo's remaining animals should be sent to other zoos throughout Germany. These animals were not good enough for his purposes, but they still had use value for the Reich. However, Heck and some of his SS friends slaughtered the animals without value to German interests as sport:

—Heck invited his SS friends to a rare treat: a private hunting party right on the zoo grounds, a spree that combined privilege with the pell-mell of exotic animals even a novice or soused gunman could bag.... Heck and a cadre of fellow hunters arrived on a sunny day, full of drink and hilarity, elated by army victories, laughing as they roamed the grounds, shooting penned and caged animals for sport.... The savagery didn't serve hunger or necessity, it wasn't a political gambit, the doomed animals weren't being culled because they'd become too abundant in the wild. Not only was the SS ignoring their value as ... creatures with unique personalities, the men didn't even credit animals with basic fear or pain. (*ZW* 95–96)

In other words the zoo's remaining animals were not killed for any real purpose beyond the lack of the necessity for their being; the Nazis imagined these beasts to be without "basic fear or pain." By slaughtering the "valueless" animals without intent even to use the carcasses, Heck and his companions construed the animals' slaughtered bodies as having no real use value even in death: they were destroyed as entities without value, their corpses without significance. While the odd body part could be mounted and displayed as a sign of the "Nazi warrior," the primary reason for the animals' death derived from their alleged genetic flaws. They existed outside of any scheme of use value, and their continued existence would endanger the Aryans' environment. In other words these animals could not be recuperated for any meaningful reason, and Heck, with his companions, enjoyed killing them. It was "sport." They derived pleasure from the experience. The question becomes, then, "how does one derive pleasure from slaughter?"[9]

Heck's behavior illustrates that the Nazi project of "Blood and Soil" had a subjective dimension coupled to its objective of removing offending parties from desired territory. The removal of offending objects was only one aspect of the project. The territory had to be "prepared" for its mythical role as Heimat; that is, the subjective dimension required the space to be reimagined as it existed in a Nazi myth of origin. Part of that reimagining, furthermore, mandated that the Nazi subject derived a kind of catharsis from the experience of slaughter. In this way slaughter became a form of aesthetic experience.

Without the subjective dimension, Heck's behavior signifies a colonial act in that he determines the values of the zoo's resources, appropriates them, sends the animals with different degrees of significance to various locations in Germany, and converts the zoo itself into a pig farm. At face value these actions seem like colonial gestures, detachable tactics that have appeared before in other contexts in which colonizers appropriate the resources of the colonized. But we have to wonder if their depiction as colonial acts would be enough to explain why Heck then went back to the zoo and slaughtered the animals that remained behind? We have to ask what motivated Heck to determine that the remaining animals lacked any kind of value for the *Volk* and why that lack demanded extermination? Why did he take the radical step of killing all of the remaining animals at the zoo? Was he simply sadistic? Was there something aberrant in him that prompted this behavior? Or was Heck applying Nazi race theory to justify a new form of destruction?

The initial steps of Heck's projects seemed in line with other projects of the period. When Heck took over the administration of the Berlin zoo from his father in 1931 (*ZW* 78), his first step was to remodel it along the lines of a very basic ideology: a celebration of indigenous German species. This action became an initial foray into his later task of "reinventing nature" (*ZW* 85). As Schama has shown, this was nothing new; eugenics was hardly a Nazi invention, and the celebration of indigenous German traditions was already a popular trend fostered by romanticism. By 1937, when Heck officially joined the National Socialist Party, he had already devoted himself to the project of resurrecting "three pure-blooded, extinct species—the Neolithic horses known as tarpans, aurochs (the wild bovine progenitor of all European cattle breeds), and the European or "forest" bison (*ZW* 80), also known legendarily as the wisent. His project was understood familiarly as the "back breeding" program.

Although Heck would later seize his desired animals, initially he purchased "wild or halfwild cattle" from specific herds across Europe so that the Berlin zoo would possess "a very large number of races of pure and crossbred cattle." From the eighty animals in the zoo's collection, Heck concluded that "breeding back to the extinct aurochs" was possible and desirable because the aurochs represented an animal in existence not only before domestication, but also specifically before "crossbreeding."[10]

An ancient beast from which all modern, domesticated cattle are descended, the *B. primigenius*, or aurochs, had been associated with the Germans since antiquity, beginning with Caesar's description of the "uroxen" in the Gallic War, which were "somewhat smaller than elephants ... [and] were as bulls." Caesar described how the Germans would kill the aurochs "zealously ... taking them in pits; by such work the young men harden themselves and by this kind of hunting train themselves, and those who have slain most of them bring the horns with them to a public place for a testimony."[11]

The beasts resonated then with another mythical narrative, one in which Teutonic warriors lived "free, pure, and untainted" by the evils of impure blood, isolated in and by nature, hunting the beasts whose capture would "harden" the warriors and whose totems would publicly identify the warriors as heroes of the people. Heck's activities suggest that he imagined a new status for himself as he slaughtered the remaining animals in their cages: like the Teutonic warrior, Heck imagined himself "the hero of the people" because of his actions.

In this way Heck proposed himself to be a "genetic hero" who would reproduce another aurochs, an "ur-calf."[12] This proposal added another mythical layer to the ideology of "Blood and Soil"; the hunter not only gained a new rank, but he was also able to dispose of the narrative of Jewish origins simultaneously. In Heck's version he would save the Volk by preventing the Jews' literal destruction of the "Golden Calf."

Lutz Heck's desire for the aurochs was part of what his brother Heinz described as a recovery project that would restore man and nature eventually to an ontological purity by overcoming the "extermination" imposed by Jews on Aryans and their totemic beasts. As Heinz described it, "Some of those kinds of animals . . . already exterminated can be brought back to life again" (ZW 82). They understood extermination here to be the impure bloodlines transmitted through "wrong breeding and domestication,"[13] that is, the animal's removal from the forest and its eventual intermingling with inferior bloodlines. The brothers wanted to recover that which "modernity," a signifier for miscegenation both between races and among species, had polluted and destroyed. By being responsible for bringing back the aurochs and other primordial beasts, the Heck brothers would return to the German people an evolutionary starting point that could count on the absence of pollutants: implicitly, Lutz Heck was searching for an evolutionary starting point that would "recover" a mythical Aryan world, Mickiewicz's "ark of species," as a literal entitlement.

The aurochs' association with an autochthonic, primordial, and mythical existence intensified Heck's belief that he could not only supply the Nazis generally with a missing link between their Aryan pretensions and the missing ancient antecedents but also that he could provide Göring with a particular link to the Aryan hunter. Like the ancient men who painted the aurochs at Lascaux, "the wild ancestors of domesticated cattle,"[14] Göring had the aurochs' close cousin the *wisent*, or bison, depicted on the walls of Carinhalle, his Schorf Heide estate east of Berlin (*LM* 71). Painted on the cave's walls, the aurochs became a signifier of the true inhabitants of the land; painted on the walls of Carinhalle, the wisent enabled Göring to impose himself, likewise, as the natural descendant of the Aryan hunter, inserting himself mythically into the pictures around him. In fact, the pictures at Schorf Heide acted emblematically to elicit Göring's identification.

This elicited identification was key, since for Heck the aurochs's pedigree intimated not only a life free of "racial mixing" but also an imagined identity that resonated with an aesthetic representation or myth of pure nature enfolding the Aryan man. Thus, "only prehistoric creatures would do, ones untainted by racial mixing.... If he concentrated the genes by breeding together animals that most resembled an extinct one, in time he would arrive at their purebred ancestor" (*ZW* 80), the ideal beast to go with Hitler's ideal Aryan. It was a myth that pushed Heck to imagine he could reintroduce the coordinates of an ancient evolutionary point, one unfettered by a contaminated existence. Moreover, it was not a desire for these animals as animals that prompted the back-breeding program; rather, it was a desire for an imagined narrative about Nazi identity. The aurochs accrued value as the signifier of Nazi myth.

Heck enlisted Göring's help with the back-breeding project in 1934 by giving him "breeding bulls" so that Göring could "begin populating his Schorf Heide estate ... with progeny produced, according to the best veterinary eugenic advice, from mating with hybrid cows" (*LM* 68). Often hunting together at Carinhalle, both men believed that the Aryan race had been degraded because of "haphazard breeding of robust and humdrum stock" and that "a race policy" was necessary "in which ruin is prevented by the elimination of 'degenerate' types" (*ZW* 85).[15]

Not unique to Heck and Göring, this belief was associated with Konrad Lorenz and other influential German intellectuals, as well as Nazi leaders.[16] Between 1938 and 1943 Lorenz argued that "changes in the instinctive behavior patterns of domesticated animals" were "symptoms of decline." Thus Lorenz "assumed a homology between domesticated animals and civilized human beings; that is, he assumed there must be similar causes for effects assumed to be similar, and he further believed that civilization was in a process of 'decline and fall.'"[17]

Lorenz's theory not only suggested the physical removal of "degenerate types," but it also sought to combat a certain kind of culture. Hence, it had both objective and subjective dimensions. To intervene in degenerate culture meant that Nazi race theory had to identify both appropriate and inappropriate cultural objects, as well as an appropriate way to imagine Aryan subjectivity, a properly Nazi aesthetic experience. An outcome of this experience was the imagining that Jews as a "type" should be mentally "sloughed off" or "discharged" so as to be no longer inferable from human experience.

In other words there were two mental functions at stake in Nazi race theory—one expressed as a "science," a knowledge, and one intuited as an imagined experience. The two functions together generated a mythical narrative about modern humanity's "haphazard breeding" and the domestication of wild beasts so that nature emerged as a signifier under threat, both blood and soil polluted by a contaminant that could not be identified beyond the suspect practices of "haphazard breeding," the suppression of Heck's "ur-calf." Nature's salvation, and, with it, the Aryan essence, became contingent on going back both to the mythical aurochs and its "pristine" beginnings. This contingency plan proposed that a significant percentage of domesticated cattle were valueless to the aurochs's recovery; they were unacceptable for the Nazis' mythical world.

But even this aspect was not simply a case of acceptability or unacceptability. Some beasts retained value for the basic needs of the Volk, and they could be suborned because of this basic value. Others were distinctly valueless, and they needed to be eliminated from existence because they posed too great a threat to the Reich's *Naturschutz*. Within this mythical narrative the mere existence of the "valueless" produced a biological strain or threat to the bloodlines of the more important and desirable mythical ontologies.[18]

The Nazis' intention to "cleanse" both "blood and soil" of biological threats prompted Pierre Lecomte de Noüy, a biophysicist, to declare in 1944 that "Germany's crime is the greatest crime the world has ever known, because it is not on the scale of history: *IT IS ON THE SCALE OF EVOLUTION.*"[19] The statement hinges on its last clause, printed in capital letters so that the statement's dramatic stress has the force of a scream, tethering Lecomte de Noüy's first assumption—"it is not on the scale of history"—to a far more disturbing axis: "*IT IS ON THE SCALE OF EVOLUTION.*" The Nazis were aiming at the mechanism of evolutionary adaptation by which new organisms came into being. By destroying biological diversity, they would save Aryan identity. Lecomte de Noüy believed the Nazis to be rewriting human biology by imposing a mythical narrative on the environment around them.

Darwin argued that species become extinct because they fail to adapt; "if any one species does not become modified and improved in a corresponding degree with its competitors, it will soon be exterminated."[20] One could infer that the Aryans failed to adapt, so they became extinct. For Heck and the Nazis, however, Aryans, like their beasts, had been "exterminated" through "haphazard breeding and domestication." Inverting evolutionary logic, the Nazis determined that what had to change was their environment—its people, animals, soil, plants—so that they could recover the Aryan genetic code. Heck's "recovery project" had its roots in this "assault on evolution."

Essentially, Nazi race theory posited the Aryans akin to a keystone species in history "whose removal leads to an even further loss from the community."[21] Such a loss would constitute the destruction of an entire environment;[22] in the Nazi case, the Aryan world of pristine Nature had ceased to exist because of the "extermination of Aryan men and beasts" by civilizing forces: the "bearers of civilization" had made them extinct. More important, the Nazis felt justified in "preying on different species" because their actions ensured the rediscovery and salvation of the mythical "ark of species."[23] With its eugenics projects Nazi race theory emerged as a necessary stratagem for restoring nature, the Final Solution, an inevitable consequence; for Lecomte de Nöuy this inevitable consequence signaled an attack on evolution and the diversity of nature. The Nazi myth legitimated the identification of Jews as a specific threat.

In "The Uniqueness of the Holocaust" Avishai Margalit and Gabriel Motzkin argue that Nazi race theory delineated two different kinds of racism. They start from the premise that the Nazis sought to exclude Jews from humanity because the Nazis viewed the Jews as an illegitimate part of evolution—not an inferior component, but an illegitimate existence.

> The Nazis did indeed seek to exclude the Jews from the human race, and not merely the German people.... The Nazis viewed the Jews through the lenses of two different kinds of race theory. One kind of racism ... that asserts that certain varieties (races) are inferior to other varieties of the same species. This kind of racism does not deny the idea of a common humanity, since it views all varieties as belonging to the same species, but it finds one kind of human superior to another, and so relativizes the ethical obligations that we presumably share toward fellows.[24]

In Margalit and Motzkin's first form of racism the Nazis legislate over a hierarchy of species. Conversely, this argument also lends itself to imagining a hierarchy among the Nazis' victims. We might even propose this as a colonial perspective in which one victim might be imagined as more valuable than another.[25] Certainly, the Nazis routinely ranked other groups according to this type of hierarchy, in which, furthermore, "the ethical obligations that we presumably share toward fellows" become "relativized," conditioned by one's interactions with specific groups and environments. In this case the Nazis justified their colonial attitudes through their "interactions" with "an inferior Other."[26]

But the Nazis' second form of racism presented the Jews outside of the human species: they were not "inferior Others": "The other kind of racism denies that humans belong to a common species. There are different races in the same way there are different kinds of animals. This kind of racism asserts that Jews are not merely an inferior race, but a different animal altogether, and that therefore, they should be treated in the way that one treats other animals."[27]

If humans do not "belong to a common species," then, an epistemological category of human could have multiple species within it, and such a variety would be inappropriate. It became the Nazis' mission to remove from this category inappropriate "objects," a way of "purging" knowledge. In the first form of racism the category of human could accommodate many inferior objects as long as they were clearly marked as such and as long as Aryan superiority remained at the top of the hierarchy. This model was the working plan for the Barbarossa campaign of 1941, in which one of the Nazis' goals was "to turn western Russia into a German paradise of 'Aryan' colonizers served by hordes of Slav helots."[28]

In the second form of racism, if a haphazardly reproduced object emerged in the category, it would destroy the category altogether. Thus, "the Nazis viewed the Jews as the paradigmatic example of a degenerative evolution, one that would lead eventually to the extinction of their race."[29] Margalit and Motzkin's analysis of Nazi race theory certainly resonates with Heck's practice of Nazi eugenics, as well as with his behavior at the Warsaw zoo.

Heck hoped to eliminate the danger of "haphazard reproduction" when he received the charge to "reinvent Nature." Moreover, the traces of "haphazardness" seemed to have tainted every level of evolution. Figuring that "the boundaries of genus and species are not fixed, that humans may well be on their way to becoming something else,"[30] the Nazis supposed that if evolution's starting point was reimagined as "reopened space," it could be wiped clean of contagion, enabling the Aryans and their mythical animals to reemerge, restarting Aryan domination; and for Heck the battle they were fighting began with an imaginary prehistory, anchored to a missing "golden calf."

This revision was the subjective stake of Heck's looting of the Warsaw zoo—those animals that were without value could be disposed of without consequence. The keys to a cleansed German nature acquired an ontological dimension as well. Those elements that polluted German ontology had to be "sloughed off" so that these foreign elements could eventually no longer be inferred from existence. They had to be essentially "discharged" from Nazi psychology, and this was not the allocation of a subjective space to which an "inferior Other" could be assigned. This was not an epistemological reorganization with hierarchies; that effect would come later as a consequence of cleansing the human subjectivity of the Jews.

In other words the Nazis' imagined subjective space did not include a space for Jews.[31] We have to ask what such a claim actually means and what the deployment of such a subjective position means after the fact.[32] For the Nazis this position gave them a mythical investment unlike any previous German appropriations and entitlements. Colonial greed appears to be secondary to the constitution of the Aryan subject: the myth was more important to Heck, Göring, and other Nazi leaders than the acquisition of natural resources and their eventual use value, although all of these elements enabled the Nazis to produce their myth.[33] After all, the mythical forest of Białowieża and the "noble aurochs, tarpans, and wisents" suggested themselves to the Nazi mind as aesthetic necessities, so much so that when the SS occupied Białowieża during Operation Barbarossa in 1941, Göring himself prevented the SS from torching "the forest to purge it of any possible shelter for partisans" (*LM* 69), declaring it a *heiliger Hain* (holy grove).[34] In this respect Göring was emblematic of the subject position emerging in Nazism. His imagined identity legitimized his actions at Białowieża, even overturning the "scorched earth" policy normally associated with Operation Barbarossa,[35] and this privileging of the myth's subjective components brings us to the entitlement Göring imagined he possessed.

In 1934, in addition to beginning his eugenics experiments with Heck, Göring made his first trip to Białowieża, and he enacted the Reich Game Law. Under the Reich Game Law, Göring became *Reichsjägermeister*, entitling him to wear the traditional garb of the mythical Aryan hunter (*LM*

68). The post gave Göring the role of guarantor and overseer of the Reich Game Law, and this entitlement meant that both his trip to Białowieża and his participation in the back-breeding program signified more than just casual hobbies. These activities were already creating a mythical space for the Aryan warrior. Göring acted as if he were the Teutonic, Aryan huntsman, "the man of the forest," a reincarnation of Hermann, whose steps he ritually reenacted when he "reentered" the *Urwald* of Białowieża.[36] This shift was reinforced routinely at every level until Göring saw his ritualized participation in the hunt as a mystical rite, putting him aesthetically in the same place— the *heilige Hain*—occupied by his imagined ancestors so that anyone who would imagine himself to be of Aryan stock, *as Göring imagined himself to be*, would likewise perform and act in the same way.

This mental step provided the ritual theater, the subjective orientation, Göring needed for his identity as Aryan and Nazi warrior, and it was part and parcel of his aesthetic experience. At its core it was the classic articulation of *subjective universality* that Kant attributed as that which underwrote the validity of judgments of taste.[37] This necessary step to aesthetic experience ended in two critical moments: the emergence of the subject and the placing of that subject within a community (*Gemeinschaft*) of like-minded individuals, predicated on their imagined likenesses to the subject.

But in Kant *subjective universality* is never empirically verifiable; as the Nazis' hijacked aesthetic experience, they inscribed an empirical component onto the experience in which the Reich, consisting of like-minded and biologically identical people, validated an imagined Nazi subject by reflecting visibly desirable physical traits. The underside of this inscription is found at the death camps themselves, where the Nazi subject erases evidence of the Jews from his palette so that he can imagine "beginning again."

Thus Göring dons his hunting costumes, visits Białowieża annually, and reenters the forest as the reincarnation of Hermann; he acts as if an autochthonic charge prompts him, and this "as if" doesn't even register the Jews' presence in the Białowieża forest. They could not be "men of the forest" because Göring, the "man of the forest," already occupied that space; the Jews were the environmental "blight" that the *Reichsjägermeister* would have to eliminate so that his "ark of species" would be preserved, uncorrupted, and awaiting its Aryan Adam.

Göring's proposed narrative, his myth, tethered his imagined identity to the belief that Białowieża was an Aryan Heimat and, as such, belonged to the Nazis; it was specifically under his guardianship. The Poles and Slavs had produced an occupation, living in the forest as poor custodians who had allowed Jewish infection to compromise the forest. Thus, the Poles and Slavs had to be redeployed farther east, but Jews had to be destroyed. This realization brings us to several necessary questions: Were the Nazis' practices colonial in nature? Did they spring from a Nazi colonial subject, or did the Nazis posit a different subject altogether when it came to Jews?

While colonialism as a practice is useful in determining how the Nazis justified their treatment of Poles and Slavs, it cannot account entirely for the subjective position associated with the Nazis in 1941. Even with the presence of similar structures within the ideology of "Blood and Soil" and within other colonial rhetorics, the logic can only go so far. For example, A. Dirk Moses cites the example of Evans and Thorpe's concept of "indigenocide": "Raymond Evans and Bill Thorpe have continued this line of thinking, proposing a new term altogether, 'indigenocide.' . . . It has five elements: the intentional invasion/colonization of land; the conquest of indigenous peoples; the killing of them to the extent that they can barely reproduce themselves and come close to extinction; their classification as vermin by the invaders; and the attempted destruction of their religious systems. Indigenocide is consistent with the continued existence of indigenous peoples where they are classified as a separate caste."[38]

One could argue that the Nazis deployed these structures against the Jews, as well as their other victims. Even with the caveat that the Nazis did not plan on Jews' "continued existence" as a separate caste, four of the five "elements" are present. However, as Moses points out, "insights come at the cost of a certain blindness, namely, blurring an important distinction and proposing a static model that bypasses rather than confronts the problem of the exterminatory consciousness."[39]

The bypassing of the "exterminatory consciousness" has concerned several post-Holocaust philosophers, most of whom focus on the use of reason in such a consciousness.[40] But in *La fiction du politique* Philippe Lacoue-Labarthe linked the Nazis' exterminatory consciousness to the idea that the Nazis imposed a "caesura" in history. Borrowing a trope from Hölderlin's aesthetics, Lacoue-Labarthe qualified that this "was not a tragic caesura" because it did not provide a politicized aesthetics but rather an aestheticized politic, a distinction that Wlad Godzich points out is key to recognizing the subjective stakes of the Nazis' project.[41] Lacoue-Labarthe's nuanced phrasing located politicized aesthetics in Hölderlin, the nineteenth-century German poet who proposed the idea of a German identity finally emerging on a national and aesthetic stage. The effect of Hölderlin's proposition was, then, the introduction of a subjective experience that triggered a national identity, a transcendence that grounded itself in a cultural-mythical project. The German subject in aesthetic experience could imagine an entire community identically and essentially formed by such an experience of transcendence, that is, a political aesthetics.[42]

By aestheticizing politics, the Nazis reversed the order. Lacoue-Labarthe suggests that this move enabled the Nazis to impose, through the political use of the caesura, a political space that had two dramatic effects. The first effect of the caesura allowed the Nazis to visualize their communal essence as a work in progress, a thing to be formed that emerged against an evacuated and blank cultural space on which they could work. From an imagined evolutionary starting point, the Nazis could work like an artist might, erasing, cutting off, destroying, eliminating those ancillary elements judged useless or detrimental to the work of art, the "sloughing off" of the useless, a necessary effect for the Aryans' ontological emergence.

The second effect of the caesura designated Auschwitz as the expression of Nazi *techné*, the death camp as the canvas on which the Nazis produced their "Judenrein" community. This effect tethered the Nazi imagination necessarily to a techné of extermination so that the Jews would constitute a detrimental element of German identity that would essentially be removed as a secondary effect of the emergence of the Nazi subject, the Jews' extermination, a by-product of Nazi catharsis. According to Lacoue-Labarthe, the caesura functions here both as a physical practice and an imagined principle—physical in the sense of the death camp, imagined in the sense of the Nazi subject's catharsis.

In this way the Nazis imposed the caesura, an "aestheticized" politics, on German history, and unlike its aesthetic ancestor, they elevated the caesura to the rank of "the concept of historicity." This elevation causes the caesura to emerge as "that which within history interrupts history and opens another possibility for history, or else closes off all possibility of history."[43] Essentially, two things are at stake in this elevation: (1) the caesura gains an epistemological status by being elevated as concept; and (2) the caesura intervenes in history as the concept of historicity, "that which within history interrupts . . . or else closes off all possibility of history."

The Nazis cut off history through the privileging of their own myth of Aryan historicity. Initially a feature of German aesthetic experience, the Nazis reproduced this "cutting off" empirically, erasing history from the public space and substituting in its place a *mythos*, a mythology of German identity, or even a mythic impulse that could reproduce itself perpetually.

Lacoue-Labarthe stresses that even though the caesura "forecloses" and "opens up a quite other history," it has only occurred "in the case of Auschwitz." This singularity intimates an aesthetic dimension:

> And this is so for the only time, I believe in modern history (this is why Auschwitz opens up, or closes, a quite other history than the one we have known up until now). With one small proviso—though this changes everything—that Auschwitz is the site of a dissociation: those who suffer the "categorical turning away" in the unprecedented figure not even of death, but of a mere purging (an unutterable degradation of *catharsis*)—are not those who desired immediacy or committed a crime, but those upon whom those who did do these things literally discharged themselves (once again, an unutterable degradation of *catharsis*—making of Auschwitz, no less literally, the *discharge* of Germany (and of Europe). (*HAP* 45–46)

Lacoue-Labarthe proposes that the physical existence of Auschwitz had a critical link to a Nazi experience of catharsis; this link exhibited the Jews' extermination, furthermore, as a discharge or purging of the Aryan subject, even though the Aryan subject's experience of catharsis stood at a distance from the purging. As such, Auschwitz was the site of a "dissociation."

For Lacoue-Labarthe this dissociation required Nazism "to present itself as myth or as the realization of a myth.... In this sense, as is perfectly clear from Lacoue-Labarthe's reading of Rosenberg, myth is ... a 'power' (*puissance*) ... a gathering together of the fundamental forces and orientations of an individual or a people, that is to say the power of a deep, concrete, embodied identity" (*HAP* 93–94). To act as such a power required the mythic to act as an art form tied mimetically to nature, "the mimetic ... always linked to the mythic," so that "the political" became imagined as "the sphere of *fictioning* of beings and communities," the production of an "onto-typology" (*HAP* 82–84). The Nazis posited the Jews outside of the human altogether, reserving for themselves ontology as type. Citing Alfred Rosenberg, Lacoue-Labarthe goes even further to illustrate the ontotypological myth of the Nazis: "The Jews do not belong to *humanitas* thus defined because they have neither dreams nor myths. Maurice Blanchot is right when he says 'the Jews embody ... the rejection of myths, the eschewing of idols, the recognition of an ethical order which manifests itself in respect for the law. What Hitler is attempting to annihilate in annihilating the Jew, and the "myth of the Jew," is precisely man liberated from myths'" (*HAP* 96).

Resonating with Margalit and Motzkin's argument, Lacoue-Labarthe also notes that the Jews existed outside the category of the human—"outside" because "they embody the rejection of myths, the eschewing of idols." The fundamental scene of this rejection is associated with Moses, who presents the Jews with "the Law" as the alternative to the mythical calf. Lacoue-Labarthe locates in Nazi typology, then, the significance of the Jews' "rejection of myths": "This 'rejection of myths' is precisely why the Jews do not constitute a type: they have, says Rosenberg, no *Seelengestalt*—and therefore no *Rassengestalt*. They are a formless, unaesthetic 'people,' which by definition cannot enter into the process of self-fictioning and cannot constitute a subject, or in other words, a being-proper (*être-propre*)" (*HAP* 96).

The relationship between *Seelengestalt* and *Rassengestalt* demonstrates how the Jews exist as "a formless, unaesthetic people." Jews exist without *Seelengestalt*, or the form of the soul, that is, without ontology. It follows that without this basic component of the human, Jews cannot produce *Rassengestalt*, a racial form. On another occasion Rosenberg declares the Jew to be "formless . . . the man of the universal abstract, as opposed to the man of singular, concrete identity," the Aryan warrior.[44] Rosenberg's contrast hinges on the Jews' "formlessness" as a sign that they are excluded from ontology or essential Being.

The Jews' incapacity for ontology leads Rosenberg to insist that Jews are not the Nazis' rivals or "counter-types" but rather that they are the Teuton's "contradiction—the very absence of type." The Jews are an illegitimate presence in the Aryan environment, one that must be eradicated for the Nazi subject to be able to fashion himself. Thus, the Nazis are justified in ruthlessly destroying this illegitimate presence.

Furthermore, an aesthetic component has been embedded all along in Nazi race theory since the Jews are ultimately "*Kulturträger*," the "bearers of civilization": "Hence their power—they who are neither *Kulturbegründer* nor *Kulturschöpfer*, but mere *Kulturträger*, bearers of civilization—to insert themselves into every Culture and State and then to live a life that is parasitic upon these, constantly threatening them with bastardization" (*HAP* 96).

When Heck descried the "extermination" of the aurochs, he blamed the bearers of civilization for the aurochs's "haphazard reproduction" and "domestication"; they had destroyed the aurochs by mixing the beast's bloodlines with inferiors and by removing it from its "ark of species," corralling it instead in domesticity. When Lorenz considered civilization, he designated it "a process of 'decline and fall,'"[45] a process that had been imposed by unseen agents again on nature. When Göring donned his "hunter's outfit," entering Białowieża, he went to reclaim it as Aryan Heimat, its symbolic value severed fundamentally from civilization. Thus, Rosenberg's identification of the Jews as the "bearers of civilization" who illegitimately "insert" themselves into all human populations, "threatening" to create a bastard population, was part and parcel of a Nazi aesthetic experience that revealed itself precisely in the myth it constructed about the Jews.

This brings us to an issue that colonial theory does not address: the Nazis' desire to exterminate Jewish identity was not exclusively genocide, but rather it was the necessary condition for Nazi aesthetic experience, the frightening aspect of Lacoue-Labarthe's "discharge of catharsis." In other words there might be many reasons for why the Nazis targeted the Jews, but the more frightening aspect of Lacoue-Labarthe's thesis suggests that the Jews' extermination was particularly advanced as a necessity of the Nazi subject's experience of catharsis. The Nazis disposed of the Jews as a necessary part of their own catharsis; moreover, the Nazis did not articulate this disposal as such, but rather they registered it as a "discharge," a throwing off of something else during the experience of catharsis. Much like Heck's disposal of the Warsaw zoo's "valueless" animals, with every discharge at the death camps, in the forests and ghettos of central and eastern Europe, the Nazi soldier could imagine himself more and more an Aryan hunter.

Therefore, while the Nazis occasionally utilized forms of colonialist thinking in relation to Poland, their treatment of the Jews could hardly be the same strategy. They completely reshifted the imagination so that Jews not only could be removed from the public and visible sphere but also could no longer be ontologically inferable—not just the absence of visibility but the absence of inferring that Jews could have ever existed beyond a statistical footnote of contagion in human history. Imagined at the aesthetic level and extended to the empirical level, this ideology's constitutive elements had to derive from thinking that went something like this: "If anyone is to be a subject like me, then that individual would have to make the same judgment I am making." As degenerate representations Jews were, then, untethered in the imagination and discarded as untenable. They were sublimely destroyed so that the Nazis could realize their Reich.[46]

As a result the Nazis did not see the Jews as a species unto themselves—a group to be colonized—but rather as an aspect of the environment that had to be removed. If we limit this to science, the Nazis were either really bad scientists or they had to ignore good science in order to posit their beliefs. Science, however, is not the issue here. In the Nazis' choices we have the outlines of an aesthetic experience in which the subject of Nazism articulates a myth of chosenness giving the Nazis "originating species" status. The Nazis were aiming at the Jews and Jewish tradition not because of what Jews owned, even though the appropriation of Jewish belongings was an acceptable side effect, but because "the Jewish religion, whether as actually practised by religious Jews or as a cultural heritage with Jewish Agnostics, represents a mortal danger."[47] It was always about the myth. In this way Nazism's major apologists, Göring and Rosenberg, as well as its minor figures, Lutz and Heinz Heck, who fantasized returning a "calf" to Germany, suggest clues about how the Nazis hoped to rewrite human biology physically so that the Jews and their God would not exist, a moment when a Jewish ontology would not be inferable at all.[48]

In contemporary studies of German history, attempts to place the Holocaust in relation to German colonialism have become increasingly common at conference venues, in recent publications, and in the German Studies classroom.[49] Indeed, many of the new generation of historians and academics working on Germany's colonial past rely heavily on arguments that claim the Holocaust as either a continuation of Germany's imperial pretensions in the nineteenth century and the twentieth, a continuation focused on "the events of 1884, 1918, and 1945," or a reflection of Germany's following a colonial pattern and precedent established by other Western societies. As Birthe Kundrus has pointed out in her contribution to this volume, "Although . . . the events of 1884, 1918, and 1945 are highly relevant for those seeking answers . . . , debates among scholars have tended to overstep the bounds these watersheds suggest."

I share Kundrus's concern that the lure of seeking historical precedent for the Nazis' actions has prompted some scholars to subtend Nazi actions as evidence of a shared genocidal predisposition inherent in Western societies so that the specific actions directed at individual groups have become reducible to the signs of colonial aggression against the Other throughout human history. From this "continuity perspective" the Herero and Nama wars are not only the "genocidal precursors" to the "German war of extermination in Eastern Europe,"[50] "a *decisive* link to the crimes of the National Socialists,"[51] but they also furnish justification for expanding the category of colonialism to include Jews, Poles, and Slavs as the Nazis' primary targets since all three groups share in the Nazis' victimization. Victimization becomes generally interchangeable, then, as we develop a narrative of colonial oppression, and it leads us to the notion that the structures of genocide appear to be part and parcel of intended actions in the ancient world, the Crusades, and early modern exploration, as well as the unintended, but no less deadly, introduction of disease to indigenous populations.[52]

Although most scholars of this perspective would distinguish qualitatively between the Holocaust and other genocides, the coupling of the Nama and Herero genocides with the experiences of Jews, Poles, and Slavs during the Holocaust implies a formal link, or at least a shared experience of genocide as form. This formal link enables researchers to examine history and genocide comparatively with a view to ascertaining the presence of the shared form of genocide in other traditions, whichever aspects of that form are indeed shared by different groups.[53] To some degree this perspective must categorize the Holocaust as one genocidal form among many in human history so that historians might "address the question if and how the 'Final Solution' can be integrated into larger conceptual and narrative frameworks, for example, the history of the twentieth century, the history of modernity."[54]

While the "definitional problem" has been at the center of these discussions,[55] Kundrus asks whether "it makes sense, in terms of the politics of memory, to heighten the perceived significance of colonial history by declaring it a prelude to National Socialism," since ultimately "we would be doing a disservice to both historical phenomena—the history of violence under German colonialism and the history of violence in the National Socialist period."[56] Kundrus identifies the real issue here: in a "politics of memory" victims are measured hierarchically against each other, damaging both victims of German colonialism and the victims of National Socialism, even when such measurement is inadvertent and unintentional.

From someone outside the discipline of German history, but whose research on the Holocaust intersects with the issues raised by this debate, I find myself wondering how we went from the *Historikerstreit* of the 1980s and 1990s to a debate over colonialism and globalization in the twenty-first century. It seems to me that we are still engaged in what Saul Friedländer has called "a conflict of memories"[57] and that current attempts to connect the Holocaust to a preexisting political disposition, whether the totalitarianism of the *Historikerstreit* debate[58] or the critique of the use of the Holocaust reflects a tendency to graft the conflicting memories of Holocaust experience on to a rational and reasonable narrative of historical precedent, and in the process, it transforms these memories into "a single, unified value"[59] so that "the event" can circulate epistemically both as an object and as a signifier. In other words, the Holocaust as a series of complex events becomes flattened out into discrete structures.

The flattening out of the Holocaust, however, severs "excessive" aspects from these events, enabling historians to place the Holocaust categorically, without addressing those excesses, what, as we have seen, Moses suggests as bypassing "the exterminatory consciousness." Researchers can emphasize the similarity of discrete structures, omitting the differences or details that might preclude their epistemological classification.

In the case of my above examples—Heck's actions in Warsaw, SS actions in Białowieża, and Göring's imagined identity as an Aryan hunter—Nazi race theory coupled with Nazi myth leads unequivocally and unmistakably to the destruction of Jews. Thus the stakes of tethering the Holocaust to German colonial theory strikes me as trying to ascribe a rational precedent, a logic, for a position forged in the caesura, a position that occludes the Nazi mythic impulse and what this subjective position means for modernity. As Lacoue-Labarthe notes, "the Extermination does not, however, correspond to this logic. Nor to that of the exclusion of the other. And this is why it is more serious; not so much on account of the will purely and simply to annihilate but on account of the very people to whom that will to annihilate applies, the Jews, in so far as they are reckoned neither to belong to the community nor to stand outside it, that is to say in so far as they are literally unlocatable or—and this comes down to the same thing—forbidden to exist from the outset" (*HAP* 75). In other words, current desires to include the Nazis' project as an instance of "excluding the other" necessarily overlook the conceptual underpinnings of the project: Jews were "reckoned neither to belong to the community nor to stand outside it." The Nazis intended to excise Jews from ontology.

Notes

1. Schama, *Landscape and Memory*, 59–60; subsequent references are cited parenthetically in the text, using the abbreviation *LM*.

2. See Sunseri, "Exploiting the *Urwald*," 9. Sunseri focuses on *Urwald* as a term signifying exploitable resources for the Kaiserreich.

3. Schama, "Stopping by the Woods," 33.

4. See Fitzpatrick, "The Pre-History of the Holocaust?" 477.

5. See Hilberg, *Perpetrators, Victims, Bystanders*; and Bartov, *Murder in Our Midst*.

6. See Shelley Baranowski's contribution to this volume.

7. Ackerman, *The Zookeeper's Wife*, 85; subsequent references are cited parenthetically in the text, using the abbreviation ZW.

8. See Kristin Kopp's contribution to this volume.

9. Although not all Nazis derived pleasure from murdering or exterminating, the experience always had an aesthetic component embedded within it.

10. See Ahrens, "Breeding Back the Auerochs."

11. See Caesar, *The Gallic Wars*, 353.

12. Ahrens, "Breeding Back the Auerochs,"266. The aurochs was worshipped as the "wild bull" of *The Epic of Gilgamesh*, the Egyptian Apis Bull, and the "golden calf" of Exodus.

13. Ahrens, "Breeding Back the Auerochs," 266.

14. See Zeuner, "The Colour of the Wild Cattle of Lascaux."

15. See also Margalit and Motzkin, "The Uniqueness of the Holocaust."

16. See Bramwell, *Blood and Soil*.

17. See Kalikow, "Konrad Lorenz's Ethological Theory," 39.

18. This is the "useless eaters thesis," advanced initially by Rafael Lemkin and echoed by A. Dirk Moses. See Moses, "Conceptual Blockages and Definitional Dilemmas in the 'Racial Century,'" 20. See also Welch, "'The Annihilation of Superfluous Eaters.'"

19. Quoted in Ackerman, *The Zookeeper's Wife*, 92. The French translation is even more forceful: "Le crime de l'Allemagne est le plus grand crime que le monde ait jamais connu parce qu'il n'est pas à l'échelle de l'Histoire: IL EST A L'ÉCHELLE DE L'EVOLUTION." See Pierre Lecomte de Nöuy, *La dignité humaine*, 47.

20. Darwin, *Origin of the Species*, 47.

21. Roughgarden, *Theory of Population Genetics and Evolutionary Ecology*, 546.

22. See Tanner et al., "Species Coexistence, Keystone Species, and Succession," 2205.

23. The "keystone predator" feeds on "competitors" who would destroy the richness of the environment, nature, and other species, because they would essentially take over those species. Thus it preserves the environment by destroying competitors.

24. Margalit and Motzkin, "The Uniqueness of the Holocaust," 71.

25. François Bédarida has called this "a quantitative approach" that "consists of counting the victims, comparing their number to that of other massacres and exterminations." See Bédarida, "The Place of the Shoah in History," 71.

26. Note Fitzpatrick's use of Kristeva's "abject Other" as a term for describing the Jewish victims of the Holocaust and the victims of colonialism. See Fitzpatrick, "The Pre-History of the Holocaust?" 478–79.

27. Margalit and Motzkin, "The Uniqueness of the Holocaust," 71.

28. See Bartov, *Germany's War and the Holocaust*, 7.

29. Margalit and Motzkin, "The Uniqueness of the Holocaust," 72.

30. Ibid.

31. See Kristin Kopp's contribution to this volume.

32. In numerous texts A. Dirk Moses analyzes the claim of the Holocaust's uniqueness both by its supporters and its critics. See, e.g., Moses, "Empire, Colony, Genocide"; and Moses, "Conceptual Blockages and Definitional Dilemmas in the 'Racial Century.'"

33. See Bartov, *Germany's War and the Holocaust*, 1–32.

34. For Operation Barbarossa see Hilberg, *Destruction of the European Jews*; and Browning, *The Origins of the Final Solution*. Hilberg also stresses that Hitler had "formulated his ideas on Jews ... in 1919, and then remained fixated on them for the rest of his life" (quoted in Bartov, *Murder in Our Midst*, 98).

35. See Bartov, *Germany's War and the Holocaust*, 9.

36. See Margalit and Margalit-Ullmann, "Holding True and Holding as True."

37. See Kant, *Critique of Judgment*, 53–54.

38. Moses, "Conceptual Blockages and Definitional Dilemmas," 25.

39. Ibid., 26.

40. See, e.g., Santner, "Freud, Zizek, and the Joys of Monotheism"; Lyotard, *Le différend*; Lacoue-Labarthe, *La fiction du politique* (translated by Chris Turner as *Heidegger, Art, and Politics*); Fackenheim, *Metaphysics and Historicity*; and Améry, *Jenseits von Schuld und Sühne*.

41. See Godzich, "The Holocaust," 140–43.

42. This was essentially Kant's theory of the French Revolution as a collective experience of the sublime.

43. Lacoue-Labarthe, *Heidegger, Art, and Politics*, 45; subsequent references are cited parenthetically in the text, using the abbreviation *HAP*.

44. See Lacoue-Labarthe and Nancy, "The Nazi Myth," 307 (quoted in Santner, "Freud, Zizek, and the Joys of Monotheism," 198).

45. Kalikow, "Konrad Lorenz's Ethological Theory," 39.

46. See Lyotard, *Heidegger et "les juifs."*

47. Bédarida, "The Place of the Shoah in History," 79.

48. See Moses, "Stigma and Sacrifice in the Federal Republic of Germany."

49. See, e.g., "Germany's Colonialism in International Perspective," conference held at San Francisco State University, Sept. 6–9, 2007 (www.sfsu.edu/~german/GCC/index.html); "War, Genocide, and Memory: German Colonialism and

National Identity," held at the University of Sheffield, Sept. 11–13, 2006 (www.c19 .group.shef.ac.uk/germancolonialismprogramme.html); and "Genocides: Forms and Consequences—the Namibian War (1904–1908) in Historical Perspective," held in Berlin, Jan. 13–15, 2005. Among a growing list of short publications dealing with German colonialism and the Holocaust see Fitzpatrick, "The Pre-History of the Holocaust?"; Janué i Miret, "Imperialismus durch auswärtige Kulturpolitik"; Kundrus, "From the Herero to the Holocaust?"; and Moses, "Conceptual Blockages and Definitional Dilemmas." Lengthier studies include Wildenthal, *German Women for Empire, 1884–1945*; Zantop, *Colonial Fantasies*; and Berman, *Enlightenment or Empire*. On classroom studies see Wildenthal, "Places of Colonialism in Writing and Teaching Modern German History."

50. See Gerwarth and Malinowski, "Der Holocaust als kolonialer Genozid?"

51. Zimmerer and Zeller, *Völkermord in Deutsch-Südwestafrika* (as quoted in Kundrus, "From the Herero to the Holocaust?" 300).

52. See Moses, "Empire, Colony, Genocide," 8.

53. Bédarida, "The Place of the Shoah in History," 71.

54. See Kansteiner, "From Exception to Exemplum."

55. See Moses, "Conceptual Blockages and Definitional Dilemmas."

56. Kundrus, "From the Herero to the Holocaust?" 300.

57. See Friedländer, "A Conflict of Memories?"

58. See Broszat, *Nach Hitler*.

59. Kertesz, "Who Owns Auschwitz?" 268.

Bibliography

Ackerman, Diane. *The Zookeeper's Wife*. New York: Norton, 2007.

Ahrens, Theodore G. "Breeding Back the Auerochs." *Journal of Mammology* 17, no. 3 (Aug. 1936): 266–68.

Améry, Jean. *Jenseits von Schuld und Sühne: Bewältigungsversuche eines Überwältigten*. Munich: Szczesny, 1967.

Bartov, Omer. *Germany's War and the Holocaust: Disputed Histories*. Ithaca, NY: Cornell University Press, 2003.

———. *Murder in Our Midst*. New York: Oxford University Press, 1996.

Bédarida, François. "The Place of the Shoah in History: Uniqueness, Historicity, Causality." *Philosophia* 30, nos. 1–4 (March 2003): 69–86.

Berman, Russell A. *Enlightenment or Empire: Colonial Discourse in German Culture*. Lincoln: University of Nebraska Press, 1998.

Bramwell, Anne. *Blood and Soil: Richard Walther Darré and Hitler's Green Party*. Buckinghamshire: Kensal Press, 1985.

Broszat, Martin. *Nach Hitler: Der schwierige Umgang mit unserer Geschichte.* Munich: Oldenbourg, 1987.
Browning, Christopher. *The Origins of the Final Solution.* Lincoln: University of Nebraska Press, 2004.
Caesar, Julius. *The Gallic Wars.* Translated by Henry John Edwards. Cambridge, MA: Heinemann, 1917.
Darwin, Charles. *Origin of the Species.* Edited by Gillian Beer. Oxford: Oxford University Press, 1996.
Fackenheim, Emil. *Metaphysics and Historicity.* Toronto: University of Toronto Press, 1961.
Fitzpatrick, Michael. "The Pre-History of the Holocaust? The *Sonderweg* and the *Historikerstreit* Debates and the Abject Colonial Past." *Central European History* 41 (2008): 477–533.
Friedländer, Saul. "A Conflict of Memories? The New German Debates About the 'Final Solution.'" Leo Baeck Memorial Lecture 31, 1–24. New York: Leo Baeck Institute for the Study of German-Speaking Jewry, 1987.
Gerwarth, Robert, and Stephan Malinowski. "Der Holocaust als 'kolonialer Genozid'? Europäische Kolonialgewalt und nationalsozialistischer Vernichtungskrieg." *Geschichte und Gesellschaft* 33 (2007): 439–66.
Godzich, Wlad. "The Holocaust: Questions for the Humanities." *Partial Answers* 7, no. 1 (2009): 133–48.
Hilberg, Raul. *Destruction of the European Jews.* New Haven, CT: Yale University Press, 2003.
——. *Perpetrators, Victims, Bystanders: The Jewish Catastrophe, 1933–1945.* New York: Aaron Asher, 1992.
Janué i Miret, Maricio. "Imperialismus durch auswärtige Kulturpolitik: Die Deutsch-Spanische Gesellschaft als 'zwischenstaatlicher Verband' unter dem Nationalsozialismus." *German Studies Review* 31, no. 1 (Feb. 2008): 109–32.
Kalikow, Theodora. "Konrad Lorenz's Ethological Theory: Explanation and Ideology, 1938–1943." *Journal of the History of Biology* 16, no. 1 (spring 1983): 39–73.
Kansteiner, Wulf. "From Exception to Exemplum: The New Approach to Nazism and the 'Final Solution.'" *History and Theory* 33, no. 2 (May 1994): 145–71.
Kant, Immanuel. *Critique of Judgment.* Edited by Werner Pluhar. Indianapolis: Hackett, 1987.
——. *Kritik der Urteilskraft.* Hamburg: Felix Meiner, 1924.
Kertesz, Imre. "Who Owns Auschwitz?" *Yale Journal of Criticism* 14, no. 1 (2001): 267–72.
Kundrus, Birthe. "From the Herero to the Holocaust? Some Remarks on the Current Debate." *Afrika Spectrum* 40 (2005): 299–308.

Lacoue-Labarthe, Philippe. *Heidegger, Art, and Politics: The Fiction of the Political.* Translated by Chris Turner. Oxford: Basil Blackwell, 1990.

———. *La fiction du politique: Heidegger, l'art et la politique.* Paris: Christian Bourgois, 1988.

Lacoue-Labarthe, Philippe, and Jean-Luc Nancy. "The Nazi Myth." *Critical Inquiry* 16 (winter 1990): 291–312.

Lecomte du Noüy, Pierre. *La dignité humaine.* Paris: Brentano, 1944.

Lorenz, Konrad. "Durch Domestikation verursachte Störungen arteigenen Verhaltens." *Zeitschrift für angewandte Psychologie und Charakterkunde* 59 (1940): 1–81.

Lyotard, Jean-François. *Heidegger et "les juifs."* Paris: Galilée, 1988.

———. *Le différend.* Paris: Editions de Minuet, 1983.

Margalit, Avishai, and Edna Margalit-Ullmann. "Holding True and Holding as True." *Synthese* 92, no. 2 (Aug. 1992): 167–87.

Margalit, Avishai, and Gabriel Motzkin. "The Uniqueness of the Holocaust." *Philosophy and Public Affairs* 25, no. 1 (winter 1996): 65–83.

Montgomery, Scott L. "What Kind of Memory? Reflections on Images of the Holocaust." *Contention* 5, no. 1 (autumn 1995): 79–103.

Moses, A. Dirk. "Conceptual Blockages and Definitional Dilemmas in the 'Racial Century': Genocides of Indigenous Peoples and the Holocaust." *Patterns of Prejudice* 36, no. 4 (2002): 7–36.

———. "Empire, Colony, Genocide: Keywords and the Philosophy of History." In *Empire, Colony, Genocide: Conquest, Occupation, and Subaltern Resistance,* edited by A. Dirk Moses, 3–54. Oxford: Berghahn, 2008.

———. "Stigma and Sacrifice in the Federal Republic of Germany." *History and Memory* 19, no. 2 (fall/winter 2007): 139–80.

Payton, Ian J., et al. "Keystone Species: The Concept and Its Relevance for Conservation Management in New Zealand." *Science for Conservation* 203 (July 2002): 23–29.

Roughgarden, J. *Theory of Population Genetics and Evolutionary Ecology: An Introduction.* New York: Macmillan, 1979.

Ruse, Michael, and Robert J. Richards, eds. *Cambridge Companion to the "Origin of Species."* Cambridge, UK: Cambridge University Press, 2009.

Saller, K. *Die Rassenlehre des Nationalsozialismus in Wissenschaft und Propaganda.* Darmstadt: Progress, 1961.

Santner, Eric. "Freud, Zizek, and the Joys of Monotheism." *American Imago* 54, no. 2 (1997): 197–207.

Schama, Simon. *Landscape and Memory.* New York: HarperCollins, 1995.

———. "Stopping by the Woods." *New Republic,* Oct. 26, 1992, 31–37.

Sunseri, Thaddeus. "Exploiting the *Urwald*: German Colonialism in Poland and Africa, c. 1900–1941." Paper presented at the "Germany's Colonialism in International Perspective" conference, San Francisco State University, Sept. 6–9, 2007.

Tanner, James E., et al. "Species Coexistence, Keystone Species, and Succession: A Sensitivity." *Ecology* 75, no. 8 (Dec. 1994): 2204–19.
Welch, Steven. "'The Annihilation of Superfluous Eaters': Nazi Plans for and Uses of Famine in Eastern Europe." Yale University Genocide Studies Program. Working Paper no. 16 (2001): www.yale.edu/gsp/publications/Annihila.doc.
Wildenthal, Lora. *German Women for Empire, 1884–1945*. Durham, NC: Duke University Press, 2002.
——. "Places of Colonialism in Writing and Teaching Modern German History." *European Studies Journal* 16, no. 2 (1999): 9–23.
Zantop, Suzanne. *Colonial Fantasies: Conquest, Family, and Nation in Precolonial Germany, 1770–1870*. Durham, NC: Duke University Press, 1999.
Zeuner, F. F. "The Colour of the Wild Cattle of Lascaux." *Man* 53 (May 1953): 68–69.
Zimmerer, Jürgen. "The Birth of the *Ostland* Out of the Spirit of Colonialism: A Postcolonial Perspective on the Nazi Policy of Conquest and Extermination." *Patterns of Prejudice* 39, no. 2 (2005): 197–219.
——. "Colonialism and the Holocaust: Towards an Archeology of Genocide." In *Genocide and Settler Society*, edited by A. Dirk Moses, 49–76. Oxford: Berghahn, 2004.
Zimmerer, Jürgen, and Joachim Zeller, eds. *Völkermord in Deutsch-Südwestafrika: Der Kolonialkrieg (1904–1908) in Namibia und seine Folgen*. Berlin: Christoph Links, 2003.

PART III

Looking East

Poland, the Ottoman Empire, and Politicized Jihadism

6

Germany's Adventures in the Orient

A History of Ambivalent Semicolonial Entanglements

Malte Fuhrmann

The question of continuities and breaks in Germany's relationship with its "Orient," that is, the regions southeast of the Kaiserreich and the Habsburg Empire, is not easy to answer, because there is no consensus among historians on how to interpret this encounter in the first place. This chapter focuses on the question of how to frame this relationship meaningfully in the context of colonialism and Orientalism. On this basis, I will briefly discuss how we can address the question of continuity without committing the fallacies either of seeing the Kaiserreich's Orient colonialism as a unique event separated from the rest of German history by unbridgeable ruptures or of creating retrospective teleologies that fall short of a close reading of historical evidence and *Zeitgeist*.

The Germans' relationship with the peoples of Southeast Europe and West Asia has historically been a multifaceted and complicated one. Common narratives of this encounter have tended toward oversimplification by reading it either optimistically as a relationship of extreme reciprocity or pessimistically as one of extreme subjugation. In the Turkish case the optimistic interpretation sees warm relations from the initial Friendship Treaty between Friedrich II and Mustafa III to the amicable relationship between Abdülhamid II and Wilhelm II, the military development aid by Prussia to the camaraderie-in-arms of World War I[1] and recent support by Federal Chancellor Gerhard Schröder for Prime Minister R. Tayyıp Erdoğan in EU negotiations. By contrast, several historians have attempted to frame the Kaiserreich's involvement in Ottoman affairs rigorously as a bona fide colonial conquest and unilateral dependency. In this narrative there exists an unbroken continuity of othering from the sixteenth century Turco-German wars to present-day German xenophobia.[2] The Prussian military aid for the Ottoman army starting in the Bismarck era, railway development, and the alliance in World War I were all part of one coordinated scheme to turn Southeast Europe and West Asia into a German colony.

Each side can muster impressive evidence for its position. On the one hand, unlike any other European Great Power, Imperial Germany never occupied or annexed any Ottoman territories. On the other hand, present-day Germany boasts all classical signs of a postcolonial relationship with the Southeast: representative museums filled to the brim with world heritage artifacts exclusively taken from the Ottoman lands, a massive and long-term immigration from the post-Ottoman countries comparable to South Asians in Great Britain, Maghrebins in France, or Yugoslavs in Austria, and continuous intense relations between Southeast Europe and Germany. The approach taken here aims not to weigh the claims of the one against the other but to find a new perspective that accommodates this apparently contradictory evidence.

Two contradictory notions informed German attitudes toward the Eastern Mediterranean in the age of imperialism: identification with the agents of imperialist expansion and identification with its victims. While in some cases opposing camps in the German government and society held these positions, at other times they combined them in an apparently paradoxical manner that has caused much of the confusion in interpreting nineteenth-century German Oriental policies. While identification with the other imperial powers is a well-established motif in the studies of German imperialism,[3] the identification with the often-slandered peoples of the East as informing Oriental policy warrants some explanation. I will therefore briefly contextualize the identification with the imperial oppressors in the Ottoman context and then continue to delineate what I mean by identification with the imperial oppressed. I will touch on a selection of particular semicolonial activities but will focus mainly on how their agents interpreted their own actions and to what larger framework they believed their actions contributed.

By 1838 the Ottoman Empire had become a semicolonial sphere of Great Powers influence. Jürgen Osterhammel, Hong Lysa, Bryna Goodman and others have coined the term *semicolonial* to describe the East Asian context.[4] While the Chinese monarchy, for example, remained official sovereign of the country, adverse terms of trade, the Treaty Port System, zones of influence declared by the Great Powers, and military interventions severely limited its powers. For the Ottoman sphere, following much criticism on the claim that the Southeast European states were far from helpless satellites, Raymond Detrez has recently reaffirmed the validity of semicolonialism to describe Western influence in the nineteenth-century Balkan kingdoms and especially in the Ottoman Empire.[5] The Great Powers intervened in all peace treaties negotiated in the region, imposed an open-door trade policy on the High Porte, demanded far-reaching exemptions from Ottoman jurisdiction and taxation, set up the Public Debt Administration to seize state revenues directly and allocate them toward foreign creditors, and incessantly paraded their gunboats around Ottoman waters to remind the locals of their place. The impositions on local sovereignty were not as grave as in the Chinese case, but there was a constant fear that the Great Powers would intensify them by enforcement of a treaty port system, specific spheres of influence, or even complete dismemberment through colonial annexation.[6] Overall, the jealousy between the imperialist rivals in this strategically sensitive region prohibited more dynamic impositions on the High Porte, but it also caused the rivals to imitate immediately almost any hegemonic project, each fearing that the other would end up one step ahead.

Accordingly, the desire to find a "place in the sun" and to be considered equal by its peers, many of whom had a more established position in Levantine trade and politics, inspired many German activities in the region.[7] Germany vied to increase trade; tried to secure its share of investments in the Ottoman Empire; sought to impress the local population with representative embassies, churches, monuments, schools, and festivities; and sent its gunboats when Europeans seemed threatened. This facet of German Oriental policy has so far gathered the most interest. Some authors derive from the fact that Germany was not very original in many of its Eastern initiatives the assumption that Berlin saw the Ottoman lands as only a sideshow and that the main interests of *Weltpolitik* lay elsewhere.[8] But this view is based on a gross overinterpretation of Bismarck's 1876 claim that the Ottoman Empire was not worth the bones of a single Pomeranian musketeer, a statement made in a distinct context—the call for intervention into Balkan uprisings that later culminated in the Russo-Turkish War. Many political factions did not share this view and clamored for intervention, and even Bismarck changed his attitude soon after, just as he did on the matter of overseas colonies, by switching to a policy of support for the Ottoman government. The apparently slow, nonspectacular steps and defensive official rhetoric in Oriental policy are a result of the intense imperialist rivalry in the region and of the need for agents to act circumspectly. If we take into account the lively public debates surrounding Oriental policy, we can hardly consider this a sideshow of German expansionism: "hardly any other foreign policy issue and certainly no colonial or world policy issue occupied and excited the German public and the political leadership of the Reich under Wilhelm II as much and led to so many publications as the Eastern Question."[9] Furthermore, "the heart of the German bourgeois beat faster when hearing the names of Asia Minor, Palestine, or Mesopotamia than at the mention of the African colonies or the Bismarck-Archipelago."[10] This brings us to the second aspect of the German Oriental adventure.

German colonialist ideology differs from French and British paradigms. One of its most remarkable characteristics is the extent to which Germans identified with the supposedly subjugated Other. Sheldon Pollack has found German Indologist readings of ancient Indian society to mirror aspirations for a future fascist German society, and Susanne Zantop has found early German colonial novels to sympathize with subjugated Native Americans.[11] This sympathy results from the German self-image of the early nineteenth century. Germans believed themselves to have first suffered cultural and then actual colonial dominance at the hands of the French, thus retarding their process of nation building and subsequent imperialist expansion. The feeling of being an upstart nation still not taken seriously by its peers overshadowed a desire to achieve equity with the foremost imperialist powers of the age, the "place in the sun."[12] Although Germans often claimed their culture, science, technology, economy, and military to be superior, they believed this had not earned them the standing in the world that they deserved. Despite economic and technological progress, their relationship to modernity remained reserved. When confronted with the supposedly semicivilized Orient, this predisposition led to interactions that were unique for an imperialist power.

From the mid-nineteenth century onward we discover a notable undercurrent of images depicting the Ottoman Empire, especially its Anatolian and Balkan parts, not as other but as an atavistic self-image. This undercurrent, in time, developed into the dominant trope, which inspired publishing activities, public opinion, collective initiatives, and, after an initial phase of reluctance, the official foreign policy of the Reich.

This paradoxical mix of assumed superiority and empathy first manifested itself in activism among German intellectuals at the time of the Greek secessionist uprising against Ottoman rule in the 1820s. While philhellenism also arose as part of an internationalist movement against absolutist systems, in many cases its conservative adherents combined it with a German paternalist and avant-gardist approach. In a letter to Freiherr von Stein, Barthold G. Niebuhr, the historian and Prussian envoy in Rome, claimed that the time was ripe for German agrarian settlements in Macedonia and Bithynia. He envisioned redirecting impoverished German emigrants heading for the Americas by offering them land, believing this initiative would manage to draw thousands to the liberated Ottoman lands and thought it necessary to wage war continuously against the Turks until Germany had driven them to the Nile Cataracts and the Persian Gulf. He even pictured his own son as such a settler-conqueror.[13] Niebuhr and his contemporaries did not believe these ideas amounted to abusing the Greek uprising for their own ends. They thought the Hellenes would welcome such initiatives, as they were directed against a common enemy, and German expertise and manpower could be an advantage.

The outcome of the war made these plans unattainable for the near future. The uprising only succeeded due to Great Power intervention, which led the major European states to dictate the political system of the Hellenic Kingdom. Through the installation of the Wittelsbachs on the Athenian throne, Greece was to be the first attempt at transforming Southeast Europe in the German image. It also brought to the surface many of the conflicts inherent in the attitude of empathy with the locals and patronizing them simultaneously. The state was not democratic but an enlightened centralist monarchy. King Otto surrounded himself with German advisers who tried to import wholesale their version of classic antiquity's legacy to modernity. German institutions of higher learning in the early nineteenth century, from the Gymnasium to the university, posited ancient Greek language, aesthetics, philosophy, and mythology as the pinnacle of human achievement and as a model for the future.[14] By consequence, the advisers at Otto's court felt themselves in touch with Greek antiquity and predestined to reimport classical ways to the Greeks who had supposedly lost the link to their roots under Byzantine and Ottoman rule. Germany installed Roman law as adapted in the German states as the basis for the country's legal system with little tolerance for preexisting modes of negotiating power and property in the southern Balkan Peninsula. Otto and his father, the king of Bavaria, adopted the initiative to recreate cities of antiquity. Eduard Schaubert and Stamatios Kleanthis, both avid followers of Karl Friedrich Schinkel, redesigned especially Athens with a classical geometrical street grid. In the end its opponents first forced the so-called *Bavarokratie* or *xenokratia*, the rule of foreign experts, to compromise and then completely ousted it. Historical comments have often simplified this period as one of good intentions but with too little communication between the rulers and the ruled. It seems, however, that much of this period of so-called foreign domination is characterized not only by the classic fallacy of supposedly knowing the natives better than they do themselves, and thus also knowing what is good for them, but also believing that what benefits oneself benefits the natives. There are indications that the *xenokratia* allowed for German colonialist settlements within the kingdom until such plans had to be withdrawn under popular pressure.[15]

After this early idealist attempt to remake Southeast Europe in the German Hellenist self-image had failed as a result of local resistance, Germany revived its imperialist aspirations toward the remaining Ottoman lands. A wave of publications called for agrarian settlements or missionary initiatives in the Levant. An interesting late variety of the attempt to fuse German characteristics into the Hellenic national character appeared in the 1860s under the name Evangelischer Verein für christliche Bildung im Orient (Evangelical Association for Christian Education in the Orient). This initiative, established by the Prussian Protestant reverend in Smyrna, Julius Axenfeld, and supported by the influential missionary and colonialist activist Friedrich Fabri, was only partially concerned with the Hellenic Kingdom; it mainly targeted the Greeks within the Ottoman Empire.

In the 1860s and early 1870s the idea that the loss of the Ottoman Aegean provinces was imminent haunted the discussion of the Eastern Question, regardless of the discussants' political preferences. Yet no one automatically assumed that the Athens-based state would simply extend its borders; the future Aegean political system still seemed open. Missionary activists saw this as a second opportunity to establish what the *Bavarokratie* had failed to achieve, owing to its paternalist approach and bad communications: a lasting

German influence among the Greek people by restructuring their religion and education via key disseminators. This was to be achieved in a highly circumspect manner that bordered on conspiracy.

Axenfeld realized that traditional missionary propaganda aimed at proselytizing would achieve little in Ottoman society, where religion was the primary marker of group identity. He developed a much more ambitious agenda that would serve the main interests of religious and imperialist expansion without outright conversions. Within the space of just a few years he developed a network connecting his own boys' school in Smyrna, an Athenian priest seminary, the elementary schools of Macedonia, and Fabri's Rheinische Missionsgesellschaft (Rhineland Missionary Society). Based on a handful of key actors both of German and of Greek origin, the network aimed at influencing the Greek Church and by consequence the Greek nation in its formative period, not directly subjugating it. Future orthodox priests were to be trained to practice their religion in a manner that came close to Protestant ways, but they were not expected to convert. Followers of Axenfeld's movement hoisted their disciples into key positions from which they could also put appropriate candidates into Greek schools in the Ottoman Empire, especially in Macedonia, the main target of Greek irredentist policy. Priests were to emphasize sermon and community, according to the Lutheran tradition, and schoolteachers were to use German pedagogic models and propagate a worldview compatible with Berlin's. One observer summarized the aim of the project, which enjoyed much sympathy among moderate conservatives in the Reich, as follows: "Then, when the last necessary step is taken and the fading crescent over the Asia Minor littoral finally gives way, Germany will have won a solid and deeply rooted influence among the local population, and this influence will serve as a base for contributing to re-establish a new Christian Greek state in the archipelago."[16]

The 1870s saw the peak of the Verein's activity, founding a priest seminary in Serres under the auspices of Axenfeld's disciple Dimitris Maroulis and buying land in Macedonia to finance its activities. The Oriental Crisis provoked a flurry of activity to attract more support in Europe for the Greek cause. By 1885, however, the German supporters of the Verein had grown disenchanted with the project, which had not made much headway into Greek society despite almost two decades of ample financing, and with its main field agent, Maroulis.[17] The Verein abandoned the scheme, and it would seem in retrospect little more than a farcical curiosity if it had not provided a blueprint for later activities aimed at Turks.

The 1880s were a turning point for German attitudes and policies toward Southeast Europe and West Asia. Philhellenism became thoroughly discredited, not only when directed to the Hellenic Kingdom, which had left many observers disenchanted after its poor performance in the Oriental Crisis, but also when taking a cultural approach, such as that of the Evangelischer Verein. More important though, Germans became increasingly weary of identifying themselves with classicism. Several German scholars of antiquity no longer unreservedly declared Hellenic civilization or Christianity the pinnacle of human achievement but introduced a strongly relativist view, focusing more intensely on the ancient Middle East. This was paralleled by trends in wider society to reflect more critically on Hellenic society, as well as its relevance to modernity, and a tendency to question the conceptualization of the West as an integral entity and particularly Germany's place in it.[18] The most popular forms of this trend culminated in *Zivilisationsmüdigkeit* (civilizational fatigue) as propagated by both Friedrich Nietzsche and Richard Wagner.[19] While this coincided with the end of patronizing solidarity with the contemporary Greeks, it did not immediately result in establishing a new "pet nation" in the Ottoman context.[20] The more immediate result tended toward German intellectual self-isolation.

Initially, this coincided with a new interest in the Aegean region as a potential "place in the sun." In 1880 Bismarck surprised his followers, who had canonized his Pomeranian musketeer statement, by dispatching civil and military advisers to Constantinople.[21] For the first time Germany proactively intervened in the Eastern Question. Bismarck had realized that the period of self-sustainable "free trade imperialism" was ending and that a more vigorous stance was necessary now to succeed in foreign markets. At the same time, in defense of his earlier statement, he founded a tradition of denial, declaring that Germany would not become embedded in the Eastern Question, as it would not be establishing lasting interests in the region. Subsequent foreign ministers incessantly reiterated statements of this kind—on the one hand, to calm the rival powers and the Bismarckian faction in the German Foreign Office and, on the other hand, to discourage more hot-headed colonialist activists. The statement became increasingly more hollow, but that did not stop its reiteration, even in times when the Baghdad Railway project had made a mockery of it.[22]

Although trade, investments, concessions for infrastructure development, and arms orders continued to increase after Bismarck's dismissal in the 1890s, no one in Berlin spoke out to declare that the Ottoman Empire had become a major site for contending with the other European Powers. In 1897 Adolf Marschall von Bieberstein, former deputy minister of the Foreign Office, was appointed ambassador to Constantinople. The energetic ambassador actively encouraged German activities in the Levant and served as the mastermind of this policy for fifteen years. He organized new arms deals, fought obstinately for infrastructure concessions, negotiated the acquisition of archaeological finds, and managed to keep Abdülhamid and later the postrevolutionary governments tied to Berlin.

Marschall, however, felt no sentimental attachment to the region. The Ottoman lands for him were clearly a theater to grab "a place in the sun." Supporting the territorial status quo and the old regime in Constantinople was simply trying to follow in the footsteps of Great Britain, which had until 1876 pursued a policy of profiting from the Ottoman state's weakness by being a strong but distant ally to the sultan.

The pioneer of reading a deeper meaning into Germany's activities in the Ottoman sphere and more strongly than before identifying with the "natives" was Colmar von der Goltz (Goltz Pasha). Goltz was sent as one of the first Prussian military advisers to Constantinople in 1882, and soon afterward he became head of the mission, a position he occupied until 1895. Like Marschall, Goltz was too ambitious to reap quietly the benefits of his position. Unlike Marschall though, he did not intend to imitate Great Britain's policies. Goltz was a typical representative of the petty aristocracy from east of the Elbe. He believed in a strongly hierarchical society but had a different vision about how to secure such a political system. Whereas the traditional aristocrats chose to treat modern social activism, diversified society, and popular politics with disdain, Goltz believed it necessary to use these elements to maintain an elitist system. Believing that war was human fate and that modern nations were locked in a Darwinist struggle to survive, he wished to include the masses not through participation but through a new kind of leadership that targeted the individual and empowered him to take responsible decisions for the common goal. His overall aim was to break down the barrier between society and the army and introduce the organization of the latter to the former, while tapping to the greatest possible extent society's manpower for the military. He summarized this vision in *A Nation in Arms*. When this failed to convince his colleagues, Goltz took on the position with the Ottoman military. While a top-to-bottom approach to reforms did not prove fruitful under the Hamidian regime, he found a more hopeful sphere in the education of cadets and managed to create a circle of close disciples among young officers, which connected him to the passive opposition against the sultan.[23]

The ideological turn of the 1880s, which doubted Europe's claim to the pinnacle of civilization, clearly influenced Goltz. He believed that new Asian empires could arise and felt vindicated when Japan defeated Russia in 1905. He preached incessantly that the Turks could follow a similar path if they were guided to a modern hierarchical political system in accordance with his recommendations for Germany in *A Nation in Arms*. In his writings the general clearly depicted the Turks not as other but as Germans' atavistic alter egos. Goltz declared that Turkish society was in a state in which Germany had found itself mere decades ago, before the onslaught of modernity. While Germans—in contrast to the English or French—had managed to remain virtuous despite the temptations of modernity because of their more hierarchical social order, the Turks were still virtuous because modernity had yet to unfold fully. Germans, the pasha argued, had the duty (or civilizing mission) to guide the Turks through the process of modernization by leading them onto a course toward a German social order. If Turks were left alone to find their path to modernity, this would result in cultural contamination, which could already be witnessed among the upper classes in the big cities, where the Francophile elites had embraced Western decadence. The German path, by contrast, should teach Turks not to embrace foreign religions, cultures, or languages but to integrate modern institutions into their traditional hierarchies. This would lay the basis for a military and civic rejuvenation of the empire.[24]

Goltz's declaration of a new civilizing mission with the aim of remaking the Turks in the German self-image fell on fruitful ground among proimperialist activists in the Reich, which had become disoriented after the official policy line had disclaimed any annexation activities in the Ottoman sphere. Especially in the times following Wilhelm's 1898 visit to Constantinople, a positive image of the Turks gained popularity in circles that otherwise were not Goltz's allies. Some even developed Goltz's characterization of the Turks as kindred spirits into the claim that Turks were racially related to the Germans.[25] Liberal journalists became ardent supporters of German-Turkish rapprochement. A wave of new publications called for a secular cultural mission to the Turks. Friedrich Naumann, Hans Delbrück, Hugo Grothe, Paul Rohrbach, and Ernst Jäckh were the best-known of the movement, which was later dubbed "peaceful imperialism." It gained momentum early in the twentieth century, when the European public became aware that imperialist expansion was no longer possible without confrontation with other Great Powers and that Germany could not hope to obtain landmasses overseas as large as those of its rivals. By consequence "peaceful imperialists" sought to direct activities toward states that were nominally independent but weak. Such states should be influenced to bind them closely to Germany in economic, political, and cultural matters. While such strategies clearly also targeted China, the other focus was the Ottoman Empire.

While the more radical organizations such as the German Colonial Society and the Pan-German League supported the policy of creating strong ties with weaker states as simply a subterfuge to establishing colonial dependency, claiming that one day, the Ottoman sultan would hold no more power than the Bey of Tunis or the Khedive of Egypt,[26] the "liberal" imperialists envisioned a different aim from the start. They emphasized that activists in the Ottoman Empire should completely rid themselves of the standard approaches of imperialist influence. In 1908, at the time of the Young Turk Revolution, an undercurrent among the peaceful imperialists clamored to intensify Turco-German relations considerably. Rohrbach and Jäckh, especially, criticized the direction German Oriental policy had taken under Marschall. According to them this policy had fixated too strongly on materially calculable benefits through major investments such as the Baghdad Railway or technocratic advisers. They claimed that such a checkbook mentality did not grasp the larger picture of what was at stake. Instead, they called for "moral conquests" targeting the hearts and souls of the population at large, thus creating deeper affections for Germany among Turks and gaining popular consent for the larger political project.[27] Germany should support Turkish national emancipation through an educational and cultural policy that also reminded the Orientals of the advantages of German civilization. Translated into modern terms, they envisioned directly installing a postcolonial mentality in a fully sovereign Turkish nation without first installing colonial dependency. If their policy succeeded, the national elites would turn to Germany for every innovation in the political, cultural, or academic field. As in the case of the *Bavarokratie* and the philhellenic activities championed by Friedrich Fabri in the 1860s, Jäckh and Rohrbach also believed that what would be good for Germany would be good for the "natives": such a policy would lead to a genuine empowerment of the Chinese and the Turks through improved access to technologies and education.[28]

Initially, the Berlin Foreign Office was skeptical of an increase in cultural activities abroad, but this soon changed as a result of the immense popularity of this policy. This new movement, which once again tried to identify with the semicolonially suppressed instead of the suppressors, was a generational and social revolt against the ruling elites in the German Reich. Its activists were bourgeois and mostly younger, whereas the older, mostly aristocratic, elites, notably Marschall von Bieberstein, had dictated the Oriental policy. The ambassador saw the coming predicament of imperialist policy in the age of Ottoman mass politics following the Young Turk Revolution of 1908. Although the new rulers demanded more aid in the form of military, bureaucratic, and educational staff, Germany would hereby grow dependent on the Young Turks. The Turkish nationalists saw their effort to reform as part of a process of nation building and thus as a step toward reclaiming sovereignty over the country. If Germany was to support their reforms, it could no longer uphold the second component of its dominance in the Eastern Mediterranean, which included autonomous schools and charity organizations. All countries with imperialist interests employed these instruments to further their position in the Ottoman Empire; the non-Muslim population made the most use of their services. From the Turkish point of view they furthered imperialist interests and offered the tools for self-empowerment via education to ethnic groups increasingly perceived as public enemies, such as the Greeks and, especially, the Armenians. The committee's plans for reclaiming sovereignty included gaining control over the autonomous foreign schools. Germany would most likely be forced to choose between one strategy and the other.

Moreover, there was no guarantee that supporting the Young Turks would further German influence. If, on the one hand, the advisers and teachers were to stress the superiority of German culture too explicitly and overtly preach German dominance, they would come into conflict with the Young Turk ideal of nationalist self-empowerment and risk being excluded from the reforms. On the other hand, if they restricted themselves to catalyzing Turkish self-empowerment without following their own agenda, there would be no clear gain in German influence. Marschall insisted that German-Turkish schools would only benefit the Reich's interests if Germans were ascribed a dominant position.[29] His *Realpolitik*, however, was no longer popular in the twentieth century, and the coming years would see the triumph of idealists and dreamers.

In 1912 Ernst Jäckh founded the German-Turkish Association (DTV), a society uniting almost all financial and industrial corporations with interests in the Eastern Mediterranean. These corporations donated considerable amounts to the DTV to further cultural rapprochement, especially guided tours to Germany for Turkish politicians and businessmen to impress them with the country's achievements, as well as educational initiatives in the Ottoman Empire. Marschall had rightfully feared a private-sector Oriental policy in "Türken-Jäckh's" initiatives and had combated them. The compromise reached by the arbitration of the Foreign Office ruled that the DTV would use the considerable funds at its disposal in coordination with the Foreign Office for expenses exceeding the Foreign Office's budget. Marschall, feeling that his control over Oriental policy was slipping, resigned in 1912. His successor was his disciple Hans von Wangenheim, but the more impressive Wangenheim soon came under the influence of Goltz's and Jäckh's followers, noticeably Hans Humann, who had been at the embassy since 1913.[30] Through Humann's letters to Jäckh, we have a clear impression of the nonpublished views this movement followed. Hans Humann had been born in Smyrna as the son of Carl Humann, the "discoverer" of the Pergamum Altar. Hans, raised in the Reich, still felt strongly attached to the Ottoman Empire, which he called "my old homestead."[31] In Constantinople he preferred the company of modern Turkish upper-middle-class families to that of fellow Europeans.[32] Despite his Turcophilia, he openly considered what he and Jäckh were doing as a form of "colonization." Under Jäckh's guidance he pushed for a close alliance, especially through his intimate friendship with Enver Pasha, who was to become war minister.[33] Besides being a radical nationalist, Enver was an enthusiastic admirer of Germany. Once the Ottomans had entered hostilities against Russia (following several months of arcane diplomacy), the partisans of "German-Turkish Friendship" were at the peak of their success. Both the German Military Supreme Command and Foreign Office now considered good relations with the Ottoman government and a lasting influence among Turks vital for the war effort, and the Germanophiles in the Ottoman administration such as Enver had created a situation in which all internal opposition to the alliance with Germany was hopeless. The German Foreign Ministry supported all cultural initiatives aimed at the Turkish population, no matter how far-fetched. There was now a German official in a key position in practically every ministry. A German in the Ministry of Education worked out a new law on basic education. Teacher training seminars were organized and a number of aspiring teachers sent to seminars in the Reich. German teachers were dispatched to certain elitist high schools. The new girls' schools had German headmistresses appointed. Twenty German professors were appointed to Istanbul University not only to teach but also to reform the institution to meet European standards. Several Turkish professionals such as lawyers or newspaper publishers were invited to Germany to gain insight into the work of their colleagues there. Hundreds of Turks were sent to the Reich for vocational training, and German instructors taught at vocational schools in Anatolia. Orchestras and theater ensembles were to be sent to Constantinople to show off German culture. The German-Turkish Association laid down the founding stone of Friendship House, a huge building to be erected on Divan Yolu, just opposite the fountain Wilhelm II had donated in 1898. The building was to house concert and movie halls; provide space for exhibitions, reading, and classrooms; and act as a showcase for German culture. A Friendship House in Berlin to promote Turkish culture was planned for a similarly prominent place on the corner of Wilhelmstraße and Unter den Linden.[34]

This list gives an impression of the changes envisioned by German and Turkish activists. It alone is insufficient, however, to indicate the extent to which the Anatolian population was expected to mimic the Central Europeans. They were supposed to admire and replicate their culture, adopt German teaching methods and subjects, restructure their university according to the imported standards, learn to organize and self-discipline themselves, and be industrious in a German way. But the transformation was to have a physical dimension. One propaganda leaflet addressed to the Turkish public was entitled "How to train (educate) strong and big bodies following the German example (A healthy and very pleasant book. Especially recommended for all household heads—men and women alike)."[35]

Another endeavor that we must interpret in light of the German identification with the Turks is the attempt to unleash an Islamic Holy War against the Entente with the help of the Ottoman government. With great naiveté advocates of this endeavor did not consider that unlocking the genie of religious hatred for the sake of imperial politics might boomerang after Germany would one day reconsider its stance in global geopolitics. Both Enver Pasha and the Jäckh camp initially resisted the project. But as the German High Command expected much from an appeal to jihad, the Ottoman government finally acquiesced.[36] The degree to which German activists in Oriental policy no longer associated themselves with the West can be grasped by the following picture: in an office of the Berlin Foreign Ministry the infidel Max von Oppenheim planned how to instruct the true believers of Islam to rise up against the infidels. German agents ignored the appeal by the Ottoman allies to leave the agitation in Persia in Turkish hands, so that Turkish and German jihadis obstructed each other more than they obstructed the enemy.[37]

Obviously, because of the close ties the cultural projects had with the war effort, they had to be abandoned once the war and the empires on the German side were lost. Many activists for greater German identification with the peoples of the East continued their activities into the years of the republic in a more circumspect manner. While some arranged themselves with the republic, others joined the camp clamoring for a return to more authoritarian forms of government.[38] During the German occupation of Southeast Europe from 1941 to 1944, history repeated itself, this time as tragedy rather than farce. While Hitler at first wished to show himself benevolent to the defeated Greeks, because he believed Germans to be descendants of ancient Greeks, this attitude changed when the occupiers realized that the Greeks did not unreservedly reciprocate these feelings. On the one hand, the Wehrmacht propaganda switched to describing the Greeks as "Negroes" and as having lost all attachment to their classical roots. This propaganda accompanied a policy of scorched earth to retaliate against partisans, a tactic that Germany had used earlier in the African colonies.[39] On the other hand, the German occupiers adopted a short-lived policy of considering the Slavic Macedonians as a lost Germanic people and setting up a marionette state for them.[40] Hitler also entertained great sympathies for the Turks and, in his *Tischgespräche* (table talk), referred to Mustafa Kemal (Atatürk) as being of Germanic descent.[41] As Germany and Turkey did not enter into hostilities or alliance, this distant admiration was not put to the test.

This paradoxical attitude of trying to attain world power status while at the same time identifying with the colonially suppressed in the Eastern Mediterranean, mainly with Greeks at one time and Turks at another, is not an ideology in itself. It is rather a predisposition that managed to influence several different ideological positions, secular philhellenism, Protestant mission, liberalism, monarchism, militarism, and later fascism. Identifying with the Oriental characterized several key persons in various academic disciplines, the church, civil society, the army, and the state. While these actors fell far short of their fantastic goals—creating a uniform Germanophile Greek or Turkish nation—we can safely assume that it was only through their keen interest in the cultural, intellectual, technological, and state-building capacities of first the one and then the other nation that Germans managed to make a considerable imprint on these two communities despite Germany's status as a latecomer in the Eastern Question. Had they remained more distant from the people of the Levant, such as the British or to a lesser degree the French colonialist agents in the region, Germanophilia would have hardly accomplished as much as it did, dominating, for example, Greek and Turkish academic traditions for a considerable time. The disappointments suffered when the Germans' paternal attitude met with resistance, however, led German activists to react with particular violence, especially to Greek reactions to German domination. While in the nineteenth century German counterreactions took on the form of slander, such as in the famous anti-Greek polemics by Jakob Ph. Fallmerayer, the rejection of the Nazi occupiers' overtures led to the atrocities described above.

Although Germany's identification with the native constitutes a *Sonderweg* in trying to gain influence in the East, one reason it has been often disregarded is that Germany after 1945 tried to portray itself as firmly rooted in the West. This helped Germany to break with many of the undesirable developments of the previous one hundred years, but it created new cases of imperial vanity now in the name of a superior Occident. It also clouded in "collective amnesia"[42] the once proclaimed proximity and familiarity between the Germans and the inhabitants of the Eastern Mediterranean, as well as the mistakes and crimes committed in the name of this familiarity. The other reason, however, is the indecipherable and paradoxical nature of the German philhellene and Turcophile activities themselves. The confusion is not only created by looking from a historical distance at a movement that seems alien to the twenty-first century. To the historian, it seems, for example, that Enver Pasha or Ernst Jäckh often lost sight of whether their actions truly benefited the Turkish or the German side, and of where their priorities lay.

This indecipherability, in combination with the "collective amnesia," has promoted an attitude of false historical innocence in German society when it comes to the historical roots of its relations with the people of southeastern Europe. The Pergamon Museum might owe its treasures to the Kaiserreich's good relationship to Abdülhamid, but neither the museum authorities nor the general public is interested in the exact circumstances of how the artifacts came to Berlin. Germany reaps the benefits of being Turkey's largest trade partner, but outside of a limited number of researchers, nobody looks for the origins of this relationship.

Scholars in the field of genocide studies have made the most pronounced attempts to break through this amnesia concerning the legacy of Germany's Oriental ambitions. Did German activists in the Ottoman Empire imprint their ideas of racial hygiene on the Turkish nationalists, precipitating if not co-orchestrating the genocide against Armenians? Or, on the other hand, did the Armenian genocide provide a blueprint for the Holocaust? While both trajectories seem plausible, research has not offered easy answers to this question. Instead, it has brought forth the divided, contradictory, and complex nature of the continuities between the two efforts at exterminating an entire people.

Approaching Germany's role in the Eastern Mediterranean region, one must avoid the simple opposition of the friendship or the colonialism paradigm as described at the beginning of this chapter. Furthermore, one must avoid the dichotomy of "us" and "them" inherent in the friendship paradigm but also in many works on colonialism. If one describes German philhellenic activities, one must keep in mind their anti-Turkish and anti-Slavic repercussions. The Turcophile activists, in turn, furthered anti-Greek and anti-Armenian sentiments, enriched with their own anti-Semitic notions from the Reich. Preferences for and degrees of interaction with the one or other peoples of the Eastern Mediterranean could change rapidly.

At an early stage postcolonial studies warned against simply projecting master-servant schemas on to colonizer and colonized and drew our attention to the in-between spaces and processes of appropriation inherent to the colonial encounter.[43] This is especially important for semicolonial spheres such as the late Ottoman Empire. In this context we must understand "empire" and "colony" not so much as objectively given realities but rather as ideals that both the Great Powers and the regional powers and political movements strived to achieve. We gain little in this context by interpreting "German colonialism through a comparative relationship to Ottoman imperialism," as propagated by Russell Berman.[44] Such East-West contrasts grew stale a long time ago.[45] It is much more promising to explore the unpredicted East-West interactions, such as the "proxy-colonialism" that Marin Braach-Maksvytis identifies in Adenauer Era West Germany's relationship with Israel. Similarly, it could be argued that both the Weimar Republic and the Third Reich cultivated a sentiment of "proxy-imperialism" for Kemalist Turkey, because the Turkish National Army managed to revoke its World War I peace treaty unilaterally and to reconquer Anatolia, goals that Germany had failed to meet.[46] To open itself to such complex investigations—taking into account a multitude of players and seeing the colonizer-colonized relationship more as a shared ideal of the involved parties than as a pregiven reality—is a promising perspective for German colonial studies. By understanding "colonialism as a phenomenon that is always global, European, national, and local at the same time,"[47] the study of the German colonial experience could evolve into entangled histories, in which postcolonial interrogations are imminent but not exclusive. Such a development would be something quite different from Berman's proposal to hijack German colonial studies' critical potential for an anticommunist and anti-Arabic agenda under the etiquette of transnationalism.[48]

Notes

1. See Laqueur, "'The Traditional Turco-German Friendship'—Fact or Fiction?"
2. Öztürk, *Alman Oryantalizmi*.
3. Schöllgen, *Imperialismus und Gleichgewicht*; Schwanitz, "Paschas, Politiker, und Paradigmen"; Mommsen, *Imperialismustheorien*.
4. See Osterhammel, "Semicolonialism and Informal Empire in Twentieth Century China," 295–96; Goodman, "Improvisations on a Semicolonial Theme"; Lysa, "'Stranger Within the Gates,'" 351–54.
5. Detrez, "Colonialism in the Balkans"; Todorova, *Imagining the Balkans*, 16–21; Deringil, *The Well-Protected Domains*.
6. Kampen, "Studien zur deutschen Türkeipolitik in der Zeit Wilhelms II"; Quataert, "The Industrial Working Class of Salonica, 1850–1912," 195.
7. Schöllgen, "'Dann müssen wir uns aber Mesopotamien sichern!'"
8. See, e.g., Schwanitz, "The German Middle Eastern Policy, 1871–1945."
9. Schöllgen, "'Dann müssen wir uns aber Mesopotamien sichern!'" 130.
10. Kampen, "Studien zur deutschen Türkeipolitik in der Zeit Wilhelms II," 84.
11. See Pollack, "Deep Orientalism?"; and Zantop, *Colonial Fantasies*, 10.
12. Schöllgen, "'Dann müssen wir uns aber Mesopotamien sichern!'" 130–45.
13. Nahmer, "Deutsche Kolonisationspläne und -erfolge in der Türkei vor 1870," 936.
14. Marchand, *Down from Olympus*.
15. See Hösch, "Die 'Bayernherrschaft' und das Problem der Modernisierungsstrategien in Griechenland"; and Nahmer, "Deutsche Kolonisationspläne und -erfolge in der Türkei vor 1870," 933, 934.
16. Stark, *Aus dem Reiche des Tantalus und Croesus*, 56–58.
17. Fuhrmann, *Der Traum vom deutschen Orient*, 126–42.
18. See Marchand, "German Orientalism and the Decline of the West."
19. See Holub, "Nietzsche's Colonialist Imagination."
20. Todorova, *Imagining the Balkans*, 118.
21. See Scherer, *Adler und Halbmond*, 434–49.
22. Kampen, "Studien zur deutschen Türkeipolitik in der Zeit Wilhelms II," 28, 29.

23. Fuhrmann, "Zwei Völker in Waffen"; Yasamee, "Colmar Freiherr von der Goltz and the Rebirth of the Ottoman Empire"; Teske, *Colmar Freiherr von der Goltz*.

24. Fuhrmann, *Der Traum vom deutschen Orient*, 157–60.

25. One notable adherent was Paul Rohrbach. See Kampen, "Studien zur deutschen Türkeipolitik in der Zeit Wilhelms II," 302, 303. See also Grothe, *Auf türkischer Erde: Reisebilder und Studien*, 272–75; and Barth, *Unter südlichem Himmel*, 32.

26. Kampen, "Studien zur deutschen Türkeipolitik in der Zeit Wilhelms II," 149.

27. Fuhrmann, *Der Traum vom deutschen Orient*, 25–27, 397.

28. Kampen, "Studien zur deutschen Türkeipolitik in der Zeit Wilhelms II"; Kloosterhuis, *"Friedliche Imperialisten"*; Pöppinghaus, *"Moralische Eroberungen"?*; Gencer, *Bildungspolitik, Modernisierung und kulturelle Interaktion*.

29. Gencer, *Bildungspolitik, Modernisierung und kulturelle Interaktion*, 142–55.

30. Humann to Jäckh, Constantinople, Dec. 22, 1913, Ernst Jäckh Papers, box 1, file 3.

31. Humann to Jäckh, Berlin, Aug. 30, 1912, Ernst Jäckh Papers, box 1, file 1.

32. Humann to Jäckh, Constantinople, Dec. 22, 1913, Ernst Jäckh Papers, box 1, file 3.

33. Bundesarchiv-Militärarchiv (BA-MA, Federal Archives–Military Archives, Freiburg) Reichsmarine 40-4, -151, -456, -457.

34. Fuhrmann, *Der Traum vom deutschen Orient*, 222–63. On wartime cultural propaganda in the Ottoman Empire see Politisches Archiv des Auswärtigen Amts (PA-AA, Political Archives of the Foreign Office Berlin) R 62841, 62842, and Konstantinopel 401, 402, 403, 405, 406, 415, 416; Bundesarchiv Berlin (BA Berlin, Federal Archives, Berlin branch) R 901-71087, -71206, -71207, -71208, -71209, -71210, -72025, -72865; Kloosterhuis, *"Friedliche Imperialisten,"* 2:623–25; Gencer, *Bildungspolitik, Modernisierung und kulturelle Interaktion*, 98–118, 139–231, 265–85; Liman v. Sanders, *Fünf Jahre Türkei*, 187–88.

35. Osmanisch-deutsche Freundschaftsbibliothek, in Gencer, *Bildungspolitik, Modernisierung und kulturelle Interaktion*, 215.

36. Enver to Moltke, Constantinople, Oct. 21, 1914, Jäckh Papers, box 1, file 14; Schwanitz, "The German Middle Eastern Policy, 1871–1945," 6–9.

37. Bundesarchiv-Militärarchiv (BA-MA, Federal Archives–Military Archives, Freiburg) Reichsmarine 40/214, 100 (black numbers): Sarre, "Report on Persian Mission," no date (June/July[?] 1916).

38. Seidt, "'When Continents Awake, Island Empires Fall!'"; and Roth, "Berlin-Ankara-Baghdad."

39. Fleischer, "Deutsche 'Ordnung' in Griechenland," 1941–1944."

40. Troebst, "Makedonischer Staat von Hitlers Gnaden?"

41. Gemein and Oezsinmaz, *Deutsche und Türken in der Geschichte*, 90.

42. Jenkins, "German Orientalism."

43. See Lüdtke, "Einleitung."
44. See Russell A. Berman's chapter in this volume.
45. See Osterhammel, *Die Entzauberung Asiens*.
46. See Martin Braach-Maksvytis's chapter in this volume. On the Turkish case consult Stefan Ihrig, ongoing PhD research project on Turkish-German relations in the twentieth century, at Churchill College, Cambridge, UK, supervised by Richard J. Evans. My thanks to the author for sharing his work on this subject.
47. See Birthe Kundrus's chapter in this volume.
48. For a discussion of the different attempts at postnational historiography see Kaelble, "Die Debatte über Vergleich und Transfer und was jetzt?" For a discussion of imperialism and colonialism in the Soviet context see ongoing discussions in the journal *Ab Imperio*. For a balanced account of Arab attitudes toward Hitler fascism see Höpp, Wien, and Wildangel, *Blind für die Geschichte?*

Bibliography

Barth, Hans. *Unter südlichem Himmel: Bilder aus dem Orient und Italien*. Leipzig: Rengersche Buchh., 1893.

Deringil, Selim. *The Well-Protected Domains: Ideology and the Legitimization of Power in the Ottoman Empire, 1876–1909*. London: I. B. Tauris, 1998.

Detrez, Raymond. "Colonialism in the Balkans: Historic Realities and Contemporary Perceptions." *Kakanien Revisited* (May 15, 2002): www.kakanien.ac.at/beitr/postcol (accessed April 23, 2009).

Fleischer, Hagen. "Deutsche 'Ordnung' in Griechenland, 1941–1944." In *Von Lidice bis Kalavryta—Widerstand und Besatzungsterror: Studien zur Repressalienpraxis im Zweiten Weltkrieg*, edited by Hagen Fleischer and Loukia Droulia, 151–224. Berlin: Metropol, 1999.

Fuhrmann, Malte. *Der Traum vom deutschen Orient: Zwei deutsche Kolonien im Osmanischen Reich, 1851–1918*. Frankfurt: Campus, 2006.

———. "Zwei Völker in Waffen: Türkisch-deutsche Interdependenzen beim nation building." In *Schnittstellen: Gesellschaft, Nation, Konflikt und Erinnerung in Südosteuropa*, edited by Ulf Brunnbauer, Andreas Helmedach, and Stefan Troebst, 231–44. Munich: Oldenbourg, 2007.

Gemein, Gisbert, and Metin Oezsinmaz. *Deutsche und Türken in der Geschichte*. Münster: Aschendorff, 2001.

Gencer, Mustafa. *Bildungspolitik, Modernisierung und kulturelle Interaktion: Deutsch-türkische Beziehungen (1908–1918)*. Münster: Lit, 2002.

Goodman, Bryna. "Improvisations on a Semicolonial Theme, or, How to Read a Celebration of Transnational Urban Community." *Journal of Asian Studies* 59, no. 4 (2000): 889–926.

Grothe, Hugo. *Auf türkischer Erde: Reisebilder und Studien.* Berlin: Allgemeiner Verein für Dt. Literatur, 1903.
Holub, Robert C. "Nietzsche's Colonialist Imagination: Nueva Germania, Good Europeanism, and Great Politics." In *The Imperialist Imagination: German Colonialism and Its Legacy*, edited by Sara Friedrichsmeyer, Sara Lennox, and Susanne Zantop, 33–50. Ann Arbor: University of Michigan Press, 1998.
Höpp, Gerhard, Peter Wien, and René Wildangel, eds. *Blind für die Geschichte? Arabische Begegnungen mit dem Nationalsozialismus.* Berlin: Das Arabische Buch, 2004.
Hösch, Edgar. "Die 'Bayernherrschaft' und das Problem der Modernisierungsstrategien in Griechenland." In *Der Philhellenismus und die Modernisierung in Griechenland und Deutschland*, edited by Institut für Balkanstudien und Südosteuropagesellschaft, 77–92. Thessaloniki: Institute for Balkan Studies, 1986.
Jäckh, Ernst. Papers. Manuscripts and Archives, Yale University Library.
Jenkins, Jennifer. "German Orientalism: Introduction." *Comparative Studies on Africa, South Asia and the Middle East* 24, no. 2 (2004): 97–100.
Kaelble, Hartmut. "Die Debatte über Vergleich und Transfer und was jetzt?" *H-Soz-u-Kult* (Feb. 8, 2005): http://hsozkult.geschichte.hu-berlin.de/forum/type=artikel&id=574 (accessed April 25, 2009).
Kampen, Wilhelm van. "Studien zur deutschen Türkeipolitik in der Zeit Wilhelms II." PhD diss., Kiel University, 1968.
Kloosterhuis, Jürgen. *"Friedliche Imperialisten": Deutsche Auslandsvereine und auswärtige Kulturpolitik, 1906–1918.* 2 vols. Frankfurt: Lang, 1994.
Laqueur, Hans-Peter. "'The Traditional Turco-German Friendship'—Fact or Fiction?" In *The First World War as Remembered in the Countries of the Eastern Mediterranean*, edited by Olaf Farschid, Manfred Kropp, and Stephan Dähne, 415–24. Würzburg: Ergon, 2006.
Liman v. Sanders, Otto. *Fünf Jahre Türkei.* Berlin: August-Scherl-Verlag, 1920.
Lüdtke, Alf. "Einleitung." In *Herrschaft als soziale Praxis*, edited by Alf Lüdtke, 9–63. Göttingen: Vandenhoeck und Ruprecht, 1991.
Lysa, Hong. "'Stranger Within the Gates': Knowing Semi-Colonial Siam as Extraterritorials." *Modern Asia Studies* 38, no. 2 (2004): 327–54.
Marchand, Suzanne. *Down from Olympus: Archaeology and Philhellenism in Germany, 1750–1970.* Princeton, NJ: Princeton University Press, 1996.
———. "German Orientalism and the Decline of the West." *Proceedings of the American Philosophical Society* 145, no. 4 (2001): 465–73.
Mommsen, Wolfgang J., ed. *Imperialismustheorien.* Göttingen: Vandenhoeck und Ruprecht, 1987.
Nahmer, Ernst v. d. "Deutsche Kolonisationspläne und -erfolge in der Türkei vor 1870." *Schmollers Jahrbuch für Gesetzgebung* 40 (1916): 915–76.

Osterhammel, Jürgen. *Die Entzauberung Asiens: Europa und die asiatischen Reiche im 18. Jahrhundert.* Munich: Beck, 1998.

———. "Semicolonialism and Informal Empire in Twentieth Century China: Towards a Framework of Analysis." In *Imperialism and After: Continuities and Discontinuities,* edited by Jürgen Osterhammel and Wolfgang J. Mommsen, 290–314. London: Allen and Unwin, 1986.

Öztürk, Ali O. *Alman Oryantalizmi: 19. yüzyıl Alman Kültüründe Türk Motifi.* Ankara: Vada Yayınları, 2000.

Pollack, Sheldon. "Deep Orientalism?" In *Orientalism and the Postcolonial Predicament: Perspectives on South Asia,* edited by C. A. Breckenridge and P. v. d. Veer, 74–103. Philadelphia: University of Pennsylvania Press, 1993.

Pöppinghaus, Ernst-Wolfgang. *"Moralische Eroberungen"? Kultur und Politik in den deutsch-spanischen Beziehungen der Jahre, 1919 bis 1933.* Frankfurt: Vervuert, 1999.

Quataert, Donald. "The Industrial Working Class of Salonica, 1850–1912." In *Jews, Turks, Ottomans: A Shared History, Fifteenth Through the Twentieth Century,* edited by Avigdor Levy, 194–211. Syracuse, NY: Syracuse University Press, 2002.

Roth, Karl Heinz. "Berlin-Ankara-Baghdad: Franz von Papen and German Near East Policy During the Second World War." In Schwanitz, *Germany and the Middle East, 1871–1945,* 181–216.

Scherer, Friedrich. *Adler und Halbmond: Bismarck und der Orient, 1878–1890.* Paderborn: Schöningh, 2001.

Schöllgen, Gregor. "'Dann müssen wir uns aber Mesopotamien sichern!' Motive deutscher Türkenpolitik zur Zeit Wilhelms II. in zeitgenössischen Darstellungen." *Saeculum* 32 (1981): 130–45.

———. *Imperialismus und Gleichgewicht: Deutschland, England, und die orientalische Frage, 1871–1914.* Munich: Oldenbourg, 1984.

Schwanitz, Wolfgang G. "The German Middle Eastern Policy, 1871–1945." In Schwanitz, *Germany and the Middle East, 1871–1945,* 1–23.

———, ed. *Germany and the Middle East, 1871–1945.* Madrid: Iberoamericana, 2004.

———. "Paschas, Politiker, und Paradigmen: Deutsche Politik im Nahen und Mittleren Orient, 1871–1945." *Comparativ* 14, no. 1 (2004): 22–45.

Seidt, Hans-Ulrich. "'When Continents Awake, Island Empires Fall!' Germany and the Destabilization of the East, 1919–1922." In Schwanitz, *Germany and the Middle East, 1871–1945,* 65–86.

Stark, Bernhard. *Aus dem Reiche des Tantalus und Croesus: Eine Reisestudie.* Berlin: Lüderitz, 1872.

Teske, Hermann. *Colmar Freiherr von der Goltz: Ein Kämpfer für den militärischen Fortschritt.* Göttingen: Musterschmidt, 1957.

Todorova, Maria. *Imagining the Balkans.* New York: Oxford University Press, 1997.

Troebst, Stefan. "Makedonischer Staat von Hitlers Gnaden? Ein nationalsozialistisches Staatsgründungsprogramm von 1944." In *Makedonien: Prägungen und*

Perspektiven, edited by Gabriella Schubert, 225–39. Wiesbaden: Harrassowitz, 2006.

Yasamee, Feroze A. K. "Colmar Freiherr von der Goltz and the Rebirth of the Ottoman Empire." *Diplomacy and Statecraft* 9, no. 2 (1998): 91–128.

Zantop, Susanne. *Colonial Fantasies: Conquest, Race, and Nation in Pre-Colonial Germany, 1770–1871*. Durham, NC: Duke University Press, 1997.

7

Arguing the Case for a Colonial Poland

Kristin Kopp

> Without a consideration of German *Ostkolonisation* and its continuation, we will never adequately understand the colonial fantasies and practices of the Germans.
> —Herbert Uerlings, "Kolonialer Diskurs und Deutsche Literatur"

In an oft-cited episode reflecting National Socialist perceptions of eastern European space during the Second World War, we follow the prominent author and president of the Reich Chamber of Literature, Hanns Johst, as he joins his close friend, SS-Reichsführer Heinrich Himmler, for a brief tour through occupied Poland during the winter of 1939 to 1940.[1] Having surveyed the scene, Johst writes: "The Poles are not a state-building nation. They lack even the most elementary preconditions for it. I drove alongside the Reichsführer-SS up and down that country. A country that has so little feeling for systematic settlement, that cannot even deal with the style of a village, has no claim to any sort of independent political status within the European area. *It is a colonial country!*"[2]

During the Second World War the National Socialists planned a fundamental reorganization of eastern European space with the intention of creating German settlement colonies there. Such depictions as Johst's, rendering this region in colonial terms as chaotic and undeveloped, unable to keep pace with modernity, and requiring external intervention in order to achieve civilizational progress, became key components of the rhetoric used to legitimize these plans. In Johst's claim that he was traveling through a "colonial country" lies the invitation to map centuries' worth of European overseas colonial experience onto adjacent European space and to structure German-Polish affairs according to conventional expectations of relationships between colonizers and colonized.

In recent years scholars of both German colonial history and National Socialism have increasingly returned to Hannah Arendt's early postwar interrogation of the ways in which these two historical experiences might have been linked.[3] One version of the question asks whether it is possible—and, if so, to what extent useful—to draw connections between the 1904 mass murder of the Herero and Nama peoples in German Southwest Africa, on the one hand, and National Socialist atrocities on the European continent, on the other. Scholars pursuing such links are interested in identifying racist ideologies or eliminationist practices that can be found in the contexts of both overseas colonization and National Socialist continental expansionism. The resulting studies have found continuities in specific practices of social governance and racial engineering and have even identified certain individuals that played active roles in both sets of events, transferring knowledge and experience developed in Africa to the European continent later in the century.[4] Others position themselves against such narratives of continuity, arguing that the inclusion of eastern Europe would extend the category of colonialism too far and result in the weakening of the term's critical acumen. At the same time, to the extent that the continuity thesis locates the Holocaust within a larger framework of colonial violence, opponents warn that it threatens to relativize the Holocaust by not taking strongly enough into account the different ideological and political intentions that structured different genocides.[5]

As different positions are staked within this debate, divergent definitions of *continuity* have spawned a pluralization of terms that have complicated discussion. At stake is whether or not one understands continuity to be an expression of causality; in other words, if one argues that there is continuity between colonial and National Socialist structures of violence, is this the same as arguing that the first *led to, caused, or paved the way for* the second? Opponents of the continuity thesis tend to position it within this causal logic by reformulating discussions about whether we can identify structures of continuity into the question of whether the practices developed in the context of the Herero massacre necessarily found their ultimate expression in the Holocaust. Pascal Grosse, for example, argues that "if German colonialism led in some causal way to National Socialism, then the German colonial order must have been different from that of its European rivals," because the other colonial powers did not return to the European continent and perpetrate mass genocides comparable to the Holocaust.[6] Grosse then argues that the German overseas colonial experience does not distinguish itself from that of other European powers, and he rightly points out that while the Germans were indeed guilty of mass killings in their colonies, they certainly were not the only colonial power to have perpetrated such violence (one need only consider the Belgian atrocities in Congo). Since German colonial violence was not unique, Grosse concludes that the colonial experience could not have led to the Holocaust, because the Holocaust *was* unique.

Grosse is easily able to reject the continuity thesis when he considers it according to the metric of causality, and it would seem that his treatment of the question could end with this finding. Yet he returns once again to the issue of commonalities, this time shifting his attention from acts of genocide to practices of racial politics, where he indeed finds convincing similarities between German practices in the overseas colonies and eastern Europe. In explaining this link Grosse usefully negotiates a noncausal model of continuity: instead of arguing that the two events were separate, and that we can draw a causal link from the first to the second, he positions the two historical experiences on more or less equal terms within a larger common historical framework. According to this model, Grosse suggests that "German colonialism was less a prerequisite for the emergence of National Socialist racial politics than an expression of the same intellectual eugenicist model at an earlier time and in a different historical setting."[7] Following Grosse's model, we might rather seek to locate both German colonialism and National Socialism within a shared historical frame, one in whose racial logic, and racialized violence, European colonial powers as a whole might well be implicated.

It is with this model of a shared conceptual framework, rather than that of causality, that I would like to engage the question of continuity between colonialism and National Socialist policies in eastern Europe. I argue that, in both cases, Germans came to construct the relationship between self and other with the aid of a conceptual apparatus that had been developed in the context of the European global colonial project (a project that, as has often been noted, Germans had helped shape as members of the larger European community). In a liberal rewording of Grosse's position I would like to suggest that certain of the National Socialist policies in Poland were expressions of the same intellectual colonial model manifested overseas. This specific claim of continuity differentiates itself from those focusing primarily on the two cases of genocide in its expanded temporal frame. Whereas most investigations trace a path from German Southwest Africa in 1904 to eastern Europe in 1939, it is crucial that we shift our explorations of German interventions in Polish space to include a much earlier period, during the time when the Herero massacre was taking place overseas. Once the spatiotemporal frame has been thus expanded, it becomes easier to see the connections between Africa and eastern Europe—connections that may ultimately aid in the comparative study of the two genocides.

The National Socialists were not the first to envision a colonial Poland. This process had begun much earlier, as the Germans simultaneously pursued two different colonial projects at the end of the nineteenth century. In 1886, just two years after Germany took its first overseas colonies in Africa, Bismarck launched the "inner colonization" campaign in Prussia's predominantly Polish eastern provinces. He designed this project to displace ethnic Poles and encourage them to relocate over the border into Russian-controlled Congress Poland so that a new population of ethnic German settlers, recruited from the western regions of the nation, could come in to "Germanize" the race and space of the East.[8] Inner colonization was accompanied by a propaganda campaign presenting the regions in question as colonial space, while fashioning the Poles as uncivilized and therefore illegitimate guardians of the land.[9] Both literary texts and the mainstream press, as well as a wide range of specialized discourse including both academic historiographies and popular colonial atlases, represented "Poland" as colonial space.[10]

This renegotiation of the East as colonial space did not succeed Germany's overseas colonial engagements but occurred simultaneously with them. Certain aspects of a relationship that scholarship has often approached diachronically (as two genocidal events separated by four decades and a continental divide) are rather best apprehended synchronically (as two spaces that were both cast in colonial terms at the same time within the same overarching conceptual framework). There were, of course, significant differences between the African and eastern European colonial variants, both in the manner in which these colonial projects were carried out and in the ways in which they were discursively rendered. Nonetheless, considering German Southwest Africa and Prussian Poland together allows us to see that both spaces were interpolated into a shared colonial worldview.

Constructions of Poland as German colonial space had been in prominent cultural and political circulation long before Hanns Johst and Heinrich Himmler made their journey eastward. Since the mid-nineteenth century, various groups and individuals promoting the eastward extension of German hegemony (be it in the form of additional territorial expansion or of the "Germanization" measures of the inner colonization campaign) had represented eastern Europe in racial and spatial terms derived from an overarching European colonial idiom. Because this colonial discourse vis-à-vis Poland had been adapted to suit the rhetorical needs of various specific historical, cultural, and political contexts, Hanns Johst could appeal to a rich set of preexisting representational models to depict the eastern region as colonial space.

Indeed, Johst is able to draw on a well-known passage from the literary canon in formulating his assessment of Poland. In claiming that the Poles lack the ability to generate a modern state on their own (and thus require colonial intervention in order to achieve and maintain this level of civilizational development), he echoes an assertion made in the best-selling German novel of the nineteenth century, Gustav Freytag's *Soll und Haben* (1855). In a pivotal scene of this novel the protagonist, Anton Wohlfart, travels into Polish lands with his employer on a mission to rescue a convoy of goods from the hoard of wild, dark-skinned Polish "natives" who have attacked it. As they travel toward their destination, Wohlfart's employer assesses the nature of the Poles and their inability to form their own state: "'There is no race more lacking in the prerequisites of social progress and no race more unable to use their capital to achieve civilizational development than the Slavic race.... It is incredible how incapable they are of generating for themselves the social class that could bring about civilization and progress, and that could unite a heap of scattered farmsteads into a proper state.'"[11]

Both Wohlfart's employer and Hanns Johst frame their colonial claims with the same concept of autonomous civilizational development, a capacity that, in their representations of Polish space, they both depict as lacking. This is, of course, one of the central tenets of European colonial ideology—the belief that non-European peoples lagged behind European civilization because, owing to an inferior nature that was essentially static and inert, non-Europeans lacked both the ability and the will to change and progress on their own.[12] The depiction of the Poles as incapable of creative innovation and thus unable to produce new technology, culture, or social practices and unable to cultivate space, make land fertile, or shape their environments as products of their collective identity describes a discursive continuity I have identified as spanning more than a century of German rhetoric on the East. This construction of the Poles allowed Germans to claim that all evidence of progress in the East was due to their own efforts in the region—efforts that were traced ever further into the past. In the second half of the nineteenth century, German historians and publicists rediscovered the medieval history of German eastward migration, which they increasingly renarrated as a colonial undertaking.[13] Over time this history was cast even further back to include the period of the *Völkerwanderung* (300–700 CE). According to the narratives produced in this discourse, the Germans/Germanic tribes were responsible for all cultural developments in the East, while the Slavs merely benefited from centuries of German colonial labor.

After Germany lost large stretches of Polish-Prussia as a result of its defeat in the First World War, the proliferation of these narratives intensified and reached ever larger audiences through the press, popular literature and historiography, and widely implemented educational materials. By the 1930s even those segments of German society not calling for the return of the territories ceded to Poland were convinced that Germans were responsible for any civilization or development achieved in the region. This conviction was so hegemonic that Hitler could use it to introduce his famous declaration of war to the Reichstag on September 1, 1939: "Representatives! Men of the German Reichstag! For months we have all been suffering the agony of a problem bestowed upon us by the dictate of Versailles that—in its deterioration and degeneration—had finally become intolerable. Danzig was and is a German city! The Corridor was and is German! All of these territories owe their cultural development exclusively to the German people, without whom the worst barbarism [*die schlimmste Barbarei*] would prevail in these eastern territories."[14] With these lines Hitler opens a speech with which he seeks to mobilize the German masses behind his war plans. The rhetorical function of these opening lines, therefore, is to establish an initial point of consensus, to unite his audience in a shared conviction from which he then derives his decision to go to war. The colonial narrative provided this point of consensus.

It also provided the point of departure for the National Socialists' plans for eastern European space. The *Generalplan Ost* was articulated as a plan for the colonization of large stretches of land occupied in the East. Although several of their measures overlapped, the *Generalplan Ost* was distinct from the "Final Solution" of the Holocaust and was more directly concerned with the role that ethnic Poles would play in the envisioned German continental empire. To summarize one version of a contested history: The *Generalplan Ost* was a plan to resettle the entire population of the region between the

Oder and Dnieper rivers, with the intention of introducing millions of German settlers into this space. The plan was envisioned in two phases: a first intense phase during the war, and a second extending over the course of the following twenty-five to thirty years. While the plan affected both ethnic Poles and Jews, it obviously did so differently: no role in the future colonial state was envisioned for the Jews, who were slated for elimination. But the Poles were to be refunctionalized: once removed from the region, individuals would either be racially reclassified as "German" and reintroduced into the population, expelled and scattered across regions much farther east (where it was expected that they would dissolve into other Slavic populations), or fed into a pool of slave laborers that would serve the Germans in both agriculture and industry (a practice already introduced in the forced-labor program during the war). To create a passive, enslaved population, the National Socialists deemed it necessary to eliminate the Polish social, political, and cultural elite, and they undertook the imprisonment and murder of these civilians on a large scale.[15] In addition, the *Generalplan Ost* resulted in the expulsion of almost a million Poles from Polish territories annexed by Germany and the resettlement of hundreds of thousands of Germans onto the land the Poles were forced to vacate.

The National Socialist plans for the East can readily be categorized as colonial, according to almost any definition of this term. Had defeat not brought an end to the plans of the *Generalplan Ost*, eastern Europe would have looked like an overseas settlement colony, replete with the exploitation of natural resources for consumption in the motherland, forceful appropriation of native land and property, subjection of the native population to undemocratic rule by an external minority, and, ultimately, elimination of the native population by both direct and indirect means. Whether one applies an economic, political, or cultural model of colonialism, the National Socialist plans for the East clearly meet the parameters. But facts on the ground were not quite as clear, because only the first steps had been undertaken and because, upon their retreat, the Nazis had destroyed many key documents, which scholars now think included all copies of the *Generalplan Ost*. It was therefore initially difficult for external investigators to make sense of what they found on the ground: in the chaos of the immediate postwar period they did not immediately understand cases of Polish dispossession and displacement as manifestations of a separate, coherent plan but instead categorized them as atrocities of occupation or as side effects of the Holocaust. The genocidal "Final Plan" had been so incomprehensible in its magnitude and extent that it had been difficult to see that Poland had been the site of more than one National Socialist project.

This initial miscategorization explains why the main architect of the *Generalplan Ost*, Konrad Meyer, was found innocent—and set free to continue his career as a professor of spatial planning—when tried by an American military court. The judges were convinced that his ideas had only been theoretical.[16] Much later, secondary documents were discovered that attested to the existence of the original *Generalplan Ost*. They provided the overall contours of the plan for the colonization of eastern Europe and provided the structural framework into which individual events could be organized. As the facts on the ground began to take shape, a coherent narrative of a second National Socialist "Plan" emerged. The belated recognition of this colonial project might also explain why it has received such little attention in interdisciplinary German colonial studies.[17]

In Poland, meanwhile, a growing discussion is taking place questioning the extent to which models of colonialism and postcolonialism might apply to various phases of the Polish-German and Polish-Russian/Soviet pasts. On the one hand, scholars debate whether we can rightfully or usefully consider German interventions during the time of the Partitions (1772–1918) and of subsequent National Socialist occupation to have been manifestations of colonialism. Izabela Surynt has led this discussion with numerous publications, including her most recent monograph, *Postęp, kultura I kolonializm: Polska a niemiecki projekt europejskiego Wschodu w dyskursach publicznych XIX wieku* (Progress, Culture, and Colonialism: Poland and the German Project in Eastern Europe in Nineteenth-Century Social Discourse), in which she not only argues that Germans cast their relationship with Poles in colonial terms but that the Poles responded to this projection in such ways as to allow one to speak of colonized subjectivities.[18] For this reason an intensified negotiation with postcolonial theory would be important for coming to terms with this phase of the Polish past. The historian Jan Kieniewicz, in contrast, argues that if colonial categories are at all useful, then they are so in the context of Soviet cold war hegemony rather than in the history of German territorial expansion. Kieniewicz argues that cultural difference is a main component of colonial relationships and finds that while the Russian-Polish difference allowed a colonial dynamic to develop, German-Polish difference was too minimal to extend beyond political categories of domination.[19]

Literary scholars would seem to disagree.[20] Recent studies have revisited such nineteenth-century canonical works as Bolesław Prus's *The Out-*

post (1886) and Henryk Sienkiewicz's *Bartek the Victor* (1882) and *Teutonic Knights* (1900) to show that postcolonial theory allows us to access these works in new ways—as responses to German colonial discourse vis-à-vis Poland. Others engage the postcolonial model of "the empire writing back" and find examples in contemporary Polish literature. Most notable in this regard is Paweł Huelle's 2004 *Castorp*, a novel that "samples" various characters and episodes from the German literary canon, including Thomas Mann's *Magic Mountain*, whose eponymous main character, Hans Castorp, is also the protagonist of Huelle's text.[21]

Scholars of German colonialism, particularly those interested in the question of colonial and postcolonial literature, have long noted that the German overseas colonial experience did not result in a significant body of postcolonial literature. They ascribe this absence in part to the relative brevity of Germany's colonial engagement but also to the low priority placed on the transmission of German language and culture to the colonized populations. We therefore know of few texts written by former German colonial subjects that engage the German colonial past or that negotiate questions of identity vis-à-vis this past.[22] In contrast, the German-Polish relationship is much more complex; its origins can be traced back to the time before either national group had formed as such. It has undergone multiple renegotiations of its social, political, and cultural parameters. The colonial variants are a relatively recent phenomenon and arose after a long period of struggle and contestation. Within German colonial history this process was unique to Polish space, and within global colonial history it was perhaps not singular (the Russian Empire contains its own variants of this particular relationship) but certainly fell outside of the typical experience. Given the recent calls to identify the particularities of the German colonial experience, we should not let that which sets the Polish case apart deter us from its consideration.[23]

Recent argumentation has warned against extending the colonial category to include Eastern Europe, citing Frederick Cooper's warning that overloading the category would make colonialism "appear everywhere—and hence nowhere."[24] Yet, even when only considered in strictly geographic terms, the reality is that colonialism *was* actually *everywhere*. In her introduction to theories of colonialism and postcolonialism, Ania Loomba reminds us that by the 1930s "colonies and ex-colonies covered 84.6 per cent of the land surface of the globe."[25] While one may question the precision of her figure (since she includes no data to support the statistic, there is no certainty about exactly which regions she includes in her colonial categories), the sheer enormity of the percentage must give us pause. Given that virtually every non-European space was, at one point, the object of some form of European colonization, would the inclusion of eastern Europe, or specific portions thereof, really threaten to dilute the category? To be sure, there are significant differences between the German colonial experiences in southwest Africa and those in Poland, differences that are worth delineating and investigating. But, given the great diversity found among the plethora of global colonial engagements, it would be difficult to argue that the eastern European variant would somehow enfeeble our intellectual apparatus were it to be included in the scholarship.

Instead, including Poland might focus additional attention on the plurality of the German colonial experience. George Steinmetz has long argued that German colonialism manifested itself differently in each of its colonies, yet scholarship tends to consider it as a homogeneous expression of a singular idea.[26] He has shown that parallel institutions in the various colonies enacted different policies regarding issues such as intermarriage, citizenship, and property rights and that the source of these differences can be traced back to local variations in ethnographic practices that preceded the official act of state-driven colonization. The differing ways in which precolonial otherness was constructed led to differing policies and practices during the colonial period. Given the length and complexity of the German-Polish "precolonial" period, as well as the various manifestations of coloniality (inner colonization, interwar "postcolonial" irredentism, National Socialist recolonization), the Polish case would certainly offer a rich source of comparison.

A more difficult argument is raised by the assessment that German representations of Poland as colonial space were manifestations of a nationalist, not colonialist, logic.[27] While this argument would be difficult to uphold for the period of the *Generalplan Ost*, the case of the decades preceding it are much less clear-cut. Inner colonization was a different project than overseas colonization, and its status as a "true" manifestation of colonialism is rightly the object of contestation. At the same time, however, the discourse that accompanied, supported, mobilized, and legitimized this project described it in unmistakably colonial terms.[28] Are we right to consider the literature arising out of this discourse "colonial literature"? Unfortunately, the scholarship on colonial literature does not provide a useful framework for resolving this most basic question. The problem lies in the definition of "colonial literature" most studies use to frame their projects, which presents us with an unhelpful tautology: colonial literature is that which portrays or derives from the colonial relationship. Elleke Boehmer's standard introduction to colonial and postcolonial literature distinguishes between two categories: "colonial literature" is "writing concerned with colonial perceptions and experience, written mainly by metropolitans, but also by creoles and indigenes, during colonial times," while "colonialist literature in contrast was that which was specifically concerned with colonial expansion. On the whole it was literature written by and for colonizing Europeans about non-European lands dominated by them. . . . Its distinctive stereotyped language was geared to mediating the white man's relationship with colonized peoples."[29] In other words, recognizing a piece of literature as either colonial or colonialist depends on the prior recognition of a given historical relationship as colonial. Accordingly, Boehmer's book is prefaced with several maps identifying the areas included within the British Empire at various historical moments, thereby introducing geographical parameters to delimit the appropriate literary object from the very outset. A second study, Ania Loomba's post-Marxist introduction to colonialism and postcolonialism, proceeds similarly. Her work opens with a detailed discussion of colonialism, imperialism, and postcolonialism, each defined in relation to modern capitalism. Loomba's model merely replaces Boehmer's imperial map with an economic one. In both cases colonial literature is identified via its relationship to a contemporary (and English-based) "commonsense" understanding of a historical colonial reality; there is nothing in these definitions that allows us to start with the literature itself and position it as colonial based on literary or discursive structures.[30]

Fortunately, the idiosyncrasies of the German overseas colonial experience have led scholars to develop more complex models to delineate it, turning Germany's overseas colonial belatedness into an opportunity to interrogate common methodological assumptions. We now know that the German production, distribution, and consumption of colonial narratives was not limited to the period during which the nation held overseas colonies but was preceded by narrations of German colonial fantasies extending at least as far back as the eighteenth century and continuing after the loss of the colonies in the form of "colonialism without colonies."[31] Such research allows us to step outside the tautology that restricts our understanding of colonial literature to that which represents already existing colonial relationships. Instead, we must begin with a definition of colonial discourse that reflects its functionality, such that we can identify as colonial literature that which brings this discursive function into narrative representation. According to Herbert Uerlings, "at the core of colonial discourse lies an axiom of inferiority that constructs ethnic difference: two entities defined as ethnically different are positioned into a relationship of unquestionable inequality." Uerlings retreats from the project of identifying further commonalities, arguing that to do justice to historical reality, "historical discourse analyses must take into account the plurality, inner heterogeneity, and instability of colonial (situations and) discourses."[32] While I obviously agree with Uerlings, I disagree that the mere indication of inequality between ethnicities is enough to indicate a colonial discourse. The decisive element is the way in which this inequality is explained: in colonial discourse, the ethnic or racial Other's inferiority is essentialized and attributed to inherent internal qualities (as opposed to approaches capable of relativizing difference or finding explanations for developmental lag in external historical contingencies). Within colonial discourse the Other is not only inferior but, because of his or her essential nature, also unable to progress without external intervention.

Identified in this way, German colonial discourse is not only identifiable but also traceable to its various synchronic and diachronic continuities: from late-nineteenth-century inner colonization to the *Generalplan Ost*, from precolonial overseas colonial fantasies to postcolonial irredentist claims, and, indeed, from German Southwest Africa to Poland.

Notes

1. See Düsterberg, *Hanns Johst*.
2. Translated and quoted in Burleigh, *The Third Reich*, 447 (my emphasis). I thank Jürgen Zimmerer for bringing this passage to my attention. See Zimmerer, "The Birth of the *Ostland* Out of the Spirit of Colonialism," 205.
3. See Arendt, *The Origins of Totalitarianism*.
4. See Zimmerer, "The Birth of the *Ostland* Out of the Spirit of Colonialism"; see also Furber, "Going East"; Klotz, "Global Visions"; and Smith, *The Ideological Origins of Nazi Imperialism*.
5. See, e.g., Grosse, "What Does German Colonialism Have to Do with National Socialism?; and Kundrus, "Von Windhoek nach Nürnberg?" See also Jürgen Zimmerer's response to Kundrus in Zimmerer, "Von Windhuk nach Warschau." Zimmerer's anthology *Von Windhuk nach Auschwitz?* will bring together several positions within the debate.
6. Grosse, "What Does German Colonialism Have to Do with National Socialism?" 118.
7. Ibid., 129.

8. For the history of the inner colonization campaign see Tims, *Germanizing Prussian Poland*, 104–32; and Broszat, *Zweihundert Jahre deutsche Polenpolitik*, 129–72.

9. See Kopp, "Constructing Racial Difference in Colonial Poland"; Ketelsen, "Der koloniale Diskurs und die Öffnung des europäischen Ostens im deutschen Roman"; and the essays collected in Nelson, *Germans, Poland, and Colonial Expansion to the East*.

10. The scare quotes ("Poland") indicate that while Poland did not exist as such following the Polish Partitions (which erased the country off the European map in 1795; it would not be reinstated until 1918), the term was nonetheless in common use to refer to predominantly Polish space in the East, including lands held by Prussia. See Kopp, *Germany's Wild East*, in which I present the results of my research on German construction of "Poland" as colonial space.

11. Freytag, *Soll und Haben*, 1:383 (my translation).

12. See Blaut, *The Colonizer's Model of the World*.

13. See Wippermann, *Der 'deutsche Drang nach Osten'*; Wippermann, "'Gen Ostland wollen wir reiten!'"; Hackmann and Lübke, "Die mittelalterliche Ostsiedlung in der deutschen Geschichtswissenschaft"; and Piskorski, "The Medieval Colonization of Central Europe as a Problem of World History and Historiography."

14. Domarus, *Hitler*, 3:1312.

15. For the history of this colonial project see Rössler and Schleiermacher, *Der "Generalplan Ost."* For a treatment of the link between inner colonization and the *Generalplan Ost* see Mai, *"Rasse und Raum"*; and Furber, "Going East."

16. Heinemann, "Wissenschaft und Homogenisierungsplanungen für Osteuropa," 67.

17. Although historians of German-Polish relations are engaging this question—see particularly the essays in Nelson, *Germans, Poland, and Colonial Expansion to the East*—the field of German colonial studies has been much more reluctant to pursue this line of questioning. None of the most prominent recent anthologies contain articles addressing the *Generalplan Ost*.

18. See also Surynt, *Das "ferne," "unheimliche" Land*.

19. See Kieniewicz, *Ekspansja, kolonializm, cywilizacja*.

20. See the recent edition of the leading Polish literary journal, *Teksty Drugie* 106, no. 4 (2007), edited by Włodzimierz Bolecki, which is devoted to the question of Polish postcolonial studies. See also the work of Hanna Gosk, whom I thank for her valuable bibliographical and conceptual contributions to my work on this topic: Gosk, "Polskie opowieści w dyskurs postkolonialny ujęte"; and Gosk, "Polskie pożytki z krytyki postkolonialnej."

21. See particularly the scholarship of Dariusz Skórczewski, who first brought Huelle's novel to my attention: "Wobec eurocentryzmu, dekolonizacji i postmodernizmu" [Considerations of Eurocentrism, decolonization, and postmodernism]; and

"Postkolonialna Polska—projekt (nie)możliwy" [Postcolonial Poland—an (im)possible project]. Huelle's novel has been translated into both German and English.

22. Nina Berman has surveyed this literature in "Colonialism and African Writing." See also the growing scholarship considering the ways in which postcolonial theory can be applied to position various minority literatures in Germany: Mani, *Cosmopolitical Claims*; Adelson, *The Turkish Turn in Contemporary German Literature*; and Cheesman, *Novels of Turkish German Settlement*. Meanwhile, scholarship treating Polish-German cultural production from a postcolonial angle remains a desideratum.

23. In his book on German Orientalism Todd Kontje includes a chapter on depictions of Eastern Europe and thereby paves the way for further research in this area; see Kontje, *German Orientalisms*, chap. 4.

24. Cooper, *Colonialism in Question*, 47. I intentionally use this oft-reproduced, and somewhat misleading, abridgement of Cooper's complete sentence, which argues not against addressing additional historical relationships within the framework of colonial studies but, instead, against extending the colonial category into purely discursive realms: "Looking for a 'textual colonization' or a 'metaphoric colonization' distinct from the institutions through which colonial power is exercised risks making colonialism appear everywhere—and hence nowhere."

25. Loomba, *Colonialism/Postcolonialism*, xiii.

26. See Steinmetz, *The Devil's Handwriting*.

27. See Kundrus's critique in her review of Ames, Klotz, and Wildenthal, *Germany's Colonial Pasts*.

28. Kundrus challenges the colonial nature of this discourse by drawing attention to the extent to which Poles were granted the agency of resistance within it. But the depiction of various forms of native resistance is a common narrative device in colonial literature. One need only consider Gustav Frenssen's depiction of Herero resistance in *Peter Moors Fahrt nach Südwest* (1906). See Kundrus, review of *Germany's Colonial Pasts*.

29. Boehmer, *Colonial and Postcolonial Literature*, 2–3.

30. See Loomba, *Colonialism/Postcolonialism*.

31. See Zantop, *Colonial Fantasies*; and Friedrichsmeyer, Lennox, and Zantop, *The Imperialist Imagination*.

32. Uerlings, "Kolonialer Diskurs und Deutsche Literatur," 18–19 (my translation).

Bibliography

Adelson, Leslie A. *The Turkish Turn in Contemporary German Literature: Toward a New Critical Grammar of Migration*. New York: Palgrave Macmillan, 2005.

Ames, Eric, Marcia Klotz, and Lora Wildenthal, eds. *Germany's Colonial Pasts*. Lincoln: University of Nebraska Press, 2005.

Arendt, Hannah. *The Origins of Totalitarianism.* New York: Harcourt Brace, 1951.

Berman, Nina. "Colonialism and African Writing." In *A Historical Companion to Postcolonial Literatures—Continental Europe and Its Empires,* edited by Prem Poddar, Rajeev S. Patke, and Lars Jensen, 225–27. Edinburgh: Edinburgh University Press, 2009.

Blaut, J. M. *The Colonizer's Model of the World: Geographic Diffusionism and Eurocentric History.* New York: Guilford, 1993.

Boehmer, Elleke. *Colonial and Postcolonial Literature.* 2nd ed. Oxford: Oxford University Press, 2005.

Bolecki, Włodzimierz, ed. *Teksty drugie* 106 (2007).

Broszat, Martin. *Zweihundert Jahre deutsche Polenpolitik.* Frankfurt: Suhrkamp, 1972.

Burleigh, Michael. *The Third Reich: A New History.* London: Macmillan, 2001.

Cheesman, Tom. *Novels of Turkish German Settlement: Cosmopolite Fictions.* Rochester, NY: Camden House, 2007.

Cooper, Frederick. *Colonialism in Question: Theory, Knowledge, History.* Berkeley: University of California Press, 2005.

Domarus, Max. *Hitler: Reden und Proklamationen.* 4 vols. Wauconda, IL: Bolchazy-Carducci, 1998.

Düsterberg, Rolf. *Hanns Johst: "Der Barde der SS"; Karrieren eines deutschen Dichters.* Paderborn: Schöningh, 2004.

Frenssen, Gustav. *Peter Moors Fahrt nach Südwest.* Berlin: G. Grote'sche Verlagsbuchhandlung, 1906.

Freytag, Gustav. *Soll und Haben.* 2 vols. Leipzig: Hirzel, 1902.

Friedrichsmeyer, Sara, Sara Lennox, and Susanne Zantop, eds. *The Imperialist Imagination: German Colonialism and Its Legacy.* Ann Arbor: University of Michigan Press, 1998.

Furber, David. "Going East: Colonialism and German Life in Nazi-Occupied Poland." PhD diss., State University of New York at Buffalo, 2003.

Gosk, Hanna. "Polskie opowieści w dyskurs postkolonialny ujęte" [Polish narratives in a postcolonial frame]. In *(Nie)obecność: Pominięcia i przemilczenia w narracjach XX wieku,* edited by Hanna Gosk and Bożena Karwowska, 74–88. Warsaw: Elipsa, 2008.

———. "Polskie pożytki z krytyki postkolonialnej: Dyskurs postzależnościowego w prozie Tadeusza Konwickiego i Doroty Masłowskiej" [Polish benefits from postcolonial criticism: Post-dependency discourse in the prose of Tadeusz Konwicki and Dorota Maslowska]. In *Dwadzieścia lat literatury polskiej, 1989–2009: Idee, ideologie, metodologie,* edited by Inga Iwasiów and Arleta Galant, 201–13. Szczecin: Wydawnictwo Naukowe Uniwersytetu Szczecińskiego, 2008.

Grosse, Pascal. "What Does German Colonialism Have to Do with National Socialism? A Conceptual Framework." In Ames, Klotz, and Wildenthal, *Germany's Colonial Pasts,* 115–34.

Hackmann, Jörg, and Christian Lübke. "Die mittelalterliche Ostsiedlung in der deutschen Geschichtswissenschaft." In *Historiographical Approaches to Medieval Colonization of East Central Europe: A Comparative Analysis Against the Background of Other European Inter-Ethnic Colonization Processes in the Middle Ages*, edited by Jan M. Piskorski, 179–217. Boulder, CO: East European Monographs, 2002.

Heinemann, Isabel. "Wissenschaft und Homogenisierungsplanungen für Osteuropa: Konrad Meyer, der 'Generalplan Ost' und die deutsche Forschungsgemeinschaft." *Wissenschaft, Planung, Vertreibung: Neuordnungskonzepte und Umsiedlungspolitik im 20. Jahrhundert*, edited by Isabel Heinemann and Patrick Wagner, 45–72. Stuttgart: Steiner, 2006.

Huelle, Paweł. *Castorp*. Translated by Antonia Lloyd-Jones. London: Serpent's Tail, 2007.

Ketelsen, Uwe-K. "Der koloniale Diskurs und die Öffnung des europäischen Ostens im deutschen Roman." In *Kolonialismus: Kolonialdiskurs und Genozid*, edited by Mihran Dabag, Horst Gründer, and Uwe-K. Ketelsen, 67–94. Munich: Wilhelm Fink, 2004.

Kieniewicz, Jan. *Ekspansja, kolonializm, cywilizacja* [Expansion, Colonialism, Civilization]. Warsaw: DiG, 2008.

Klotz, Marcia. "Global Visions: From the Colonial to the National Socialist World." *European Studies Journal* 16, no. 2 (1999): 37–68.

Kontje, Todd. *German Orientalisms*. Ann Arbor: University of Michigan Press, 2004.

Kopp, Kristin. "Constructing Racial Difference in Colonial Poland." In Ames, Klotz, and Wildenthal, *Germany's Colonial Pasts*, 76–96.

———. *Germany's Wild East*. Ann Arbor: University of Michigan Press, forthcoming.

Kundrus, Birthe. Review of *Germany's Colonial Pasts*, edited by Eric Ames, Marcia Klotz, and Lora Wildenthal. *H-Soz-u-Kult* (March 1, 2007): http://hsozkult.geschichte.hu-berlin.de/rezensionen/2007-1-006 (accessed May 3, 2010).

———. "Von Windhoek nach Nürnberg? Koloniale 'Mischehenverbote' und die nationalsozialistische Rassengesetzgebung." In *Phantasiereiche: Zur Kulturgeschichte des deutschen Kolonialismus*, edited by Birthe Kundrus, 110–31. Frankfurt: Campus, 2003.

Loomba, Ania. *Colonialism/Postcolonialism*. London: Routledge, 1998.

Mai, Uwe. *"Rasse und Raum": Agrarpolitik, Sozial- und Raumplanung im NS-Staat*. Paderborn: Schöningh, 2002.

Mani, B. Venkat. *Cosmopolitical Claims: Turkish-German Literatures from Nadolny to Pamuk*. Iowa City: University of Iowa Press, 2007.

Nelson, Robert L., ed. *Germans, Poland, and Colonial Expansion to the East: 1850 Through the Present*. New York: Palgrave Macmillan, 2009.

Piskorski, Jan M. "The Medieval Colonization of Central Europe as a Problem of World History and Historiography." *German History* 22, no. 3 (2004): 323–43.

Prus, Bolesław. *Placówka* [*The Outpost*]. 1886. Edited by Tadeusz Żabski. Wrocław: Zakład Narodowy im. Ossolińskich, 1987.

Rössler, Mechtild, and Sabine Schleiermacher, eds. *Der "Generalplan Ost": Hauptlinien der nationalsozialistischen Planungs- und Vernichtungspolitik*. Berlin: Akademie, 1993.

Sienkiewicz, Henryk. *Bartek zwycięzca: Nowela*. 1882. Bielsko-Biała: Beskidzka Oficyna Wydawnicza, 1998.

———. *The Teutonic Knights*. Translated by Alicia Tyszkiewicz. Edited by Mirosław Lipiński. New York: Hippocrene, 1993. Originally published as *Krzyżacy* (1900).

Skórczewski, Dariusz. "Postkolonialna Polska—projekt (nie)możliwy" [Postcolonial Poland—an (im)possible project]. *Teksty drugie* 97–98 (2006): 100–112.

———. "Wobec eurocentryzmu, dekolonizacji i postmodernizmu: O niektórych problemach teorii postkolonialnej i jej polskich perspektywach" [Considerations of Eurocentrism, decolonization, and postmodernism: On various problems of postcolonial theory and its Polish perspectives]. *Teksty drugie* 109–10 (2008): 33–55.

Smith, Woodruff D. *The Ideological Origins of Nazi Imperialism*. New York: Oxford University Press, 1986.

Steinmetz, George. *The Devil's Handwriting: Precoloniality and the German Colonial State in Qingdao, Samoa, and Southwest Africa*. Chicago: University of Chicago Press, 2005.

Surynt, Izabela. *Das "ferne," "unheimliche" Land: Gustav Freytags Polen*. Dresden: Thelem, 2004.

———. *Postęp, kultura I kolonializm: Polska a niemiecki projekt europejskiego Wschodu w dyskursach publicznych XIX wieku* [Progress, Culture, and Colonialism: Poland and the German Project in Eastern Europe in Nineteenth-Century Social Discourse]. Wrocław: Centrum Studiów Niemieckich I Europejskich im. Willy Brandta Uniwersytetu Wrocławskiego, 2006.

Tims, Richard Wonser. *Germanizing Prussian Poland; the H-K-T Society and the Struggle for the Eastern Marches in the German Empire, 1894–1919*. New York: AMS Press, 1966.

Uerlings, Herbert. "Kolonialer Diskurs und deutsche Literatur: Perspektiven und Probleme." In *(Post-)Kolonialismus und deutsche Literatur: Impulse der angloamerikanischen Literatur- und Kulturtheorie*, edited by Axel Dunker, 17–44. Bielefeld: Aisthesis, 2005.

Wippermann, Wolfgang. *Der "deutsche Drang nach Osten": Ideologie und Wirklichkeit eines politischen Schlagwortes*. Darmstadt: Wissenschaftliche Buchgesellschaft, 1981.

———. "'Gen Ostland wollen wir reiten!' Ordensstaat und Ostsiedlung in der historischen Belletristik Deutschlands." In *Germania Slavica* 2, edited by Wolfgang Fritze, 187–235. Berlin: Duncker und Humblot, 1981.

Zantop, Susanne. *Colonial Fantasies: Conquest, Family, and Nation in Precolonial Germany, 1770–1870*. Durham, NC: Duke University Press, 1997.

Zimmerer, Jürgen. "The Birth of the *Ostland* Out of the Spirit of Colonialism: A Postcolonial Perspective on the Nazi Policy of Conquest and Extermination." *Patterns of Prejudice* 39, no. 2 (2005): 197–219.

———. *Von Windhuk nach Auschwitz? Beiträge zum Verhältnis von Kolonialismus und Holocaust*. Münster: LIT, 2007.

———. "Von Windhuk nach Warschau: Die rassische Privilegiengesellschaft in Deutsch-Südwestafrika—ein Modell mit Zukunft?" In *Rassenmischehen, Mischlinge, Rassentrennung: Zur Politik der Rasse im deutschen Kolonialreich*, edited by Frank Becker, 97–123. Stuttgart: Steiner, 2004.

8

Colonialism, and No End

The Other Continuity Theses

Russell A. Berman

Growing scholarly attention to German colonialism has provided a welcome correction to previous paradigms that focused too exclusively on internally and narrowly national processes. An extensive consideration of the history of the disciplines, above all literature and history, might be able to trace the source of that conventionally national and now increasingly outdated paradigm, in German Studies as well as in other fields. Literary fields are grappling with the challenge of "world literature," as historiography tries to understand what a "world history" might mean. The widened perspective, in any case, which surpasses those national constraints, despite their lingering influence, has resulted from engagement with new questions, in particular ours: what is German colonialism? In terms of disciplinary history, one can describe this shift from national to transnational investigations as an innovative transformation of the field, if not strictly speaking a broadening (except of course in a spatial and geographic sense) but a de facto displacement, for in an era of constrained or even shrinking resources (numbers of teaching and research personnel) the addition of this new topic (German colonialism) will necessarily lead to the disappearance of older ones. This process of displacement is a defining component of any innovation, in principle worth embracing, conditional on efforts to make the right intellectual choices. Adding a new subfield inescapably implies reducing or eliminating others: about this we should be honest. Hence the urgency to pose the question in the most productive manner. Yet—and this is the fundamental claim of this chapter—the potentially transformative strategies of German colonial studies so far have been, if anything, insufficiently innovative because the field has not gone far enough in relinquishing anachronistically national paradigms. In effect, the pertinent change of the field has only involved making some limited room for the study of colonialism in the Wilhelmine period (and a few decades on either side) as a footnote to national history, but it has so far missed out on the more profoundly transformative intellectual opportunities implied by the colonial question, if it were to be posed in a boldly comparative framework, without debilitating historicist and geographical constraints. The questions nationally bound historians—and literary historians—now pose are only slightly larger than in the past, hardly less indebted to national-historiographic paradigms and certainly no place in the sun. National history has taken on some transnational characteristics, but it is far from comparative and rarely global in scope.[1] Explaining such intellectual caution, if not to say timidity, is truly *ein weites Feld*. (Fontane's phrase itself was an overdetermined metaphor of imperial ambition.)[2]

Academics are generally not risk takers and rarely rock the boats of their particular disciplinary conventions. Moreover, German culture arguably also has its own penchant for provincialism and the coziness of the *kleine Welt*, which may carry over to the scholars who study it, whatever their individual provenance. In addition, we should not ignore how the importation of postcolonial studies from other national fields (British rule in India) carried with it congenital limitations already well established there. By and large, studies of colonialism and empire during recent decades have concerned nearly exclusively the non-European colonial territories of western European powers, and research has therefore been historically restricted to the study of phenomena of Western modernity—as if colonies and empires had existed nowhere else. This selective treatment of the potentially much more multifaceted topic of empire reflects in part the guilt culture that operates in parts of the western European academic world and in part the lingering influence of the Leninist paradigm of imperialism, which has rarely been subjected to serious critical examination: the only empires worth studying are the empires of European capitalism as part of a strategy to denounce those economies. By accepting this limitation, contemporary scholarship narrows its research and misses opportunities to broaden the discussion to include comparative and contrasting cases that could add considerable depth to our understanding. "German colonial studies" could have been the transnationalizing vehicle allowing an escape from the obsolete terms of national literary study or the nineteenth-century narrowness of a field like "German history." Yet so far scholarship has achieved little more than an enhanced national paradigm with a new topic, ripe for exploitation (an ironically colonial relationship to literally colonial material), with a touch of comfortable political correctness: a focus on German (and other Western European) colonial practices in the non-European world but on no other empires and no other colonies. The current critique of European colonialism remains thoroughly Eurocentric. This intellectual inconsistency in contemporary colonial and postcolonial studies might be taken as an ideological underdevelopment, an inability to think beyond national and European constraints, or it might indicate an unexpected durability of precisely those categories—nation and Europe—that would deserve an elaborate reflection; that, however, would go beyond the scope of this essay.

The opportunity to theorize colonies and empire across wider expanses of space and time was excluded from the start of the current wave of scholarly engagement. For England and France and their empires this framework could at least stretch back into early modernity. For Germany this limitation necessarily confined the discussion to decades around 1900 (unless one follows Susanne Zantop, who builds her case on literary representations alone, without bona fide extra-European colonial enterprises, an argument that can only go so far: there is, *pace* discourse theory, an existential distinction between genuine practices of external power projection and fictional depictions produced for domestic audiences).[3] German colonial studies therefore remain stuck, still, in a Wilhelmine historiography spruced up with some exoticizing colonial supplements. While colonial studies properly turns attention to what transpired in the colonies, it treats this new knowledge as thoroughly part of German history: the historiography of imperialism has become the highest stage of the national paradigm rather than a vehicle to surpass the nationalist epistemology altogether.

What kinds of questions, largely silenced to date at least within German colonial studies, might be posed to emancipate historiography from national structures? An answer requires a conceptual articulation of the object of study that would abstract from the specific Eurocentric experience of high imperialism and describe instead transnational—or, more appropriately, given the historical limitations even on the category of "nation"—transregional expansions of power through the direct use of violence, as well as the extension of symbolic networks of economics and culture; this broader, post-Foucauldian understanding of power not only indicates that colonialism was not merely about gunboats and invasions but that the obsessive binary of colony and metropolis, too, has to be dismantled to explore extensive and multidirectional networks of control and collaboration. An initial definition endowed with this sort of suppleness would allow scholarship to follow through on the intellectual promise of transnationality to work toward an effectively global and postparochial treatment of problems of empire, which then would enable us to gauge the character of nineteenth-century European imperialism and the specific features of German colonialism within a rich comparative field. It would also force a confrontation with many of the core conceptual, evaluative, and especially political presuppositions that define the field, often in unreflected ways. In other words, if German colonial studies is to be more than just the latest subfield within an unquestioned and quaintly linear national cultural historiography, it should be considered comparatively in relation to processes often quite far afield. We not only have to draw on models other than the exclusively West European empires of modernity; we also have to interrogate the credibility of the geographical terms that creep into our paradigms: why hold onto the primacy of national structures, if we are insisting on the importance of global processes?[4] In order to clarify these matters, I want first to review several intellectual and contextual components that determined the structure of current studies of German colonialism in order, secondly, to describe how research agenda could be enhanced through a comparative framework before, finally, suggesting two continuity theses, two big questions regarding German colonialism that would move the discussion out of conventional Wilhelmine limitations and lead to an engagement with major issues of considerable interest to a wide intellectual audience.

The recent studies of German colonialism emerged in the fields of literary and cultural scholarship, rather than in political or social history. Zantop's *Colonial Fantasies* marked an important turning point and opened up the topic for the wider fields associated with German Studies, especially although by no means exclusively in the United States. It is useful to reflect on the internal dynamic of this cross-disciplinary paradigm change. A set of research questions that developed outside of German Studies, in particular in postcolonial studies of Anglophone material, was imported into the German discussion. Interdisciplinarity often takes shape involving the lateral move of a cross-disciplinary borrowing in order to enhance the interpretive capacities of the scholar's initial community. Postcolonialism first focused primarily on the British Empire, especially the relationship between England and the Indian subcontinent, but quickly expanded to other regions as well. Parallel developments took place in the field of French with growing attention to African *francophonie*, which could not fail to raise questions of colonialism. While the hegemonic role of English within the study of literature in the United States goes a long way to explaining why smaller fields would soon follow suit, a full intellectual history of this transition has to address more than this imitative dependency and turn instead to several developments in philosophy, demography, and geopolitics which, in various ways, continue to mark the German discussion and frame efforts to define German colonialism as a scholarly topic.

The initial turn toward questions of German colonialism took place—among literary scholars in the United States long before historians anywhere—during the 1980s, when, in the era of high literary theory, the critique of colonialism, understood as the imperial practices of Western states during the nineteenth century, was rapidly conflated with a deconstructive critique of Western metaphysics, a connection articulated most forcefully by Gayatri Spivak, building on Derrida and Heidegger: Heidegger's post-Nietzschean suspicion of Western philosophy since Socrates somehow (such was the inflationary spirit of the decade) could seem congruent with resistance to practices of Western politics and economics identified as colonial or imperialist.[5] Not very far below the surface, an important inversion was taking place, a profound reconfiguration of anticolonial discourse, for the association of which with deconstructive philosophical paradigms was surely counterintuitive. The anticolonial advocates at the Versailles Treaty, who quickly grew deeply disappointed with the outcome of those negotiations, whether pertaining to Africa or China, argued in the name of Western ideals—humanism, liberty, democracy—which they took at face-value as properly pertaining to all of humanity, including the colonial subjects who were understood as aspiring for freedom. Making the world safe for democracy was taken to imply the need for democratic change not only in Germany but also in China and Africa and therefore the end to colonial rule. That, however, was notoriously not the victors' choice at Versailles, and contemporary critics of colonialism, such as W. E. B. Du Bois, could point out the hypocrisy when Western democrats refused to live up to their own stated ideals, ideals that Du Bois also embraced.[6] In contrast, late-twentieth-century academic anticolonialism, with its deconstructive and postmodern sensibility, frequently regarded those very same categories of humanism, liberty, and democracy as gravely problematic. Anticolonialism was no longer a matter of the hypocritical failure to apply these values; rather, these values were treated as carrying a specific internal logic that generated imperialist inflections: Western idealism was condemned as necessarily complicit with domination. Even "human rights" could therefore come to be seen as tainted by an irrevocably flawed "humanism," which from a post-Heideggerian perspective guaranteed the continuity of subject-object distinctions, a blindness to existence, and ultimately a master-slave relationship that underpinned imperialist hegemonies.

This philosophical turn took place in the context of a demographic transformation in the flow of labor and capital, typically addressed under the rubric of globalization. Traditional ideological representations of the population of the European states as ethnically homogeneous, which were certainly never accurate owing to the vitality of minority communities and long-standing practices of migration, became unsustainable given the scope of population flows in the second half of the twentieth century. These population displacements resulted from disparate causes and far-flung dislocations: intra-European refugees in the wake of World War II or resulting from Communist dictatorships in the East; workers seeking employment in the robust economies of European industrial powers (the foreign laborers from Yugoslavia, Italy, Greece and Turkey); former European colonial populations following economic promise from Algeria to France or from Morocco to Holland or fleeing postcolonial nationalism (East African Indians arriving in Britain); political refugees (from the Greek junta or the Allende regime in Chile); or the extensive and more general push from the global South to enter the global North. This demographic transition, which would periodically generate political attention, for example during the citizenship debate in Germany, or public concern regarding the annual deaths of Africans who drown while attempting to cross the Mediterranean to Spain or Italy, also impacted the scholarly sphere: the insularity of parochially national narratives became increasingly obsolete in the face of the undeniable transformation of the population.

Yet if these aspects of globalization subverted traditionally ethnonational paradigms and implied the necessity for directing scholarly attention to transnational processes, then one has to view the turn to the colonial problematic in literary studies or in history as one of the cultural consequences of globalization. Indeed, the era of high colonialism is best understood not as some absolute and fully pejorative binary that stands in simplistic contrast to an emancipated "postcolonial era" but as a prehistory to contemporary structures of transnationality, including globalization, international governance structures, and human rights discourse. Contemporary paradigms of globalization or transnationality inherit more from the geographic vision of colonialism than conventionally progressive scholars may be willing to concede. Both share a constitutive aversion to restrictive national models for narration and interpretation.

A third vector in this disciplinary transformation toward a recognition of colonialism and its importance in German cultural history concerns geopolitics. To be sure, this is not without irony. German colonialism itself was a specifically geopolitical move, a strategy designed to insert the newly established German nation-state into a world imperial system, which, dominated by England and France but also including Holland, Italy, Portugal and Spain, had been developing at least since the late fifteenth century. Elements in German society pushed the Bismarckian state, against its own conservative predispositions, to participate as well. The scholarly echo, a century after the "Scramble for Africa," has been for German Studies to scramble to insert itself into the colonial discussion as well, belatedly catching up with other literary fields. Yet this disciplinary geopolitics has taken place in an environment altogether different from the one that surrounded the imperial strategy of the nineteenth century: of primary relevance here is not the disciplinary environment of German Studies (a topic frequently discussed elsewhere) but the vicissitudes of the German "nation-state," divided and then unified, at the very moment of the colonial turn in scholarship. Context matters.

Discourses of postcolonialism drew on many heterogeneous sources (including the post-Heideggerian deconstruction referred to above), but they also internalized the rhetoric of Leninist anti-imperialism, which conflated the specifically colonial discussion with a characteristically dogmatic anti-capitalism and the politicized "internationalism" that had long been a defining ideological element of Communist culture. This whole convolute has informed aspects of the discussion of colonialism, and understanding this genealogy could mean exploring the urgent questions of political activism in scholarship as well as a hypothetical anticapitalist bias in the intelligentsia, intriguing topics that, nonetheless, point far beyond the scope of this essay. The germane point here, however, is that the very question "What is German colonialism?" (that is, the colonial turn in German Studies) draws on a critique of Western colonialism that itself had long been occupied by Communist discourse, as far back as Lenin, and this discourse functioned as a propagandistic vehicle for Soviet interests during the mid-twentieth-century processes of decolonization.[7] This strand in the genealogical derivation of anticolonialism therefore explains the stunning blindness of "German colonial studies": correctly, if belatedly identifying the participation of Wilhelmine Germany in European colonial practices, it has largely refused to interrogate the history of discursive representations of Germany itself as an object of colonialism, a standard trope of early-twentieth-century nationalist rhetoric, especially in the wake of the Versailles Treaty and the status of the German states after the Second World War, in particular the subordination of East Germany to the Soviet Union. After the collapse of the Soviet Empire the question has to be asked: can anti-imperialism be decolonized from the Leninist legacy? Intellectual integrity demands this sort of interrogation of the unreflected presuppositions that continue to structure and distort scholarly practice.

Understanding these constitutive constraints on the field can help clarify a more promising approach to the topic. Placing Wilhelmine colonialism in a nonpresentist and non-Eurocentric comparative framework would be an auspicious beginning. A more complex definition of German colonialism, which would include the appropriations of the 1880s but not be limited to them (and therefore in effect extrapolate from Zantop's paradigm), could continue to build on the 1980s philosophical turn and the hypothetical convergence of Western colonialism and Western metaphysics. Yet that metaphysical tradition obviously long predates late-nineteenth-century colonialism, so it would hardly be implausible to test the claim by examining older evidence and imperial formations. The early modern empires of Spain, England, France, and Portugal provide rich examples.[8] Yet precisely the German fields—in literature and history alike—could approach the colonial problem through a genealogical examination of older imperial discourse in an equally significant but radically different way, via the symbolism of the Holy Roman Empire, and its own appropriation of ancient Rome. Heidegger's philosophical account places considerable weight on the translational gap between Greek and Latin, and, in the era of high imperialism, Weber points to the imperial Roman transformation of the forms of Greek polity as defining of Western political rationality.[9] This intellectual and political engagement with ancient empires also plays out in the German classical engagement with

Greece and especially with the movement for Greek independence: was German support for Greek nationalists against Ottoman rule an early example of anticolonial sentiment or evidence of a Western Orientalism hostile to an Islamic state? The reassuring binary of a safe distinction between colonialism and anticolonialism may prove to be unstable, unsustainable, or just intellectually impoverished (in particular with regard to Western advocacy for oppressed minorities in non-Western regimes).[10]

Yet there is still more in the premodern era that can help define German colonialism, such as the occupation of central Europe by Roman forces, the names of whose settlements testify to the colonial project: *Köln* comes from *colonia*. The challenge to contemporary scholarship would be to open, or reopen, the study of this conflict between Rome and the northern European populations without succumbing to the nationalist narratives that dwelt on this material in the nineteenth century and that Heine parodied so trenchantly in *Deutschland, ein Wintermärchen*. A further element of this agenda to study German colonial discourse involves the transformation from an object of colonial power (Rome) into a colonial power on its own, especially in the various endeavors to expand German settlements in eastern Europe. It makes little sense to focus exclusively on the barely thirty years of Wilhelmine colonialism in Africa and the Pacific, or even the forty-five years of Russians in East Germany, while ignoring the longer and complicated involvement in violent transnational processes of power within Europe. Of course, there is scholarly work on all these topics: the point, though, is that they remain largely segregated from one another. What is needed is a genuinely comparative and global discussion of colonialism and empire that would draw on a wide diversity of cases.

The Roman Empire, as point of reference, provides a rich foil for discussing modern empires and their particular transnational dynamics. Through multiple refractions Germany inherited Roman paradigms (as did England, France, Italy, and Russia as well, in their own ways), and its structures of authority and codes of power stand in that tradition: this is exactly the implication of the various accounts of Western cultural continuity, especially the critical ones, such as Heidegger's or Horkheimer and Adorno's *Dialectic of Enlightenment*. In contrast the investigation into German (and more broadly European) empires could benefit from comparisons with other examples. The rise of Islam in the seventh century, the establishment of unified cultural and political regimes between Spain and central Asia, and the eventual establishment of Ottoman rule surely stand out as key examples with which to contrast European formations for multiple reasons: the physical presence in Europe (the Balkans and Spain), the long history of military conflict, the self-understanding of Europe in relation to the "Orient," and the later integrative discourse of Turkey as notionally part of Europe. As I will elaborate below, the significance for understanding German colonialism is particularly important given the status of the Middle East in Wilhelmine foreign policy.

For cultural approaches, however, the Ottoman Empire allows for a needed complication of Edward Said's thesis of orientalism: while exoticizing representational practices were crucial to European empires, can there be empires without orientalism?[11] Or did a similar semiotic exoticism operate elsewhere, outside of European conventions of representation? Is exoticism a function of empire in general or a peculiarity of Europe? As long as we are unwilling to interrogate German colonialism through a comparative relationship to Ottoman imperialism, let alone examples further afield, scholarship will remain cloistered within an arbitrarily and oddly anachronistic national interpretive frame. The inertia of conventional historiography resists comparisons between European and non-European political formations and, for whatever reasons, reserves studies of imperialism solely for the western European empires in order to condemn them; the consequence of this selection is a systemic blindness to Russian imperialism, including its Soviet aftermath, as well as a strikingly Eurocentric disregard to metaregional structures of power elsewhere. Malte Fuhrmann's blunt proscription of a comparative discussion of Turkish and German imperialisms leads him, moreover, to dodge the most salient topic for each, the genocides of Armenians and Jews, even though the very invention of the term *genocide* to describe the Holocaust drew explicitly on the Armenian precedent. Yet a historiography that can only marginalize the most important questions in the respective fields has clearly reached an epistemological dead end. Unless colonial studies escape national strictures, connections such as this, a history of imperialism from the standpoint of the victims, remain inaccessible.

A comparative study of empire very quickly points to a defining geographical problem: whether the extension of political rule takes place across contiguous or noncontiguous territories. The European colonizations of Africa in the late nineteenth century all involved noncontiguous appropriations of space: the colonies were at considerable distance from the respective "motherlands." This topography contrasts with expansionism on land through bordering, if increasingly distant territories: German and Austro-Hungarian extensions into eastern and southeastern Europe; Czarist Russian incorporation of central and East Asian territories as well as pan-Slavic ambitions in Europe; the growth of the Chinese Empire toward the north (Korea), the west (Tibet), and the south (Vietnam). The westward expansion of the United States, famously under the guise of "manifest destiny," lends itself to comparison with this set as well. Noncontiguous expansion requires naval capacity, which loomed large as a contested topic in late-nineteenth-century Germany. Contiguous expansionism is a function of military power on land, with ramifications for the structures of empire, as Carl Schmitt pointed out.[12] To date, German colonial studies appear to restrict interest primarily to noncontiguous examples, thereby excluding consideration of intra-European examples, such as the eighteenth-century partitions of Poland. Yet in what sense were Prussia, Russia, and Austria not participating in imperial rule?[13] The point is not to say that the structures of occupation were identical in German-ruled Africa but, precisely, to inquire into commonalities and differences. Just as distant colonies may resist settlers, contiguous imperial systems are inherently susceptible to irredentist resistance, efforts by borderlands to escape centralizing power. Vietnam was able to escape the Chinese Empire, while Tibet remains disputed; Poland's vicissitudes between two imperial spaces, Germany and Russia, bears comparison, involving anxieties that remain obviously and anxiously contemporary. Indeed, the whole Eastern European corridor between the *Großraum* of the European Union and Russia clearly remains susceptible to de facto imperial pressures from the East and the West. The study of German colonialism can only mature when it gives full transnational consideration to Warsaw and Kaliningrad, treating their relationship to German political power in a comparative field that includes Windhoek and Tsingtao.

"Colonialism" and "empire" are evidently used as critical categories in contemporary discourse; they are taken not only to designate transregional structures of domination but also to level an accusation at them. Territories should not be colonized, such is the implication, and powers should not be imperial. If the implicit values inherent in those claims seem uncontroversial, scholarship has largely refrained from providing a grounding for the judgment, and there is surely a significant difference between a consistently anarchist rejection of any exercise of power, for example, and a specific refusal of transregional power. If the point is (as is likely) the latter, the implication follows that power should be regional, not transregional, or, put more bluntly, the opposite of imperial rule may turn out to be nationalism. That, in any case, is the historical answer provided by the collapse of Austro-Hungary, which poses particular problems for colonial studies. Short of succumbing to Hapsburg nostalgia, we require a political-theoretical clarification to explain the a priori preferability of "nation" as an organizing principle over and against "empire." The name of the political program to emancipate nations from Hapsburg imperialist domination was Wilsonianism: the division of the lumbering multinational regime into units defined (more or less) in terms of segregated ethnicity and language on a plebiscitary basis. Nationalism as the aftermath of empire elsewhere sometimes became a tragic element of decolonization processes, and it stands in a tautly dialectical relationship to contemporary globalization, the current form of transregional organization. As far as the scholarly interrogation of German colonialism goes, it is perplexing to say at the least that the critique of empire can effectively imply the endorsement of nationhood—the postcolonial nation—as category, a further indicator of a conceptual inability to break out of the national paradigm. In fact, the whole line of thought draws stunningly close to the reactionary German nationalist rejection of Western imperialism.

Transregional rule initially implies a dynamic of expansion and therefore "bloody borders."[14] Yet it simultaneously involves the potential for an internal variegation in which a primary regime organizes, but does not obliterate or homogenize, the set of heterogeneous regions that make up the space of empire. It is here that the contrast between nation-state and empire is most pronounced, insofar as the former emphasizes a fundamentally homogenous population that finds its representation in a state structure (leaving the question of minorities for subsequent constitutional and political deliberation), while the latter is defined in terms of the diversity and inequality of its constituent parts. While a nation-state system tends toward centralized rule (with Jacobin France serving as the paradigmatic example), an imperial system tilts toward federal arrangements, some historically and politically contested distribution of power between local institutions and central authority. This is the framework in which German colonialism, particularly of the Wilhelmine era, has to be theorized, for the Reich was itself established, more than a decade prior to the overseas colonial expansion, precisely as a metaregional structure. There was undoubtedly a significantly unequal distribution of power between Prussia and the other units, yet it would be wrong to describe the German Empire in terms of Prussian centralism in the way that power in France came to be concentrated in Paris. The history of post-Napoleonic Germany involved the gradual spread of direct Prussian power, as well as the integration of institutional networks across a complex territory of significantly different and semiautonomous units. The categorical differentiations between national unification, territorial acquisition, colonialism, and empire are difficult to define: the Prussian annexation of Hanover in 1866, the integration of Alsace-Lorraine after the Franco-Prussian war, the character of Prussian rule over the non-German populations in the East (let alone the large Polish immigration from the East into the Ruhr region: an indicator of the metanational diversity of the imperial regime, the tendency for colonized populations to be drawn into the economic dynamism of the colonizing power, and the complicated process of largely successful assimilation). The populations in the German colonies provide additional examples of the complexity of the Reich: the administration in Cameroon was not the same as in Southwest Africa.

Political rule in the era of German colonialism therefore cannot be described in terms of a homogenous nation-state or a transparent centralization of power, undertaking simple acquisitions of foreign territory. To understand "German colonialism," we have to examine the multiple dimensions of German rule in Africa and the Pacific, but that cannot be uncoupled from the various institutions and multiple practices of Prussian administration of diverse regions of central Europe. Moreover, in addition to this textured political-legal landscape, scholarship of German colonialism is remiss in not considering the overwhelming demographic development of the period, the constant emigration of ethnic Germans to the United States, Canada, Australia, and South Africa, as well as to parts of South America. This enormous participation of "Germans" in the settlement of the various countries that received the great population flow out of Europe during the nineteenth century is a crucial component of the overall transformation and the dissemination of European power, understood complexly. Colonial propagandists agitated for German colonies precisely in order not to relinquish this population to demographic growth in the United States and the British Empire: better to settle in German Africa than in Wisconsin or Texas, they pleaded, albeit with little success.[15] German colonialism ultimately failed in this endeavor because it could not align its overseas territorial acquisitions with the emigration ambitions of the population.

These four points of reference—the Roman Empire and its tradition, the question of contiguous or noncontiguous expansion, nationalism as the alternative to Austro-Hungarian imperial rule, and the complexities of German federalism coupled with emigration patterns—indicate how much broader a scholarship on transregional power networks could become and how colonial studies could grow into more than a minor supplement to Wilhelmine history. Yet German colonial studies could also achieve greater complexity while escaping a historicist narrowing by paying attention to "continuity theses," that is, claims regarding continuity in German history, the consequences and afterlives of colonialism. Continuity theses have often figured prominently in German historiography, a feature of the field that results presumably from radical regime changes, which have necessarily provoked the skeptical question as to how much ever truly changes and whether structures and institutions (let alone personnel) survive across the dramatic historical ruptures. Continuity allegations between the Kaiserreich and the Weimar Republic have typically addressed the stability of the government infrastructure, with the implication that the imperial officialdom retained sufficient power to limit, resist, and eventually undermine democratic developments; continuity claims from Weimar to the Nazis involve assertions regarding industrial power and economic leaders, although the Frankfurt School notoriously also impugned aspects of Weimar cinematic culture as already anticipating if not laying the way for Hitler; and continuity theses across the divide between 1945 and the establishment of the two Germanys in 1949 largely served polemical purposes in the context of the cold war.

Yet just because a continuity thesis has rhetorical power does not mean it is irrelevant. Some continuity may be genuine and substantive, even if such a claim goes against the grain of received opinion. (The very rhetorical structure of continuity claims makes a polemical effect likely, since they involve the assertion of a durable identity against presumptions of disruption and innovation.) Two such theses are particularly pertinent to the study of German colonialism: one involves the genealogy of Communist internationalism and the other the resilience of Nazi ideological tropes.

A key starting point for a discussion of German colonialism and continuities in German history is Hannah Arendt's *The Origins of Totalitarianism* precisely because it spans pre- and postcolonial European political formations, and it devotes one of its three structural segments to the question of imperialism. Such a prominent focus on overseas expansionism alone is a relative rarity: while scholars of German colonialism still complain that the topic was marginalized until fairly recently, Arendt addressed it head-on more than half a century ago with the claim that imperialism had to be integrated into any discussion of the core developments in European history. Of course, her approach benefits from her particular cross-national argument, moving from British imperialism to German totalitarianism, a methodology that continues to irritate scholars trapped in national paradigms. That she could articulate a critique of colonialism from her vantage point as a conservative thinker—one can accurately describe her position as anticolonial from the right—makes it all the more remarkable and a world apart from the standard neo-Leninist denunciations of imperialism as the "highest stage" of capitalism. While Arendt and Lenin, obviously, share a concern with the same topic—imperialism—the similarity ends there: there is a world of difference between his economistic determinism and her neo-Aristotelian ethics.[16]

The Arendtian thesis that colonial violence paved the way, at least in political thinking, from extermination of indigenous populations in Africa to the war of annihilation against the Jews of Europe, a hypothesis of a de facto continuity between colonialism and National Socialism, is discussed elsewhere in this volume.[17] Her overall argument suggests, however, another bold thesis, equally if not more controversial since it concerns the roots of Communist foreign policy as an effect of imperialism. To highlight this thesis requires retracing her core argument.

Although *The Origins of Totalitarianism* is often read as a comparative description of Nazi Germany and Stalinist Russia, it pursues a different agenda: a descriptive account of the concept of totalitarianism as a new political form, an addition to a short list of political types that, according to Arendt, had remained stable since antiquity: democracy, tyranny, monarchy, aristocracy. Insistent that the totalitarianism of Germany and Russia had to be distinguished from the normal dictatorships of the past, which she claims pursued a rational and utilitarian, if often brutal, maintenance of power, she traces the elaboration of more radical goals under Hitler and Stalin. Without claiming a simplistic identity between Nazism and Communism, she does assert a profound comparability, which won her the enmity of the left, typically reluctant to engage in critiques of Communism. Although Arendt's presentation ranges over several European national histories, she does not make truly national-historical claims: her argument does not concern a continuity between the German nineteenth century and the German twentieth, and there is next to no discussion of nineteenth-century Russia, despite the extensive focus on the Bolshevik regime and its consequences. The overall argument rather involves the trans-European transformation of political-theoretical categories as refracted through and reflected in the historical experience of modernity. The examination of anti-Semitism in the first section of her book focuses on France through the Dreyfus affair. Her point, however, is not the history of French prejudice but rather how liberal civic thought in Europe underwent a profound degradation, which paved the way for the exclusion of Jews from citizenship a few decades later in Germany and, by extension, the wholesale erosion of the category of citizenship in totalitarianism. Similarly, if Arendt were writing parochially national histories, it would make little sense to focus, as she does in the second section, on British imperialism to explain twentieth-century German and Russian behavior. This incongruity disappears, however, once one recognizes the character of her argument, which involves the transformation of Europe-wide political thinking, not the vicissitudes of national institutions. Changes in one country have ripple effects across the political-theoretical continent. It is this transnational argument about imperialism and totalitarianism that has an explosive ramification for German colonial studies.

The core of the argument about imperialism involves the ambitions of the bourgeoisie to expand: to grow, to acquire, and, in particular, to stretch national sovereignty into new territories. In contrast to Lenin, Arendt avoids dubious economic hypotheses about an alleged objective need to export surplus capital. On the contrary, her description builds on an Aristotelian critique of imprudent expansion and, hence, gives expression to a conservative anti-imperialism. It is this specifically modern pursuit of the infinite that transgresses national borders and develops an international agenda that takes the shape of the "Scramble for Africa." Through that imperial experience Europe acquires a capacity for administrative bureaucracy, which boomerangs back to the home countries, undermining civic virtue and amplifying the power of the state. It is also in the imperialist setting that racism becomes virulent: this, too, returns to Europe in doctrines of a master race and subhumanity. Yet if that element of imperialism, in Arendt's description, finds its afterlife in the totalitarianism of race—Nazi Germany—imperialism is also reborn and transfigured in the alternative totalitarianism of class, Stalinist Russia, where the postnational transgressiveness of bourgeois imperialism in the nineteenth century is resurrected as internationalism in the service of Soviet foreign policy in the twentieth century.

An argument for some continuity between the European nineteenth century and the European twentieth would require no big leap of faith, since it would not challenge the bias toward the primacy of national definitions. To argue a continuity between nineteenth-century imperialism and twentieth-century Nazism is a more specific assertion, more susceptible to greater skeptical scrutiny, but it would not irritate standard value judgments: one evil, colonialism, is hypothetically set in relation to another evil, Nazi Germany.

Connecting imperialism to Stalinism seems trickier, however—Arendt's overall argument in *The Origins of Totalitarianism* implies this connection, but she does not spell it out—not only because of the displacement from one national history to another (this never seems to bother her, and it holds for all the elements of her cross-national accounts) but because of a still lingering effort to spare Communism and even Stalinism the most stringent criticism, in particular any "anti-imperialist" criticism (although the accusation that the Soviet Union pursued Russian hegemonic ambitions under the guise of internationalism has hardly been absent from Chinese political thought). Nonetheless, the claim is compelling: for Arendt the imperialism of bourgeois acquisitiveness generated visions of world conquest, subverting Westphalian respect for territorial borders and issuing into world-domination fantasies based on either race or class. Soviet internationalism inherited the Czarist prison house of nations; instead of liberating them, Communism redefined the justification for empire through the ostensibly progressive pretext of an internationalist doctrine of world liberation: hence the occupation of the Baltics, the massacre at Katyn, the Brezhnev doctrine in the Prague Spring or the invasion of Afghanistan, let alone efforts at noncontiguous expansion throughout the Third World.

If this repressive internationalism derives from the transnational ambitions of nineteenth-century imperialism, repackaged as progressive revolution, then the research agenda of German colonialism suddenly faces the obligation to examine its "left" ramifications, and not only the "right." As far as literary studies go, this could mean, for example, that colonial discourse analysis should not limit itself to, for example, Hans Grimm, whose *Volk ohne Raum* was the foundational novelistic plea for a post-Versailles German colonial agenda in Africa; it should also address figures on the other end of the political spectrum, such as Bertolt Brecht, even if such a suggestion runs thoroughly counter to standard literary-historical assumptions. It is, nonetheless, well established that Brecht drew liberally and productively from the imperialist poet par excellence, Rudyard Kipling.[18] The insinuated ideological continuity from Kipling to Brecht is hard to fathom, to be sure, owing to the alternative political locations as much as to the conventional literary-historical categorizations—the Victorian Kipling versus the modernist Brecht—unless one takes note of their transnational ambitions. In the case of Kipling, whom George Orwell famously dubbed the "prophet of imperialism," the case is clear; yet it is equally clear that in *The Measures Taken* Brecht notoriously stages an argument for the exportation of revolution or, more specifically, a heroization of the intrusion of agents of Russian foreign policy into China. The play has primarily elicited a discussion of the morality of political agitation, the conflict between subjective identification with suffering and the obligations to the party; but, from the standpoint of colonial discourse analysis, it undertakes a stunning elision between a transformative agenda to change the world and a transnational, imperial agenda to conquer the world: "We came as agitators from Moscow," the central figures declare at the outset, and this spatial extension is nowhere interrogated by the text.[19] The agenda of world conquest is accepted without question or criticism, and from this German colonial fantasy—Brecht's vicarious participation in Russian extraterritorial expansion—it is a short step to the intellectual challenge to examine Germany itself as colonized territory in the case of the GDR. "We came as agitators from Moscow" might as well have been the slogan of the Communist leadership that returned to Berlin after 1945. Lacking any genuine nation-state autonomy and extensively integrated into the institutional apparatus of a transnational system dominated by the Soviet Union, the GDR provides a contrastive foil to the forms of colonial rule that developed in the Wilhelmine era. This material belongs to the field of study subsumable under the rubric of German colonialism: Germany as colonized, in addition to Germany as colonizer, as well as the ambiguity of those two positions, yielding, however, a complexity that resists incorporation into the sort of simplistic political agenda that sometimes hovers around scholarship on colonial topics.

This argument for an expanded account of German colonialism traces a continuity from imperialism to totalitarianism, following Arendt, but shifts that genealogy from National Socialism to Communism, on the basis of their shared, if alternative world-conquest ambitions. The specifically German inflections of postimperialist internationalism as a covert practice of colonialism involve the vicissitudes of Communism in multiple locations, not only on the periphery of the USSR, but especially in East and Central Europe and, of interest to us, in East Germany. How did this variant of transnationality operate within the confines of the "sub-nation-state" of the GDR? The very parochialism of East Germany, its claustrophobic stuffiness, depended on a congenital internalization and inversion of the world-transforming ambitions inherent in the heroic rhetoric of Communist internationalism, which, as hegemonic ideology, justified the Soviet occupation. A vicarious identification with "world revolution" and the Soviet superpower provided ideological compensation in the carceral state behind the Wall with its panoptical *Stasi*.

No doubt some scholars dismiss any account of Soviet imperialism as "anticommunist" (Fuhrmann); they then owe us an explanation as to why the Russian occupation of East and Central Europe in the name of internationalism does not deserve to be sanctioned as a colonial process. Whoever does not want to talk about Katyn should not talk about Sétif.[20]

A second continuity thesis traces parallel legacies of Nazi ideology along a temporal spectrum, leading backward to elements of Wilhelmine foreign-policy aspirations in the Eastern Mediterranean and forward to strands of radicalism in the wider Middle East, which are of particular interest to scholars of German culture, at the very least as understudied examples of the international reception of German material. At stake here are the German imperialist ambitions in regard to the Ottoman Empire and in competition with other imperial powers, a complex history that involves commercial networks, Protestant missionary activity, characteristically nineteenth-century grand schemes, such as the Berlin-to-Baghdad railroad project, and Wilhelm's own personal sense of grandeur evidenced in his elaborately staged 1898 entry into Jerusalem through Jaffa Gate. Yet all of this was framed, ultimately, by the German efforts to compete with England, France, and Russia on the world stage, and this factor of interimperial rivalry continued after 1918 and after 1933 as well. Inheriting German strategies for the region established during Weimar, the National Socialist state initially pursued a foreign policy in the Middle East tempered by efforts to minimize hostility with England; in other words, it viewed the region, and Palestine in particular, as a bargaining chip for European relations rather than as a terrain for specific undertakings. Within a few years, however, German policy underwent a radicalization—consistent with a broader radicalization of National Socialism—as the plausibility of an alliance with England declined, which led Germany to begin to support the anticolonial movement against England, especially the newly formed Muslim Brotherhood. The specific complexity of these politics derives from the elision of the imperialist (if not specifically colonial) external projection of the power of a European state (Germany) with an emerging anticolonial movement: Berlin supported the Egyptian opponents of its enemy in London. Despite this stark reversal of course, the German agenda still involved an instrumentalization of the Middle East for intra-European goals: the erstwhile effort to accommodate England metamorphosed into an increasingly belligerent competition with England, but it was England that remained the point of reference.

This hardly subtle Machiavellian geometry of alliances took on a new and profoundly transformative significance, however, that surpassed conventional models of interimperialist competition as a result of the accelerating radicalism of the Nazi agenda and the racial extremism of the ideological content. The German connection to anti-British activists not only channeled financial support to the Middle East; it also contaminated the Arab anticolonial movement with the obsessiveness of Nazi anti-Semitism, significantly influencing the indigenous anticolonialism, which took on a specifically anti-Jewish character. Needless to say, German intrusion could not thoroughly determine the complex and multifaceted character of Arab politics.[21] It could however influence it sufficiently to reorient its development. Thus, Arab anticolonial activism shifted away from the major population arena, British-dominated Egypt, which might have provided fertile territory as the primary candidate for agitation, turning instead to a peripheral territory, Palestine, where German influence with its programmatic anti-Semitism allowed for an amplification of hostility to the Jewish settlers because they were Jews. Instead of waging an anticolonial war against the British Empire, Arab forces, supported by Nazi propaganda and other resources, redirected their anticolonialism into a war against the Jews. While it is hardly surprising that, as Derek J. Penslar has pointed out, Arab anti-Semitism obviously differed in ways from European anti-Semitism, some of those distinctive features, especially traditionally Judeophobic elements in Islam, catalogued in detail by Andrew Bostom, proved fertile ground for Nazi rhetoric.[22] Matthias Küntzel and Klaus Gensicke have traced this connection from the original German support for the Muslim Brotherhood in Cairo and the Grand Mufti of Jerusalem, who would eventually relocate to Berlin in order to provide propaganda broadcasts on Nazi radio to the Arab world during the war.[23] In his *Nazi Propaganda for the Arab World* Jeffrey Herf provides extensive documentation of the interplay between propaganda and warfare in the era.[24] This confluence of Nazi ideology and Arab extremism was later solidified by the several Nazi figures who found safe haven in Egypt and Syria after the war, sometimes attaining influence in the political sphere, as did the former Free Corps member and Nazi author Johann von Leers, who became an adviser to the Information Department in Cairo. He embodies the second continuity thesis, the transition from Wilhelmine imperialist aspirations through Nazi policy shifts to the ideological influencing of parts of Arab nationalism with a programmatic anti-Semitism, which remains a painful problem in contemporary debates over Israel and Palestine.

Of course, Arab nationalism, anticolonialism, and even anti-Zionism extend beyond the specific legacy of Nazi ambitions in the region; National Socialism was not the sole source of Arab anti-Zionism, nor, however, should one be blind to the Nazi impact on Arab politics or naively suggest that a critique of the dissemination of Nazi ideology in the Middle East is somehow "anti-Arab" (Fuhrmann). To claim that the violent attacks on the refugee population of the Yishuv during the 1930s were simply anticolonial and not also anti-Jewish—or simply xenophobic—is akin to describing the Nazi boycott of Jewish stores in Germany on April 1, 1933, as expressions of anticapitalism without anti-Semitism or treating the book burnings as disinterested literary criticism. The scope of the anti-Jewish potential in the politically active segment of the Arab population in Palestine was considerable, frequently linked to pro-German and pro-Hitler sympathies, especially as Rommel's army made headway across North Africa. Had he not been defeated at El Alamein, German forces might very plausibly have been able to cross the Suez Canal and occupy Palestine. In that case the SS *Einsatzkommando Rauff* stood prepared to oversee an extension of the genocide then under way in Europe and for which it could certainly count on the murderous assistance of local collaborators, as was the case in eastern Europe. Indeed, Hitler had explicitly endorsed the spread of anti-Jewish terror in Palestine in advance of the anticipated Rommel victory and the goal of putting an end to the plan for a Jewish state.[25]

Yet Rommel met defeat, and the SS could not extend the Shoah to Palestine, to the disappointment of Germany's Arab admirers; Arendt reported how, as the Eichmann trial opened years later in Jerusalem, "a broadcast from Cairo . . . even injected a slightly anti-German note into its comments, complaining that there was not 'a single incident in which one German plane flew over one Jewish settlement and dropped one bomb on it throughout the last war.' "[26] While the anti-Jewish agenda failed and the Yishuv was not eradicated, the German *Umfunktionierung* of Arab anticolonialism in Palestine had considerable repercussions elsewhere in the region. In the wave of decolonization that followed the Second World War, Arab nationalism could easily make room for Christians, as well as Muslims; indeed, the movement was largely modernizing and secular (in stark contrast to the subsequent Islamization of politics in the region), and Christian Arabs could even play a prominent role in Arab anti-Zionism. Yet Arab nationalism, having learned its German lessons, had no need for Arab Jews: the long-standing communities of indigenous Jewish populations from North Africa to Baghdad were expelled to Israel, where, today, the majority of the Jewish population traces its background to the Arab world. To be sure, those mass expulsions reflected characteristic tendencies toward a modernizing homogenization in the spirit of postcolonial nationalism that typically has little tolerance for minority communities and by no means solely in the Arab world.[27] The underlying assumption, however, that Jews could not be at home in majority Arab countries and that they were effectively deemed foreigners who belonged elsewhere rendered them vulnerable targets of populist rage, in Cairo as much as in Baghdad: part of the legacy of the Nazi influence, a vestige of an ideological colonization that had promoted a simplistic identification of Zionism and Jews and, therefore, of anti-Zionism and anti-Semitism. The results were as tragic for the Jewish communities throughout the Arab world as they remain for the prospects for political reconciliation.

While Communist internationalism eventually redirected the question of German colonialism internally onto Germany itself in the GDR, the afterlife of Nazism introduced a toxic German heritage into the Middle East. Both lineages deserve examination and therefore indicate the importance of avoiding a narrow and chronologically foreshortened concept of German colonialism: colonialism involves the external projection of power by various means, not only military occupation or economic domination, and cultural or ideological penetrations can have greater durability than particular state structures. The necessity for a complex and variegated understanding of the transnational deployment of power may frustrate a historiography still trapped within the model of the nineteenth-century nation-state. The salutary attention that scholarship has directed toward colonialism and imperialism in the past two decades therefore offers an opportunity for a thoroughgoing paradigm shift beyond the model of national historiography, although this will imply profound restructurings of important areas of scholarship, not only in terms of content of their institutional arrangements. Colonial studies should not be trivialized as the latest footnote to that sort of national historiography; it is, rather, a step forward toward a postnational and global hermeneutics that forsakes the fetishization of national territory or nation-states as the non plus ultra of political or cultural communities. Reforming structures of scholarship is never easy, but the opportunities for vibrantly comparative and transnational perspectives are extraordinary. Too much is at stake in terms of the possibilities of understanding in the age of globalization for us to fall back comfortably into past bad habits, which would only conceal the multiple and far-reaching consequences of nineteenth-century imperialism for transnational processes in the twentieth and twenty-first centuries.

Notes

1. The essays in the noteworthy volume *Das Kaiserreich transnational* demonstrate the liminal position of recent historiography, addressing transnational matters but still within a fundamentally national paradigm.

2. "A broad field" or "a large topic" is the leitmotific disclaimer of the father of the eponymous heroine of *Effi Briest*, the best-known novel of German realism by Theodor Fontane. The phrase indicates a culture of repression in which difficult topics are declared too large for consideration, but it also points to a rhetoric of space that underpins the novel and that in various ways points to a thematic concern with Wilhelmine imperialism.

3. See Zantop, *Colonial Fantasies*, 17–42.

4. Instead of arguing that (European) nations appropriate (non-European) colonies, the more dynamic argument involves the subversion of traditional nationality precisely through the imperial process: imperialism undermines the imperialist nation. While this trope is consistent with Hannah Arendt's discussion in *The Origins of Totalitarianism*, it has been rearticulated recently in Hardt and Negri, *Empire*.

5. See Spivak, *In Other Worlds*.

6. See Lewis, *W. E. B. Du Bois*, 564–80.

7. See Lenin, *Imperialism*.

8. See Pagden, *European Encounters with the New World*.

9. Heidegger, "The Origin of the Work of Art," 22–24; and Weber, "Politics as Vocation," 96.

10. See my *Enlightenment or Empire*, 203–39.

11. Said, *Orientalism*; see also Warraq, *Defending the West*.

12. See Schmitt, *The Nomos of the Earth in the International Law of the "Jus Publicum Europaeum,"* 172–84. Of course, such expansionism does not depend on military power alone but on complex forms of cultural appropriation as well, as has been demonstrated in George Steinmetz's seminal study, *The Devil's Handwriting*.

13. In this volume A. Dirk Moses addresses the contrast between overseas colonialism and the imperial rule of Austro-Hungary, Germany, and Russia in eastern Europe. Indeed, all variants belong in the discussion. Moses, however, attempts to undercut the relevance of the experience of German colonialism in Africa for the subsequent history of the Holocaust, suggesting that the pertinent background was the intra-European structure of empire. Arendt, however, moved unproblematically between the two types in her analyses of imperialism and its consequences for the emergence of totalitarianism, which is the relevant point here. For recent treatments of the German colonization of Poland and "the East" see Nelson, *Germans, Poland, and Colonial Expansion to the East*.

14. See Huntington, *The Clash of Civilizations and the Remaking of World Order*.

15. For a definitive example of a demographic argument for colonization see Fabri, *Bedarf Deutschland der Colonien?* See also Bade, *Friedrich Fabri und der Imperialismus in der Bismarckzeit*.

16. Of course, Arendt was an admirer of Rosa Luxemburg, who, however, can hardly be viewed as Leninist. Arguably, it is precisely the aspects of Luxemburg's thought that are farthest from Bolshevism that intrigued Arendt. It is worth considering whether a line can be drawn between Luxemburg's own critique of the Russian Revolution and Arendt's dissection of its legacy in *The Origins of Totalitarianism*. See Spencer, "From Rosa Luxemburg to Hannah Arendt."

17. See, e.g., A. Dirk Moses's chapter.

18. Lyon, *Bertolt Brecht and Rudyard Kipling*.

19. Brecht, *The Measures Taken and Other Lehrstücke*, 9.

20. Zaslavsky, *Class Cleansing*; Diner, *Gegenläufige Gedächtnisse*, 64–103; see also Moses, this volume.

21. Wildangel, *Zwischen Achse und Mandatsmacht*; Höpp, Wien, and Wildangel, *Blind für Geschichte?*

22. Penslar, "Anti-Semites on Zionism"; Bostom, *The Legacy of Islamic Antisemitism*. See also Sivan, *Islamic Fundamentalism and Antisemitism*, 18.

23. Küntzel, *Jihad and Jew-Hatred*; Klaus Gensicke, *Der Mufti von Jerusalem und die Nationalsozialisten*.

24. Herf, *Nazi Propaganda for the Arab World*.

25. Mallmann and Cüppers, "'Beseitigung der jüdisch-nationalen Heimstätte in Palästina,'" 160.

26. Arendt, *Eichmann in Jerusalem*, 13.

27. Diner, *Gegenläufige Gedächtnisse*, 102–3.

Bibliography

Arendt, Hannah. *Eichmann in Jerusalem*. Middlesex: Penguin, 1965.

Bade, Klaus J. *Friedrich Fabri und der Imperialismus in der Bismarckzeit: Revolution, Depression, Expansion*. Freiburg: Atlantis, 1975.

Berman, Russell A. *Enlightenment or Empire: Colonial Discourse in German Culture*. Lincoln: University of Nebraska Press, 1998.

Bostom, Andrew. *The Legacy of Islamic Antisemitism: From Sacred Texts to Solemn History*. New York: Prometheus, 2008.

Brecht, Bertolt. *The Measures Taken and Other Lehrstücke*. New York: Arcade Press, 1977.

Conrad, Sebastian, and Jürgen Osterhammel. *Das Kaiserreich transnational: Deutschland in der Welt, 1871–1914*. Göttingen: Vandenhoeck und Ruprecht, 2004.

Diner, Dan. *Gegenläufige Gedächtnisse: Über Geltung und Wirkung des Holocaust.* Göttingen: Vandenhoeck und Ruprecht, 2007.

Fabri, Friedrich. *Bedarf Deutschland der Colonien?—eine politisch-ökonomische Betrachtung.* Gotha: F. Perthes, 1884.

Gensicke, Klaus. *Der Mufti von Jerusalem und die Nationalsozialisten: Eine politische Biographie Amin el-Husseinis.* Darmstadt: Wissenschaftliche Buchgesellschaft, 2007.

Hardt, Michael, and Antonio Negri. *Empire.* Cambridge, MA: Harvard University Press, 2000.

Heidegger, Martin. "The Origin of the Work of Art." In *Poetry, Language, Thought.* New York: Harper and Row, 2001.

Herf, Jeffrey. *Nazi Propaganda for the Arab World.* New Haven, CT: Yale University Press, 2009.

Höpp, Gerhard, Peter Wien, and René Wildangel, eds. *Blind für Geschichte? Arabische Begegnungen mit dem Nationalsozialismus.* Berlin: Klaus Schwarz, 2004.

Huntington, Samuel P. *The Clash of Civilizations and the Remaking of World Order.* New York: Simon and Schuster, 1996.

Küntzel, Matthias. *Jihad and Jew-Hatred: Islamism, Nazism and the Roots of 9/11.* New York: Telos, 2007.

Lenin, V. I. *Imperialism: The Highest Stage of Capitalism.* London: Pluto, 1996.

Lewis, David Levering. *W. E. B. Du Bois: Biography of a Race, 1868–1919.* New York: Henry Holt, 1993.

Lyon, James K. *Bertolt Brecht and Rudyard Kipling: A Marxist's Imperialist Mentor.* The Hague: Mouton, 1975.

Mallmann, Klaus-Michael, and Martin Cüppers. "'Beseitigung der jüdisch-nationalen Heimstätte in Palästina': Das Einsatzkommando bei der Panzerarmee Afrika, 1942." In *Deutsche, Juden, Völkermord: Der Holocaust als Geschichte und Gegenwart,* edited by Jürgen Matthäus and Klaus-Michael Mallmann, 153–76. Darmstadt: Wissenschaftliche Buchgesellschaft, 2006.

Nelson, Robert L., ed. *Germans, Poland, and Colonial Expansion to the East: 1850 Through the Present.* New York: Palgrave, 2009.

Pagden, Anthony. *European Encounters with the New World: From Renaissance to Romanticism.* New Haven, CT: Yale University Press, 1994.

Penslar, Derek J. "Anti-Semites on Zionism: From Indifference to Obsession." *Journal of Israeli History* 25, no. 1 (March 2006): 13–31.

Said, Edward W. *Orientalism.* New York: Parthenon, 1978.

Schmitt, Carl. *The Nomos of the Earth in the International Law of the "Jus Publicum Europaeum."* New York: Telos, 2003.

Sivan, Emmanuel. *Islamic Fundamentalism and Antisemitism.* Jerusalem: Shazar Library, 1985.

Spencer, Philip. "From Rosa Luxemburg to Hannah Arendt: Socialism, Barbarism and the Extermination Camps." *European Legacy* 11, no. 5 (2006): 527–40.

Spivak, Gayatri Chakravorty. *In Other Worlds: Essays in Cultural Politics*. New York: Methuen, 1997.

Steinmetz, George. *The Devil's Handwriting: Precoloniality and the German Colonial State in Qingdao, Samoa, and Southwest Africa*. Chicago: University of Chicago Press, 2007.

Warraq, Ibn. *Defending the West: A Critique of Edward Said's "Orientalism."* Amherst, NY: Prometheus Books, 2007.

Weber, Max. "Politics as Vocation." In *From Max Weber: Essays in Sociology*, edited by H. H. Gerth and C. Wright Mills, 77–128. New York: Oxford University Press, 1958.

Wildangel, René. *Zwischen Achse und Mandatsmacht: Palästina und der National-Sozialismus*. Berlin: Klaus Schwarz, 2007.

Zantop, Susanne. *Colonial Fantasies: Conquest, Family, and Nation in Precolonial Germany, 1770–1870*. Durham, NC: Duke University Press, 1997.

Zaslavsky, Viktor. *Class Cleansing: The Massacre at Katyn*. New York: Telos, 2008.

PART IV
Of Missionaries, Economics, and Intranational Self-Perception

9

The Purpose of German Colonialism, or the Long Shadow of Bismarck's Colonial Policy

Hartmut Pogge von Strandmann

Recent economic news has suggested that China's rising industrial strength threatens Germany's position as the world's leading exporter of manufactured goods. The expansion of Germany's industrial economy started in the middle of the nineteenth century, as did its drive to increase its share in world trade. Germany soon became one of the leading exporters, a position the country has kept up to the present, despite losing two world wars in the twentieth century. The country's exports and imports reached their initial peak during the last thirty years before World War I. Compared with the figures of 1880, they had more than trebled. By 1913 nearly 70 percent of Germany's exports consisted of manufactured goods, whereas 58 percent of its imports were raw materials and semifinished products. A continuous search for new markets and cheap sources of much-needed raw materials accompanied Germany's conversion from a predominantly agricultural economy in the early nineteenth century to an industrial one at the end of the century. Most economic expansion in Europe and overseas was due to new economic opportunities and the emergence of an early global economy. Before the First World War, Germany's share of world exports had reached 13 percent, whereas by 1928 it had fallen to less than 10 percent, a figure that had been even lower three years earlier.¹

Although most mid-nineteenth-century businessmen operated under the flag of free trade, German steel and iron industrialists and agrarians campaigned after the crash of 1873 for a reintroduction of protective tariffs to fend off cheaper foreign competition. In this climate it was natural for business circles to expect governmental assistance in creating nationally secured overseas markets. The campaign for cooperation in this field had been going on for several years when the government finally followed other European powers and acquired a number of colonies. Although it was a sudden governmental decision to acquire the first colonies between 1883 and 1885, the business community had been anticipating this action for some time. From the point of view of German businessmen it looked as if Germany had virtually grown into the position of a colonial state. The annexation of colonial territories was not the result of a war of conquest, nor did its colonial possessions lead to any immediate international conflicts. Germany's overseas ventures received international recognition by the Berlin Africa Conference in 1884–85 and by bilateral agreements with Britain and France. Nonetheless, this development in international relations should not deflect from the mainly economic origins of the political decision to acquire colonies.²

In their influential study of the 1960s, *Africa and the Victorians*, Robinson and Gallagher argued strongly in favor of political over economic motives for the scramble for Africa.³ They denied the influence of business, missionary societies, and other colonial interests on the decision-making process of imperialist policy makers. Consequently, they concluded that there was no "unofficial mind" of imperialism and that imperialist theories could not prove that business interests influenced or guided governments. Although their arguments were mainly Anglocentric, the two authors implied that their interpretations were also valid for other countries, such as France or Germany.

As far as Germany is concerned, however, neither their view nor any other that concentrates on the political side alone can be maintained. One must take into account different power constellations and different complexities when analyzing German policies in the metropolis, as well as later in its overseas empire. In addition, the historiography of German imperialism has largely isolated and overstated the role of Bismarck.⁴ I would contend that Germany grew into its role of becoming a colonial power. The first steps toward an overseas empire in 1884–85 did not find the country unprepared.

The mainly liberal pressure for German unification and the foundation of a strong German nation-state corresponded with a long-standing desire, again strongly supported by the liberals, for an overseas dimension of the future empire.[5]

I will briefly discuss six factors to shed some light on the growing procolonial atmosphere in German society. The first one is emigration, which Germans widely regarded as a loss to the nation's strength.[6] The migratory stream was somewhat undirected and was one of the most important characteristics of German society in the nineteenth century. How much stronger, so the argument ran, could Germany become if at least part of the emigrating stream could be settled in territories controlled by a powerful German state? The millions who left Germany between the 1830s and the 1890s would no longer be a loss to the nation. Emigration societies lobbied for the establishment of German settlement colonies, and over the years various projects were widely discussed in the public realm.

The next factor was Germany's rising position as a trader in world markets. German trade volume had been roughly doubling every fifteen years. As a consequence the "commercial group of the population grew faster than any other."[7] In the early 1880s those engaged in trade and transport accounted for one tenth of the population, a figure that rose to one eighth by 1907, from 4.5 million to 8.3 million. The growth of Germany's trade was only part of a worldwide trend, but its shipping, exports, and imports underscored the fact that the country had become a leading player on the stage of international trade.[8] The public had become acutely aware of this position through the press and was able to keep informed of the country's commercial involvement overseas.[9]

The third factor is the growth of the missionary societies.[10] Missionaries visiting churches in small towns and in the countryside were able to relate events in precolonial and colonial areas, thereby helping church congregations to understand Germany's growing role outside Europe. In this connection the campaign to end slavery and the slave trade in Africa were of special importance.[11]

Fourth, a brief reference must be made to the effects of geographical exploration and the burgeoning geographical societies all over Germany. They were not mass organizations, but their growing membership and publications made it clear that exploration of unknown territories and overseas travel reports were relatively popular subjects.[12] The exploratory reports were a stimulus to exotic fantasies.[13]

Fifth, after this general buildup in "globalized" concerns, it was no surprise to see a number of colonial pressure groups being founded. These groups channeled the growing interest in colonial possessions and in the overseas realm in general into political and economic lobbying efforts. Within a short time five pressure groups were founded, some of which were linked to the local geographical societies, chambers of commerce, and the business world in general.[14] The purpose of these groups was to increase public awareness of the need for overseas activities and put pressure on politicians and ministers to take positive action.

Part of this general buildup was colonial propaganda, which brings us to our sixth factor. The authors of a number of books, brochures, and pamphlets were beating the drum for Germany's overseas expansion.[15] These outpourings fit in well with an earlier literature that "had continuously argued for a German imperialist capacity throughout the nineteenth century."[16] This type of literature had little to do with the flights of fantasy of earlier periods. It was part of the ascendency of German liberalism for which overseas expansion was an integral part of the building of a nation-state. The liberals' aim was to secure and boost German economic activities in competition with other European nations, which either possessed or were about to dominate non-European lands. Concern for the populations in these territories was rarely expressed, and the racist belief in the white man's superiority was widely accepted.

The six factors discussed in brief above all contributed to the increasing public appetite for expansionist action by the state. Although the number of voices in favor of colonization had been growing, it could nevertheless not obliterate the opposition in left-liberal and social democratic circles. On the contrary, the opposition to colonial aspirations intensified in the late 1870s and early 1880s in proportion to the growing pressure for state-supported overseas activities.

The general atmosphere and the special activities of the imperialist lobby also affected the business world. We can gauge some of its interests by checking the membership lists of various imperialist associations and their correspondence, where available, as in the case of Gerson von Bleichröder.[17] Membership, however, does not say much about the actual level of involvement. Apart from providing some financial support, the business members of the associations hoped mainly to benefit from advanced knowledge and the emerging potential of colonial annexations. This disposition applied to bankers, merchants, and industrialists alike, so we find some of their names on the membership lists. There was also the opportunity to gain contacts with the ministerial bureaucracy, which many considered important for various overseas activities. As a number of businessmen regarded the campaigns for overseas lands as progressive and liberal, they were keen to publicize this activity. The business membership of these pressure groups and their support for a general bid for colonies was an indication of what these men might expect should Germany ever acquire overseas lands in the future.[18]

They expected to integrate the economies of these areas into the German economy as well as into the Europe-dominated world economy. They showed little enthusiasm in promoting civilizing aspects of colonialism, although occasionally references to such efforts could be found. Broadly speaking, business interests in overseas economic activities were in harmony with the government's intentions to foster enterprises overseas. Businessmen were not looking for "private colonies"; they were primarily keen on cooperation with the government, governmental "protection," and consular institutions. Because of growing international competition, businessmen sought the help of the state to provide a greater degree of security and possibly even financial "encouragement." The introduction of protective tariffs to help heavy industry and the great agrarians in the late 1870s might have provided the model for such state help. Bismarck's attempt to safeguard German economic dominance in the South Seas by working out a comprehensive rescue package for the bankrupt Godeffroy venture was in line with interventionism but took a new direction.[19] The leading German banks were willing to re-fund the bankrupt enterprise but expected the German state to subsidize their planned action by a dividend guarantee of 4.5 percent. This meant that the public purse would pay three hundred thousand marks in subsidies per year to a company that had significant private financial backers. In April 1880 a narrow majority of left liberals in the Reichstag rebuked the government's preparedness to come to the rescue of a German enterprise overseas. Although the government was defeated, the episode did not end the government's intentions of helping German business overseas. Nor did the banks withdraw from the South Seas. Instead, they set up a new company that operated successfully without state subsidies. In fact, a state protection of a kind was installed in 1899 when the government took over the administration of New Guinea, at the same time as Samoa became a German colony. Bismarck's original willingness to provide state subsidies was significant, as it heralded a new departure in Berlin politics. Perhaps one is justified in interpreting the so-called Samoan Bill as the beginning of Germany's intent to become more active on the stage of colonial and world politics. Bismarck's defeat in the Reichstag is well documented. It is less well-known that a few months later Adolph von Hansemann, the leading executive of the Disconto Banking Group and the architect of the second successful attempt to rescue the Godeffroy enterprise, submitted a memorandum about Germany's future policy in the South Seas. Von Hansemann wrote about the possible acquisition of parts of New Guinea and the South Sea Islands and about what sort of state protection German enterprises would need if they went in. This memorandum was to provide the guidelines for German policies in the South Sea arena, the foundation of the New Guinea Company, and the acquisition of part of the island in 1885.[20]

The Samoan episode demonstrates that the chancellor was not as strongly committed to the anticolonialist cause as has been often claimed. There are several by now well-known quotations that seem to support an anticolonial attitude, but they must not be overinterpreted in view of his actions between 1883 and 1885. He was supportive of business ventures overseas and hoped these enterprises would eventually administer any colonial areas themselves under governmental protection against the competition from foreign intervention, be that of a private or governmental nature.

As it turned out, the South Seas affair was not the end of the German governmental intervention in overseas matters. The next venture was to follow the French initiative and introduce shipping subsidies in Africa. But the Hamburg shipping merchants objected to the subsidizing of shipping lines in competition with their own operations in East Africa.[21] The next initiative in the run for German colonies came from Adolph Woermann himself, who alerted Berlin to the partitioning of west Africa among British and French authorities.[22] This alarmed Bismarck much more than repeated calls from leading liberals for an active colonial policy. The subsequent declaration of protectorates in west Africa fit in well with the government's intentions to protect German businesses from foreign encroachments. Bismarck adhered to this principle even if the enterprises in question were relatively small. A case in point is Lüderitz's rowboat undertakings in what is today southern Namibia. A protectorate was declared to prevent the Cape Colony from annexing the region.[23]

The term *protection* had nothing to do with providing the indigenous population with help against exploitation or the brutal excesses of the colonizers. It was clear from the outset that the German government only regarded commercial enterprises as candidates for protection against outside interference, as well as against legal complications inside the protected areas. The declared preference was initially for a commercial regime to run the colonies. Those who had benefited from the creation of protectorates should run the administration as a kind of quid pro quo. This was to keep the costs down for the treasury and involve the merchants more in the early phase of colonial policy. Bismarck aimed at imperialism on the cheap. He was easily persuaded of the advantages of the rule by chartered companies and hoped that any state involvement in running colonies would be kept to a minimum.[24] How much he miscalculated the situation in west and later east Africa is well known. Only Hansemann's expansion into the South Seas and the foundation of the New Guinea Company would satisfy the government's original intentions.[25] In west Africa the merchants showed an unwillingness to run any official administration and only offered to give advice on local matters. In east Africa the chancellor's plans foundered as well. To rescue Carl Peters's collapsed enterprise was one thing, but to juggle the interests of the German state in a region in which Britain, the Sultan of Zanzibar, the Hamburg merchants in Zanzibar, and the coastal Afro-Arab elites were major players complicated the establishment of German rule.[26] On top of that came the Bushiri Uprising, which threatened the budding German influence in east Africa and put commercial operations at risk. Rather than give up German influence, the government was forced to start military operations in 1888, which thus laid the foundation for a full-fledged state administration there. All this was against Bismarck's original plans, but acquiring and maintaining colonies did boost national prestige. Not for a moment did Bismarck seriously consider giving up these new additions to the Reich. Consequently, he was prepared to ask the Reichstag for public funding and establish official administrations. In the end, entry onto the stage of *Weltpolitik* came at a price.

Bismarck, in fulfilling national expectations and reacting to an atmosphere of pressure, regarded himself as an economic pragmatist, but he was without a consistent plan. He granted the state's protection wherever the applicant could demonstrate it made economic sense. Thus, economic activities provided the rationale for expansionist politics. The result was a haphazard collection of the colonial territories, or, in Max Weber's words, there were "accidental single business enterprises in West Africa and individually gathered lands through accidental pioneering deeds in East Africa."[27]

For Weber, chance seemed to be the underlying feature of the motley collection of German acquisitions in Africa and the Far East. They were the result of the government's reliance on existing local enterprises as a precondition for any governmental action. There was no equivalent to the dream of a Cape to Cairo link. There was nothing similar to the strategic safeguarding of the route to India; however, there was talk of aiming for a German *Mittelafrika* before the First World War, and Mittelafrika became part of the war aims program later.[28] There was an agreement with Britain concerning the future of the Portuguese colonies should Portugal ever want to sell them.[29] The reason Germany wanted to acquire parts of Angola was economic and linked to German business activities in Angola. Thus, Bismarck's insistence on business reasons for the official declaration of protectorates cast a long shadow. Concern for the national economy had become the main reason for expansionism. Even after the chancellor's departure, his legacy helped to shape colonial policy in the German colonies. An economic rationale strongly influenced the political culture in the colonies, but the priority of economic thinking was not restricted to the colonies. Business concerns heavily shaped the structure of decision making in Berlin. In the *Kolonialrat* (colonial council), which had been planned in the Bismarck era and which was finally set up in 1891, business interests continued to exert significant influence on the making of colonial policy.[30]

None of the other European colonial powers had similar institutionalized economic concerns. The French carried out their colonial policy under the banner of a civilizing mission. As Alice Conklin has recently argued, from 1895 Republican French colonialism adopted the pursuit of civilization as the official imperial doctrine. According to French interpretation, civilization did not simply restrict itself to the mastery of other peoples.[31] She concluded that the French concept was based on the concept of mastery over nature, which meant health over disease, reason over instinct, and knowledge over ignorance. As the colonial populations lacked the ability to master these matters, they were regarded as being in need of a civilizing influence. The French revolutionary tradition of having overcome "oppression and superstition to form a democratic and rational government" strongly influenced French colonial ideology.[32] With the belief in their civilizing mission and racial superiority, the French administrators were able to overcome any contradiction between democracy and running a colonial empire. What was included in the belief of mastery was the creation of new economic opportunities once the phase of military conquest was complete. Whatever problems the French had with their concept and whatever the historical difficulties might have been, German colonialism did not operate under a concept of this nature. Civilizing—if one wanted to use this term at all—in the German context did not lead to the introduction of civil society in the colonies, nor did Germany mean for it to do so. What most Germans wanted was to force the indigenous populations to work—the notorious *Erziehung zur Arbeit* (educate to work)—for German employers and according to European concepts of the work ethic.[33] This kind of *Erziehung* (education) meant little education and a great amount of hard work. Economic exploitation under European dominance was essential. Slavery continued to exist in east Africa and the Cameroons, although a growing labor market gradually replaced it before 1914.[34] Forced-labor schemes replaced slavery, but the laborers themselves did not always benefit from their freed status in any particular way. The difference between colonial methods among the various powers was not very significant; forced labor schemes operated in most African colonies. In other colonies African-owned farming played a growing role, especially in west Africa, whereas it took much longer to be acceptable in Germany. The first colony where this happened was Togoland.[35] During the Dernburg years in east Africa, Germany put more emphasis on encouraging the African farming sector as a greater factor in the colonial economy.[36]

Apart from forced labor schemes, there were other similarities between the French and German colonial policies. Military power played a special role in both empires; state-sanctioned violence conquered and subjugated the colonial hinterlands. Any resistance or uprising was brutally squashed, but the similarities ended there. On the French side there seem to have been no genocidal wars on the scale of the Herero War. Racial superiority seems to have underpinned all colonial rule, but the French administration constantly referred to their *mission civilisatrice* in order to implement certain measures. Yet many Frenchmen dreaded the prospect of a limited assimilation, which was to be the result of the civilizing process, though such a thing was still far away by 1914.[37] The war was to help the process when the French started to recruit increasingly African troops to defend the values of the Third Republic on the western front. Critics pointed out that military recruitment would not help the civilizing mission; it would tend to keep the Africans in an inferior role and increase resistance to French colonial rule. All of this was true, but assimilation eventually became possible for a number of individual Africans.

One aspect of the civilizing mission still requires our attention, however brief. The French colonial government had emphasized that economic exploitation was part of the policy of *mise en valeur*.[38] Production, trade, communications, and the improvement of health conditions contributed to France's colonial mission. The economic activities were not an end in themselves; rather they were part of the civilizing process.

This last point highlights the differences between German and French colonial policies. The French had an imperial doctrine for Africa, whereas the Germans were mainly concerned with economic exploitation, profits, formal rule, and subjugation. In Bismarck's time the French had not yet developed the concept of a civilizing mission. He believed that French colonial rule was too bureaucratic. By contrast Bismarck gave priority to the business side of colonial politics. This was not a personal whim, nor was it borne out of an unwillingness to negotiate with the *Reichstag*. The model for his thinking was the British Empire, with its concept of informal rule and chartered companies. Such companies had made more than 75 percent of British colonial acquisitions south of the Sahara in the 1880s, and Britain's informal sway kept British influence supreme until France, Germany, and Leopold of Belgium challenged it.[39] Bismarck did not stand alone in Germany in supporting informal rule; advocates of German colonialism echoed it. In 1882 the Colonial Association was founded in support of the idea of establishing trading posts under the "protection of the Reich."[40] In the founding document of the *Kolonialverein*, the association had offered to help the government "to attract in suitable cases governmental protection for German enterprises to fend off any foreign intervention."[41]

German business concerns, however, went further than was demonstrated by the support of the Colonial Association. The notorious Carl Peters, an early colonial pioneer, once wrote that all "colonial foundations are in essence a business [*Geschäft*] for the states." Theodor Leutwein towed the same line when he wrote: "The main purpose of all colonization is, if one leaves all made-up idealism and humanitarianism aside, a business. The colonizing race does not want to bring happiness to the indigenous population but looks after its own advantage and profit. So therefore there is only one guide-line for colonization and that is the pursuit of profitable business."[42]

The pursuit of business was the common denominator among those in the Bismarck administration and those interested in making Germany a colonial power. What happened to the primacy of economic concerns in the post-Bismarck era? What was the interplay between the private and the public sector? What structures would be put into place to make sure that essential aspects of that cooperation would function in a way that would satisfy both sides? A few merchants would have been happy with having their economic activities restricted to coastal operations and leaving the hinterland to missionaries and African traders, but this was not enough for those who wanted to build a colonial economy with plantations, mining companies, railways, roads, and possibly even white farming settlements. When the last vestiges of chartered rule broke down in east Africa and the state began to establish full colonial administration there, the business world in Berlin lobbied successfully for closer cooperation with the government in colonial policy on a more regular footing. As a result, the *Kolonialrat* was set up in 1891. From then until 1906 most essential aspects of colonial policy went through the Colonial Council. That included, for instance, colonial budgets, administrative decrees, and business initiatives. In looking back at the first *Kolonialrat* over the fifteen years of its actual existence (1891–1906), historians are afforded the rare opportunity of studying some of the aspects of the "unofficial mind of imperialism," the gradual development into a formal colonial empire, and the growth in certain areas of direct rule. The members of the *Kolonialrat* had a strong interest in all these issues, as they regarded an expanding colonial government in the colonies as the precondition for successful economic exploitation and economic growth.[43]

Prominent members of the council included the Berlin banker Adolph von Hansemann, the Hamburg sea merchant Adolf Woermann, the Cologne banker Simon Alfred Freiherr von Oppenheim, Karl von der Heydt (a banker in Elberfeld and in Berlin), the banker and industrialist Wilhelm Oechelhäuser, the Hamburg lawyer Julius Scharlach, the Berlin publisher Erich Vohsen, the investor Dr. Max Schoeller, and Heinrich Wiegand, managing director of the Bremen shipping line Norddeutsche Lloyd, to name but a few. Their aim was not only to look after their special business interests in the colonies but also to work for continuous growth of state funding for the military, infrastructure, land concessions, communications, and the exploitation of the African labor force. The private sector was also interested in joint projects and public interest guarantees to make sure private investments were profitable. With the exception of two members, the council supported big business and its involvement in the German colonies. The much-bemoaned disinterest of German capitalists in the colonies in the 1880s and early 1890s did apply to Africa but not to the South Seas. The Diskonto Bank, the Bleichröder bank, and the Deutsche Bank operated successfully there. Once railway construction, copper and diamond mining, and the operations of large landowning companies were under way in Africa in the early twentieth century, the large banks and industrial concerns had taken control of most colonial investments.

This was the case in Africa, New Guinea, the Shantung Province in China, and some of the phosphate and copra-producing South Sea Islands. Apart from railway construction, investments were relatively small by European or American standards, but they mattered for the colonial economies and represented a beginning of further developments. Thus, one year before the First World War, the Oberhausen steelworks concern, Gutehoffnungshütte, discovered that the east African market (Kenya, German East Africa, and Mozambique) would take twenty-five hundred tons of steel girders annually, a size for which the company thought worthwhile organizing a supply business.[44]

The *Kolonialrat* was also the forum where merchants such as Karl Vietor challenged the European economic monopoly from Bremen, who argued that boosting an African farming economy might be of greater benefit to the colonies than the influence of white planters or the financial operations of the big banks. The first colonial secretary, Bernhard Dernburg, and even the electrotechnical industrialist Walther Rathenau—neither of whom were keen on small German planters and their political influence in the African colonies—entertained similar thoughts.[45] Together with the governor, Dr. Albrecht Freiherr von Rechenberg, they believed in the potential of an economy based on African input under European guidance. The construction of railways would not only secure German rule militarily but might help African cash crop production. This shift of colonial emphasis ran into determined opposition in Africa and Berlin and was to some extent even reversed. By the outbreak of the war, about 46 percent of east Africa's agrarian exports came from African farmers.[46] This did not give German colonial rule a different character, nor did it make colonial policy more humane, but it demonstrated that German colonialism had become economically and politically much more complex.

Dernburg's appointment signaled another shift in colonial politics. A banker from a leading bank took over the Colonial Department (*Kolonialabteilung*), which a few months later changed into an independent Colonial Office (*Kolonialamt*). Now a businessman of the first order, Dernburg gave economic concerns top priority in colonial policy. His ability to rationalize the administrative system in Berlin, as well as in the colonies, proved to be vital for the growing profitability of German colonial enterprises. Dernburg can be regarded as one of the strongest advocates of a more modernized primacy of economics. With him in power the government committed itself to a considerable increase in colonial expenditures. Unlike earlier times the Reichstag after 1907 would go along with that policy. Thus, the business circles had achieved what they had always wanted, namely that the government would augment its colonial budgets. With that goal achieved, there was no longer any need for the *Kolonialrat*. Dernburg confirmed this position when he wrote that the main reason for the dissolution was the "economic upswing of the colonies." As Chancellor Bülow put it to the Kaiser: "The Kolonialrat had outlived itself and it was therefore recommended not to re-convene it."[47]

After Dernburg's resignation, his successor as colonial secretary, Friedrich von Lindequist (not a member of the business community), reconvened a colonial council that was to support the Colonial Office in finding solutions to economic problems within a given framework.[48] One such problem was the question as to whether it was worthwhile to set up a credit organization in Namibia. This was very different from the influence of the old *Kolonialrat*, although Lindequist had expressed his wish to cooperate with the "big banks, commerce and modern industry" to strengthen the colonial economies. These meetings led to the establishment in 1913 of a state-owned agricultural mortgage bank, since the private sector had proved unwilling to lend to farmers on a long-term basis at low interest rates.[49]

Wilhelm Solf, the last imperial colonial secretary (who also had no direct links to the business world), tried to benefit from the advice of financiers and industrialists in a new council. At the meeting of this third council in 1913, members discussed the question of how to prevent the establishment of fraudulent business ventures in the colonies. This council was to meet again in 1914, but the outbreak of the war prevented another session. The dilatory way with which this question was dealt indicated that there was no urgent need for a solution. But the contacts among the colonial government, the business world, and pressure groups were well established, and some of the basic principles of colonial policy had been laid down and followed. One of those was the emphasis on economic exploitation by German enterprises under the umbrella of state "protection," which had been Bismarck's starting point back in the 1880s.

After 1919, when Germany had lost her overseas empire at the Versailles Peace Conference, German exports took several years to approach prewar levels, but then Germany had lost all her foreign assets and some of her foreign markets as well. It was no wonder that the public and the government of the day demanded a return of the colonies. The political campaign for restoring German colonies led to "revisionism" as a political goal in the Weimar Republic. The support for revisionism highlighted the transitory character of Germany's first democracy and the problem of compatibility between democracy and imperialist ambitions. As revisionism did not lead to any successes, the colonial movement began to turn to the National Socialist Party for a possible radical support of its demands. Although Hitler was willing to endorse colonial revisionism for tactical reasons, he was never a keen advocate of adding German overseas colonies to the German Empire. Instead, his favored expansionist drive was to be directed to the east, to Poland and Soviet Russia. The business community was keen on a different expansion into southeastern Europe based on informal empire building and trade dependencies. This was part of an economic *Großraum*, which did not mesh with the Nazi idea of *Lebensraum*, and which was going to be directed more toward Poland and Russia. It included racialist considerations, the settlement of German settlers, and ultimately the extermination of the east European Jewry. What had started as a bid for revising the Peace Treaty ended up as a bid for political and economic hegemony on the European continent. This was a departure of the overseas imperialism of the prewar decades and the beginning of a land-based expansionism eastward. Thus, between the 1880s and 1945 Germany had followed two imperialist drives, the first one overseas and the second one to the east in the Second World War. Both attempts failed disastrously and created unlimited human suffering. So what was left for Germany? The foreign minister, Gustav Stresemann, declared in 1925: "The last thing that makes us a great power is our economic power and it is that we have to use to make foreign policy." After the Second World War West Germany resumed its industrial rise and became the leading power in industrial exports, a campaign that did not aim at political hegemony.[50]

Some of the more recent literature, referred to in the wide-ranging introduction to this book, has concentrated on the possible connections between the genocidal war in German Southwest Africa (Namibia) and the Holocaust of the Third Reich. The two authors focus on the historical aspects of continuity and discontinuity and emphasize the question of causality in German colonialism. They are, however, very much aware that it remains difficult to establish a cogent link between military campaigns in the colonies and the Final Solution beyond the general reference to the term *genocide*. According to recent interpretations the mass massacres in Namibia were the consequence of a brutal war between the German military forces and the Hereros, who had challenged German domination. The campaign, which the military fought, did not escape criticism in Germany at the time, although it was popular to give money to the German civilian victims of the uprising.⁵¹ This, of course, excluded the Hereros.

According to German colonial law any resistance against German rule carried the death sentence. The forces under General von Trotha did not apply this law exclusively against the Herero and Nama leaders but against all the Hereros, including wives and children, and thereby all but exterminated the Herero and Nama peoples. The reaction in Germany was mixed, but eventually Trotha was replaced. The widespread belief in the white man's superiority and the justification for colonialism did not result in any warnings about the rise of racism. As far as is known, the German atrocities were not interpreted as a prelude to worse things to come. Only in England did some observers link the military actions in Namibia to the German military atrocities in Belgium and northern France at the beginning of the First World War.⁵² The German actions were seen only in military terms. Even the German Jew Walther Rathenau, who was assassinated after the First World War, and who, as a critic of his times, was concerned about the rise of anti-Semitism, did not allude to links between German colonial brutalities and the rise of anti-Semitism. The character of the campaign in Namibia was the consequence of the ubiquitous racist belief in the "white man's superiority" and the relatively low esteem given to the pursuit of "civilisatory" values.

All European powers had fought brutal colonial wars against their colonial populations. In some cases it could be defined as genocidal because they turned against civilian populations as well. In all these European powers anti-Semitism was widespread, but none except the National Socialist regime in Germany went on to organize the Holocaust in Europe. Recognition of this fact could lead to a revival of the *Sonderweg* thesis, but the mixture of racism and violence points to another important consideration. It looks as if the brutal actions against civilians in the First World War and the plans for ethnic cleansing prepared the ground for more violent forms of anti-Semitism. The assassination of Walther Rathenau in 1922 by right-wing young officers may have been one of the first signs of an increasingly violent anti-Semitism that eventually peaked in the state-organized Holocaust.

In the discussions in England about the German atrocities in Belgium and northern France in August and September 1914, no reference to German racism was made. The campaign of mass racist murder the Turks waged on the Armenians during the Great War may have prepared the ground for more violence, this time in the form of anti-Semitism, which could be carried out in a war and against sections of the domestic society. So it looks as if the widespread violence used against the civilian populations in the war was the harbinger for the rise of violent anti-Semitism. The use of violence against civilians in a war requires further investigations. The pursuit of this topic, however, is beyond the scope of this chapter.

The relationship between empires and genocidal wars, important as this discussion is, should not push into the background the analysis of European imperialism in general and the purpose of German colonialism in particular. And here there are still two major fertile fields for investigation. The first one would deal with the effects German rule had on the colonial populations in Africa, the South Seas, and China, the second with colonial politics in Germany. The latter should also include the quest for an enlargement of the empire. The recent historiographical emphasis on cultural aspects has demonstrated the effects colonialism had on various sectors of German society, their imaginations and beliefs.[53] This has become a rich seam for research. Jens Jäger has argued recently that the possession of colonies became "an integral part of the imperial nation."[54] However valuable these new fields of investigation are, it is still necessary and desirable for the debate about colonial politics in its widest sense to continue. It forms an essential part of the political culture in Wilhelmine Germany. Important fields remain to be explored, such as the history of the Colonial Society. We need a comprehensive and systematic analysis of this important agitational pressure group focusing on both the center in Berlin and the regional branches in Germany.

Notes

1. Statistisches Reichsamt, *Deutsche Wirtschaftskunde*, 193–98.

2. See Barth, *Die deutsche Hochfinanz und der Imperialismus*; Wehler, *Bismarck und der Imperialismus*; Wehler, *Deutsche Gesellschaftsgeschichte*, vol. 3; Hampe, *Die ökonomische Imperialismustheorie*; Gründer, *Geschichte der deutschen Kolonien*; and Stoecker, *Drang nach Afrika*.

3. Robinson and Gallagher, *Africa and the Victorians*, 462–72; and Robinson, "The Conference in Berlin and the Future in Africa, 1884–1885." See also Owen and Sutcliffe, *Studies in the Theory of Imperialism*.

4. For this view see Pflanze, *The Period of Fortification, 1880–1898*, 113–42.

5. Fitzpatrick, *Liberal Imperialism in Germany*.

6. See Bade, "German Transatlantic Emigration in the 19th and 20th Centuries"; Bade, *Europa in Bewegung*; and Grant, *Migration and Inequality in Germany, 1870–1913*.

7. Clapham, *The Economic Development of France and Germany, 1815–1914*, 365.

8. Scholl, "Shipping Business in Germany in the Nineteenth and Twentieth Centuries."

9. Darwin, *After Tamerlane*, 237–45; Rostow, *The World Economy*, 43–75; Hobsbawm, *The Age of Empire from 1750 to the Present Day*, 18, 349; and Borchardt, "The Industrial Revolution in Germany, 1700–1914."

10. Gründer, *Christliche Mission und deutscher Imperialismus*; Heyden and Stoecker, *Mission und Macht im Wandel politischer Orientierungen*.

11. Gründer, *Christliche Mission und deutscher Imperialismus*, 357–64; Gründer, *Geschichte der deutschen Kolonien*, 68–70.

12. Schulte-Althoff, *Studien zur politischen Wissenschaftsgeschichte der deutschen Geographie im Zeitalter des Imperialismus*; Essner, *Deutsche Afrikareisende im neunzehnten Jahrhundert*; Marx, "*Völker ohne Schrift und Geschichte*"; Fabian, *Out of Our Minds*; and Pogge von Strandmann, *Ins tiefste Afrika*.

13. For this see Zantop, *Colonial Fantasies*.

14. The five societies were the African Society in Germany (founded 1878), which was the result of a merger of two earlier organizations; the Central Association for Commercial Geography and the Furthering of German Interests Abroad (founded 1878); the West German Association for Colonization and Export (founded 1879); the German Colonial Association (founded 1882); and the Society for German Colonization (founded 1884), which merged with the Colonial Association to become the German Colonial Society in 1887. See Gründer, *Geschichte der deutschen Kolonien*, 39–43; Bendikat, *Organisierte Kolonialbewegung in der Bismarckära*; Soénius, *Koloniale Begeisterung im Rheinland während des Kaiserreichs*; Eley, *Reshaping the German Right*; Bade, *Friedrich Fabri und der Imperialismus in der Bismarckzeit*, 136–89, 287–309; and Demhardt, *Deutsche Kolonialgesellschaft, 1888–1918*.

15. Gründer, *Geschichte der deutschen Kolonien*, 33–39; Fröhlich, *Imperialismus*, 20–31; Wehler, *Bismarck und der Imperialismus*, 142–55.

16. Fitzpatrick, "Bürgertum ohne Raum," 161.

17. Stern, *Gold and Iron*, 394–435.

18. See Bade, "Imperial Germany and West Africa."

19. See Hiery, *Die Deutschen und die Südsee, 1884–1914*; Stern, *Gold and Iron*, 396–402; and Wehler, *Bismarck und der Imperialismus*, 215–23.

20. Hansemann to Auswärtiges Amt, Nov. 11, 1880, Federal Archives Berlin, Reichskolonialamt 2927.

21. Washausen, *Hamburg und die Kolonialpolitik des Deutschen Reiches, 1880–1890*, 43–53.

22. Ibid., 138–54; see also Jaeck, "Die deutsche Annexion."

23. Kaulich, *Die Geschichte der ehemaligen Kolonie Deutsch-Südwestafrika (1884–1914)*, 43–61.

24. Jaeck, "Die deutsche Annexion," 81–84; Stoecker, *Drang nach Afrika*, 58–59.

25. Gründer, *Geschichte der deutschen Kolonien*, 90–94.
26. Ibid., 85–87; Perras, *Carl Peters and German Imperialism, 1856–1918*, 46–66; Koponen, *Development for Exploitation*, 45–85.
27. Weber, *Gesammelte politische Schriften*, 32.
28. Stoecker, *Drang nach Afrika*, 222–33; Gründer, *Geschichte der deutschen Kolonien*, 100–106.
29. Drechsler, *Südwestafrika unter deutscher Kolonialherrschaft*, 199–202; Fröhlich, *Imperialismus*, 95–99. For a different emphasis see also Tschapek, *Bausteine eines zukünftigen deutschen Mittelafrikas*, 211–15, 245–64.
30. See Pogge von Strandmann, *Imperialismus vom Grünen Tisch*, chaps. 2, 3.
31. See Conklin, *A Mission to Civilize*.
32. Ibid., 6.
33. Beck and Spittler, *Arbeit in Afrika*; and Koponen, *Development for Exploitation*, 323–30.
34. Deutsch, *Emancipation Without Abolition in German East Africa, c. 1884–1914*.
35. Knoll, *Togo Under Imperial Germany, 1884–1914*; Sebald, *Togo, 1884–1914*; and Erbar, *Ein "Platz an der Sonne?"*
36. Koponen, *Development for Exploitation*, 223–29.
37. Conklin, *A Mission to Civilize*, 75, 168–69.
38. Ibid., 41–42.
39. Flint, "Chartered Companies and the Transition from Informal Sway to Colonial Rule in Africa," 71–77.
40. Pogge von Strandmann, "Consequences of the Foundation of the German Empire," 114.
41. Ibid., 115.
42. Peters, *Zur Weltpolitik*, 115; Leutwein, *Elf Jahre Gouverneur in Deutsch-Südwestafrika*, 541.
43. For the Kolonialrat see Pogge von Strandmann, *Imperialismus vom Grünen Tisch*.
44. Gussmann's report of May 27, 1913, Rhenish Wesphalian Business Archive Cologne, Archive of the Gutehoffnungshütte (HA/GHH 30000030/23).
45. Koponen, *Development for Exploitation*, 258–314.
46. Tetzlaff, *Koloniale Entwicklung und Ausbeutung*, 177.
47. Dernburg to Bülow, July 8, 1907; Bülow to the Kaiser, July 11, 1907; and the Kaiser's reply, July 17, 1907; all in Federal Archives Berlin, Reichskanzlei 914.
48. Pogge von Strandmann, *Imperialismus vom Grünen Tisch,* chap. 12.
49. Kaulich, *Die Geschichte der ehemaligen Kolonie*, 403–7.
50. Pogge von Strandmann, "Imperialism and Revisionism in Interwar Germany"; Laak, "Ist je ein Reich, das es nicht gab, so gut verwaltet worden?" See also Snyder, *Myths of Empire*, 105–9.

51. It may suffice here to refer to the works by Isabel Hull and Jürgen Zimmerer, which are discussed briefly in the introduction.
52. Horne and Kramer, *German Atrocities, 1914*, 167–69, 423.
53. See Kundrus, *Phantasiereiche*.
54. Jaeger, "Colony as *Heimat*?"

Bibliography

Bade, Klaus J. *Europa in Bewegung: Migration vom späten 18. Jahrhundert bis zur Gegenwart*. Munich: C. H. Beck, 2000.

———. *Friedrich Fabri und der Imperialismus in der Bismarckzeit: Revolution, Depression, Expansion*. Freiburg: Atlantis, 1975.

———. "German Transatlantic Emigration in the 19th and 20th Centuries." In *European Expansion and Migration: Essays on the International Migration from Africa, Asia, and Europe*, edited by Pieter C. Emmer and Magnus Mörner, 126–36. New York: Oxford University Press, 1992.

———. "Imperial Germany and West Africa: Colonial Movement, Business Interests, and Bismarck's 'Colonial policies.'" In Förster, Mommsen, and Robinson, *Bismarck, Europe, and Africa*, 121–47.

Barth, Boris. *Die deutsche Hochfinanz und der Imperialismus: Banken und Außenpolitik vor 1914*. Stuttgart: Franz Steiner, 1995.

Beck, Kurt, and Gerd Spittler. *Arbeit in Afrika*. Munich: C. H. Beck, 1996.

Bendikat, Elfi. *Organisierte Kolonialbewegung in der Bismarckära*. Brazzaville: Kivouvo, 1984.

Borchardt, Knut. "The Industrial Revolution in Germany, 1700–1914." In *The Emergence of Industrial Societies*. Vol. 4 of *The Fontana Economic History of Europe*, edited by Carlo Maria Cipolla, 1:75–160. Los Angeles: Collins Fontana, 1973.

Clapham, John H. *The Economic Development of France and Germany, 1815–1914*. 4th ed. Cambridge, UK: Cambridge University Press, 1963.

Conklin, Alice L. *A Mission to Civilize: The Republican Idea of Empire in France and West Africa, 1895–1930*. Stanford: Stanford University Press, 1997.

Darwin, John. *After Tamerlane: The Global History of Empire*. London: Allen Lane, 2007.

Demhardt, Imre J. *Deutsche Kolonialgesellschaft, 1888–1918: Ein Beitrag zur Organisationsgeschichte der deutschen Kolonialbewegung*. Wiesbaden: Olms, 2002.

Deutsch, Jan-Georg. *Emancipation Without Abolition in German East Africa, c. 1884–1914*. Athens: Ohio University Press, 2006.

Drechsler, Horst. *Südwestafrika unter deutscher Kolonialherrschaft: Die großen Land- und Minengesellschaften (1885–1914)*. Stuttgart: Franz Steiner, 1996.

Eley, Geoff. *Reshaping the German Right*. New Haven, CT: Yale University Press, 1980.

Erbar, Ralph. *Ein "Platz an der Sonne?" Die Verwaltungs- und Wirtschaftsgeschichte der deutschen Kolonie Togo, 1884–1914*. Stuttgart: Franz Steiner, 1991.

Essner, Cornelia. *Deutsche Afrikareisende im neunzehnten Jahrhundert: Zur Sozialgeschichte des Reisens*. Wiesbaden: Franz Steiner, 1985.

Fabian, Johannes. *Out of Our Minds: Reason and Madness in the Exploration of Central Africa*. Berkeley: University of California Press, 2000.

Fitzpatrick, Matthew P. "Bürgertum ohne Raum: The Oneiric Empire of German Liberalism, 1848–1884, 1918–1943." PhD diss., University of New South Wales, 2005.

———. *Liberal Imperialism in Germany: Expansionism and Nationalism, 1848–1888*. Oxford: Berghahn, 2008.

Flint, John. "Chartered Companies and the Transition from Informal Sway to Colonial Rule in Africa." In Förster, Mommsen, and Robinson, *Bismarck, Europe, and Africa*, 69–83.

Förster, Stig, Wolfgang J. Mommsen, and Ronald Robinson, eds. *Bismarck, Europe, and Africa*. Oxford: Oxford University Press, 1988.

Fröhlich, Michael. *Imperialismus: Deutsche Kolonial- und Weltpolitik, 1880–1914*. Munich: Deutscher Taschenbuch, 1994.

Grant, Oliver. *Migration and Inequality in Germany, 1870–1913*. Oxford: Oxford University Press, 2005.

Gründer, Horst. *Christliche Mission und deutscher Imperialismus: Eine politische Geschichte ihrer Beziehungen während der deutschen Kolonialzeit (1884–1914) unter besonderer Berücksichtigung Afrikas und Chinas*. Paderborn: Schöningh, 1982.

———. *Geschichte der deutschen Kolonien*. 2nd ed. Paderborn: Schöningh, 1991.

Hampe, Peter. *Die ökonomische Imperialismustheorie: Kritische Untersuchungen*. Munich: C. H. Beck, 1976.

Heyden, Ulrich van der, and Holger Stoecker, eds. *Mission und Macht im Wandel politischer Orientierungen: Europäische Missionsgesellschaften in politischen Spannungsfeldern in Afrika und Asien zwischen 1800 und 1945*. Stuttgart: Franz Steiner, 2005.

Hiery, Hermann J., ed. *Die Deutschen und die Südsee, 1884–1914: Ein Handbuch*. 2nd ed. Paderborn: Schöningh, 2002.

Hobsbawm, Eric. *The Age of Empire from 1750 to the Present Day*. London: Weidenfeld and Nicolson, 1987.

Horne, John, and Alan Kramer. *German Atrocities, 1914: A History of Denial*. New Haven, CT: Yale University Press, 2001.

Jaeck, Hans-Peter. "Die deutsche Annexion." In *Kamerun unter deutscher Kolonialherrschaft*, edited by Helmuth Stoecker, 33–87. Berlin: Rütten und Loening, 1960.

Jaeger, Jens. "Colony as Heimat? The Formation of Colonial Identity in Germany around 1900." *German History* 27, no.4 (Oct. 2009): 467–89.

Kaulich, Udo. *Die Geschichte der ehemaligen Kolonie Deutsch-Südwestafrika (1884–1914)*. Frankfurt: Peter Lang, 2002.

Knoll, Arthur J. *Togo Under Imperial Germany, 1884–1914: A Case Study in Colonial Rule*. Stanford: Stanford University Press, 1978.

Koponen, Juhani. *Development for Exploitation: German Colonial Policies in Mainland Tanzania, 1884–1914*. Helsinki: Lit, 1994.

Kundrus, Birthe, ed. *Phantasiereiche: Zur Kulturgeschichte des deutschen Kolonialismus*. Frankfurt: Campus, 2003.

Laak, Dirk van. "Ist je ein Reich, das es nicht gab, so gut verwaltet worden?" Der imaginäre Ausbau der imperialen Infrastruktur in Deutschland nach 1918." In Kundrus, *Phantasiereiche*, 71–90. Frankfurt: Campus, 2003.

Leutwein, Theodor. *Elf Jahre Gouverneur in Deutsch-Südwestafrika*. 1906. Windhoek: Namibiana Buchdepot, 1997.

Marx, Christoph. *"Völker ohne Schrift und Geschichte": Zur historischen Erfassung des vorkolonialen Schwarzafrikas in der deutschen Forschung des 19. und frühen 20. Jahrhunderts*. Stuttgart: Franz Steiner, 1988.

Owen, Roger, and Bob Sutcliffe, eds. *Studies in the Theory of Imperialism*. London: Longman, 1972.

Perras, Arne. *Carl Peters and German Imperialism, 1856–1918: A Political Biography*. Oxford: Oxford University Press, 2004.

Peters, Carl. *Zur Weltpolitik*. Berlin: Verlag von Karl Siegismund, 1912.

Pflanze, Otto. *The Period of Fortification, 1880–1898*. Vol. 3 of *Bismarck and the Development of Germany*. Princeton, NJ: Princeton University Press, 1990.

Pogge von Strandmann, Hartmut. "Consequences of the Foundation of the German Empire: Colonial Expansion and the Process of Political-Economic Rationalization." In Förster, Mommsen, and Robinson, *Bismarck, Europe, and Africa*, 105–20.

———. "Imperialism and Revisionism in Interwar Germany." In *Imperialism and After: Continuities and Discontinuities*, edited by Wolfgang J. Mommsen and Jürgen Osterhammel, 90–119. London: Allen and Unwin, 1986.

———. *Imperialismus vom Grünen Tisch: Deutsche Kolonialpolitik zwischen wirtschaftlicher Ausbeutung und "zivilisatorischen" Bemühungen*. Berlin: Christoph Links, 2009.

———, ed. *Ins tiefste Afrika: Paul Pogge und seine präkolonialen Reisen ins südliche Kongobecken*. Berlin: Trafo, 2004.

Robinson, Ronald. "The Conference in Berlin and the Future in Africa, 1884–1885." In Förster, Mommsen, and Robinson, *Bismarck, Europe, and Africa*, 1–32. Oxford: Oxford University Press, 1988.

Robinson, Ronald, and John Gallagher, with Alice Denny. *Africa and the Victorians: The Official Mind of Imperialism*. London: Macmillan, 1965.

Rostow, Walt Whitman. *The World Economy: History and Prospect*. Austin: University of Texas Press, 1978.

Scholl, Lars U. "Shipping Business in Germany in the Nineteenth and Twentieth Centuries." In *Business History of Shipping*, edited by Tsunehiko Yui and Keiichiro Nakagawa, 185–213. Tokyo: University of Tokyo Press, 1985.

Schulte-Althoff, Franz-Josef. *Studien zur politischen Wissenschaftsgeschichte der deutschen Geographie im Zeitalter des Imperialismus.* Paderborn: Schöningh, 1971.

Sebald, Peter. *Togo, 1884–1914: Eine Geschichte der deutschen "Musterkolonie" auf der Grundlage amtlicher Quellen.* Berlin: Akademie, 1988.

Snyder, Jack. *Myths of Empire: Domestic Politics and International Ambition.* Ithaca, NY: Cornell University Press, 1991.

Soénius, Ulrich S. *Koloniale Begeisterung im Rheinland während des Kaiserreichs.* Cologne: Rheinisch-Westfälisches Wirtschaftsarchiv, 1992.

Statistisches Reichsamt, ed. *Deutsche Wirtschaftskunde: Ein Abriß der deutschen Wirtschaftsstatistik.* Berlin: Reimar Hobbing, 1930.

Stern, Fritz. *Gold and Iron: Bismarck, Bleichröder, and the Building of the German Empire.* London: George Allen and Unwin, 1977.

Stoecker, Helmuth, ed. *Drang nach Afrika: Die deutsche koloniale Expansionspolitik und Herrschaft in Afrika von den Anfängen bis zum Verlust der Kolonien.* 2nd ed. Berlin: Akademie, 1991.

Tetzlaff, Rainer. *Koloniale Entwicklung und Ausbeutung: Wirtschafts- und Sozialgeschichte Deutsch-Ostafrikas, 1885–1914.* Berlin: Duncker und Humblot, 1970.

Tschapek, Rolf P. *Bausteine eines zukünftigen deutschen Mittelafrikas: Deutscher Imperialismus und die portugiesischen Kolonien; Deutsches Interesse an den südafrikanischen Kolonien Portugals vom ausgehenden 19. Jahrhundert bis zum Ersten Weltkrieg.* Stuttgart: Franz Steiner, 2000.

Washausen, Helmut. *Hamburg und die Kolonialpolitik des Deutschen Reiches, 1880–1890.* Hamburg: Hans Christians, 1968.

Weber, Max. *Gesammelte politische Schriften.* Munich: C. H. Beck, 1921.

Wehler, Hans-Ulrich. *Bismarck und der Imperialismus.* Cologne-Berlin: Kiepenheuer und Witsch, 1969.

———. *Deutsche Gesellschaftsgeschichte.* Vol. 3, *Von der 'Deutschen Doppelrevolution' bis zum Beginn des Ersten Weltkriegs, 1849–1914.* Munich: C. H. Beck, 1995.

Zantop, Susanne. *Colonial Fantasies: Conquest, Family and Nation in Precolonial Germany, 1770–1870.* Durham, NC: Duke University Press, 1997.

10

Christian Missionary Societies in the German Colonies, 1884/85–1914/15

Ulrich van der Heyden

Probably the longest lasting and most controversial debate over German colonialism has been the decades-long debate about its relationship to the Christian mission. In mission historiography there has been an equally long debate about how closely the Christian mission is connected to colonialism and how close it ought to be. The discussions, which question the very legitimacy of mission work, are revisited repeatedly.[1] Even the Christian churches have criticized the practice and content of Christian missionary activity of the past and sometimes the present.

The most common question in these debates is whether one should consider the Christian missionaries as forerunners of European colonial rule. Research commonly answers this question in the affirmative, since missionaries often took over sovereign tasks of colonial administration or used their infrastructure in their zealous fight against the traditional customs and cultures of overseas people if they did not fit the colonizer's picture of "Christian civilization." The work was often criticized after the 1960s and too frequently in an indiscriminate way,[2] without considering that missionary work was a very complex and ambivalent process.

Since then, scholars have widely recognized that we cannot deny a close connection between the spread of the Christian missions and the expansion of European power; alongside Buddhism and Islam, Christianity is by its nature a missionary religion.[3] Both processes—mission and colonialism—ran almost parallel in time in various regions in the nineteenth century, known as the century of the mission and as the century of European colonial expansion.[4]

It is worthy of mention that during the period of direct German colonial rule between 1884/85 and 1918/19 the German missionary societies usually had no objection when colonial propaganda publications praised their activities abroad "in the peaceful war for cultured behavior, improvement and refinement of mankind."[5] Colonial rulers declared their activities an integral part of the process of colonization and an important instrument for maintaining colonial rule. It should come as no surprise that in colonial literature (and in mission literature as well) there was a perception that there was "a very simple division of work between mission and colonization."[6]

Were the missionaries really agents of colonialism? Did the missionaries actually destroy the cultural identity of entire ethnic groups? This did happen, to be sure, and it can be proved, but can one establish sweeping theories? From the point of view of the victims, the European missionaries "brought the Bible and took the land," an expression that for good reason has become almost a proverb in the whole of Africa.[7] We must be allowed to ask whether in many cases the missionaries even knew that colonial politicians and administrators later misused their knowledge and experience, drawn from many years' work. The missionaries' attitude toward the colonizing process was not always as unambiguous as in the characterization by the director of the Berlin Mission Society, Hermann Theodor Wangemann, in the mid-nineteenth century. He admitted candidly that the missionaries "reported freely on the intentions and movements of the indigenous enemy which no one else could have done."[8] This attitude on the part of the European missionaries is not altogether surprising; they had a completely Eurocentric worldview, so it seemed appropriate not merely to reject "heathen" cultures but also to legitimize an active battle against them.

Much more common than direct support of colonial rule, which contemporary literature admits, however, was an apparent indirect use of the knowledge gained through missionary activity in the colonies. As a Russian academic once frankly stated, right at the start of the direct phase of European colonization around the mid-1880s, Christian propaganda became a direct instrument of colonial expansion, and the missionaries, irrespective of their subjective will, became its defenders.[9]

For extensive joint action by missionaries and colonizers abroad, it was necessary to create or strengthen the appropriate ideological prerequisites, particularly among the German public, which financed the mission through donations averaging fifty-four million marks a year in support of the societies' personnel resources. Through their paternalistic and sometimes racist fundamental attitude to the Africans and other "natives" in the German colonial areas, most European missionaries already possessed the characteristics essential for effectively supporting and driving the process of colonization. These ideological principles could be realized only in harmony with and not in conflict with the colonialization process.[10]

An argument often used to defend missionary activity abroad is that along with the Gospel the missionaries also brought civilization, whatever one may wish to understand by civilization. As a rule, it means education—reading and writing skills that undoubtedly enabled the colonized people to gain an awareness of the world and helped them to create a connection with modernity.[11] The non-Europeans' contributions to medical advances, which at that time took place primarily in Europe, are sometimes considered part of this process, as some research findings were made in the colonies.[12]

Of course, a few particularly zealous missionaries also understood "civilization" to mean supposed "European values," which were often transferred with violence and usually meant the most effective methods of subduing and exploiting the non-European peoples. Apologists, in particular those who exclusively take the side of the missionaries in discussions, often state that there would not have been any progress in what is known today as the "developing world" without European missionaries. However, a definition of *progress* is often neglected. Technological progress? Did progress not largely serve the colonial masters? Did the non-Europeans not live perhaps better but above all with more self-determination before the arrival of the Europeans?

In his groundbreaking work, the theologian Karl Hammer was one of the first people in Germany to analyze the links in the history of ideas between the Christian mission and colonialism. A few years later, the historian Klaus Bade put the fundamental issues of this relationship explicitly at the center of his research. In various publications, the historian Horst Gründer set the groundwork for a discussion of this broadly composed complex of themes, not only relative to the German colonies but also with a primary focus on them.[13]

In the 1950s und 1960s, historians from the GDR initiated a critical historiography of colonization, challenging and inspiring their West German colleagues.[14] However, they very seldom dealt with the combination of mission and colonialism,[15] or they did so in a one-sided way. An example of this is Heinrich Loth, who judged the relationship between mission and colonialism very critically for years. In 1960 he published *Kolonialismus unter der Kutte* (Under the Robes of Colonialism), without acknowledging at all the humane elements and the criticism of the colonies that were evident in the missionaries' actions, practices, publications, lectures, and letters. This acknowledgment occurred only years later in his subsequent publications.[16]

A much more interesting question is the problem that was already being discussed before the beginning of European colonial rule, namely, to what extent the missionaries could be "the natives' advocates" in dealing with the colonial administration, or to what extent they should have been, in light of their self-perception. We can give an adequate answer to this only if we consider time, place, and space, as well as the individual characteristics of the people involved, from a present-day perspective. Even the most engaged "advocates of the natives," however, did not question the colonial system as a whole; their criticism was always inherent to the system and for the most part dealt only with concrete shortcomings in the practice of colonial rule.[17]

To overcome entrenched arguments of the past, the Berlin Society for Mission History was founded in the mid-1990s. With the help of its series of writings, in particular the "Archive of Mission History," and its international academic conferences, the gaps that existed in academic debates between "critics and defenders" of the Christian missionary activity overseas have largely been bridged.

German Missionary Societies in the German Colonies

It seems appropriate here to provide at least an outline of those German missionary societies that were active in the German colonies in Africa, Asia, and the South Seas, describe what their intentions and real successes were, and elucidate what recent research informs us about them. It can only be a rough overview; it would be simply impossible here to consider adequately the 331 protestant missionary societies in Germany at the end of the nineteenth century that employed around one thousand missionaries.[18]

Historians generally assume that German colonial history began with the division of Africa at the Berlin Congo-Conference of 1884/85. However, this assumption is accurate only for the beginning of the phase of direct German colonial rule overseas. One should view the activities of German missionary societies in the colonial areas conquered by Germany in connection with the start of religious missionaries and warriors at the start of early modernity, even if the initial impulse came exclusively from the Catholic Church.[19]

Few people know that centuries before the beginning of direct colonial rule, German companies, adventurers, and noble rulers had sought to gain colonial territories.[20] Such attempts, however, were ultimately fruitless or achieved only short-lived success. Only the elector Friedrich Wilhelm of Brandenburg founded, by hoisting the Brandenburg flag on January 1, 1683, on the West African coast, a trading colony that existed for several decades and was sold to the Dutch East India Trading Company in 1717.[21] This attempt to gain a trading colony, however, was not accompanied by attempts to convert the African population, as was typical practice later in the nineteenth century. According to the mission inspector of the Gossner church, Karl Plath, who lived during the beginning of German colonial rule in Africa, this was the reason the Prussian colonial venture did not last.[22] Here we have the widespread opinion of the nineteenth and twentieth centuries explicitly expressed: the Christian mission was a prerequisite for maintaining European colonial rule overseas.

In considering the German colonies, in particular in Africa, we can see that in most cases Christian missionaries worked in the areas that Germany later seized as colonies. All in all, most of the missionary societies were active in their mission areas much longer than the colonial masters ruled these territories. This was also the case in the German colonial areas founded in the mid-1880s, where as a rule missionary societies were in fact present, even if they were foreign ones. The German colonial politician Paul Rohrbach also praised non-German missionary societies for their contributions to establishing and maintaining colonial rule, as they had played "a role at the founding of the German colonial efforts."[23]

The large Protestant German missionary societies that already existed at this time in Basel, Berlin, and Bremen are also much older than the German colonies.[24] The German Protestant missionaries developed a specific set of ideas and concepts, albeit generally later than their coreligionists in the "classic colony countries" like England and France, and were influenced by the social situation in a Germany that had only been united in 1871. In a detailed study Thorsten Altena has characterized these missionaries in the sociocultural, political, and religious contexts of their time, with careful consideration of their careers, and has related this to their daily routines. He has created a multifaceted, vivid, and complex picture of missionary thought and action, in particular with regard to the working conditions in the mission field and the mission's relationship with colonial seizure of land.[25] The Catholic missions, in contrast, were organized internationally and ultimately controlled by the Vatican, even though many of their missionaries were Germans.

The following overview should make clear not only that the Christian missionary societies were already present in the later colonies of the German Empire before direct colonial rule was achieved but also that their influence continued to have an effect when the colonial masters began their retreat with the end of the First World War.

In the period of direct German rule, beginning in 1884/85, the leading representatives of the German missionary movement generally not only expressed a "fundamental approval of German colonial politics"[26] (some of them were even vocal proponents, like Friedrich Fabri[27]), but they also cooperated with colonial traders and merchants, a phenomenon that has hardly been studied up to the present day.[28]

Over the past several years, a significant number of publications about the history of Christian missions have appeared in Germany. Whether short case studies or book-length inquiries, these publications are primarily interested in the relationship between missions and colonialism. The changes of the indigenous societies through the process of Christianization have received attention in scholarship as well. As a theoretical frame, research has referenced the studies by Jean und John Comaroff. It is important to note that the Comaroffs' case studies have been performed among the Tswana in South Africa. Of course, there is a difference in the changes between indigenous societies under direct and indirect colonial rule. Additionally, when evaluating the influence of European forms of colonial power on traditional societies of Africa, we have to consider the national character of the colonial rulers. We also have to pay attention to the denomination of the missionary societies, who send their missionaries overseas. The Portuguese colonial ruler had a different relationship with the African population than the Germans or the French. Finally, it is significant in the evaluation of the influence of Christian missionaries on indigenous societies, to address the aspect if the missionaries or their missionary base came from the country that was colonized in Africa.

Southwest Africa

The first contact by German missionaries in the colonial areas later claimed by Germany was in German Southwest Africa, present-day Namibia. At that point most German missionaries still worked for the London Mission Society.[29] Later the Protestant Rhenish Missionary, which had its headquarters in Wuppertal, directly employed the missionaries.[30]

When in April 1884 South West Africa became a German colony, the Rhenish missionaries had already been working there for forty-two years. Until the start of the Herero War, in 1904, they had successfully defended their position of monopoly, in particular against Catholic attempts to get a foothold in the region. Tilman Dedering has pointed out that not only the Herero but also other ethnic communities resisted German colonialism, although they had close contact with the Christian religion and the mission.[31]

In addition to their actual task of spreading the Christian faith, the Protestant missionary societies took on the job of ending the constant intraethnic disputes of the native population over land in southwest Africa, not least in order to be able to fulfill their mission more effectively. This involvement benefited not only the missionary work but also the later colonization process. In historiography Heinrich Loth first criticized this cooperative behavior, and it was viewed, particularly in the 1960s and 1970s, as an example of the close relationship between the mission and colonialism.[32]

The missionaries viewed the settlement of nomadic cattle breeders in permanent mission stations as a means of accomplishing the task they had set themselves. The natives were "re-educated" as settled farmers.[33] For this reason the missionary Samuel Hahn had already introduced the plow to the Nama. The missionary leaders gave particular attention to the education and training of young Africans.[34] To make this process more effective, they pushed ahead with the translation of the Bible; current research has shown that the African wife of a missionary played a great part in the success of this project.[35] The Nama, under their chief, Jonker Afrikaner, were initially those on whom the missionaries could rely in spreading the Christian faith. When Jonker Afrikaner turned his back on Christianity, however, the Rhine Missionaries set their hopes on the Herero, whose political organization was much less mature. In the so-called Missionary Peace Settlement of 1870, limits could be fixed on the areas of settlement and spheres of influence of the two ethnic communities before the beginning of German colonial rule. In this way the missionaries could strengthen and even extend their influence over the Africans.

The hoped-for success of having created the foundations for a long-term secure peace did not come about, however. The Herero achieved political and economic dominance over the Nama, which caused the missionaries great problems.[36] They longed for a strong regime to guarantee that the Christian mission would develop and prosper, and it was unimportant to them whether this regime came from Great Britain or Germany. When the German Empire took on the "protectorate" over the estates and business enterprises acquired by the Bremen merchant Adolf Lüderitz, Germany set up direct colonial rule over large parts of the territory of what is today the Republic of Namibia. The local German missionaries and the mission leadership back home immediately welcomed this development.[37]

In German Southwest Africa the colonial administration could rely on the experience and influence of the missionaries among the African population.[38] It was largely due to their contributions, as Horst Gründer puts it, "that the loose protectorate of the German Empire turned into a largely stabilized colonial regime and that through military action the two large tribes, the Herero and Nama, were 'at peace' and their attempts at independence were suppressed."[39]

Of course, the Herero and Nama War (1904–7) had a decisive effect on the success of the missionary work of the Rhenish Missionary Society.[40] The violent suppression of the African resistance to colonial conquest, described by many historians as genocide,[41] brought the prerequisite for the expansion of the mission, combined with a general enhancement in the social status of those involved in German Southwest Africa.

Recent literature refers to the close relationship between the mission and colonialism that emerged in the war, as well as its place in the genocide debate.[42] The missionaries spoke out vehemently against the plans of the colonial administration to turn the subjugated Africans into a proletariat[43] and supported preserving the native population in their "tribal culture" as the most valuable treasure of the colony.[44] They were able in only a very few cases, however, to improve the living conditions of the African population directly. Recent literature deals with this less explicitly than with the fact that the missionary society set up or ran transit camps and reserves for imprisoned or expelled Africans.[45]

When the Herero-Nama War ended, the Catholic mission also became active in German Southwest Africa. Until that time the Rhenish Missionary Society had been able to retain its position of monopoly by appealing to the "Protectorate Law" of September 10, 1900, which only allowed religious denominations recognized by the German Empire unimpeded activity in the colonies. In 1896 the missionary congregation "Oblates of Mary Immaculate" (Hünfeld Oblates) had already tried to venture into Ovamboland, which was not yet under colonial rule. Because of joint protest by the Rhenish society and the Finnish missionary society, both of whom intended to carry out missionary work there, the Catholics had to give up their project two years later.[46] With the Marienberg Oblates (Salerians), however, they were able to continue working, providing pastoral care for the Catholic members of the German *Schutztruppe*.

The outbreak of war in 1904 surprised the Catholic missionaries as much as it did the Rhenish. Both groups succeeded in keeping some ethnic communities from taking part in the war and even prevented some groups of Tswana from fighting on the German side.

From the end of the war to the beginning of the First World War in 1914, the number of Africans baptized by the Rhenish Missionary Society grew almost threefold.[47] There were even rumors of mass baptisms. According to the historian Horst Gründer, these were not so much the manifestation of a sudden awakening of religious feeling as an expression of a "national all-embracing movement."[48]

In fact, after armed conflict had ended, the twenty-two mission stations of the Rhenish Mission Society, with their regulated daily routines, easy to comprehend hierarchies, relative safety, and offers of help from missionaries and other community members in other regions of the world, became relatively safe social and political sanctuaries. The Africans, who had just escaped the atrocities of the war, could reorient themselves and receive help and support from the well-meaning, if mostly paternalistic, Europeans.

Some of the altogether twenty-nine German missionaries no longer sympathized as much with the Africans as before, however; quite a few of their charges, including former close colleagues and friends of the missionaries, took part in battles against the Germans. These events, they said, had now deeply shaken their trust in the Africans. The extensive break in communication between the mission central office and the area of mission activity also led to this. As Richard Pierard has put it: "World War I was the greatest crisis in the history of Protestant world missions."[49]

The shattered "trust" led to a strengthening of the German paternalistic idea of missions, which resulted in a certain "susceptibility of colonial German Protestantism to National Socialism" and became "a significant expression of the continued existence of this colonial self-perception."[50] Not just susceptibility to, but direct collaboration with, National Socialism could be found in this tradition of the German missionaries. Scholarly debates on this subject were not possible for decades until Werner Ustorf initiated academic discussions about it.

German East Africa

Missionaries from Germany were also active in the German colony of East Africa before the German Empire officially assumed "protectorate" status. This happened relatively late. The private German East African Society administered the largest of the German colonies based on a letter of imperial safe conduct and was not under the administration of the German Empire until January 1, 1891. Before German missionary societies were officially active there, two German missionaries working for the Anglican Church missionary society entered east African territory and reported on country, culture, and people. They were Johann Ludwig Krapf and Johannes Rebman, who reached the hinterlands in 1848 from Mombasa.[51] The success of the two in missionary work was very modest, though, in contrast to their services to the geographic research of east Africa. Both of them had undertaken several exploratory trips in the hinterlands of what is today Tanzania, and they can be regarded to a certain extent as pioneer missionaries.[52]

Other German missionaries followed, mostly of the Catholic faith. They included the Bavarian missionaries that Father Matthias Ittameyer had sent out. The Scottish explorer and missionary David Livingstone, about whom many books have been published, had much more success in his work in east and central Africa. His written reports, as well as those of Henry Morton Stanley, John H. Speke, Richard Burton, and other Africa researchers, drew the attention of German missionaries and others to the east African region. The first German Protestant missionaries came to east Africa, however, after Catholic missionaries had started their work in Zanzibar in 1860 and later on the mainland, almost at the same time as the precursors of European colonial rule arose in the early 1880s.[53]

Hearing the "call" to missionary work, at that time young men in particular, with the support of the German East Africa Colonial Company, founded the German East Africa Missionary Society in the German capital, which also became known as Berlin III. Berlin III was not a rival; it had a completely different missionary work method than did Berlin I, the Berlin missionary society founded in 1824. Berlin III was founded in 1886, shortly after the German East Africa colony became a territory of the German Empire. Berlin III did not send trained missionaries but young pastors who had trained specifically for the mission with Pastor von Bodelschwingh in Bethel near Bielefeld. The mission organization Berlin III had a presence in east Africa in the two large harbors, Dar-es-Salaam and Tanga, and pushed forward from there to the interior of the country. It established additional stations in the lowland plain of Usaramo and in the Usambara Mountains.

The Berlin Missionary Society, which had until now only worked in south Africa, eyed the rival with mistrust and founded hospitals with missionaries they had trained themselves in Zanzibar and later in Dar-es-Salaam. According to the mission historian Julius Richter, these hospitals "benefited Germans moving out to the colony more than natives."[54] Because of costs and because they came to the realization that the mission required the "institutionalization of mission work,"[55] the mission organization Berlin III had to give up the east African area of activity again. The Berlin Missionary Society was not prepared to take over the hotel in Dar-es-Salaam, a structure that today has been restored to its former glory. They were determined, however, to develop a new sphere of activity in east Africa because of the strong colonial mood in the German public. The former south African missionary and missions inspector Alexander Merensky suggested to the leadership of the Berlin Missionary Society that they extend their missionary work to the newly emerging colony of German East Africa in the heart of the continent.[56] It was not the coastal region that was the goal but precisely the area at the north bank of Lake Nyssa, a long inland sea that marked the boundary of the German colonial area in the southwest.

Julius Richter has formulated significant reasons for this location change: "The area [was located] so centrally in the middle of the Western border of the German sphere of influence, that they could choose from there whether to extend their work to the North, East, or Southeast."[57]

The missionaries from Berlin came across an African population on their expedition that no longer lived in precolonial conditions. Because of the slave trade and the Islamic influence, the traditional communities were in the process of regrouping if not disintegrating.[58] We may assume that Merensky was not alone with the reason he gave so often for Christianization in that region, that "the Africans ... [should] be protected from Islam."[59] This was probably the real reason the Berlin Missionary Society started working in east Africa.

Kondeland, situated by the Nyassa, was a highland region with a favorable climate inhabited by African ethnic groups that had not had continual contact with the Europeans. Aboriginal societies, uninfluenced by European "civilization," were the favored goal of the missionaries because this "cultural situation" made their missionary work easier. For successful missionary work, as it says in the *Berliner Missions Reports*, "heathen naturalness and an organic state" were always beneficial.[60] The population by Lake Nyassa, which was previously almost untouched by European influence, was the target from the beginning.

As revealed in a report from the time, the decision to start working in this area was reached "after careful consideration and detailed information had been provided to the most competent authorities."[61] On the shores of the lake, almost in the hinterlands of the newly founded colony, there was a meeting of—as Alexander Merensky has formulated it—"the well-understood interests of the European colonist, merchant, and politician with the efforts and work of the Christian mission supporter and mission worker."[62]

Besides a few Protestant rivals for a new mission field in east Africa, the Berlin missionary leadership in the region saw a serious danger to its work in the Catholic orders and congregations, who were also trying with some success to reach the untapped interior of the country on the mainland where it was easier.[63] Nevertheless there were seven other German Protestant mission societies in the east African colony whose work has not all been researched in-depth. They were the rather small Bielefeld, Herrnhut, Leipzig, Neukirchen, and Schleswig-Holstein mission societies, as well as the Adventists and the Protestant Africa Society. Together they had 89 stations with 112 missionaries, 76 European helpers—mostly doctors and craftsmen—and 41 mission sisters.[64]

In judging the missionary work of the German missionary societies in east Africa, one must also consider the nationalist character of the missionaries' engagement.[65] The strong presence of German missionary societies in the east African region aimed to prevent more British societies from penetrating into the "protectorate" claimed by Germany. The extensive involvement of German missionaries in the educational system played a special role in trying to strengthen their position against British influence.[66] Although the Berlin competitors praised the work of some British missionary societies, they criticized in particular the London mission, which, according to Alexander Merensky, was ill qualified for "difficult work in the middle of enemy territory.

According to its independentistic rules, disorder is a matter of principle."[67] The Germans counterbalanced the relatively strong presence of the English missions, "who had passively resisted the German colonial competition in East Africa for many years."[68]

At around the same time the Berlin Missionary Society was preparing to add a new mission field, the Moravian Brethren decided to start working in the emerging colony of German East Africa. The missions expert Gustav Warneck was pleased to inform the German readership, who were interested in missions although probably also a bit skeptical, in the *Allgemeine Missions-Zeitschrift*, which he had founded and published, "The Brethren and Berlin will [shortly begin] a new mission project in the German East African protectorate. After careful consideration and detailed information was provided to the competent authorities, they both decided to make their starting point at the north end of the Nyassa, adjacent to the mission field of the Scottish Free Church."[69] The German colonial administration supported the work of the Christian missionaries. After the Arab uprising under Bushiri in 1888–89 the missionaries worked openly with the colonial administration and with the German colonists who were to develop the land.[70] Mission stations could rely on the military protection of the administration in later armed conflicts. In such situations, missionaries often willingly gave information on the whereabouts of "enemy forces" or placed themselves at the disposal of the German forces as guides or medical orderlies.[71] Circumstances were similar during the Maji Maji War of 1905 to 1907.[72] The territory of what is today the state of Rwanda also belonged to the German protectorate. The German researcher, doctor, and freethinker Richard Kandt lived in the capital Kigali from 1907 to 1913.[73] He was not an absolute supporter of Christian missionary work; however, neither was he an outspoken opponent of their activities. He appreciated the missionaries as mediators in communication with the colonial powers and as representatives of an important disciplinary authority.[74]

All in all, the success of German missionary work and that of other foreign societies in German East Africa, like the Catholic White Fathers, was relatively minor.[75] For the whole colony of German East Africa, we can say that after the end of the Maji Maji war, in the last decade of German colonial rule in east Africa, the missionaries more or less subordinated themselves to the German administration, acknowledged their sovereignty in the colony,[76] and profited from the "protectorate."[77]

Cameroon

Even before Germany established a "protectorate" in Cameroon in 1884, part of the Cameroonian population had been in contact with Christian missionaries forty years earlier. The English Baptist Missionary Society had found its sphere of activity here on the coast. From here missionary work proceeded to the interior of the country. The English missionaries tried to secure their home government as a protectorate, but it refused. Nevertheless, the German government regarded the English missionaries with suspicion from the start of its "protectorate" in Cameroon on July 14, 1884. For this reason, but in particular because of the unfavorable climate, the Baptist Missionary Society ended its work in Cameroon a year later. The Baptist mission gave over its sphere of activity to the Basel missionary societies, who were considered German because they received the greater part of their financing and most of their missionaries from Württemberg. Altogether, the Basel mission maintained twenty-three stations in Cameroon, where thirty-eight missionaries and twenty-two other Germans worked. The work of the Basel Mission was very successful up to the end of the century; in 1887 the mission had seven main stations and ninety-one substations, as well as eighty-eight schools with more than twenty-one hundred pupils.[78]

In conflict with the native population, the German colonial administration, which no longer had to show consideration for the English colonial competition, tried constantly "to impose order in the hopeless conditions of Douala."[79] With the expansion of the German colonial administration into the interior of the country, the missionaries moved away from the coast. They pushed onwards to the grasslands, where they encountered ethnic minorities that, it was later stated, would have found their way to Christianity even without the European missionaries.[80] This thesis cannot ultimately be proven, but it is interesting and innovative. African Christians founded their own churches—like the Native Baptist Church—early on, generally before the beginning of missionary work by the Basel Mission and by the Board of Foreign Missions of the Presbyterian Church (USA), who were also active in Cameroon. From this and other offshoots of the European missionary societies, the first independent African churches emerged on the continent.[81]

Overall, there was a very close relationship between colonial power and mission in Cameroon, since the exponents of the two institutions pursued the same goal, even if they did not share intentions, but "despite the mutual benefit of colonial development and extension of missionary activity, there was in no way a relationship on a partnership basis between the Basel Mission and the colonial government."[82] At the end of 1898 an open and protracted dispute broke out between the Basel Mission and the German administration. It was over the ill-treatment and expropriation of Africans that had occurred and become public knowledge, as well as over missionary property on Mount Cameroon and in the Bula district. This event has been researched thoroughly in the relevant literature.[83]

Togo

After the Togo coast in west Africa had become a German colony in 1884, the missionaries who had been working in the region since 1847 and the North German Mission Society, which had its headquarters in Bremen, continued working there.[84] In the forty years of their work, until 1887, the mission's main station was destroyed four times. Out of 112 missionaries, 59 died from the consequences of the tropical climate, and 41 had to go back to Europe for health reasons; by 1887 only 14 people were working for the missionary society in Togo.[85]

The work of the North German Missionary Society showed three characteristic specialties: (1) the close connection between the mission and the Bremen chamber of commerce;[86] (2) the missionaries' focus on the educational system;[87] and (3) the focus of missionary activity on one ethnic group, the Ewe. Initially the North German Missionary Society, in particular their leader, Franz Michael Zahn, had refused to allow the society to become a colonial mission.[88] He could not, however, prevent the missionaries from becoming "water carriers," as Edward G. Norris has formulated it, of the colonial state.[89]

At first there were no missionary stations located in the area claimed by the German colonial administration. It was not until the Helgoland-Zanzibar Treaty, between the German Empire and Great Britain, of July 1, 1890, which also settled the border question in West Africa,[90] that the first two stations of the North German Missionary Society belonged to the territory of the German colony of Togo. Up until the beginning of the First World War the missionary activity of the North German Missionary Society of Togo expanded, although it was concentrated on the southern third of the colony.

At the center of missionary activity was the Ewe population, who now lived in part under German and in part under British colonial authority.

Around 1902 the number of Ewe Christians in the German protectorate exceeded the number of indigenous Christians in the English Gold Coast Colony.[91] The North German Missionary Society concluded its work after Germany lost Togo in the Versailles Treaty.[92]

A distinctive feature of the early missionary activity in Togo was that those Africans the missionaries regarded as "suitable" went to Germany for training.[93] This had a considerable influence on the attainment of Christian independence that led to the founding of an independent Ewe church in 1922 in Togo.[94]

Despite this exceptional development in the relationship between colonial authority and Christian mission in what was described as a "model colony" in the "protectorate" of the German Empire in west Africa, the North German Missionary Society profited considerably from Togo in that it was connected as a colony through the German administration. It remained without real competition, because the Basel Missionary Society did not start working in northwestern Togo until the end of German colonial rule. There were only disputes with the mission order of the "Society of the Divine Word" after 1892.

The North German Missionary Society became more involved than other missionary societies as "an advocate of the natives," and in a few cases, it came into conflict with the colonial administration or individuals among their own representatives.[95] Despite the one mentioned above and other conflict areas, according to Thorsten Altena, "the missionary work in Togo was smoother and, with regard to the attainment of independence by African Christians, more successful than in the other German African colonies."[96]

Kiatchou

The colonial history of the territory of Kiatchou (also known as Qinghai, Tsingtao) differed from the German colonies in Africa in that it was under the administration of the imperial marines and was the only German overseas naval base.[97] It also had a number of special features that we cannot discuss in detail here.[98]

In general, China remained an object of desire for the European colonial powers until the second half of the nineteenth century; the European powers were unable to sustain a colonial presence there. Germany also directed its colonial endeavors there. It needed Asia because unlike Africa, the Europeans had not divided it up diplomatically among themselves, and rival Great Britain had already taken significant areas under its control, in particular the Indian subcontinent. This was a good pretext for making an impressive demonstration of German rights there and if possible asserting them. Germany needed a spectacular opportunity in Berlin to make its territorial desires clear to the Chinese emperor and the colonial competition. The missionaries inadvertently provided this opportunity. On November 1, 1897, members of the Society of the Long Knives murdered two fathers of the Catholic Steyler mission in South Shantung.[99] When Emperor Wilhelm II learned of this, he immediately ordered a fleet demonstration in the Bay of Kiatchou (also known as Jiao Zhou).

It was by no means the first incident to befall Christian missionaries in the Chinese Empire, nor was it the first to have been reported back to Berlin. "Every case reported back to Berlin and evaluated there was only considered to see whether political capital could be made of it."[100] The occupation of Kiatchou Bay on November 14, 1897, took place without active participation by German missionaries.[101] The reason given by the German government was that these measures served as a punishment for the murder of the missionaries. Representatives of the Catholic mission laid great store by the fact that "it was the murder of two missionaries that provided a reason for the occupation of Kiatchou," as a result of which Germany had found a means of interfering in domestic affairs.[102]

From the beginning of the eighteenth century, missionaries, in particular Catholic, had been working to convert Chinese people to Christianity, although most of the missionaries had been deported from the country in 1725. Around the middle of the nineteenth century there was a resurgence of missionary work in China.[103] The diplomatic representatives of the foreign powers regarded the missionaries of the different societies as cultural pioneers who contributed to spreading "European, North American culture" in China.[104]

Statistically, the results of the Christian mission in China toward the end of the nineteenth century were, as the British missions historian Stephen Neill expressed it, "not at all impressive."[105] The Chinese regarded European and North American missionaries foremost as the spearhead of "Western civilization." On March 6, 1898, after the "government of Kiatchou" had fallen to Germany for ninety-nine years by contract with China, a second event in the region shook the German public, which was relatively well informed about events in China.[106] The event was known as the Boxer

Uprising. Neither the spatial nor the chronological connection between the occupation of Kiatchou and the outbreak of the Boxer Uprising can be assessed, even though it was much disputed on the German side in news reports of the time and in later portrayals.[107]

Even though the history of the German colony has been extensively researched in all its facets,[108] only case studies exist on the missionary societies and their relationship to the colonial administration, some more detailed than others. Examples include one on the Berlin Mission Society, which was active beginning in 1898, and on the Rhenish Missionary Society, which occasionally worked there.[109] Besides the Lutheran Berlin Missionary Society, the General Evangelical Protestant Society, the Catholic Steyler Mission, and the American Protestant Mission Society worked in Tsingtao and the Kiatchou area. The missionary work in China differed from other overseas activities across the world in that the missionaries were aware that Chinese culture was an "old and independent structure equal to the Western one in many aspects."[110] Those responsible in the missionary societies took as their starting point that the Chinese should be converted not just through a sermon but also through an intercultural religious discussion. This included efforts to translate the Bible and religious writings into Chinese, concentration on special mission foci such as native women,[111] and influencing the educational system[112] or medical assistance and training[113] in the medium term. Altogether, we could describe these goals as unattainable for the directors of the mission societies in Germany, as well as others. Both the Christian mission and the far-fetched goals of the European strategists failed. In particular, the "cultural mission" run by the Germans could not be realized.

Despite this clear defeat, most of the missionaries remained in their racist, patriarchal world of ideas, convinced of the superiority of their own culture. This integration of missionary thinking into the Western awareness of superiority and colonial mentality made an independent reconciliatory Christianity seem unrealistic. The German missionaries in Asia preferred to rely on the Asian "cannon boat diplomacy" of the Western protection forces.[114]

The South Seas

The failure of the colonial mission in Asia was the opposite of the "triumph" of Christianity in Oceania, also known as the South Seas.[115] Christianity had gained a foothold on the islands of the South Seas even before the Germans arrived. The various colonial bases of the German Empire were spread over a large area. The German claim stretched from 131 to 173 degrees longitude east and from the equator to latitude 21 degrees north. Northeast New Guinea made up the biggest area.[116] Here the Germans encountered, according to the mission expert Julius Richter, "a morally low, cannibalistic heathendom and it was... almost a polar question to the spiritual strength of Christianity, whether [Germans] could control this unruly heathen wildness."[117]

Besides this, the islands of the Bismarck Archipelago, the northern Solomon Islands, the Marshall Islands with the Nauru isles, Palau, the Caroline Islands, and the Marianas, also known as Micronesia, belonged to the German colonies. Later Western Samoa was also part of German colonial territory.[118]

In 1882, two years before the Germans seized New Guinea, missionaries of the Catholic Heart of Jesus Foundation had already settled there. In 1896 Catholic communities came to New Guinea with the Steyler Mission.[119] German missionary societies had only discovered the South Sea as an area of activity after various attempts to gain a foothold in the Malaysian Islands had failed.[120]

Mission work on the mainland of German New Guinea, known as Kaiser Wilhelm Land, proved to be particularly difficult. The Rhenish missionaries who had been working in the area since 1887 had their first modest successes here; they did not win over believers with their sermons but through the quantity and usefulness of the many tools the Europeans brought and other things that were useful for the natives, like medical supplies.[121] Not least because the Rhenish Missionary Society was too close to the colonial regime, their missionaries acquired a bad reputation; they also made themselves seem like "the advocates of a harsh regime and an extended arm of the New Guinea Company."[122] Of the fifty-three men and women the Rhenish mission had sent to this region, six died before 1913, and eighteen gave up.

Primarily American and Spanish missionaries were present on the Caroline Islands when the Germans arrived. The German administration did not like this and tried to bring German missionaries to the islands. Beginning in 1907, missionaries of the Liebenzell Mission took over the work of the foreign societies. However, a few Catholic fathers and sisters were scattered around the group of islands.[123]

Largely because of the decentralized situation among the scattered South Sea Islands and the different missionary societies in the Pacific, it is impossible to draw firm general conclusions about the activities of German missionary societies at the time of German colonial rule. Nevertheless, I will make a few short concluding comments on this subject. In February 1887 the first German missionary from the Rhenish Missionary Society arrived in German New Guinea;[124] then in July 1890 the first four Heart of Jesus missionaries landed in New Pomerania, followed by a few Steyler missionaries in August 1896. In March 1899 the Marists established the first mission station on the Shortland Islands that were still under German rule, but they were only able to lay the groundwork and make initial contact with the native population.[125]

The Liebenzell mission started its work shortly before the outbreak of the First World War.[126] The situation was different in Micronesia. Here the missionary work, carried out mostly by protestant missionaries from the United States, became markedly political.[127] The missionaries of the various societies and denominations became advocates for the small number of communities living on the island, when they came into conflict with the colonial administration. The primary target of the mission was the chiefs, who became important mediators between the cultures and religions.[128]

Although analysis shows a few fundamental commonalities in the relationship between Christian missions and colonialism in the German colonies in the time that they existed from 1884/85 until 1918/19, we should avoid sweeping judgments from today's perspective. First, an assessment of the relationship between German missionaries and the colonial administrations of other European states would turn out quite differently from an assessment of the relationship between German missionaries and the German colonial administration. Second, as Wilfried Wagner pointed out years ago, the idea of "the missionary" is an idealized construction, in the same way that "the mission" or "the colonies" never existed.[129] Valid assessments always depend on the person, institution, time, and place.

In mission history research over the past several years, often described as interdisciplinary or revisionist mission historiography,[130] there have been other questions at the center of debate, such as the significance of the emergence of an aboriginal Christianity[131] or the role of the missionary as a researcher of different cultures or his or her contribution to the creation of transcultural knowledge.

Scholars have also increasingly adopted the importance of women in overseas mission work as a theme.[132] In addition, research has examined the role of the missionary as a mediator between cultures and thus his or her role in transcultural history.[133] The indigenous mission helper and the effects of the presence of missionary families among indigenous societies are also playing an increasing role in debates.[134] In general, a significant branch of mission historiography is apparently reemerging in the historiography of non-European Christianity, which, in light of the strengthening of Christianity in the so-called third world, is not only vital for political science but may have already yielded interesting conclusions.[135]

Notes

1. On the field of British Empire studies see Porter, *Religion versus Empire?*
2. See, e.g., Paczensky, *Teurer Segen.*
3. For more on the difficult intrachurch transition process from mission to ecumenism see Neill, *Mission zwischen Kolonialismus und Ökumene.*
4. Gründer, "Mission und Kolonialismus."
5. Ritter, *Der Kampf um den Erdraum,* 239 (my translation; unless otherwise indicated, all translations are my own).
6. Rohrbach, "Die Mission in den deutschen Kolonien," 180.
7. Balz, "Mission und Kolonialismus," 175.
8. Wangemann, *Südafrika und seine Bewohner nach den Beziehungen der Geschichte, Geographie, Ethnologie, Staaten- und Kirchen-Bildung, Mission und des Racen-Kampfes,* 46.
9. Sarajevskaja, *Starye i Novye Religii Tropieskoj i Juznoj Africi,* 229.
10. Lange, *Kontinent der kurzen Schatten,* 178.
11. See Geiss, "Mission, Imperialismus und Kolonialismus."
12. Eckart, "Robert Koch"; Eckart, *Medizin und Kolonialimperialismus, Deutschland 1884–1945*; Grundmann, "Die ärztliche Mission"; and Grundmann, *Gesandt zu heilen!*
13. See Hammer, *Weltmission und Kolonialismus*; Bade, *Imperialismus und Kolonialmission*; and Gründer, "Mission und Kolonialismus."
14. See Heyden, "Kolonialgeschichtsschreibung in Deutschland."
15. The standard work of the GDR on German colonial history is Stoecker, *Drang nach Afrika* (German Imperialism in Africa).
16. See Loth, *Kolonialismus unter der Kutte*; Loth, *Im Schatten des Sternenbanners*; Loth, *Kolonialismus und Religion*; and Loth, *Zwischen Gott und Kattun.*
17. Gründer, *Mission und Kolonialismus,* 26.
18. For an overview see Heyden, "Missions."
19. See Gründer, *Welteroberung und Christentum.*
20. See, e.g., Gründer, *"—da und dort ein junges Deutschland gründen"*; Hundt, *"Woraus nichts geworden"*; Heyden, "Brandenburg-Preußens Streben in die Welt";

and Volberg, *Deutsche Kolonialbestrebungen in Südamerika nach dem Dreißigjährigen Kriege*.

21. Heyden, *Rote Adler an Afrikas Küste*.
22. See Plath, *Deutsche Kolonialmission*, 10.
23. Rohrbach, "Die Mission in den deutschen Kolonien," 181.
24. Ustorf, "Mission als Vorhut des Kolonialismus?"
25. Altena, *"Ein Häuflein Christen mitten in der Heidenwelt des dunklen Erdteils."*
26. Gründer, *Christliche Mission und deutscher Imperialismus*, 100.
27. See Bade, *Friedrich Fabri und der Imperialismus in der Bismarckzeit*; Bade, "Imperialismus und Kolonialmission"; Schmidt, *Mission, Kirche und Reich Gottes bei Friedrich Fabri*.
28. Pierard, "A Case Study in German Economic Imperialism," 164; Braun, *Die Rheinische Missionsgesellschaft und der Missionshandel im 19. Jahrhundert*; Heinrich, "Mission und Handel im missionarischen Selbstverständnis und in der kirchlichen Praxis."
29. See Dedering, *Hate the Old and Follow the New*.
30. Oermann, *Mission, Church and State Relations in South West Africa Under German Rule (1884–1915)*.
31. Dedering, "Hendrik Witbooi"; Bühler, *Der Namaaufstand gegen die deutsche Kolonialherrschaft in Namibia von 1904–1913*.
32. Loth, *Die christliche Mission in Südwestafrika*; Drechsler, *Let Us Die Fighting*, 18–22.
33. Gründer, "Deutsche Missionsgesellschaften auf dem Weg zur Kolonialmission."
34. Panzergrau, *Die Bildung und Erziehung der Eingeborenen Südwestafrikas durch die Rheinische Missionsgesellschaft von 1842–1914*.
35. See Trüper, *Die Hottentottin*.
36. See Henrichsen, "Die Hegemonie der Herero in Zentralnamibia zu Beginn der deutschen Kolonialherrschaft."
37. Engel, *Kolonialismus und Nationalismus im deutschen Protestantismus in Namibia, 1907 bis 1945*.
38. Oermann, "'Hochwerter Herr Gouverneur.'"
39. Gründer, *Christliche Mission und deutscher Imperialismus*, 120.
40. Glocke, *Zur Geschichte der Rheinischen Missionsgesellschaft unter besonderer Berücksichtigung des Kolonialkrieges von 1904 bis 1907*; Pierard, "The Rhenish Mission and the Colonial War in German Southwest Africa."
41. Zimmerer and Zeller, *Genocide in German South-West Africa*; Wassink, *Auf den Spuren des deutschen Völkermordes in Südwestafrika*; Gewald, *Herero Heroes*; Brehl, *Vernichtungskrieg der Herero*.
42. Krüger, *Kriegsbewältigung und Geschichtsbewusstsein*; Spraul, "Der 'Völkermord' an den Herero"; Dedering, "The German-Herero-War of 1904."
43. Grienig, "'Ein äusserst schwer zu bedienendes Missionsobjekt.'"

44. Gründer, *Christliche Mission und deutscher Imperialismus*, 130.
45. See Spiecker-Salazar, "Mission und Kolonialherrschaft aus der Sicht eines Missionsinspektors."
46. Miettinen, "'Living on the King's Land and Drinking the King's Water'"; Weiss, "The Beginning of Finnish Missionary Activity in Northern Namibia and Its First Setbacks, 1869–1872."
47. See Engel, *Kolonialismus und Nationalismus im deutschen Protestantismus in Namibia, 1907 bis 1945*.
48. Gründer, *Christliche Mission und deutscher Imperialismus*, 134.
49. Pierard, "World War I, the Western Allies, and German Protestant Mission," 361.
50. Gründer, *Christliche Mission und deutscher Imperialismus*, 134.
51. See Krapf, *Reisen in Ostafrika, ausgeführt in den Jahren 1837–1855*; Gütl, *Johann Ludwig Krapf*.
52. Triebel, "Evangelische Mission in Tanzania im Kontext von Kolonialismus und afrikanischer Tradition," 102.
53. Von Sicard, "Missionary Attitudes and Approaches to Muslims, Zanzibar 1864–1890."
54. Richter, *Geschichte der Berliner Missionsgesellschaft, 1824–1924*, 633.
55. Faschinger, "Mission braucht Institution."
56. See Merensky, *Erinnerungen aus dem Missionsleben in Transvaal (Südafrika), 1859 bis 1882*; and Heyden, "Zu den politischen Hintergründen der Njassa-Expedition von Alexander Merensky."
57. Richter, *Geschichte der Berliner Missionsgesellschaft, 1824–1924*, 633.
58. Pesek, "Kreuz oder Halbmond."
59. Merensky, *Deutsche Arbeit am Nyassa*, 11.
60. *Berliner Missionsberichte*, 245.
61. Warneck, "Zwei neue deutsche Missionen in Deutsch-Ostafrika," 79.
62. Merensky, *Deutsche Arbeit am Nyassa*, 11.
63. See Lemke, "Zu Methoden und Wirkungen der katholischen Missionskongregationen in der ehemaligen Kolonie Deutsch-Ostafrika, 1885–1918."
64. Rohrbach, "Die Mission in den deutschen Kolonien," 182; Fitzner, *Deutsches Kolonialhandbuch*.
65. Fiedler, *Christentum und afrikanische Kultur*.
66. Eggert, *Missionsschule und sozialer Wandel in Ostafrika*; Becher, "Ora et labora?".
67. Merensky, *Deutsche Arbeit am Nyassa*, 17.
68. Loth, "Auseinandersetzungen im religiösen Gewand," 371.
69. Warneck, "Zwei neue deutsche Missionen in Deutsch-Ostafrika," 79.
70. Gründer, *Christliche Mission und deutscher Imperialismus*, 183.
71. Niesel, "Kolonialverwaltung und Missionen in Deutsch-Ostafrika, 1890–1914."

72. Niesel, "Mit Kreuz und Krone"; and Niesel, "Kolonialverwaltung und Missionen in Deutsch-Ostafrika zur zeit des Maji-Maji-Aufstandes, 1905–1907."

73. Bindseil, "Richard Kandt und die indirekte Kolonialherrschaft in Ruanda"; and Bindseil, *Ruanda und Deutschland seit den Tagen Richard Kandts.*

74. Becher, "Die deutsche evangelische Mission."

75. Wright, *German Missions in Tanganyika, 1891–1941.*

76. Gründer, *Christliche Mission und deutscher Imperialismus*, 232.

77. Nzalayaimisi, "The Berlin Mission and the Destabilization of Power and Local Politics in Eastern and Southern Tanzania, 1887–1918."

78. Gründer, *Christliche Mission und deutscher Imperialismus*, 174.

79. Richter, *Geschichte der evangelischen Mission in Afrika*, 173; see also Eckert, *Grundbesitz, Landkonflikte und kolonialer Wandel.*

80. Balz, *Where the Faith Has to Live.*

81. Ludwig, "Afrikanische prophetische Bewegungen."

82. Altena, *"Ein Häuflein Christen mitten in der Heidenwelt des dunklen Erdteils,"* 43.

83. See, e.g., Rennstich, "The Understanding of Mission, Civilisation and Colonialism in the Basel Mission."

84. Sebald, *Togo, 1884–1914*, 469–505.

85. Altena, *"Ein Häuflein Christen mitten in der Heidenwelt des dunklen Erdteils,"* 139.

86. Tell and Heinrich, "Mission und Handel im missionarischen Selbstverständnis und in der kolonialen Praxis."

87. Adick, *Bildung und Kolonialismus in Togo.*

88. Ustorf, *Die Missionsmethode Franz Michael Zahns und der Aufbau kirchlicher Strukturen in Westafrika.*

89. Norris, *Die Umerziehung des Afrikaners*, 90–93.

90. Schneppen, "Der Helgoland-Sansibar-Vertrag von 1890."

91. Altena, *"Ein Häuflein Christen mitten in der Heidenwelt des dunklen Erdteils,"* 48.

92. Schöck-Quinteros and Lenz, *150 Jahre Norddeutsche Mission, 1836–1986.*

93. Azamede, "Von Komla-Kuma zu Albert Wilhelm Binder"; Heyden, "Lebensgeschichten der afrikanischen Diaspora in Deutschland."

94. Njoku, "The Missionary Factor in African Christianity"; Koschorke, "Emanzipationsbestrebungen indigen-christlicher Eliten in Indien und Westafrika um die Jahrhundertwende"; Ludwig, "African Independent Churches in West Africa Around 1900."

95. See Pabst, *Mission und Kolonialpolitik.*

96. Altena, *"Ein Häuflein Christen mitten in der Heidenwelt des dunklen Erdteils,"* 51.

97. Nuhn, *Kolonialpolitik und Marine*, 128–36.

98. See Steinmetz, *The Devil's Handwriting*.

99. Tiedemann, "Christian Missions in Shandong in the Context of China's National and Revolutionary Development."

100. Gründer, *Christliche Mission und deutscher Imperialismus*, 277.

101. Von Mende, "Für Gott und Vaterland?"

102. Gründer, "Die Rolle der christlichen Mission beim Ausbruch des Boxeraufstandes." See also Dabringhaus, "Der Boxeraufstand in China (1900/09)."

103. Klein, "Aktion und Reaktion?"

104. Ballin, "Colonial Imperialism and Christian Mission in China."

105. Neill, *Geschichte der christlichen Missionen*, 225.

106. Gerber, *Von Voskamps "heidnischem Treiben" und Wilhelms "höherem China"*; Wünsche, *Feldpostbriefe aus China*.

107. Mühlhahn, "Deutschlands Platz an der Sonne?"

108. Mühlhahn, *Herrschaft und Widerstand in der "Musterkolonie" Kiautschau*.

109. Jörgensen, "Zum wechselvollen Verhältnis von Mission und Politik"; Jörgensen, "Funktionalisierung der Mission durch chinesische Christen."

110. Rohrbach, "Die Mission in den deutschen Kolonien," 183.

111. Boetzinger, *"Den Chinesen ein Chinese werden"*; and Freytag, *Frauenmission in China*.

112. Kim, *Deutscher Kulturimperialismus in China*; Mehnert, "Regierungs- und Missionsschulen in der deutschen Kolonialpolitik (1885–1914)."

113. Eckart, *Deutsche Ärzte in China, 1897–1914*.

114. Graichen and Gründer, *Deutsche Kolonien*, 236.

115. Gründer, *Welteroberung und Christentum*, 429.

116. Schütte, "Lokale Reaktionen auf evangelische Missionsbemühungen im kolonialen Neu Guinea, 1887–1914."

117. Richter, "Mission und Kolonisation," 353.

118. Gründer, "Die Etablierung des Christentums auf Samoa."

119. Steffen, "Die katholischen Missionen in Deutsch-Neuguinea."

120. Wagner, "Historiographische Anmerkungen zur Geschichte deutscher Missionstätigkeit in der Malayischen Welt."

121. Schütte, *Der Ursprung der Messer und Beile*; Pech, "Deutsche evangelische Missionare in Deutsch-Neuguinea, 1886–1921"; Eckart, "Medicine and German Colonial Expansion in the Pacific."

122. Graichen and Gründer, *Deutsche Kolonien*, 177; see also Bade, "Culture, Cash, and Christianity."

123. Christmann, Hempenstall, and Ballendorf, *Die Karolinen-Inseln in deutscher Zeit*, 115–25.

124. Pech, "Die Rheinische Mission in Deutsch-Neuguinea (1887–1921)."

125. Steffen, "Die Maristenmission in den deutschen Salomonen."

126. Pech, "Die Liebenzeller Mission auf Manus (1914)," 413.

127. Knoll, "Die amerikanische-protestantische Mission im deutschen Mikronesien."

128. Käser, "Eine Legende auf Chuuk."

129. Wagner, "Plädoyer für eine profane Geschichtsschreibung," 13.

130. Heyden, "Missionsgeschichte im heutigen Verständnis multi- und interdisziplinärer Forschung"; Schulze, "Neure, interdisziplinäre Ansätze in der Missionsgeschichtsschreibung," 100.

131. Koschorke, "Kirchengeschichte, Missionsgeschichte, transnationale Christentumsgeschichte"; Koschorke, "Außereuropäische Christentumsgeschichte (Asien, Afrika, Lateinamerika)."

132. Prodolliet, *Wider die Schamlosigkeit und das Elend der heidnischen Weiber*; Konrad, *Missionsbräute*; Bowie, Kirkwood, and Ardener, *Women and Missions*; Theil, *Reise in das Land des Todesschattens*; Wendlandt-Hamann, *Zugvögel kennen ihre Zeit*; Töpperwien, *Seine "Gehülfin."*

133. Klein and Zöllner, *Karl Gützloff (1803–1851) und das Christentum in Ostasien*; Koschorke, *"Christen und Gewürze."*

134. Comaroff and Comaroff, *Of Revelation and Revolution*; Liebau, *Die indischen Mitarbeiter der Tranquebarmission (1706–1845)*; Heyden, *Martinus Sewushan*; Johnson, *Schwarze Missionare—weiße Missionare*.

135. Ludwig, "Profile der afrikanischen Christentumsgeschichte."

Bibliography

Adick, Christel. *Bildung und Kolonialismus in Togo: Eine Studie zu den Entstehungszusammenhängen eines europäisch geprägten Bildungswesens in Afrika am Beispiel Togos (1850–1914)*. Weinheim: Beltz, 1989.

Adick, Christel, and Wolfgang Mehnert. *Deutsche Missions- und Kolonialpädagogik in Dokumenten: Eine kommentierte Quellensammlung aus den Afrikabeständen deutschsprachiger Archive 1884–1914*. Frankfurt: IKO-Verlag für Interkulturelle Kommunikation, 2001.

Alt, Josef, ed. *Arnold Janssen SVD: Briefe nach Neuguinea und Australien*. Nettetal: Steyler, 1996.

Altena, Thorsten. *"Ein Häuflein Christen mitten in der Heidenwelt des dunklen Erdteils": Zum Selbst- und Fremdverständnis protestantischer Missionare im kolonialen Afrika, 1884–1918*. Münster: Waxmann, 2003.

Azamede, Kokou. "Von Komla-Kuma zu Albert Wilhelm Binder: Die Autobiographie eines afrikanischen Pastors aus Deutsch-Togo, 1858–1934." In *Jahrbuch für Europäische Ethnologie*, edited by Görres Gesellschaft, 81–96. Paderborn: Schöningh, 2006.

Bade, Klaus J. "Culture, Cash, and Christianity: The German Colonial Experience and the Case of the Rhenish Mission in New Guinea." *Pacific Studies* 10, no. 3 (1987): 53–71.

———. *Friedrich Fabri und der Imperialismus in der Bismarckzeit: Revolution, Depression, Expansion.* Freiburg: Atlantis, 1975.

———. "Imperialismus und Kolonialmission: Das Erbe Friedrich Fabris (Rheinische Mission)." In *Seelenfischer: Mission, Stammesvölker und Ökologie,* edited by Peter E. Stüben, 21–35. Giessen: Focus, 1994.

———, ed., *Imperialismus und Kolonialmission: Kaiserliches Deutschland und koloniales Imperium.* Wiesbaden: Steiner, 1982.

Ballin, Ursula. "Colonial Imperialism and Christian Mission in China: The Cases of the German Missionaries Gützlaff, Anzer and Wilhelm." In *Deutschland und China: Beiträge des Zweiten Internationalen Symposiums zur Geschichte der deutsch-chinesischen Beziehungen Berlin 1991,* edited by Heng-yü Kuo and Mechthild Leutner, 191–214. München: Minerva, 1994.

Balz, Heinrich. "Mission und Kolonialismus: Thesen." *Zeitschrift für Mission* 17, no. 3 (1991): 175–81.

———. *Where the Faith Has to Live: Studies in Bakosi Society and Religion.* Berlin: Dietrich Reimer, 1995.

Becher, Jürgen. "Die deutsche evangelische Mission—eine Erziehungs- und Disziplinierungsinstanz in Deutsch-Ostafrika." In *Alles unter Kontrolle: Disziplinierungsprozesse im kolonialen Tansania (1850–1960),* edited by Albert Wirz, Andreas Eckert, and Katrin Bromber, 141–69. Cologne: Rüdiger Köppe, 2003.

———. "Ora et labora? Evangelische Missionen und ihr Ringen um Erziehungs- und Disziplinierungsstrategien in der Kolonie Deutsch-Ostafrika." In *Mission und Moderne: Beiträge zur Geschichte der christlichen Missionen in Afrika anläßlich der Jahrestagung der VAD und des 12. Afrikanistentages vom 3.–6. Oktober 1996 in Berlin,* edited by Ulrich van der Heyden and Jürgen Becher, 21–38. Cologne: Rüdiger Köppe, 1998.

Bergunder, Michael, ed. *Missionsberichte aus Indien im 18. Jahrhundert: Ihre Bedeutung für die europäische Geistesgeschichte und ihr wissenschaftlicher Quellenwert für die Indienkunde.* Halle: Verlag der Franckeschen Stiftungen, 1999.

Berliner Missionsberichte. Berlin: Heimatdienstverlag, 1889.

Bindseil, Reinhart. "Richard Kandt und die indirekte Kolonialherrschaft in Ruanda." In *"—Macht und Anteil an der Weltherrschaft": Berlin und der deutsche Kolonialismus,* edited by Ulrich van der Heyden and Joachim Zeller, 149–54. Münster: Unrast, 2005.

———. *Ruanda und Deutschland seit den Tagen Richard Kandts: Begegnungen und gemeinsame Wegstrecken; Historischer Abriß der deutsch-ruandischen Beziehungen mit einer biographischen Würdigung des einstigen deutschen kaiserlichen Residenten.* Berlin: Dietrich Reimer, 1988.

Boetzinger, Vera. *"Den Chinesen ein Chinese werden": Die deutsche protestantische Frauenmission in China, 1842–1952.* Stuttgart: Steiner, 2004.

Bowie, Fiona, Deborah Kirkwood, and Shirley Ardener, eds. *Women and Missions: Past and Present: Anthropological and Historical Perceptions.* Providence, RI: Berg, 1993.

Braun, Thomas. *Die Rheinische Missionsgesellschaft und der Missionshandel im 19. Jahrhundert.* Erlangen: Verlag der Evangelisch-Lutherischen Mission, 1992.

Brehl, Medardus. *Vernichtungskrieg der Herero: Diskurse der Gewalt in der deutschen Kolonialliteratur.* Munich: Wilhelm Fink, 2007.

Brose, Winfried, and Ulrich van der Heyden, eds. *Mit Kreuz und deutscher Flagge: 100 Jahre Evangelium im Süden Tanzanias; Zum Wirken der Berliner Mission in Ostafrika.* Münster: Lit, 1993.

Bühler, Andreas Heinrich. *Der Namaaufstand gegen die deutsche Kolonialherrschaft in Namibia von 1904–1913.* Frankfurt: IKO-Verlag für Interkulturelle Kommunikation, 2003.

Christmann, Helmut, Peter Hempenstall, and Dirk Anthony Ballendorf. *Die Karolinen-Inseln in deutscher Zeit: Eine kolonialgeschichtliche Fallstudie.* Münster: Lit, 1991.

Comaroff, Jean, and John Comaroff. *Of Revelation and Revolution.* 2 vols. Chicago: University of Chicago Press, 1991, 1997.

Dabringhaus, Sabine. "Der Boxeraufstand in China (1900/09): Die Militarisierung eines kulturellen Konflikts." In *"Barbaren" und weiße Teufel: Kulturkonflikte und Imperialismus in Asien vom 18. bis zum 20. Jahrhundert,* edited by Eva-Maria Auch and Stig Förster, 123–44. Paderborn: Schöningh, 1997.

Dech, Uwe Christian. *Mission und Kultur im alten Neuguinea: Der Missionar und Völkerkundler Stephan Lehner.* Bielefeld: Transcript, 2005.

Dedering, Tilman. "The German-Herero-War of 1904: Revisionism of Genocide or Imaginary Historiography." *Journal of Southern African Studies* 19, no. 1 (1993): 80–88.

———. *Hate the Old and Follow the New: Khoekhoe and Missionaries in Early Nineteenth-Century Namibia.* Stuttgart: Steiner, 1997.

———. "Hendrik Witbooi: Religion, Kollaboration und Widerstand in Deutsch-Südwestafrika." In Heyden and Liebau, *Missionsgeschichte, Kirchengeschichte, Weltgeschichte,* 325–42.

Drechsler, Horst. *Let Us Die Fighting: The Struggle of the Herero and Nama Against German Imperialism (1884–1915).* London: Zed, 1980.

Eckart, Wolfgang U. *Deutsche Ärzte in China 1897–1914: Medizin als Kulturmission im Zweiten Deutschen Kaiserreich.* Stuttgart: G. Fischer, 1989.

———. "Medicine and German Colonial Expansion in the Pacific: The Caroline, Mariana, and Marshall Islands." In *Disease, Medicine, and Empire: Perspectives on Western Medicine and the Experience of European Expansion*, edited by Roy McLeod and Milton Lewis, 80–102. London: Routledge, 1988.

———. *Medizin und Kolonialimperialismus, Deutschland 1884–1945*. Paderborn: Schöningh, 1997.

———. "Robert Koch: Ein Bakteriologe für die Kolonien." In *Kolonialmetropole Berlin: Eine Spurensuche*, edited by Ulrich van der Heyden and Joachim Zeller, 102–6. Berlin: Berlin Edition, 2002.

Eckert, Andreas. *Grundbesitz, Landkonflikte und kolonialer Wandel: Douala, 1880 bis 1960*. Stuttgart: Steiner, 1999.

Eggert, Johanna. *Missionsschule und sozialer Wandel in Ostafrika: Der Beitrag der deutschen evangelischen Missionsgesellschaft zur Entwicklung des Schulwesens in Tanganyika 1891–1939*. Bielefeld: Bertelsmann Universitätsverlag, 1970.

Engel, Lothar. *Kolonialismus und Nationalismus im deutschen Protestantismus in Namibia, 1907 bis 1945: Beiträge zur Geschichte der deutschen evangelischen Mission und Kirche im ehemaligen Kolonial- und Mandatsgebiet Südwestafrika*. Bern: Peter Lang, 1976.

Ethnographie und Herrnhuter Mission—Völkerkundemuseum Herrnhut. Katalog zur ständigen Ausstellung im Völkerkundemuseum Herrnhut, Dresden. Staatliches Museum für Völkerkunde, 2003.

Faschinger, Gerald. "Mission braucht Institution: Missionsgesellschaften im späten 19. und frühen 20. Jahrhundert." In *Im Zeichen des Kreuzes: Mission, Macht und Kulturtransfer seit dem Mittelalter*, edited by Bernd Hausberger, 151–78. Wien: Mandelbaum, 2004.

Fiedler, Klaus. *Christentum und afrikanische Kultur: Konservative deutsche Missionare in Tanzania, 1900 bis 1940*. Gütersloh: Gütersloher Verlagshaus, 1983.

Fitzner, Rudolf. *Deutsches Kolonialhandbuch: Nach amtlichen Quellen bearbeitet*. 2 vols. Berlin: Hermann Paetel, 1901. Reprint, Wolfenbüttel: Melchior, 2000.

Freytag, Miriam. *Frauenmission in China: Die interkulturelle und pädagogische Bedeutung der Missionarinnen untersucht anhand ihrer Berichte von 1900 bis 1930*. Münster: Waxmann, 1994.

Geiss, Imanuel. "Mission, Imperialismus und Kolonialismus." In Heyden and Liebau, *Missionsgeschichte, Kirchengeschichte, Weltgeschichte*, 69–87.

Gerber, Lydia. *Von Voskamps "heidnischem Treiben" und Wilhelms "höherem China": Die Berichterstattung deutscher Protestantischer Missionare aus dem deutschen Pachtgebiet Kiautschou 1898–1914*. Hamburg: Ostasien, 2002.

Gewald, Jan-Bart. *Herero Heroes: A Socio-Political Study of the Herero of Namibia*. Oxford: James Currey, 1999.

Glocke, Nicole. *Zur Geschichte der Rheinischen Missionsgesellschaft unter besonderer Berücksichtigung des Kolonialkrieges von 1904 bis 1907*. Bochum: N. Brockmeyer, 1997.

Graichen, Gisela, and Horst Gründer. *Deutsche Kolonien: Traum und Träume.* Berlin: Ullstein, 2005.
Gremels, Georg, ed. *Die Hermannsburger Mission und das "Dritte Reich": Zwischen faschistischer Verführung und lutherischer Beharrlichkeit.* Münster: Lit, 2005.
Grienig, Ingrid. "'Ein äusserst schwer zu bedienendes Missionsobjekt': Farmarbeiter in Deutsch-Südwestafrika." In Heyden and Becher, *Mission und Gewalt,* 435–48.
Gründer, Horst. *Christliche Heilsbotschaft und weltliche Macht: Studien zum Verhältnis von Mission und Kolonialismus; Gesammelte Aufsätze.* Münster: Lit, 2004.
———. *Christliche Mission und deutscher Imperialismus: Eine politische Geschichte ihrer Beziehungen während der deutschen Kolonialzeit (1884–1914) unter besonderer Berücksichtigung Afrikas und Chinas.* Paderborn: Schöningh, 1982.
———. *"—da und dort ein junges Deutschland gründen": Rassismus, Kolonien und kolonialer Gedanke vom 16. bis zum 20. Jahrhundert.* Munich: Deutscher Taschenbuch, 1991.
———. "Deutsche Missionsgesellschaften auf dem Weg zur Kolonialmission." In Bade, *Imperialismus und Kolonialmission,* 68–79.
———. "Die Etablierung des Christentums auf Samoa: Konfessionelle Rivalität und politische Implikationen." In Hiery, *Die deutsche Südsee, 1884–1914,* 636–48.
———. "Die Rolle der christlichen Mission beim Ausbruch des Boxeraufstandes." In Gründer, *Christliche Heilsbotschaft und weltliche Macht,* 147–57.
———. "Mission und Kolonialismus: Historische Beziehungen und strukturelle Zusammenhänge." In Wagner, *Kolonien und Mission,* 24–37.
———. *Welteroberung und Christentum: Ein Handbuch zur Geschichte der Neuzeit.* Gütersloh: Gerhard Mohn, 1992.
Grundmann, Christoffer H. "Die ärztliche Mission: Promotorin in der höheren medizinischen Ausbildung in Asien und Afrika." In Heyden and Liebau, *Missionsgeschichte, Kirchengeschichte, Weltgeschichte,* 259–71.
———. *Gesandt zu heilen! Aufkommen und Entwicklung der ärztlichen Mission im 19. Jahrhundert.* Gütersloh: Gerhard Mohn, 1992.
Gütl, Clemens. *Johann Ludwig Krapf: "Do' Missionar vo' Deradenga" zwischen pietistischem Ideal und afrikanischer Realität.* Münster: Lit, 2001.
Hammer, Karl. *Weltmission und Kolonialismus: Sendungsideen des 19. Jahrhunderts im Konflikt.* Munich: Kösel, 1978.
Heinrich, Uwe. "Mission und Handel im missionarischen Selbstverständnis und in der kirchlichen Praxis." In Ustorf, *Mission im Kontext,* 257–92.
Henrichsen, Dag. "Die Hegemonie der Herero in Zentralnamibia zu Beginn der deutschen Kolonialherrschaft." In *Namibia—Deutschland: Eine geteilte Geschichte; Widerstand, Gewalt, Erinnerung,* edited by Larissa Förster, Dag Henrichen, and Michael Bollig, 44–59. Wolfratshausen: Edition Minerva, 2004.

Heyden, Ulrich van der. "Alexander Merenskys Beitrag zur ethnographischen und historischen Erforschung der Völkerschaften Südafrikas." *Ethnographisch-Archäologische Zeitschrift* 32, no. 2 (1991): 263–68.

———. "Brandenburg-Preußens Streben in die Welt." In *Preußen 1701—Eine europäische Geschichte: Essays*, edited by Deutsches Historisches Museum und Stiftung Preußische Schlösser und Gärten Berlin-Brandenburg, 139–46. Berlin: Henschel, 2001.

———. "Kolonialgeschichtsschreibung in Deutschland: Eine Bilanz ost- und westdeutscher Kolonialhistoriographie." *Neue Politische Literatur: Berichte über das internationale Schrifttum*, no. 3 (2003): 401–29.

———. "Lebensgeschichten der afrikanischen Diaspora in Deutschland—einige wissenschaftsgeschichtlichen Anmerkungen." In *Unbekannte Biographien: Afrikaner im deutschsprachigen Europa vom 18. Jahrhundert bis zum Ende des Zweiten Weltkrieges*, edited by Ulrich van der Heyden, 10–22. Berlin: Kai Homilius, 2008.

———. *Martinus Sewushan: Nationalhelfer, Missionar und Widersacher der Berliner Missionsgesellschaft im Süden Afrikas*. Neuendettelsau: Erlanger Verlag für Mission und Ökumene, 2004.

———. "Missions." In *A Historical Companion to Postcolonial Literatures: Continental Europe and Its Empires*, edited by Prem Poddar, Rajeev S. Patke, and Lars Jensen, 247–48. Edinburgh: Edinburgh University Press, 2008.

———. "Missionsgeschichte im heutigen Verständnis multi- und interdisziplinärer Forschung." In *Missionspädagogik im Diskurs: Eine Ausstellung in der Kritik*, edited by Anette Scheunpflug, 64–83. Hamburg: Universität der Bundeswehr, 2000.

———. *Rote Adler an Afrikas Küste: Die brandenburgisch-preußische Kolonie Großfriedrichsburg in Westafrika*. 2nd ed. Berlin: Selignow, 2001.

———. "Zu den politischen Hintergründen der Njassa-Expedition von Alexander Merensky." In Brose and Heyden, *Mit Kreuz und deutscher Flagge*, 89–95..

Heyden, Ulrich van der, and Heike Liebau, eds. *Missionsgeschichte, Kirchengeschichte, Weltgeschichte: Christliche Missionen im Kontext nationaler Entwicklungen in Afrika, Asien und Ozeanien*. Vol. 1. Stuttgart: Steiner, 1996.

Heyden, Ulrich van der, and Holger Stoecker, eds. *Mission und Macht im Wandel politischer Orientierungen: Europäische Missionsgesellschaften in politischen Spannungsfeldern in Afrika und Asien zwischen 1800 und 1945*. Stuttgart: Steiner, 2005.

Heyden, Ulrich van der, and Jürgen Becher, eds. *Mission und Gewalt: Der Umgang christlicher Missionen mit Gewalt bei der Ausbreitung des Christentums in Afrika und Asien in der Zeit von 1792 bis 1918/19*. Stuttgart: Steiner, 2000.

Hiery, Hermann Joseph, ed. *Die deutsche Südsee, 1884–1914: Ein Handbuch*. 2nd ed. Paderborn: Schöningh, 2002.

Hundt, Michael. *"Woraus nichts geworden": Brandenburg-Preußens Handel mit Persien (1668–1720)*. Hamburg: Abera, 1997.

Johnson, Samuel D. *Schwarze Missionare—weiße Missionare: Beiträge westlicher Missionsgesellschaften und einheimischer Pioniere zur Entstehung der Baptistengemeinden in Kamerun (1841–1949)*. Kassel: Oncken, 2004.

Jörgensen, Helle. "Funktionalisierung der Mission durch chinesische Christen: Die protestantische Rheinische Missionsgesellschaft im Kreis Dongguan in der Provinz Guangdong." In Leutner and Mühlhahn, *Deutsch-chinesische Beziehungen im 19. Jahrhundert*, 219–60.

———. "Zum wechselvollen Verhältnis von Mission und Politik: Die Berliner Missionsgesellschaft in Guangdong." In Leutner and Mühlhahn, *Deutsch-chinesische Beziehungen im 19. Jahrhundert*, 183–218.

Käser, Lothar. "Eine Legende auf Chuuk. Friedrich Kärcher—ein deutscher Missionar in Mikronesien." In *Das Zeitalter des Kolonialismus*, edited by Redaktion DAMALS, 93–96. Stuttgart: Theiss, 2007.

Kim, Chun-Shik. *Deutscher Kulturimperialismus in China: Deutsches Kolonialschulwesen in Kiautschau (China) 1898–1914*. Stuttgart: Steiner, 2004.

Klein, Dieter, ed. *Jehova se nami nami: Die Tagebücher der Johanna Diehl; Missionarin in Deutsch-Neuguinea 1907–1913*. Wiesbaden: Harrassowitz, 2005.

Klein, Thoralf. "Aktion und Reaktion? Mission und chinesische Gesellschaft." In Leutner and Mühlhahn, *Kolonialkrieg in China*, 32–42.

Klein, Thoralf, and Reinhard Zöllner, eds. *Karl Gützloff (1803–1851) und das Christentum in Ostasien: Ein Missionar zwischen den Kulturen*. St. Augustin: Institut Monumenta Serica/Steyler Verlag, 2001.

Knoll, Arthur. "Die amerikanische-protestantische Mission im deutschen Mikronesien." In Hiery, *Die deutsche Südsee, 1884–1914*, 570–82.

Konrad, Dagmar. *Missionsbräute: Pietistinnen des 19. Jahrhunderts in der Basler Mission*. 2nd ed. Münster: Waxmann, 2001.

Koschorke, Klaus. "Außereuropäische Christentumsgeschichte (Asien, Afrika, Lateinamerika): Forschungsstand und Perspektiven einer neuen Disziplin." *Jahrbuch für Überseegeschichte* 2 (2002): 137–64.

———, ed. *"Christen und Gewürze": Konfrontation und Interaktion kolonialer und indigener Christentumsvarianten*. Göttingen: Vandenhoeck und Ruprecht, 1998.

———. "Emanzipationsbestrebungen indigen-christlicher Eliten in Indien und Westafrika um die Jahrhundertwende." In *Aneignung und Selbstbehauptung: Antworten auf die europäische Expansion*, edited by Dietmar Rothermund, 203–16. Munich: R. Oldenbourg, 1999.

———. "Kirchengeschichte, Missionsgeschichte, transnationale Christentumsgeschichte." *Zeitschrift für Missionswissenschaft und Religionswissenschaft* 79 no. 2 (1995): 134–44.

Krapf, Johann Ludwig. *Reisen in Ostafrika, ausgeführt in den Jahren, 1837–1855*. 1858. Facsimile reprint, edited by Werner Raupp. Münster: Lit, 1994.

Krüger, Gesine. *Kriegsbewältigung und Geschichtsbewusstsein: Realität, Deutung und Verarbeitung des deutschen Kolonialkrieges in Namibia (1904–1907)*. Göttingen: Vandenhoeck und Ruprecht, 1999.

Lange, P. Werner. *Kontinent der kurzen Schatten*. Leipzig: Urania, 1987.

Lemke, Michael. "Zu Methoden und Wirkungen der katholischen Missionskongregationen in der ehemaligen Kolonie Deutsch-Ostafrika, 1885–1918." In Brose and Heyden, *Mit Kreuz und deutscher Flagge*, 127–39.

Leutner, Mechthild, and Klaus Mühlhahn, eds. *Deutsch-chinesische Beziehungen im 19. Jahrhundert: Mission und Wirtschaft in interkultureller Perspektive*. Münster: Lit, 2001.

———. *Kolonialkrieg in China: Die Niederschlagung der Boxerbewegung, 1900–1901*. Berlin: Christoph Links, 2007.

Liebau, Heike. *Die indischen Mitarbeiter der Tranquebarmission (1706–1845): Katecheten, Schulmeister, Übersetzer*. Tübingen: Max Niemeyer, 2008.

———. "Mission und Forschung." In *Geliebtes Europa—Ostindische Welt: 300 Jahre interkultureller Dialog im Spiegel der Dänisch-Halleschen Mission; Jahresausstellung der Franckeschen Stiftungen zu Halle 2006*, edited by Heike Liebau, 160–62. Halle: Verlag der Fanckeschen Stiftungen, 2006.

Loth, Heinrich. "Auseinandersetzungen im religiösen Gewand: Kirchlicher Kolonialismus und ideologische Formen des Widerstands—mit einem Dokumentenanhang." In *Philosophie der Eroberer und koloniale Wirklichkeit: Ostafrika 1884–1918*, edited by Heinrich Loth and Kurt Büttner, 369–424. Berlin: Akademie, 1981.

———. *Die christliche Mission in Südwestafrika: Zur destruktiven Rolle der Rheinischen Missionsgesellschaft beim Prozess der Staatsbildung in Südwestafrika, 1842–1893*. Berlin: Akademie, 1963.

———. *Im Schatten des Sternenbanners: 200 Jahre amerikanische Politik und Mission in Afrika*. Berlin: Union, 1979.

———. *Kolonialismus und Religion: Historische Erfahrungen im Raum des Indischen Ozeans*. Berlin: Union, 1987.

———. *Kolonialismus unter der Kutte*. Berlin: Dietz, 1960.

———. *Zwischen Gott und Kattun: Die Berliner Konferenz 1884/85 zur Aufteilung Afrikas und die Kolonialismuskritik christlicher Missionen*. Berlin: Union, 1985.

Ludwig, Frieder. "African Independent Churches in West Africa Around 1900." In *Transkoloniale Beziehungen in der Geschichte des Außereuropäischen Christentums*, edited by Klaus Koschorke, 259–72. Wiesbaden: Harrassowitz, 2002.

———. "Afrikanische prophetische Bewegungen." In Wagner, *Kolonien und Mission*, 294–308.

——. "Profile der afrikanischen Christentumsgeschichte." In *Periplus 2006: Jahrbuch für außereuropäische Geschichte*, edited by Christoph Marx, 35–60. Berlin: Lit, 2006.

——. *Zwischen Kolonialismuskritik und Kirchenkampf: Interaktionen afrikanischer, indischer und europäischer Christen während der Weltmissionskonferenz Tamboran 1938.* Göttingen: Vandenhoeck und Ruprecht, 2000.

Mehnert, Wolfgang. "Regierungs- und Missionsschulen in der deutschen Kolonialpolitik (1885–1914)." *Bildung und Erziehung* 46, no. 3 (1993): 251–66.

Merensky, Alexander. *Deutsche Arbeit am Nyassa.* Berlin: Verlag der Berliner evangelischen Missionsgesellschaft, 1894.

——. *Erinnerungen aus dem Missionsleben in Transvaal (Südafrika), 1859 bis 1882.* 1898. Edited by Ulrich van der Heyden. Berlin: Edition Ost, 1996.

Miettinen, Kari. "Living on the King's Land and Drinking the King's Water": Evolution of the Relationship Between Finnish Missionaries and Ondonga Kings, 1870–1920." In Heyden and Becher, *Mission und Gewalt*, 449–60.

Mühlhahn, Klaus. "Deutschlands Platz an der Sonne? Die Kolonie "Kiautschau." In Leutner and Mühlhahn, *Kolonialkrieg in China*, 43–48.

——. *Herrschaft und Widerstand in der "Musterkolonie" Kiautschau: Interaktionen zwischen China und Deutschland, 1897–1914.* Munich: R. Oldenbourg, 2000.

Neill, Stephen. *Geschichte der christlichen Missionen.* 2nd ed. Erlangen: Verlag der Evangelisch-Lutherischen Mission, 1990.

——. *Mission zwischen Kolonialismus und Ökumene: Die Aufgabe der Kirche in der sich wandelnden Welt.* Stuttgart: Evangelisches Verlagswerk, 1962.

Niesel, Hans-Joachim. "Kolonialverwaltung und Missionen in Deutsch-Ostafrika, 1890–1914." Diss., Freie Universität Berlin, 1971.

——. "Kolonialverwaltung und Missionen in Deutsch-Ostafrika zur Zeit des Maji-Maji-Aufstandes, 1905–1907." In *Mit Zauberwasser gegen Gewehrkugeln: Der Maji-Maji-Aufstand im ehemaligen Deutsch-Ostafrika vor 100 Jahren*, edited by Hans-Martin Hinz, Hans-Joachim Niesel, and Almut Nothnagle, 77–88. Frankfurt: Otto Lembeck, 2006.

——. "Mit Kreuz und Krone: Die deutschen Missionen im Kriegsgebiet." In *Der Maji-Maji-Krieg in Deutsch-Ostafrika 1905–1907*, edited by Felicitas Becker and Jigal Beetz, 100–114. Berlin: Christoph Links, 2005.

Njoku, Chukwudi A. "The Missionary Factor in African Christianity, 1884–1914." In *African Christianity: An African Story*, edited by Ogbu U. Kalu, 218–55. Pretoria: Department of Church History, University of Pretoria, 2005.

Norris, Edward Graham. *Die Umerziehung des Afrikaners: Togo, 1895–1938.* Munich: Trickster, 1993.

Nuhn, Walter. *Kolonialpolitik und Marine: Die Rolle der Kaiserlichen Marine bei der Gründung und Sicherung des deutschen Kaiserreiches 1884–1914.* Bonn: Bernhard und Graefe, 2000.

Nzalayaimisi, Gabriel K. "The Berlin Mission and the Destabilization of Power and Local Politics in Eastern and Southern Tanzania, 1887–1918." In Heyden and Stoecker, *Mission und Macht im Wandel politischer Orientierungen*, 211–27..

Oermann, Nils Ole. "'Hochwerter Herr Gouverneur': Zum Verhältnis von Mission und deutschem Kolonialstaat im Zeitalter des Imperialismus." In *Weltmission und religiöse Organisationen: Protestantische Missionsgesellschaften im 19. und 20. Jahrhundert*, edited by Artur Bogner, Bernd Holtwick, and Hartmann Tyrell, 589–614. Würzburg: Ergon, 2004.

———. *Mission, Church and State Relations in South West Africa Under German Rule (1884–1915)*. Stuttgart: Steiner, 1999.

Ottow, Johannes C. G., and Helga Ottow. *Im Namen Gottes betreten wir dieses Land: Die ersten Missionare Carl Wilhelm Ottow und seine Frau Auguste unter den Kannibalen auf Neu-Guinea (1855–1862)*. Münster: Lit, 2004.

Pabst, Martin. *Mission und Kolonialpolitik: Die Norddeutsche Missionsgesellschaft an der Goldküste und in Togo bis zum Ausbruch des Ersten Weltkrieges*. Munich: Verlagsgemeinschaft Anarche, 1988.

Paczensky, Gert. *Teurer Segen: Christliche Mission und Kolonialismus*. 2nd ed. Munich: Knaus, 1991.

Pakendorf, Gunther. "Der Missionar als Anthropologe: Albert Kropf und 'Das Volk der Xosa-Kaffern.'" In Heyden and Liebau, *Missionsgeschichte, Kirchengeschichte, Weltgeschichte*, 161–76.

Panzergrau, Kurt. *Die Bildung und Erziehung der Eingeborenen Südwestafrikas durch die Rheinische Missionsgesellschaft von 1842–1914: Ein Beitrag zur Beziehung von Pädagogik und Kolonialismus*. Munich: Akademischer, 1998.

Pech, Rufus. "Deutsche evangelische Missionare in Deutsch-Neuguinea, 1886–1921." In Hiery, *Die deutsche Südsee, 1884–1914*, 384–416.

———. "Die Liebenzeller Mission auf Manus (1914)." In Hiery, *Die deutsche Südsee, 1884–1914*, 413–14.

———. "Die Rheinische Mission in Deutsch-Neuguinea (1887–1921)." In Hiery, *Die deutsche Südsee, 1884–1914*, 403–12.

Pesek, Michael. "Kreuz oder Halbmond: Die deutsche Kolonialpolitik zwischen Pragmatismus und Paranoia in Deutsch-Ostafrika, 1908–1914." In Heyden and Becher, *Mission und Gewalt*, 97–112.

Pierard, Richard V. "A Case Study in German Economic Imperialism: The Colonial Economic Committee, 1896–1914." *Scandinavian Economic History Review* 16, no. 2 (1968): 155–67.

———. "The Rhenish Mission and the Colonial War in German Southwest Africa." In Heyden and Stoecker, *Mission und Macht im Wandel politischer Orientierungen*, 389–401.

———. "World War I, the Western Allies, and German Protestant Mission." In Heyden and Liebau, *Missionsgeschichte, Kirchengeschichte, Weltgeschichte*, 361–72.

Plath, Karl Heinrich Christian. *Deutsche Kolonialmission*. Berlin: Verlag der Goßnerschen Mission, 1887.
Poewe, Karla. "The Spell of National Socialism: The Berlin Mission's Opposition to and Compromise with the Völkisch Movement and the National Socialism: Knak, Braun, Weichert." In Heyden and Becher, *Mission und Gewalt*, 267–90.
Porter, Andrew. *Religion versus Empire? British Protestant Missionaries and Overseas Expansion, 1700–1914*. Manchester: Palgrave Macmillan, 2004.
Prodolliet, Simone. *Wider die Schamlosigkeit und das Elend der heidnischen Weiber: Die Basler Frauenmission und der Export des europäischen Frauenideals in die Kolonien*. Zurich: Limmat, 1987.
Rennstich, Karl. "The Understanding of Mission, Civilisation and Colonialism in the Basel Mission." In *Missionary Ideologies in the Imperialist Era, 1886–1920*, edited by Torben Christensen and William R. Hutchison, 98–102. Aarhus: Aros, 1982.
Richter, Julius. *Geschichte der Berliner Missionsgesellschaft, 1824–1924*. Berlin: Verlag der Buchhandlung der Berliner Evangelischen Missionsgesellschaft, 1924.
——. *Geschichte der evangelischen Mission in Afrika*. Gütersloh: C. Bertelsmann, 1922.
——. "Mission und Kolonisation." In *Das Buch der deutschen Kolonien*, edited by the former Governors of German East Africa, German Southwest Africa, Kamerun, Togo, German New Guinea, 352–58. Berlin: Wilhelm Goldmann, 1937.
Ritter, Paul. *Der Kampf um den Erdraum: Kolonien vom Altertum bis zur Gegenwart*. 4th ed. Leipzig: Reclam, 1939.
Rohrbach, Paul. "Die Mission in den deutschen Kolonien." In Zache, *Die deutschen Kolonien in Wort und Bild*, 179–85.
Sarajevskaja, Berta I. *Starye i Novye Religii Tropieskoj i Juznoj Africi*. Moscow: Nauk, 1964.
Schmidt, Wolfgang R. *Mission, Kirche und Reich Gottes bei Friedrich Fabri*. Wuppertal: Verlag der Rheinischen Mission, 1965.
Schneppen, Heinz. "Der Helgoland-Sansibar-Vertrag von 1890." In *Kolonialismus hierzulande: Eine Spurensuche in Deutschland*, edited by Ulrich van der Heyden and Joachim Zeller, 185–89. Erfurt: Sutton, 2008.
Schöck-Quinteros, Eva, and Dieter Lenz, eds. *150 Jahre Norddeutsche Mission, 1836–1986*. Bremen: Selbstverlag Norddeutsche Mission, 1986.
Schulze, Andrea. "Neure, interdisziplinäre Ansätze in der Missionsgeschichtsschreibung." In *Leitfaden Ökumenische Missionstheologie*, edited by Christoph Dahling-Sander, Andrea Schultze, Dietrich Werner, and Henning Wrogemann, 47–110. Gütersloh: Gütersloher Verlagshaus, 2002.
Schütte, Heinz. *Der Ursprung der Messer und Beile: Gedanken zum zivilisatorischen Projekt rheinsicher Missionare im frühkolonialen Neuguinea*. Hamburg: Abera, 1995.

———. "Lokale Reaktionen auf evangelische Missionsbemühungen im kolonialen Neu Guinea 1887–1914." In *Rassendiskriminierung, Kolonialpolitik und ethnisch-nationale Identität: Referate des Zweiten Internationalen Kolonialgeschichtlichen Symposiums 1991 in Berlin,* edited by Wilfried Wagner, Ulrich van der Heyden, et al., 497–509. Münster: Lit, 1992.

Sebald, Peter. *Togo, 1884–1914: Eine Geschichte der deutschen "Musterkolonie" auf der Grundlage amtlicher Quellen.* Berlin: Akademie, 1988.

Spiecker-Salazar, Marlies. "Mission und Kolonialherrschaft aus der Sicht eines Missionsinspektors: Das Tagebuch der Afrikareise von Pfarrer Johannes Spieker." In Wagner, *Kolonien und Mission,* 426–40.

Spraul, Gunter. "Der 'Völkermord' an den Herero." *Geschichte in Wissenschaft und Unterricht* 39 (1988): 713–39.

Steffen, Paul. "Die katholischen Missionen in Deutsch-Neuguinea." In Hiery, *Die deutsche Südsee, 1884–1914,* 343–83.

———. "Die Maristenmission in den deutschen Salomonen." In Hiery, *Die deutsche Südsee, 1884–1914,* 371–77.

———. *Missionsbeginn in Neuguinea: Die Anfänge des Rheinischen, Neuendettelsauer und Steyler Missionsarbeit in Neuguinea.* Nettetal: Steyler, 1995.

Steinmetz, George. *The Devil's Handwriting: Precoloniality and the German Colonial State in Qingdao, Samoa, and Southwest Africa.* Chicago: University of Chicago Press, 2007.

Stoecker, Helmuth, ed. *Drang nach Afrika: Die koloniale Expansionspolitik und Herrschaft des deutschen Imperialismus in Afrika von den Anfängen bis zum Ende des Zweiten Weltkrieges.* Berlin: Akademie, 1977. Translated by Bernd Zöllner as *German Imperialism in Africa: From the Beginnings to the Second World War* (London: Hurst, 1987). German 2nd edition published as *Drang nach Afrika: Die deutsche koloniale Expansionspolitik und Herrschaft in Afrika von den Anfängen bis zum Verlust der Kolonien* (Berlin: Akademie, 1991).

Tell, Birgit, and Uwe G. Heinrich. "Mission und Handel im missionarischen Selbstverständnis und in der kolonialen Praxis." In Ustorf, *Mission im Kontext,* 257–92.

Theil, Ilse. *Reise in das Land des Todesschattens: Lebensläufe von Frauen der Missionare der Norddeutschen Mission in Togo/Westafrka (von 1849 bis 1899); Eine Analyse als Beitrag zur pädagogischen Erinnerungsarbeit.* Berlin: Lit, 2008.

Tiedemann, Gerhard. "Christian Missions in Shandong in the Context of China's National and Revolutionary Development." In Heyden and Liebau, *Missionsgeschichte, Kirchengeschichte, Weltgeschichte,* 387–404.

Töpperwien, Annemarie. *Seine "Gehülfin": Wirken und Bewährung deutscher Missionarsfrauen in Indonesien, 1865–1930.* Köln: Rüdiger Köppe, 2004.

Triebel, Johannes, ed. *Der Missionar als Forscher: Beiträge christlicher Missionare zur Erforschung fremder Kulturen und Religionen.* Gütersloh: Gütersloher Verlagshaus, 1988.

———. "Evangelische Mission in Tanzania im Kontext von Kolonialismus und afrikanischer Tradition." In *Tanzania: Koloniale Vergangenheit und neuer Aufbruch*, edited by Ulrich van der Heyden and Achim von Oppen, 102–17. Münster: Lit, 1996.

Trüper, Ursula. *Die Hottentottin: Das kurze Leben der Zara Schmelen (ca. 1793–1831): Missionsgehilfin und Sprachpionierin*. Cologne: Rüdiger Köppe, 2000.

Ustorf, Werner. *Die Missionsmethode Franz Michael Zahns und der Aufbau kirchlicher Strukturen in Westafrika: Eine missionsgeschichtliche Untersuchung*. Erlangen: Erlanger Verlag für Mission und Ökumene, 1987.

———. "Im Streit um koloniale Kompetenz: Evangelische Mission und Nationalsozialismus im Spiegel der Missionsarchive." In *Studien zur Geschichte des deutschen Kolonialismus in Afrika: Festschrift zum 60. Geburtstag von Peter Sebald*, edited by Peter Heine and Ulrich van der Heyden, 562–84. Pfaffenweiler: Centaurus-Verlagsgesellschaft, 1995.

———. "Mission als Vorhut des Kolonialismus? Das Beispiel der Norddeutschen Mission." In *Afrika und der deutsche Kolonialismus: Zivilisierung zwischen Schnapshandel und Bibelstunde*, edited by Renate Nestvogel and Rainer Tetzloff, 41–53. Berlin: Dietrich Reimer, 1987.

———, ed. *Mission im Kontext: Beiträge zur Sozialgeschichte der Norddeutschen Missionsgesellschaft im 19. Jahrhundert*. Bremen: Übersee-Museum Bremen, 1986.

———. *Mission im Nationalsozialismus*. Berlin: Selignow, 2002.

———. *Sailing on the Next Tide: Mission, Missiology, and the Third Reich*. Frankfurt: Peter Lang, 2000.

———. "'Survival of the Fittest': German Protestant Missions, Nazism, and Neocolonialism, 1933–1945." *Journal of Religion in Africa* 28, no. 1 (1998): 93–114.

Volberg, Heinrich. *Deutsche Kolonialbestrebungen in Südamerika nach dem Dreißigjährigen Kriege*. Cologne: Böhlau, 1977.

Von Mende, Erling. "Für Gott und Vaterland? Die christlichen Missionen." In *Tsingtau: Ein Kapitel deutscher Kolonialgeschichte in China 1897–1914*, edited by Hans-Martin Hinz and Christoph Lind, 66–71. Berlin: Deutsches Historisches Museum, 1998.

Von Sicard, Sigvardi. "Missionary Attitudes and Approaches to Muslims, Zanzibar 1864–1890." In Heyden and Becher, *Mission und Gewalt*, 113–37.

Wagner, Wilfried. "Historiographische Anmerkungen zur Geschichte deutscher Missionstätigkeit in der Malayischen Welt." In *Bürgerliche Gesellschaft—Idee und Wirklichkeit: Festschrift für Manfred Hahn*, edited by Eva Schöck-Quinteros, 313–29. Berlin: Trafo, 2004.

———, ed. *Kolonien und Mission: Referate des 3. Internationalen Kolonialgeschichtlichen Symposiums 1993 in Bremen*. Münster: Lit, 1994.

———. "Plädoyer für eine profane Geschichtsschreibung." In Wagner, *Kolonien und Mission*, 11–15.

Wangemann, Hermann Theodor. *Südafrika und seine Bewohner nach den Beziehungen der Geschichte, Geographie, Ethnologie, Staaten- und Kirchen-Bildung, Mission und des Racen-Kampfes.* Berlin: Selbstverlag der Berliner Missionsgesellschaft, 1881.

Warneck, Gustav. "Zwei neue deutsche Missionen in Deutsch-Ostafrika." *Allgemeine Missions-Zeitschrift* 18 (1891): 79–96.

Wassink, Jörg. *Auf den Spuren des deutschen Völkermordes in Südwestafrika: Der Herero-Nama-Aufstand in der deutschen Kolonialliteratur; eine literarhistorische Analyse.* Munich: Meidenbauer, 2004.

Weiss, Holger. "The Beginning of Finnish Missionary Activity in Northern Namibia and Its First Setbacks, 1869–1872." In Heyden and Becher, *Mission und Gewalt*, 539–54.

Wendlandt-Hamann, Luise. *Zugvögel kennen ihre Zeit: Als Missionarsfrau in vier Erdteilen.* Erlangen: Verlag der Ev.-Luth. Mission/Missionshandlung, 1987.

Wendt, Reinhard, ed. *Sammeln, vernetzen, auswerten: Missionare und ihr Beitrag zum Wandel europäischer Weltsicht.* Tübingen: Gunter Narr, 2001.

———, ed. *Wege durch Babylon: Missionare, Sprachstudien und interkulturelle Kommunikation.* Tübingen: Gunter Narr, 1998.

Wright, Marcia. *German Missions in Tanganyika, 1891–1941: Lutherans and Moravians in the Southern Highlands.* Oxford: Oxford University Press, 1971.

Wünsche, Dietlind. *Feldpostbriefe aus China: Wahrnehmungs- und Deutungsmuster deutscher Soldaten zur Zeit des Boxeraufstandes 1900/1901.* Berlin: Christoph Links, 2008.

Zache, Hans, ed. *Die deutschen Kolonien in Wort und Bild.* 2nd ed. Berlin: Wilhelm Andermann, 1926. Reprint, Wiesbaden: Marix, 2004.

Zimmerer, Jürgen, and Joachim Zeller, eds. *Genocide in German South-West Africa: The Colonial War of 1904–1908 in Namibia and Its Aftermath.* Monmouth: Merlin Press, 2008.

11

German Colonialism and the British Neighbor in Africa Before 1914

Self-Definitions, Lines of Demarcation, and Cooperation

Ulrike Lindner

If we address German colonialism within an imperial and international context, we see that the fact of Germany's being a latecomer in the colonial sphere shaped the whole German colonial enterprise. We could define the wish to attain the same prestige as other European imperialists as a crucial feature of German rule in the colonial world. In this context Russell A. Berman's interpretation of German colonialism as a form of secondary colonialism with the major aim of measuring up to the other colonial powers proves highly revealing.[1] Or as Birthe Kundrus has pointed out in her article in this volume, discussions of "the German imperial dilemma of the nineteenth and twentieth centuries ... always revolved around something that Germany didn't have."[2]

In the case of German colonialism, the British Empire, with its global size and its long-standing experience, was the most important role model and the key reference point. The French example, which had been highly influential for the shaping of German nationalism in the nineteenth century, was not as prominent in the realm of the colonies.[3] For example, in an article of the *Deutsche Kolonialzeitung* of 1897, the authors explicitly stated that Germany had to colonize in a British and not in a French way if Germany was to accrue benefits and blessings.[4] Thus, for the German colonialists the tension between imitating the experienced British colonizer and distinguishing themselves from the British is obvious throughout the period of German colonialism. This is also true for the period of colonial revisionism, during which German colonial enthusiasts still tried to prove that they had been much better colonizers than the British, who had taken over most of the German colonies after World War I.[5] The argument of prestige, of being a power of equal standing to Britain, is a keynote of the entire German colonialist discourse.

In spite of these obvious influences, such aspects of German colonial history have rarely been the focus of research.[6] Approaches drawn from comparative history and transfer studies have been limited. Instead, research has interpreted German colonialism usually within the context of Germany's exceptional development during the nineteenth and twentieth centuries.[7] Hence, I will take up some of these comparative issues in the following pages and examine aspects of German colonialism in relation to the British "role model."[8] First, I will look into mutual reception as colonial powers in the colonial discourses of Germany and Britain. Thus, I will demonstrate that the development of Germany's colonial concepts or colonial style was heavily influenced by processes of imitation and demarcation from the British and was also affected by the colonial neighbor's view on German colonialism. Second, I will address some examples of interactions between German and British colonizers in neighboring African colonies to reveal Germany's connection to the colonial world and to show how this influenced German exceptionalism.

These relations I analyze in the form of an entangled history,[9] by looking at interactions and mutual reception on the level of the neighboring colonies and on the level of the metropoles, thereby creating multiple intersecting views. Such an approach allows for a novel perspective on the German colonial enterprise, replacing it within the framework of European imperialism. Thus, I will be able to address some of the questions in the wider context of this volume—for example, in what respect did German colonialism differ from other European colonialist styles, and what forms of continuity can we observe in the relations and interactions between Germany and the other imperial powers?[10] In pursuing this line of argument, I also follow Russell A. Berman's plea in this volume to analyze German colonialism with a transnational approach and to position German colonialism in the context of other nineteenth-century colonial empires in order to broaden the rather narrow discussion on German colonialism.[11]

German Self-Definition as Colonizer and the British View on the German Colonial Enterprise in Africa

As a new colonizing nation in Africa, the German colonizers observed their neighbors with great attention. We detect this phenomenon in the colonial administration, in the colonial press, and in publications of various colonial societies and enthusiasts.[12] The discussion in Germany benefited from the great number and enormous variety of colonial and literary publications—inversely proportional to the duration and spread of the German Empire.[13] Within this setting one can hardly overestimate the impact of British colonialism on Germany's self-definition as a colonial ruler. German publicists, colonial enthusiasts, but also administrators in the colonies, as well as in Berlin, defined and outlined Germany's identity as colonizer using a transnational view on the British counterpart. The power and magnitude of the British Empire and the geographical position of the British and German colonies were the reason for such an orientation. Especially in Africa, both colonizers were neighbors on the "new continent"—be it in the west, east, or south.[14]

When analyzing the German perception of British colonialism, we can identify two significant threads of discourse, which sometimes also overlap.[15] The German view oscillated between two poles—an admiration for the British as experienced colonizers and a criticism of British colonial policy—in order to define more clearly Germany's own concepts of colonization. An important example of the strong admiration for British colonialism is Bernhard Dernburg, who held the office of colonial secretary from 1906 to 1910. He visited several British colonies in Africa, constantly referred to the fact that he wanted to learn from the British colonizers, and cited Britain's administration of its colonies as exemplary in many of his speeches, as well as in his directives issued to the colonial administration.[16] Germany was a newcomer that had to learn from the experienced British; many publications voiced this argument in terms similar to Franz Josef von Bülow's, who described his stay in German Southwest Africa in the 1890s: "It is true that 'young-Germany' has only planted the fresh sprig of its colonies whereas 'Old-England' can rely on hundreds of years of experience in the colonial world. It is true that we are a people of poets and intellectuals whereas England can use its practical experience as a merchant's and shopkeeper's nation in the colonial realm; but why should we not learn from English experiences?"[17]

The admiration for the British colonizers was often connected with a bemoaning of German provinciality and narrow-mindedness: the German imagination was perceived as limited by the European coasts, whereas the British mind embraced the world.[18] In a similar vein Carl Peters complained that he wished to belong to a "true master race" with experience in the whole world. He did not appreciate when British and other European colonizers addressed him to behave like a "real Englishman" in the colonies.[19]

There was also a significant critical discourse, however, demarcating German colonialism from the British example and focusing on the allegedly too liberal and flexible approach of British colonial rule. German colonial experts and enthusiasts connected this criticism with the wish to develop a unique, better, and more rigid style of German colonialism. In particular, the Germans judged the "native policy" in British colonies as misguided and denounced British liberality as "false."[20] Even Paul Rohrbach, a German colonial publicist and enthusiast who generally admired British colonization, championed the view that too much leniency when treating the indigenous population—as could be witnessed especially in the British Cape colony—would lead to a debacle. A partial access to education as offered in the Cape colony he deemed particularly disastrous.[21]

If one examines the British side, colonial discourse did not heavily focus on German colonies. Nevertheless, Britain constantly monitored its colonial neighbors in Africa and did not lose sight of Germany, its most important rival in Europe: "the advent of a new Colonial Power is not unnaturally a matter of intense interest to a leading Colonial Power of the age."[22] In contrast with the size of the British Empire, colonial discourse in Britain was less specialized and varied than on the German side. Indeed, leading newspapers such as the *Times* or weekly and biweekly journals such as the *Fortnightly Review* or the *Nineteenth Century* discussed most of the colonial issues.[23]

The discourse on German colonialism covered a number of aspects. First, the British view reveals the attitude of the experienced colonizer, able to distinguish itself from the newcomer, Germany, and thus capable of styling its own endeavors in the colonial world as a better form of colonial rule. British observers were critical of German militarism, of overregulation and rigid administration in the colonies. Some criticized these aspects as ill-adapted to colonial circumstances, as Richard Meinertzhagen wrote in his *Kenya Diary*: "British rule is more elastic and takes the native character into account. German regulations are based on Western ideas and ride roughshod over native prejudices and customs."[24] The British used transnational observations, as well, to sharpen a unique identity as colonizer. Brutality against the indigenous population was a leitmotiv of British discourse on German colonialism: "The German is apt to be harsh, overbearing and cruel to natives, partly as a result of military discipline at home, which in the Colonies often leads him to be tyrannical to his subordinates whether black or white. Such excesses have been dubbed 'Tropencholer' [sic] a euphemism for love of beating blacks.... The system of bureaucracy, taxation, rules, regulations for muzzling dogs and extinguishing lights at a certain time has unhappily been introduced with full force into the Colonies. Anything more diametrically opposite to the first principles of colonial policy would be hard to find."[25]

British observers stressed such topics particularly during and after the Herero and Nama war in German Southwest Africa. The cruelty of German conduct remained a major point of criticism in the British press. General von Trotha's ruthless warfare strategies and his extermination policy particularly upset British commentators.[26] The failure of the German colonial administration, which had not managed to introduce a "reasonable handling" of the indigenous population, was indicted as triggering the outbreak of the war.[27] The editorials reveal a certain concurrent ambiguity, however, because articles—often in the same newspapers—showed some compassion for the "misfortunes of the Germans."[28] The weekly *African World* even published portraits to honor the German officers who had died in the battle at the Waterberg against the Herero in 1904.[29] This hints at the fact that Germany was still a fellow colonial power whose superiority over the African people had to be maintained also for their own sake—despite all criticism.

Still, the discourse on German brutality in the African colonies did not cease and became very dominant after World War I when German Southwest Africa came under South African mandate and German East Africa under British mandate. The cruelty of German methods—especially in German Southwest Africa—was used in the Versailles Treaty as a major justification for depriving Germany of its colonies. Even if the British politicians employed the argument as an excuse to remove the colonies from Germany, some real concern about German methods in southwest Africa had developed during the last years before 1914. British groups, who fought for the rights of indigenous people in Africa as the Aborigines Protection Society under Eugene D. Morel, had mostly focused on the cruelties in Belgian Congo and had even proposed to bring the Congo under German colonial rule. Around 1914 these groups also started to recognize and discuss German atrocities.[30] The 1918 British report on the "treatment of natives" in German colonies is considered the most important document in this context. Even at that point the German Colonial Office tried to counteract, publishing a document proving that Germany's rule in the colonies had been just and the treatment of the indigenous population fair.[31]

Besides this rather critical approach, however, a second thread of discourse emerged before 1914. British colonial administrators and experts displayed a rather obvious admiration for German advances in the colonies, especially in terms of the scientific exploration of colonial aspects. Articles and publications praising German achievements, especially in east Africa, were manifold and increased particularly during the last decade before World War I.[32] Even Lord Lugard, one of the most important British colonial administrators and theorists, who published many books on colonial rule, including his famous work *Dual Mandate in British Tropical Africa*,[33] praised the German colonial project in East Africa: "The endeavour to create in East Africa a prosperity which may contrast in favour with that of our German neighbours will be a worthy ambition for him to whom the administration may be entrusted. Hitherto they have set us an example in the thorough and practical way in which they set about to develop their territories."[34] Of course, such discourses on German and British colonialism reflect well-known stereotypes that had already been present in British-German relations for a long time and survived well into the twentieth century. The German side tended to portray the flexible British as cultivating a laissez-faire attitude and a lack of thoroughness that would generate problems. In parallel, however, there had always been a great admiration for British economic progress and for the development of British society, often connected with a wish for similar conditions in Germany.[35] On the British side the picture of the systematic, scientifically oriented German was not only connected with the colonies but also with a more general view on Germanness. The British depicted militarism and bureaucracy as important aspects of the German character in general and reproduced these stereotypes in the colonial area. Nevertheless, the colonial discourse added new elements—such as the brutality of German conduct—and applied existing assumptions to a new field.[36]

If we examine German self-definition and the British definition of German colonialism, we could conclude that the German habit of measuring itself up against other colonial powers, and especially against the British Empire, certainly intensified the wish to be a "better," more thorough, colonizer with a well-organized administration. German colonial politicians perceived the attempt to outdo the British Empire's economic prowess in the German colonies as a rather futile undertaking. Instead, the German colonizers' only hope of excelling in the colonial sphere was proving to be better administrators, to be more systematic, less perfunctory, and less neglectful. This certainly led to an overemphasis on strict regulations in the colonies that could easily pave the way for a radicalization of colonial rule.

German Racial Concepts in Interaction with the British "Fellow Colonizer"

Such radicalization was most obvious in the southwest African colony. Here, after the Herero and Nama war (1904–7)—as often described, particularly by Jürgen Zimmerer—German rule developed into a form of state racism with a complete repression of the indigenous population, strict demarcation lines between "black" and "white," new bans on mixed-race relations, and most significant, on mixed-race marriages.[37] In 1907 the colonial administration of German Southwest Africa issued ordinances that forbade the African population to own land and significantly restricted indigenes' freedom of movement. From then on Africans had to wear identification badges and live in separate locations.[38] Additionally, from 1907 onward the ban on mixed marriages that Deputy Governor Tecklenburg first introduced in 1905 was also applied to marriages recorded before the prohibition. These mixed marriages were pronounced invalid, and the children of these marriages were automatically reduced to "native" status.[39] Such regulations were quite exceptional in the colonial world at the end of the nineteenth century. Despite a growing racism in most African colonies, bans in other countries tended to aim at relationships between white women and indigenous men—the ultimate danger in terms of upholding white superiority in the colonial world.[40] Normally, however, marriages between European men and indigenous women remained unaffected. Furthermore, such relationships in their nonlegal form were a common feature in all colonial societies, emphasizing the power of the European patriarch.[41] But in German Southwest Africa the colonizer's wish to be outstandingly thorough in the shaping of the racial future of the colony led to rather exceptional regulations that created not only problems with some of the old-established German settlers, whose marriages were suddenly ruled invalid, but also with the British neighbors.[42]

Regular reports drafted by the resident magistrate of the British enclave Walfish Bay and, from 1909 onward, reports of the British consul stationed in the town of Lüderitzbucht informed the adjacent Cape colony and the British administration in London of the developments in the German colony.

Moreover, British citizens who had earlier moved from the Cape to the southwest African territory and who were affected by the new regulations wrote complaints to British authorities. The British consul generally commented on the new regulations: "The children of British subjects who had married in accordance with English or Cape colonial law and were resident in German South West Africa before the Germans took it over, have been degraded to the ranks of aborigines, whose legal status is as low as it is possible to be short of slavery."[43] Thus, administrators of the Cape colony and later of the Union of South Africa, as well as the officials in the British Foreign Office, were aware of the new regulations, their consequences, and the ensuing problems.[44]

Such issues reflect the case of the Hill family.[45] Hill, a British citizen from the Cape, moved to southwest Africa in the 1870s and married a local mixed-race woman. He became the owner of a huge estate; when he died, he left a farm of some six hundred thousand acres and other property in German Southwest Africa. He raised his children as white persons providing them with a "good education." The children inherited his huge property, but the new laws and ordinances classified the marriage of their parents as invalid and reduced their legal status to "natives"—raising doubts about their right to own the estate. At the same time, the German tax authorities went to court against the Hills, claiming they had obtained part of the land illegally, and tried to downsize the estate to make space for a military station. The court, however, ruled that the Hill children were "native," creating a de facto recusal because the new regulations prohibited trials for "natives" before a "European" court. Therefore, the case remained undecided.[46] Finally, the Hill heirs sued the German tax authority about the verification of their estate, and they were eventually ascertained as its owners. In the meantime the Hill children—who saw themselves as British citizens and asked for support from the British authorities—informed the British consul in Lüderitzbucht about the case. He decided to intervene on behalf of the family, and this no doubt contributed to the Hills' success.[47] Finally, despite their being of mixed race, the German governor granted the Hill family their property. The German administration had not anticipated the initiative of the Hill children or the interventions of the British consul, and it had to concede certain rights and make exceptions.[48]

The British administration of the Cape and the Foreign Office in London did not accept German redefinitions of *white* and *native*. The British ambassador Granville stated in a communiqué to the *Auswärtige Amt* that the new German terms were not to affect British citizens. They had to retain their former status, even when they were mixed-race individuals. Furthermore, children from valid marriages with British subjects had to be treated as British and were not to fall under German native law.[49]

One might have expected that the interactions with the Cape colony and the British Foreign Office would have led to a less stringent application of the new regulations in the German colony, because it apparently generated huge problems with local inhabitants and in interactions with the British neighbors. It appears, however, that British criticism only strengthened the German wish to demarcate its own policy. Correspondence between the Colonial Office and the Foreign Office between 1911 and 1913 on the issue of mixed marriages in the colonies reveals that the Germans were adamant about their regulations. The more the Foreign Office tried to avoid any definite statements regarding mixed marriages in British colonies, the more the German side insisted on exact answers.[50] The British government viewed the problem of mixed marriages as something that should be skirted, even if the colonial administration and the Colonial and Foreign Office generally opposed these relationships.[51] In contrast, German policy aimed at regulating the whole issue in detail.

One could thus argue that the constant comparison and interaction with the neighboring colonizer tended to fuel the wish of the Germans to introduce a stricter, more systematic, concept of racial rule than the rules prevalent in the adjacent British colonies.

Cooperation Between British and German Colonizers in the African Colonies

The constant measuring up to British colonizers and the steadfast wish to be a "better" colonizer certainly aggravated some features of German colonialism. Even so, British and German colonial administrators cooperated significantly before 1914, with the ultimate aim of upholding white European superiority over the African population. In this context German and British colonizers were inclined to tolerate each other's conduct in the colonial sphere.[52]

Generally, British criticism of German behavior rarely ended in any official complaints against the Germans, even when the German military or German colonial administrators treated Africans from British territories badly. In this respect, a good example is the story of Johannes, the so-called post runner (mail carrier) between the British town of Walfish Bay, situated in an enclave in German Southwest Africa, and the German town of Swakopmund. Johannes, who had been employed by the British Walfish Bay postal authorities doing his rounds for more than two months, was suddenly arrested by a German officer in Swakopmund. The Germans claimed he was a runaway prisoner. Johannes was locked up, flogged without trial, and relieved of his mailbag. The post runner managed to escape during the same night and came back to Walfish Bay. As the Lüderitzbucht postmaster wrote in a report, he showed "traces of moderately severe punishment."[53] He made a sworn statement to the British authorities about his mistreatment: "He [the German officer] next ordered me to lie across a bench. I did so. Four Hereros held me in position—one man to each arm and leg and a fifth Herero ordered by the German officer and in the presence of that officer beat me across the bare buttocks with a sjambok. I received 15 cuts. When they had finished flogging me the officer said 'to-day you get a beating, to-morrow early you will be sent to Windhoek to be hanged.'"[54]

The following correspondence between the German Foreign Office and the German Colonial Office about this incident is quite revealing. First, the British postmaster in Walfish Bay protested about the handling of his mail carrier: "As regards to the German contention that Johannes was on this occasion recognised as an escaped prisoner of war I may say that during his regular employment with me he remained always one night and sometimes more in Swakopmund.... So the German authorities had ample opportunities of recognising him for three months past. As I do not think from what I have seen of runaway prisoners from German territory that they will under any circumstances venture in to the 'lion's den' once more."[55]

Accordingly, the British administrators asked for an explanation for this obviously unlawful treatment. Without further explanation or excuse the Germans just said that he was recognized as an escaped Herero prisoner and that the flogging was justified. The British Foreign Office was not satisfied and asked for an apology but only received a rather perfunctory statement. Finally, the Foreign Office gave up corresponding with the Germans and an internal communication stated "that an apology is due from the German authorities, if not for their wrongful treatment of a mail-carrier in British employ at least for their treatment of the British mail." Finally, the issue with the mail was solved. The German administration returned the British mailbag to the postmaster in Walfish Bay, and, afterward, the British decided not to pursue the case further.[56] In this case, as in many others, the

British administration indeed criticized the German treatment of the indigenous population. Nevertheless, the British authorities certainly perceived the issues of Africans as less important than maintaining peace with their German neighbors and acted cautiously to avoid alienating their fellow colonizer. Here it meant that as long as the issue of tampering with British mail was sorted out, the rest (that is, the maltreatment of the African) could be overlooked. Similar attitudes of imperial consent—sometimes grudgingly given but nevertheless granted—exist not only in cases of mistreatment of African people but also during wars against the indigenous population.

In east Africa British criticism of German conduct was only prevalent during the first years of interaction, when British publications and British officials from the Foreign and Colonial Office disapproved of Carl Peters's brutal expeditions.[57] It was especially the German campaign against the Wachagga—an African people living at the border between British and German East Africa—that the British heavily criticized. Nevertheless, when the German administration implied that British missionaries had supported the Wachagga, something that in fact had never happened, the British authorities felt obliged to remove the missionary station of the British Church Missionary Society on the Wachagga territory near Moshi in order to appease the German colonial administration.[58] Later, German and British colonizers acknowledged that both neighboring colonies in east Africa had to tackle similar problems when dealing with the indigenous population. British press organs celebrated German soldiers from east Africa as shining examples of military bravery, such as in a story about Hermann Wissmann, published in the *African World* in 1913.[59] The British side avoided commentary on German brutality during the suppression of the Maji Maji rebellion of 1905–7. Instead, the British government perceived it as a necessary measure to bring the colony under control.

Furthermore, even during the genocidal Herero and Nama war in southwest Africa, which the British press heavily criticized, we witness cooperation between the British and German colonial administrations. On the one hand, Cape mounted police officers wrote critical reports to the Cape administration about the conduct of the German military during the war, about soldiers who regularly shot fleeing Africans in the back and also about wounded women and children. These reports, however, were only sent to the Foreign Office in London, and criticism did not reach the government in Berlin.[60] On the other hand, the British army attached an officer to General Trotha's headquarters, Colonel Trench, who wrote altogether thirty reports of approximately twenty pages each to the War Office in London between 1905 and 1906. His successor, Major Wade, pursued this task for another half year.[61] The Foreign Office and the Cape administration also read the reports. Trench's and Wade's accounts hardly indicted German conduct. Trench addressed the topic only three times within the hundreds of pages he wrote—most famously when he scathingly described one of the German prisoner camps on Haifisch Island and compared it to Dante's Inferno.[62] Otherwise, his accounts and descriptions were instruments for the transfer of military knowledge between the colonizers. He gave information on strategy, communication, and combat techniques and on colonial warfare in general. Such knowledge exchange became increasingly important for the European colonizers before World War I. Although Trench was personally rather critical of the Germans, since he saw them as a potential danger for the neighboring Cape colony, he also acknowledged a certain degree of consent and cooperation between the two imperial powers in the campaign against the Herero and Nama.[63]

Even if such forms of direct cooperation stopped with the outbreak of World War I, transfer of knowledge on Africa between Germany and other European powers reemerged during the interwar period.[64] From an even broader perspective we can trace imperial cooperation in Africa again after World War II, when Germany tried to reintegrate into a European project to develop and "open up" Africa in the context of the European Community.[65]

Concluding Remarks

A high degree of interaction and connectedness between Germany and other European powers was certainly an important feature of German colonialism during the age of imperialism. The German colonial enterprise in Africa was intertwined with the actions of its colonial neighbors. It quickly became apparent that Germany had to negotiate its colonial self-definition not only in the face of the challenges posed by the African population but also with British fellow colonialists. Such relations shaped German colonialism to a significant degree. What British observers singled out and what the German discourse of demarcation and self-definition then emphasized was a "better," more systematic, albeit inflexible form of colonization.

Germany's attempt to reach a similar standing in the colonial world as the British role model certainly led to an overemphasis on a distinct German style. The need for improvisation and the rather chaotic initial attempts in colonial Africa between the 1880s and 1890s led to a drive on the German side to stress an allegedly systematic form of colonization. This in turn gave rise to a radicalization of German colonial rule. We observe this in the forms taken by racist policy and in the overregulation of society, especially in German Southwest Africa.

At the same time, we must consider another factor. When we view German colonialism within the context of imperial cooperation, some features of German exceptionalism become rather a matter of degree. At least in the eyes of the fellow colonizer, German atrocities were partially classified as necessary colonial warfare to uphold European superiority in Africa.[66]

Furthermore, some forms of cooperation continued, despite the demise of the German colonial empire. Indeed, cooperation between (ex-)European colonial powers in Africa reemerged after both wars. Perceptual patterns between the colonizers also enjoyed a long-term continuity in British-German relations. Altogether, we can conclude that the British fellow colonizer and role model shaped the German colonial enterprise to a much greater extent than generally acknowledged.

Notes

1. Berman, "Der ewige Zweite," 28.
2. See Birthe Kundrus's contribution to this volume.
3. Muhs, Paulmann, and Steinmetz, "Brücken über den Kanal?" 11.
4. "Was lehrt uns die englische Kolonialpolitik?" *Deutsche Kolonialzeitung*, Aug. 28, 1897, 347.
5. Maß, *Weiße Helden, schwarze Krieger*, 50; Louis, *Das Ende des deutschen Kolonialreiches*.
6. Laak, "Kolonien als 'Laboratorien der Moderne'?"
7. A lot of research focuses on the continuities and discontinuities between colonialism in German Southwest Africa, with its extremely racist rule, the Herero and Nama war, and the Herero genocide and National Socialism. See, e.g., Melber, "Kontinuitäten totaler Herrschaft"; and Kundrus, "Von Windhoek nach Nürnberg?" Colonies other than German Southwest Africa and particularly comparative studies are rather underrepresented in German research. See Lindner, "Plätze an der Sonne?" 509–10.
8. This view on colonial interactions is also in line with recent research on the British Empire. See Thompson, "The Power and Privileges of Association"; and Lester, *Imperial Networks*.

9. On the concept of *entangled history* see Conrad and Randeria, "Einleitung." For a discussion of transfer and comparison in general see Kaelble, "Die interdisziplinären Debatten über Vergleich und Transfer."

10. The research in the United Kingdom, South Africa, and Namibia was made possible by the Alexander von Humboldt Foundation and the GHI London; I would like to thank them for their support.

11. See Russell A. Berman's contribution to this volume.

12. Rohrbach, *Der deutsche Gedanke in der Welt*; and Brandt, *Die englische Kolonialpolitik und Kolonialverwaltung*.

13. Pogge von Strandmann and Smith, "The German Empire in Africa and British Perspectives," 759–60. Informative newspapers and journals include *Deutsche Kolonialzeitung*, *Deutsches Kolonialblatt*, *Koloniale Rundschau*, *Zeitschrift für Kolonialpolitik*, and *Kolonialrecht und Kolonialwirtschaft*.

14. Newbury, "Great Britain and the Partition of Africa, 1870–1914," 647.

15. For a more comprehensive view on British and German colonial concepts see Lindner, "Colonialism as a European Project in Africa Before 1914?"

16. See Bundesarchiv Berlin-Lichterfelde (hereafter BAB), R 1001/6938, passim; Dernburg to colonial governors, Nov. 17, 1906, BAB, R 1001/6882/1, 36–37; Dernburg on questions of native policy, Feb. 18, 1908, BAB, R 1001/6938; Dernburg cites British colonies as a role model for a more reasonable economic policy and for a better treatment of "natives."

17. Bülow, *Drei Jahre im Lande Hendrik Witboois*, 218–19.

18. Rohrbach, *Deutsche Kolonialwirtschaft*, 30–31.

19. Peters, *Gesammelte Schriften*, 1:450.

20. Schütze, *Schwarz gegen Weiß*, 38: "Der südafrikanische Neger wurde bisher von den Engländern mit Glacéhandschuhen angefasst."

21. See, e.g., Rohrbach, *Deutsche Kolonialwirtschaft*, 83. This type of widespread criticism in the German press and literature did not escape the attention of the Foreign Office in London, as can be witnessed in a communication from Hartwright to Grey. See Hartwright to Grey, July 26, 1906, National Archive, Public Record Office, Kew, (hereafter TNA, PRO), FO 367/12, 487.

22. Tilby, "Germany as a Colonising Factor."

23. Special colonial issues were addressed in the *Journal of the Royal Colonial Institute*. The journal, however, rarely dealt with foreign colonies, and it was only after its relaunch as *United Empire* in 1910 that it regularly reported on the colonies of other European powers.

24. Meinertzhagen, *Kenya Diary, 1902–1906*, 314.

25. Hamilton, "The German Colonies in 1909," 408.

26. "The Rising in German South West Africa," *Times* (London), Nov. 14, 1904.

27. Villiers Foreign Office to Lascelles, Berlin, Herero Rising, Report by John Cleverly, Aug. 23, 1904, TNA, PRO, FO 244/640.

28. Editorial, *Times* (London), Sept. 16, 1905.

29. See "The Herero Revolt," *African World*, Jan. 30, 1904, 650; and ibid., Feb. 20, 1904, 81. For the portraits of German officers see "German Officers Killed in the Storming of the Waterberg," *African World*, Aug. 27, 1904, 107.

30. On Morel and the Aborigines Protection Society see Cline, *E. D. Morel, 1873–1924*. On the late reception of German atrocities see Louis, "Great Britain and German Expansion in Africa, 1884–1919," 38–39.

31. *Report on the Natives of South West Africa and Their Treatment by Germany*. For the German response see Reichskolonialamt, *Die Behandlung der einheimischen Bevölkerung in den kolonialen Besitzungen Deutschlands und Englands*.

32. See, e.g., Hamilton, "The German Colonies, 1910–1911"; and Crabtree, "German Colonies in Africa."

33. See Lugard, *Dual Mandate in British Tropical Africa*.

34. Lugard, *The Rise of Our East African Empire*, 1:402.

35. Mommsen, "Zur Entwicklung des Englandbildes der Deutschen seit dem Ende des 18. Jahrhunderts," 375.

36. On these stereotypes see Alter, "Herausforderer der Weltmacht."

37. See Zimmerer, *Deutsche Herrschaft über Afrikaner*; and Zimmerer, "Der koloniale Musterstaat?" On the issue of mixed marriages see Kundrus, *Moderne Imperialisten*, 219–80; and Becker, *Rassenmischehen, Mischlinge, Rassentrennung*.

38. For the native decrees of 1906 and 1907 in German Southwest Africa see Zimmerer, *Deutsche Herrschaft über Afrikaner*, 77–83.

39. Kundrus, *Moderne Imperialisten*, 119.

40. On the Dutch East Indies see Stoler, *Carnal Knowledge and Imperial Power*, 75–76. On British colonies in Africa see Cornwell, "George Webb Hardy's 'The Black Peril' and the Social Meaning of 'Black Peril' in Early Twentieth-Century Africa," 443–44.

41. Levine, "Sexuality, Gender and Empire," 140.

42. For a more comprehensive analysis of the German regulations in an international context see Lindner, "Contested Concepts of 'White'/'Native' and Mixed Marriages in German South-West Africa and the Cape Colony, 1900–1914"; and Kundrus, "Transgressing the Colour-Line."

43. Memorandum on the Status of Natives in German South West Africa, April 12, 1911, National Archives of South Africa, National Archives Repository, Pretoria (hereafter NAR SA), GG 276 4/42.

44. Office of the Governor-General of South Africa, "Marriages Between White and Coloured Persons in GSWA," 1913, NAR SA, GG 278 4/129.

45. See Gouvernement Deutsch-Südwestafrika, Fiskus vs. Hill heirs, 1907–1914, National Archives of Namibia (hereafter NAN), BKE 307 G 154.

46. Hintrager to Bezirksamtmann Keetmanshoop, Feb. 20, 1909, NAN, BKE 317 G 154.

47. Agnes Hill, Groendoorn, to British Consul, Lüderitzbucht, Feb. 12, 1911, NAN, BCL 21; British Consul to A. Hill, Groendoorn, Aug. 19, 1911, NAN, BCL 21.

48. There were many other cases in which British people living in the German colony came into conflict with the German marriage regulations. See Lindner, "Contested Concepts of 'White'/'Native,' and Mixed Marriages in German South-West Africa and the Cape Colony, 1900–1914," 66–71.

49. Ambassador Granville to Kiderlen-Waechter, Oct. 11, 1912, BAB, R 1001/5417, 259.

50. Lichnowsky, German embassy London, to Grey, Foreign Office, March 6, 1913, TNA, PRO, FO 367/328, no. 10928; Grey, Foreign Office, to Lichnowsky, German embassy London, April 18, 1913, TNA, PRO, FO 367/328, no.16146. For an analysis of the discussion see Lindner, "Contested Concepts of 'White'/'Native,' and Mixed Marriages in German South-West Africa and the Cape Colony, 1900–1914," 71–74.

51. See minutes in Proceedings of Landesrat GSWA, Aug. 20, 1912, TNA, PRO, FO 367/276, no. 35013.

52. This would also support Dirk Moses's argument and his interpretation of Hannah Arendt in this volume. He sees German overseas colonialism rather in the context of European imperialism and does not overemphasize the continuities between German overseas colonialism and National Socialism.

53. Hutchinson to Governor of GSWA, Oct. 22, 1906, TNA, PRO, FO 367/12, 669.

54. Johannes' Statement, Oct. 11, 1906, TNA, PRO, FO 367/12, 677.

55. Postmaster to Magistrate Walfish Bay, Oct. 15, 1906, TNA, PRO, FO 367/12, 685–86.

56. Minutes from a discussion in the Foreign Office, April 8, 1907, TNA, PRO, FO 367/41.

57. See, e.g., Sir Gerald Portal Zanzibar to C. S. Smith, Feb. 12, 1892, Rhodes House, Oxford, Portal Papers, 12.

58. See Soden, Gouverneur Ostafrika to Caprivi, Dec. 20, 1892, BAB, R 1001/857, 99–101; Bishop of East Africa to Mr. Lang, Feb. 9, 1892, University of Birmingham Special Collections, CMS G3 A5 O 1892; Lord Salisbury to Sir E. Malet, Dr. Peters, and Moshi Missionaries, June 2, 1892, TNA, PRO, FO 244/495.

59. *African World*, special edition, German East Africa, Nov. 15, 1913, Politisches Archiv des Auswärtigen Amtes, Berlin, R 14817.

60. Major Eliott to Commissioner of Cape Mounted Police, May 19, 1906 (copy), TNA, PRO, FO 367/12, 122–23.

61. See TNA, PRO, WO 106/268 and WO 106/269, passim.

62. Colonel Trench, attached to the German Forces in SWA, Lüderitzbucht, to Chief Staff Officer, Cape Colony, Nov. 24, 1905, TNA, PRO, WO 106/268.

63. Memorandum (secret), March 7, 1906, TNA, PRO, FO 367/8, 366–67; Colonel Trench, Extracts from Report, Dec. 26, 1905, TNA, PRO, FO 367/9, 144. See especially the British and German cooperation when capturing Morenga, one of the Nama leaders who resisted the Germans for a long time.

64. Stoecker, *Afrikawissenschaften in Berlin von 1919 bis 1945*, 176–215. Cooperation emerged mainly in the context of the International Institute of African Languages and Cultures.

65. Laak, *Über alles in der Welt*, 167.

66. See again, in this volume, Dirk Moses's interpretation of Hannah Arendt, which would support this view.

Bibliography

Alter, Peter. "Herausforderer der Weltmacht: Das Deutsche Reich im britischen Urteil." In *Das Deutsche Reich im Urteil der Großen Mächte und europäischen Nachbarn (1871–1945)*, edited by Klaus Hildebrand, 159–78. Munich: Oldenbourg, 1995.

Becker, Frank, ed. *Rassenmischehen, Mischlinge, Rassentrennung: Zur Politik der Rasse im deutschen Kolonialreich*. Stuttgart: Steiner, 2004.

Berman, Russell A. "Der ewige Zweite: Deutschlands sekundärer Kolonialismus." In Kundrus, *Phantasiereiche*, 19–34.

Brandt, Max von. *Die englische Kolonialpolitik und Kolonialverwaltung*. Halle: Gebauer-Schwetschke, 1906.

Bülow, Franz Joseph von. *Drei Jahre im Lande Hendrik Witboois: Schilderung von Land und Leuten*. Berlin: Mittler, 1896.

Cline, Catherine Anne. *E. D. Morel, 1873–1924: The Strategies of Protest*. Belfast: Blackstaff Press, 1980.

Conrad, Sebastian, and Shalini Randeria. "Einleitung: Geteilte Geschichten—Europa in einer postkolonialen Welt." In *Jenseits des Eurozentrismus: Postkoloniale Perspektiven in den Geschichts- und Kulturwissenschaften*, edited by Sebastian Conrad and Shalini Randeria, 9–49. Frankfurt: Campus, 2002.

Cornwell, George. "George Webb Hardy's 'The Black Peril' and the Social Meaning of 'Black Peril' in Early Twentieth-Century Africa." *Journal of Southern African Studies* 22 (1996): 441–53.

Crabtree, W. A. "German Colonies in Africa." *Journal of the African Society* 14 (1914): 1–14.

Hamilton, Louis. "The German Colonies, 1910–1911." *United Empire* 3 (1912): 969–72.

———. "The German Colonies in 1909." *United Empire* 1 (1910): 404–8.

Kaelble, Hartmut. "Die interdisziplinären Debatten über Vergleich und Transfer." In *Vergleich und Transfer: Komparatistik in den Sozial, Geschichts- und Kulturwis-*

senschaften, edited by Hartmut Kaelble and Jürgen Schriewer, 469–94. Frankfurt: Campus, 2003.

Kundrus, Birthe. *Moderne Imperialisten: Das Kaiserreich im Spiegel seiner Kolonien.* Köln: Böhlau, 2003.

———, ed. *Phantasiereiche: Zur Kulturgeschichte des deutschen Kolonialismus.* Frankfurt: Campus, 2003.

———. "Transgressing the Colour-Line: Policing Colonial 'Miscegenation.'" In *Gender History in a Transnational Perspective*, edited by Oliver Janz and Daniel Schönpflug. New York: Berghahn, forthcoming.

———. "Von Windhoek nach Nürnberg? Koloniale 'Mischehenverbote' und die nationalsozialistische Rassengesetzgebung." In Kundrus, *Phantasiereiche*, 110–31.

Laak, Dirk van. "Kolonien als 'Laboratorien der Moderne'?" In *Das Kaiserreich transnational*, edited by Sebastian Conrad and Jürgen Osterhammel, 257–79. Göttingen: Vandenhoeck und Ruprecht, 2004.

———. *Über alles in der Welt: Deutscher Imperialismus im 19. und 20. Jahrhundert.* Munich: Beck, 2005.

Lester, Alan. *Imperial Networks: Creating Identities in Nineteenth-Century South Africa and Britain.* London: Routledge, 2001.

Levine, Philippa. "Sexuality, Gender and Empire." In *Gender and Empire*, edited by Philippa Levine, 134–55. Oxford: Oxford University Press, 2004.

Lindner, Ulrike. "Colonialism as a European Project in Africa Before 1914? British and German Concepts of Colonial Rule in Sub-Saharan Africa." *Comparativ* 19 (2009): 88–106.

———. "Contested Concepts of 'White'/'Native' and Mixed Marriages in German South-West Africa and the Cape Colony, 1900–1914: A histoire croisée." *Journal of Namibian Studies* 6 (2009): 57–79.

———. "Plätze an der Sonne? Die Geschichtsschreibung auf dem Weg in die deutschen Kolonien." *Archiv für Sozialgeschichte* 48 (2008): 487–510.

Louis, William Roger. *Das Ende des deutschen Kolonialreiches: Britischer Imperialismus und die deutschen Kolonien, 1914–1919.* Düsseldorf: Bertelsmann, 1971.

———. "Great Britain and German Expansion in Africa, 1884–1919." In *Britain and Germany in Africa: Imperial Rivalry and Colonial Rule*, edited by Prosser Gifford and William Roger Louis, 3–46. New Haven, CT: Yale University Press, 1967.

Lugard, Frederick D. *Dual Mandate in British Tropical Africa.* Edinburgh: William Blackwood and Sons, 1922.

———. *The Rise of Our East African Empire.* 2 vols. London: William Blackwood and Sons, 1893.

Maß, Sandra. *Weiße Helden, schwarze Krieger: Zur Geschichte kolonialer Männlichkeit in Deutschland, 1918–1964.* Cologne: Böhlau, 2006.

Meinertzhagen, Richard. *Kenya Diary, 1902–1906.* Edinburgh: Oliver and Boyd, 1957.

Melber, Henning. "Kontinuitäten totaler Herrschaft: Völkermord und Apartheid in 'Deutsch-Südwestafrika.'" *Jahrbuch für Antiseminitismusforschung* 1 (1992): 92–114.

Mommsen, Wolfgang J. "Zur Entwicklung des Englandbildes der Deutschen seit dem Ende des 18. Jahrhunderts." In *Studien zur Geschichte Englands und der deutsch-britischen Beziehungen: Festschrift für Paul Kluke*, edited by Lothar Kettenacker and Paul Kluke, 375–95. Munich: Fink, 1981.

Muhs, Rudolf, Johannes Paulmann, and Willibald Steinmetz. "Brücken über den Kanal? Interkultureller Transfer zwischen Deutschland und Großbritannien im 19. Jahrhundert." In *Aneignung und Abwehr*, edited by Rudolf Muhs, Johannes Paulmann, and Willibald Steinmetz, 7–20. Bodenheim, Germany: Philo, 1998.

Newbury, Colin. "Great Britain and the Partition of Africa, 1870–1914." In *The Oxford History of the British Empire*. Vol. 3, *The Nineteenth Century*, edited by Andrew Porter, 624–50. Oxford: Oxford University Press, 1999.

Peters, Carl. *Gesammelte Schriften*. 3 vols. Munich: Beck, 1943.

Pogge von Strandmann, Hartmut, and Alison Smith. "The German Empire in Africa and British Perspectives: A Historiographical Essay." In *Britain and Germany in Africa: Imperial Rivalry and Colonial Rule*, edited by Prosser Gifford and William Roger Louis, 755–73. New Haven, CT: Yale University Press, 1967.

Reichskolonialamt, ed. *Die Behandlung der einheimischen Bevölkerung in den kolonialen Besitzungen Deutschlands und Englands: Eine Antwort auf das englische Blaubuch von August 1918*. Berlin: Engelmann, 1919.

Report on the Natives of South West Africa and Their Treatment by Germany. London: HMSO, 1918, Cd. 9146.

Rohrbach, Paul. *Der deutsche Gedanke in der Welt*. Düsseldorf: Langewiesche, 1912.

———. *Deutsche Kolonialwirtschaft: Kulturpolitische Grundsätze für die Rassen- und Missionsfragen*. Berlin: Buchverlag der Hilfe, 1909.

Schütze, Woldemar. *Schwarz gegen Weiß*. Berlin: Schwetschke, 1908.

Stoecker, Holger. *Afrikawissenschaften in Berlin von 1919 bis 1945: Zur Geschichte und Topographie eines wissenschaftlichen Netzwerkes*. Stuttgart: Steiner, 2008.

Stoler, Ann. *Carnal Knowledge and Imperial Power: Race and the Intimate in Colonial Rule*. Berkeley: University of California Press, 2002.

Thompson, Andrew. "The Power and Privileges of Association: Co-Ethnic Entworks and Economic Life of the British Imperial World." *South African Historical Journal* 56 (2006): 43–59.

Tilby, Wyatt. "Germany as a Colonising Factor." *United Empire* 3 (1912): 57–59.

Zimmerer, Jürgen. "Der koloniale Musterstaat? Rassentrennung, Arbeitszwang und totale Kontrolle in Deutsch-Südwestafrika." In *Völkermord in Deutsch-Südwestafrika*, edited by Jürgen Zimmerer and Joachim Zeller, 26–44. Berlin: Christoph Links, 2003.

———. *Deutsche Herrschaft über Afrikaner: Staatlicher Machtanspruch und Wirklichkeit im kolonialen Namibia*. Münster: Lit, 2001.

PART V
Postcolonial German Politics

12

"Kalashnikovs, Not Coca-Cola, Bring Self-Determination to Angola"

The Two Germanys, Lusophone Africa, and the Rhetoric of Colonial Difference

Luís Madureira

One of the most incongruous sights I encountered during my first trip to Havana—a city renowned for its eye-popping, positively jaw-dropping, incongruities—was an old bus (no doubt donated to the Cuban government by the former Democratic Republic of Germany), lumbering through the dilapidated streets of the Caribbean capital with its original East German destination sign still in place. For one fleeting moment it loomed improbably as a powerful emblem of tragic exile, at once the metonym and the negation of Alejo Carpentier's "marvelous real," doomed to search, until the very end of its operating days, for some unpronounceable borough of East Berlin in the heart of Havana's El Vedado district. Odd as it was, the sight of that smoke-spewing paragon of Soviet bloc engineering—and the uncanny, unremembered history it inexorably embodied (despite, or maybe because of, the rather prosaic nature of its current employment)—seemed at the same time strangely familiar to me. It may well have reminded me of other partially repressed histories, other peculiar juxtapositions of Central European technology and the tropics, perhaps harking all the way back to my childhood in colonial Mozambique. Maybe the tropical exile of that East German bus called to mind the G3 automatic rifles wielded by Portuguese colonial soldiers in the early 1970s, the MP5 submachine guns that were standard issue to Special Forces units, the *Unimog* personnel carriers that transported those troops to the front, the *Luftwaffe* T-6G warplanes that escorted troop convoys and provided air support to infantry patrols engaging with the insurgent bands, and finally the fighter-bombers that later dropped napalm on the remote regions and peoples of Mozambique, as well as Angola and Guinea-Bissau. To be sure, any comprehensive study of the colonial wars in Lusophone Africa ought to address the role cold war alliances and alignments played in enabling Portugal to sustain a thirteen-year-long war effort that mobilized 15 percent of its military-age male citizens and consumed nearly half its national budget. Given that Portugal was a small, semi-industrialized country, one of the most backward in Europe, as many of the anticolonial militants of the time insisted on calling it, such an inquiry assumes particular relevance.

According to the Portuguese sociologist Boaventura de Sousa Santos, the protracted armed struggle between the insurgents and the Portuguese colonial army was in effect "dictated" by "the conflicts and mutual conveniences of core capitalist countries" who took advantage of Portugal's weaknesses and used it "as a stopper against the Soviet danger to control Africa, and, above all, to protect South Africa without being charged with colonialism."[1] As Amílcar Cabral, the leader of the anticolonial armed resistance movement in Guinea-Bissau declared in 1971, Portugal would probably have been defeated in the African wars of independence had it not been able "to rely on the effective political and material support of its NATO allies."[2] Yet for a brief period in October 1964, Portugal was forced to withdraw its American war jets (F-86F Sabres, for the most part) from Guinea-Bissau. In response to the Salazar regime's diversion to its colonies of aircraft supplied under U.S. military aid programs with the strict proviso that they would be assigned to NATO for the defense of Europe, the Lyndon Johnson administration reaffirmed its commitment to maintaining good relations with the newly independent African states by issuing a series of formal protests. It subsequently began to apply unrelenting diplomatic pressure, going so far as to block shipments of aircraft replacements and spare parts.

After suffering heavy losses during its attacks on guerrilla bases in Guinea-Bissau, where it often faced Soviet antiaircraft machine guns, the Portuguese air force was compelled to replace not only its American F-86s but also its aging fleet of German T-6Gs. When it thus found itself in urgent need of dispatching fighter-bombers to deal with the escalating insurgencies in Angola and Mozambique, it was the Federal Republic of Germany that opportunely came to its assistance. In 1966 the West German government approved the transfer to Portugal of forty FIAT G.91 jet planes, which had originally been developed as the standard tactical fighter-bomber for NATO air forces. Several of these aircraft were immediately sent—still in their *Luftwaffe* camouflage—to Guinea-Bissau. The rest were deployed in Mozambique and Angola, donning a new "tropical-grey" finish.[3] In all, West Germany provided ninety million dollars in direct financial aid to the Salazar regime in the early 1960s. It invested heavily in the construction of Mozambique's Cahora Bassa Dam by providing extensive credits and loans to the colonial regime.[4] It was almost certainly the Western power that afforded the highest level of military assistance to the dictatorship. By the time Portugal's authoritarian regime collapsed in 1974, it had sold more than two hundred war jets, as well as large stocks of napalm to the Salazar regime.[5]

From the late 1950s, however, East Germany regularly provided aid and support to the liberation movements. Perhaps no other member of the former Socialist bloc (including the former USSR) was as actively engaged in Africa as the GDR. Even before 1960, in fact, Guinea-Bissau's Amílcar Cabral had allowed cadres of the PAIGC (Partido Africano para a Independência de Guiné e Cabo Verde, Guinea-Bissau's liberation movement) to be trained in the German Democratic Republic. East Germany was the first state in the Soviet bloc to publish the statutes of Angola's independence movement (MPLA) in 1961, in the journal *Deutsche Außenpolitik*.[6] Most of the independence movement leaders from Lusophone Africa visited East Germany repeatedly before independence, including Cabral, Angola's Agostinho Neto, Mozambique's Samora Machel and São Tomé, and Príncipe's Manuel Pinto da Costa.

Throughout the 1960s the GDR increased its support of liberation movements in Lusophone Africa, not only by offering military aid but also by sponsoring training programs, scholarships, and cultural exchanges and by regularly printing political propaganda and distributing educational materials in Africa. Throughout the 1960s especially following the onset of Frelimo's[7] armed struggle against Portugal's colonial rule in 1964, the GDR steadily increased its military and logistical support for the liberation movement.[8] By 1969 several NVA (Nationale Volksarmee, or National People's Army) officers were reportedly operating in Frelimo guerrilla camps in Tanzania. In addition, East Germany delivered shipments of infantry weapons and munitions to both Frelimo and the MPLA.[9] Indeed, as a recent study indicates in reference to Angola, "kein anderes afrikanisches

Land hatte jemals jährliche Hilfe diesen Umfangs von der DDR erhalten" (no other African country had ever received yearly assistance of this scope from the GDR).[10] According to an earlier source, and as the popular NVA rhyme that provides the title for this chapter presumably confirms, in 1973, the same year when the two German states were admitted into the United Nations, the GDR government had signed a military agreement with the MPLA that also contained provisions for training guerrilla units in Congo-Brazzaville, as well as medical treatment in East Berlin for the gravely wounded.[11] So considerable were the GDR's military commitments in Africa (the number of military advisers having at one point reached as many as five thousand), that in the late 1970s Western journalists and political commentators went so far as to revive the loaded term *Afrikakorps* to describe its engagement with sub-Saharan Africa.[12]

It is telling, in this respect, that the mutilated liberation war veteran who is the protagonist of possibly the most iconic story about Angola's anticolonial struggle, Manuel Rui Monteiro's "O Relógio" ("The Watch"), reveals that he will be receiving a prosthetic leg from a "friendly country [*um país amigo*]. The German Democratic Republic, it seems."[13] A curious, if relatively minor, consequence of these close relations between the GDR and the liberation movements of Lusophone Africa was that some of the texts that went on to become classics of Lusophone African resistance literature were published and disseminated in German translation before they became widely available in the original Portuguese. This was the case with a few short stories by Angola's Luandino Vieira. Another, perhaps even less expected, outcome of this assistance and cooperation was that East German composers contributed significantly to the music of most of Lusophone Africa's national anthems. The score of the Mozambican anthem, for example, was reportedly "retouched" (*überarbeitet*) in the GDR after its initial composition by a Mozambican musician.[14]

I recall these half-forgotten fragments of historical data connected to what one of Portugal's most prominent philosophers has memorably called "the longest-lasting and most peculiar colonial adventure on the planet"[15] in order to broach, from an admittedly oblique or "peripheral" vantage point, the recent resurgence of a vigorous debate in the emerging field of German (post)colonial studies. I refer, of course, to the polemic concerning the question of the exclusive path—the *Sonderweg*—supposedly defining not only Germany's experience of empire but also its colonial history as a whole. With respect to the colonial empire, the *Sonderweg* supposedly stems from both its arguably limited size and its relatively short duration. From my admittedly partial acquaintance with the field, two crucial arguments usually appear to underpin the debate regarding the purported relationship between the genocide of the Herero and the Holocaust: on the one hand, the proposition that Germany's colonial project (specifically the genocide of the Herero in southwest Africa) establishes the fundamental preconditions for the Holocaust. A second and frequently related aspect of this polemic pertains to the uniqueness or peculiarity of this genocidal past (the so-called *Sonderweg*). Although the first argument is not necessarily a correlative of the second, critics of the Sonderweg trope tend to conflate the two. Hence, in her critique of the genocidal continuity hypothesis, Birthe Kundrus, for instance, reduces the broad range of procontinuity arguments to the single postulation of "a specifically German genocidal disposition, which emerged for the first time in the genocide perpetrated against the Herero and culminated in the German catastrophe of World War II."[16] Yet one of the historians whose work she regards as embodying this proclivity (Jürgen Zimmerer, who is generally regarded as one of the premier scholars of German colonialism) unequivocally rejects the notion of a uniquely German path from Namibia to Auschwitz: "Aber sind dies nun deutsche Kontinuitäten, gibt es also hier einen 'Sonderweg'? Die Antwort ist nein" (But if these are now German continuities, is there then here a "Sonderweg"? The answer is no).[17]

Nevertheless, Zimmerer argues forcefully for the consideration of Germany's colonial history as coterminous with the Holocaust, even in the context of more recent brutal attacks on immigrant groups. Ironically, one of the first victims of antiforeigner violence in the former East Germany was a twenty-eight-year-old Mozambican contract worker murdered by a gang of neo-Nazi East German youths who pushed him from a moving trolley in the city of Dresden in April 1991. A few months later, in September 1991, a mob of six hundred skinheads firebombed a home for foreign workers and then physically assaulted two hundred Vietnamese and Mozambican laborers in the streets of Hoyerswerda, while their neighbors applauded. More than likely, the former German Democratic Republic had recruited these foreign workers to compensate for its labor shortage in the 1980s. As Matthes and Voß succinctly put it, "Mosambik hatte Arbeitslose und die DDR unbesetzte Arbeitsplätze" (Mozambique had unemployed people and the GDR job vacancies).[18] By 1989 there were more than sixteen thousand Mozambican workers in East Germany.[19] For Jürgen Zimmerer, this kind of racist violence obliges us to ask whether the unimaginable crimes of the Holocaust ultimately occlude the broader racist tendencies in German history. To pose Zimmerer's question in a slightly different fashion, are we not foreclosing a sustained exploration of how modalities of colonial power can endure into the present, when we concentrate exclusively on the link between the Herero wars and the Holocaust? To what extent, then, did the contract labor policies of the GDR, which made possible the presence in Germany of those Mozambican and Vietnamese victims of xenophobic violence, not reproduce colonial labor practices and attitudes? Given that one of the chief objectives of this export of labor to the GDR was the acquisition of hard currency by the Mozambican state,[20] is there not at least a structural similarity between these accords and the colonial state's exploitation of contract workers for South Africa's mines for foreign currency? Are such parallels not reaffirmed by the fact that almost all foreign contract workers were employed as production workers in several industries, performing low-skilled, unattractive work, with few or no chances for promotion, and that labor agreements did not allow family members to join the hired workers or that labor contracts seldom if ever envisaged permanent residence for the laborers?[21]

I will return to this question in the last section of this chapter. For now, let me recall that contrary to Zimmerer, Kundrus regards the establishment of any such links as a reduction of Germany's complex and unique colonial enterprise. In the final analysis, she asserts, to claim this sort of continuity decontextualizes what was always a peculiar experience of empire.[22] Similarly, for Hartmut Pogge von Strandmann Germany's colonial difference resides in the degree to which the economic objectives and the profit motive defined German colonial policy as opposed to any clearly defined and articulated notion or ideology of a civilizing mission.[23] It might nonetheless behoove us to keep in mind, in this specific regard, that the claim to colonial difference is always readily available to every colonial power. As Robert Young asserts, the differences in colonial history and administration were of scarce importance to anticolonial revolutionaries for whom "empire looked very much the same everywhere": Postcolonial critique tends to take the same point of view, Young continues, because it identifies with the subject position of anticolonial activists, not because of its ignorance of the infinite variety of colonial history from the perspective of the colonizers.[24]

In this particular context a significant discrepancy emerges in the development of Kundrus's argument concerning the unacknowledged factors rendering it unlikely that the Nazis "consciously" modeled themselves after General von Trotha.[25] When she adduces the "insight" that both Germany's colonial past in general, and the Herero wars of 1904–8 in particular, may have been erased "from collective memory,"[26] she is apparently overlooking an argument she herself makes elsewhere regarding the pervasiveness of the colonial experience in the German metropole: "although the epoch of colonial rule was quite short, the 'colonial' mentalities and practices that developed in Germany even without formal colonial possessions continue to have a lasting effect up to the present day."[27] The continuity Kundrus appears to be proposing in this fragment may be fundamentally distinct from the one Zimmerer posits. Nonetheless, her suggestion that "colonial desires and projections" persist under "varying historical conditions" in present-day Germany, notwithstanding the brevity of its colonial rule,[28] indicates in turn that it is utterly possible, not to say worthwhile, to uncouple the genocidal continuity hypothesis from the Sonderweg position. More specifically, her apparent oversight enables us provisionally to postulate—even in the absence of any "conscious" or direct Nazi allusions to the colonial "pacification" campaigns, or von Trotha's infamous *Vernichtung* proclamation—that there may well be structural and ideological similarities, even "continuities," between the horrors of the Holocaust and the horrors of colonialism. As Zimmerer's deliberate separation between the genocidal continuity argument and the Sonderweg trope therefore indicates, the second essential step we ought to take in considering whether the Holocaust and the annihilation of the Herero are coterminous is precisely to split the continuity hypothesis from the fundamentally different question of Germany's purportedly unique genocidal proclivities.

Even if we start out with the presupposition that these two arguments are distinct, critics of the continuity hypothesis nevertheless impute attempts to connect the genocide of the Herero with the Holocaust for their failure to provide compelling empirical backing for such a relationship. Not surprisingly perhaps, Kundrus, again, declares emphatically in this respect, "there is no indication that the [Nazis] consciously referred to the Herero genocide as a kind of model."[29] In a more nuanced overview of genocidal continuity arguments, Matthew Fitzpatrick concludes similarly that "there are no records of Hitler or indeed any high-ranking Nazi referring to von Trotha's genocidal proclamation."[30] I would submit, in a preliminary moment, that to require specific empirical evidence of an ideological and structural relationship between the destruction of over 80 percent of the Herero population and the atrocities perpetrated by the Nazis might ultimately obfuscate what, from a postcolonial perspective, should be the central question. As the late

Martinican poet Aimé Césaire contends in his classic 1955 essay *Discourse on Colonialism*, this question revolves around the provocative assertion that liberal European humanism regarded the Holocaust as an unforgivable crime precisely because the Nazis "applied to Europe colonialist procedures which until then had been reserved exclusively for the Arabs of Algeria, the coolies of India, and the blacks of Africa."[31] In light of this fundamental point the singularity of Germany's road to genocide becomes, in the final instance, far less pertinent than this broader and more crucial point. As Hannah Arendt recognized more than four decades ago, the logic of modern genocide is generated and eventually unfolds in the colonies. As she contends in her magisterial study of imperialism, racist violence along with the ideology of white supremacy inherent to colonial rule set the stage "for all possible horrors. Lying under anybody's nose, she famously concludes, were many of the elements which gathered together could create a totalitarian government on the basis of racism."[32]

More recently, Mahmood Mamdani has refined Arendt's argument by pointing out that if Arendt was correct that genocide needed to be related to race ideology as well as bureaucratic efficiency in order to be comprehended, "she was mistaken in thinking that race was a singular South African, Boer, discovery. Had she added to the list of imperial horrors the genocide of the Amerindians and the centuries-long trans-Atlantic slave trade, she would have come to a different conclusion."[33] For Mamdani, then, it is less important to inquire whether there is a direct connection between Namibia and the Holocaust than to seek to ascertain the extent to which "the prototype of settler violence in the African colonies was the German annihilation of ... the Herero population" (10). If, then, "the genocide of the Herero was the first genocide of the twentieth century" (10), its connections with the Holocaust must surpass the building of concentration camps and the execution and annihilation policies, for the "link that connects the genocide of the Herero and the Nazi Holocaust ... is *race branding*, whereby it became not only possible to set a group apart as an enemy, but also to exterminate it with an easy conscience" (12).

As Mamdani specifies, echoing Césaire's polemical assertions from more than half a century ago: "The bipolar division of humanity provided the rationale for the elimination of entire peoples. More than the design to eliminate an entire people, it was the fact that this ghastly endeavor for the first time targeted a people in the heart of Europe that made the Holocaust unique in the imagination of the West. Nazi ideology having cast the Jewish people as a race apart from Europeans, Nazi power set out to eliminate them as a people. The imperial chickens, as it were, came home to roost" (77–78).

In a related sense, to search for indisputable empirical evidence of institutional or discursive links between the Holocaust and the annihilation of the Herero presupposes, as does Hannah Arendt, for instance, a relatively straightforward connection with settlers' genocide. As Mamdani shrewdly notes, however, "when the Nazis set out to annihilate the Jews, it is far more likely that they thought of themselves as natives and Jews as settlers" (13). Even though the genocidal logic informing the Holocaust is grounded in colonial history, the particular genocidal "impulse" the Nazis embodied may best be grasped as a sort of perverse nativism,[34] undertaken by self-anointed pure "natives" against tainted and polluting "settlers." In this sense the proposition Kundrus makes toward the end of her critique of the genocidal continuity hypothesis regarding the alleged "a-temporality" of genocidal warfare—a "mode of behavior" that can arguably "be retraced [to] numerous wars since antiquity"[35]—seems ultimately to lead us to somewhat contradictory conclusions. On the one hand, it validates, in the broadest possible sense, the connection between colonial history and the Holocaust. On the other, it so universalizes the conception of modern genocide as to expunge every trace of its historical specificity (or specific historical provenance). A similar historical specificity should, for example, also inform the persistence of "colonial mentalities and practices," which Kundrus identifies in German society and culture long after the formal dissolution of its colonial empire.[36] Just like these colonial desires and projections, modern genocide, too, has a long and particular history, and it is all the more vital that we heed it.

It is, in fact, to the complex ways in which the legacy of colonial power continues to define the foreign relations between the two Germanys and Africa in the post–World War II period that I now wish to turn. To recall the contest for predominance in Africa during the cold war is inevitably to revive a now somewhat outmoded ideological dispute about the alleged continuities of colonial domination—what Arendt termed "the unexpected revival of imperialist policies and methods" by the main contenders in that prolonged struggle.[37] In this context the inter-German competition in Africa represented more than a patent extension of cold war rivalries and hostilities between the two Germanys—that is a concerted effort by the GDR to gain international legitimacy and enhance its global stature and thus release itself from the isolationism to which West Germany consistently sought to relegate it. East Germany's professed solidarity with and unwavering support for liberation movements, its attendant, indeed de rigueur denunciations of West Germany's "neocolonialist" involvement in the continent, its so-called *Afrikapolitik*, in brief, may be grasped concurrently as a determined attempt to erase any lingering traces of both the Nazi as well as colonial past. At the same time, it sought consistently to link the Bonn government precisely to that imperial history.[38] In effect, a "scientific" report produced for the East German Foreign Affairs Ministry in the early 1960s maintains that the regime's development of commercial, social, and cultural ties with the newly independent African nations must be grasped in the context of its opposition to "West German imperialism and militarism."[39] The report underscores that the main task of the GDR's Africa strategy was to unmask the colonial underpinnings of the "Bonn regime's" dealings with Africa (that is, "die 'Entlarvung der Kolonialbestrebungen der Bonner Regierung' ").[40] Significantly, this *soi-disant* "international demystification campaign" specifically addressed West Germany's unstinting support for Portugal's colonial rule in Angola, Guinea-Bissau, and Mozambique.[41] Thus, Erich Honecker, addressing an international conference on national liberation held in East Berlin in 1980, confidently proclaims that, having succeeded in establishing "friendly relations on an equal footing" with African, Asian, and Latin American countries, "the German Democratic Republic has broken with the German imperialist past once and for all."[42] Referring to another conference on Africa, which took place five years later, *Neues Deutschland*, the ruling SED's official organ, declared it "the antithesis" of Bismarck's Berlin Conference convened one hundred years before.[43]

By contrast, at least in the eyes of anticolonialist militants, West Germany's policies with regard to Africa, especially their continued support for colonial and minority white regimes in South Africa and Rhodesia, signified precisely a continuum with Germany's imperial rule. In the early 1960s, for example, both Amílcar Cabral and Uria T. Simango, at the time vice president of Mozambique's Frelimo, while praising the GDR for its solidarity with the freedom struggle, sharply denounced West Germany's military and financial support for the "tottering Salazar dictatorship."[44] In his 1967 play condemning Portugal's retrograde colonial enterprise (*Gesang vom Lusitanischen Popanz*), Peter Weiss suggested that the FRG's financial backing of the Salazar regime disclosed a link not just with its own colonial period but with the Nazi regime as well. In one of the play's final scenes a German bank director pledges a line of credit of "170 million Deutschmarks" to the

Portuguese dictator (the "Lusitanian bugbear"), and cynically commends him for the humanism (*humanistische Gesinnung*) and profound sense of justice (*hochausgeprägtes Rechtsbewußtsein*) that inspired him, during the last world war, to leave intact German assets located on Portuguese soil: "indem Sie nach dem letzten Krieg unsere auf Ihren Hoheitsgebieten stehengebliebenen Guthaben unangetastet ließen."[45] The critique of the FRG's "neocolonialism" was by no means restricted to the expected proclamations of GDR officialdom, or the assessments of national liberation leaders and radical left in the West, however. Indeed, as late as 1974 the UN Commissioner for Namibia formally censured the Bonn government for carrying out actions in the protectorate that were in direct violation of the UN Charter and contributed to racial discrimination.[46]

To reconsider the history of the rivalries between the two Germanys in Africa during the cold war enables us concomitantly to reinsert Germany's peculiar experience of empire into the broader dynamic of subalternization of cultures and forms of knowledge and subjugation of peoples that Aníbal Quijano has defined as the "coloniality of power" (*colonialidad del poder*). In brief, Quijano's notion establishes colonial difference as the condition of possibility for sustaining and legitimating specific modes of political, economic, and epistemological hegemony. According to Walter Mignolo's iteration of the concept, coloniality of power resides in the capacity to project "European local knowledge and histories" as global designs (from Christocentrism to Hegel's "universal history" and recent ideologies of development).[47] The crucial point that both Quijano and Robert Young make is that from the perspective of the subaltern, it becomes difficult to endorse the thesis that historical exactitude demands that we pay heed to the irreducible specificities of German imperialism.

From such a perspective the absence of a clearly formulated ideology of a civilizing mission, or indeed the alleged peculiarities of Germany's colonial enterprise, would not perforce constitute a crucial difference with the English brand of colonial domination, as Pogge von Strandmann and Kundrus argue, for instance. In fact, with respect to a "subaltern" colonial power, such as Portugal purportedly is, the force and scope of Germany's power was not easily distinguishable from those of the British Empire. Hence, during the initial stages of the so-called scramble for Africa, in 1898, Britain and Germany signed a secret agreement (known as the Treaty of Westminster), which provided for the partitioning of Angola and Mozambique between them, should Portugal prove unable to hold on to its colonies. The treaty would be confirmed in 1913, and a year later a German consortium would acquire a holding company (Nyassa Consolidated) whose principal aim was to exploit a vast swathe of Mozambican territory as a labor reserve. "Germany had in effect purchased a territory," as Leroy Vail mordantly put it.[48] It is unclear what effect, if any, these early historical circumstances might have had on the rumors, widely circulated in the international press a little more than two decades later, concerning the sale of Angola to the Third Reich. So rife were these reports, in fact, that Salazar himself felt the need to dispel them in one of his official addresses to the nation in 1937. With characteristic bluster, the Portuguese dictator concluded: "We will not sell, we will not cede, we will not lease, and we will not share out our colonies. . . . Our constitutional laws do not allow it; and, in their absence, our national consciousness would not allow it."[49] Whatever truth there may have been behind these rumors, the fact remains that the reason why they were so readily accepted as fact by the European press had to do precisely with the relatively subordinate position Portugal occupied in relation to the northern European powers. This "subalternity" was manifest not just in the wake of the Berlin Conference but on the eve of the Second World War. It endured into the 1960s, in fact, when West Germany's financial support and direct military aid enabled Portugal to prosecute its low-intensity yet costly counterinsurgency campaigns on three different fronts.

West Germany's geopolitical and epistemic supremacy thus exerts itself differentially yet consistently in two distinct and interrelated ways. First, it unveils itself in the German Reich's ability to "purchase" large portions of Portugal's colonial possessions and sign a secret accord with what was then the world's superpower for the eventual partition of Portugal's African colonies in the late nineteenth century. Its second expression is the Federal Republic's financial wherewithal that arguably enabled the Salazar regime to finance and prosecute its quixotic colonial wars for more than a decade. Examined under this light, many of the specific contours of Germany's postcolonial relations exhibit unequivocal continuities with its colonial past. And this "coloniality of power" continues to define its interactions not just with the "subaltern colonizer" but also with the postindependence regimes in Lusophone Africa. A case in point was the Bonn government's demand, at a time when it was fiercely vying for political and economic influence in Africa with the GDR, that the newly independent Lusophone countries accept the so-called *Land* Berlin Clause of the Lomé Convention, which made recognition of Berlin as an integral part of the Federal Republic of Germany mandatory. This represented in essence an iteration of the Hallstein Doctrine of 1955, which aimed at precluding so-called third world states from according diplomatic recognition to East Germany by threatening, among other things, to withdraw economic assistance. This requirement was of course never part of any agreement signed with the Soviet Union or other East European countries. Both the growing economic plight of Angola and Mozambique, as well as their need to gain access to European capital markets, finally led them to accede to the clause in the early 1980s.

Coloniality of power is usually associated with capitalist expansion, yet we can discern its lineaments in the GDR's policies toward Afro-Marxist regimes, in spite of its professed commitment to relate on an "equal footing" with the developing world. For all the reassuring rhetoric about solidarity and "mutual economic advantages,"[50] much of the economic "cooperation" that took place in the 1970s between the GDR and the People's Republic of Mozambique was fundamentally driven by the former's persistent need for hard currency and raw materials.[51] In this regard, and despite President Samora Machel's formal request for favorable exchange terms, the GDR imposed a series of onerous conditions on Mozambique's payment of its exports, including the demand that they effect such payments in U.S. dollars and the imposition of a 5 percent or higher annual interest rate.[52] Additionally, in exchange for the heavy agricultural and road-building machinery, as well as consumer goods delivered by the GDR, Mozambique was expected to ship back, within a year, raw materials such as tea, citrus, and groundnuts. These export schemes were, in effect, chiefly to blame for Mozambique's large foreign debt to the GDR (and the FRG, after unification).[53] As an East German high official remarks in a closed meeting on African affairs at the East German Ministry of Foreign Relations, "es kann nicht vernünftig sein, dass man nur Geld in diese Länder hinein pumpt, ohne dass man irgend etwas da rauskriegt" (it cannot be sensible for us just to pump money into these [African] countries without getting something back in return).[54]

To ask again a question I posed above: to what extent do the bilateral trade agreements and labor recruitment contracts the GDR established with Afro-Marxist regimes like Mozambique and Angola reproduce the logic of colonial extraction and exploitation? A similar question arises in relation to the large-scale agricultural projects the GDR undertook in Mozambique in the 1970s. Like their colonial forerunners, these massive schemes evinced a familiar division of labor: Africans were to provide the manual labor, Europeans the technical know-how and expertise. In another apparent echo from the colonial period, the GDR required 50 percent of the production from these state farms to be shipped back as payment for exports. Moreover, the East German planners possessed scant or no knowledge of the conditions in situ and hardly took into account Mozambique's interests or the effects that these immense transformations might have on local populations.[55] The onslaught of Renamo's terror campaign against the civilian population in 1979 precluded these projects from ever getting off the ground.[56] As Hans-Joachim Döring indicates, however, had the civil war not broken out, it remains doubtful whether they could ever have succeeded.[57]

From a political or epistemological standpoint we can identify an analogous process of subalternization in the theoretical formulations of East German intellectuals concerning the revolutionary processes in African countries, which expectedly relegated them to an inferior or lower status in relation to the East European countries. By the mid-1980s, in fact, tensions had arisen between Frelimo cadres in Mozambique and their counterparts from the socialist bloc, particularly from East Germany, with respect to the relevance and application of orthodox Marxism-Leninism to the concrete social and historical realities of Mozambique. As a result, the teaching of Marxism-Leninism was suspended at Mozambique's national university in 1983. It is probably no coincidence that it was at this time precisely that economic and political relations between Mozambique and East Germany began to be significantly curtailed or "moderated."[58] Significantly, Mozambique's gradual turn toward localism and self-reliance in the area of political training and policy making preceded the Frelimo government's formal repudiation of Marxism-Leninism in 1989. Perhaps this vigorous questioning of the social efficacy of some of the rigid developmentalist policies aggressively "exported" by the GDR[59] indicates a tacit acknowledgment that by operating under the conviction that social revolution could be imposed from above, the Afro-Marxist state was itself effectively building on the legacy of colonial power. Their revolutionary nationalism is thus just as caught up in the coloniality of power dynamic. It evinces the contradictoriness that defines emergent national discourses, according to Partha Chatterjee, namely, the tendency to reproduce an order of knowledge whose structure of representation corresponds to the very power regimes that nationalist thought attempts to reject. In this crucial structural sense the legacy of colonialism extends to the postindependence states themselves. Indeed, as Mahmood Mamdani contends in reference to "radical African states," the conviction that social revolution can be imposed from above builds on the legacy of colonial power. With respect to its abrogation of local forms of authority, the fledgling Marxist-Leninist Mozambican state ultimately proved itself one of "the true inheritors of the colonial tradition of rule by decree and rule by proclamation, or subordinating the rule of law to administrative justice so as to transform society from above."[60] Given the ambivalence and multifaceted intricacy of colonialism's enduring legacy to which these examples attest, it may finally prove as futile to look for direct and indisputable empirical evidence of links connecting the genocide of the Herero to the Holocaust as it was for that old East German bus to search for Alt-Hohenschönhausen in the middle of Havana.

Notes

1. Santos, "Between Prospero and Caliban," 20.
2. Cabral, *A Acção armada e os métodos militares 21*, 10.
3. Much of the information included herein about the aircraft used in Portugal's counterinsurgency campaigns in Africa is culled from Johnson, "COIN [Counterinsurgency]."
4. Engel and Schleicher, *Die beiden deutschen Staaten in Afrika*, 56.
5. Isaacman and Isaacman, *Mozambique*, 104–5.
6. Cited in Winrow, *The Foreign Policy of the GDR in Africa*, 123.
7. Frelimo (Frente para a Libertação de Moçambique [Mozambique Liberation Front]) was founded in 1964 and fought a ten-year-long guerrilla war against Portugal. It has been the country's ruling party since independence.
8. Matthes and Voß, "Die Beziehungen der DDR zur Volksrepublik Mosambik in der Afrikapolitik der DDR," 40, 42.
9. Winrow, *The Foreign Policy of the GDR in Africa*, 125.
10. Engel and Schleicher, *Die beiden deutschen Staaten in Afrika*, 109 (my translation; unless otherwise indicated all translations are my own).
11. Winrow, *The Foreign Policy of the GDR in Africa*, 130.
12. Engel and Schleicher, *Die beiden deutschen Staaten in Afrika*, 363.
13. Rui, *Sim, Camarada*, 50.
14. Ragozat, *Die Nationalhymnen der Welt*, 160.
15. Lourenço, *O Labirinto da saudade*, 129.
16. "From the Herero to the Holocaust?" 301.
17. Zimmerer, "Kein Sonderweg im Rassenkrieg?" 340.
18. Matthes and Voß, "Die Beziehungen der DDR zur Volksrepublik Mosambik in der Afrikapolitik der DDR," 46.
19. Ibid.

20. Ibid.

21. One might easily expand the range of this question to encompass the fraught relations between West and East Germany after 1989, though such a discussion would well exceed the scope of this chapter.

22. See Kundrus in this volume.

23. See Pogge von Strandmann in this volume.

24. Young, *Postcolonialism*, 19.

25. See Kundrus, "From the Herero to the Holocaust?" 304.

26. Ibid., 305.

27. Kundrus, "Blind Spots," 99–100.

28. Ibid., 86.

29. Kundrus, "From the Herero to the Holocaust?" 304.

30. Fitzpatrick, "The Pre-History of the Holocaust?" 494.

31. Césaire, *Discourse on Colonialism*, 14.

32. Arendt, *Imperialism*, 101.

33. Mamdani, *When Victims Become Killers*, 78; subsequent references are cited parenthetically in the text.

34. For Mamdani the Rwandan genocide needs to be understood precisely as a natives' genocide; see ibid., 14.

35. Kundrus, "From the Herero to the Holocaust?" 304.

36. See Kundrus, "Blind Spots," 99–100.

37. Arendt, *Imperialism*, xiii.

38. Whether the policy succeeded in allaying the burden of two devastating global conflicts and the horrors that accompanied them must, of course, remain an open question.

39. Engel and Schleicher, *Die beiden deutschen Staaten in Afrika*, 95–96.

40. Ibid., 96.

41. Ibid., 103.

42. Winrow, *The Foreign Policy of the GDR in Africa*, 196.

43. Ibid.

44. Cited in ibid., 197.

45. Weiss, *Gesang vom Lusitanischen Popanz*, 257.

46. Engel and Schleicher, *Die beiden deutschen Staaten in Afrika*, 56.

47. Mignolo, *Local Histories / Global Designs*, 17.

48. Cited in Newitt, *A History of Mozambique*, 359, 405.

49. Salazar, *Discursos e notas políticas*, 2:264. The Portuguese dictator scrupulously monitored these rumors, as a perusal of his personal papers discloses. The materials related to Angola's alleged sale to Hitler collected in the Salazar archive range from the transcription of a conversation between Portugal's minister of foreign affairs and the French prime minister (who cunningly reminds the Portuguese high official that "les allemands ne veulent pas acheter [votre Angola] avec

de l'argent" [the Germans do not wish to purchase (your Angola) with money]) to letters and reports cautioning that "every German in Angola is a spy" stirring up anticolonial sentiment among the natives and their sympathizers and preparing a "peaceful assault" on or "infiltration" of the colony. One secret report contends, however, that "Communist elements" stoked these rumors in order to create an insurrectionist "anti-German mood" in Portugal. (I am grateful to the Luso-American Foundation for its generous support of my research in the Torre do Tombo, Portugal's National Archive.)

50. Matthes and Voß, "Die Beziehungen der DDR zur Volksrepublik Mosambik in der Afrikapolitik der DDR," 45.

51. Engel and Schleicher, *Die beiden deutschen Staaten in Afrika*, 110.

52. Döring, "Freundschaftsform Ökonomie?" 76, 78.

53. Ibid., 78. As Döring notes, this debt was finally forgiven by postunification Germany in 2003; see ibid., 210n12.

54. Ibid., 78.

55. Ibid., 81–83.

56. Resistência Nacional Moçambicana (Mozambique National Resistance), now Mozambique's main opposition party, started out as a mercenary unit created by the Special Branch of the former Rhodesia's colonial army. For seventeen years it carried out a brutal armed struggle against the Maputo government that eventually grew into a formidable movement and, by 1986, had extended its sphere of activity to 80 percent of the national territory. The 1992 Roma Peace Accords negotiated an end to the civil war and established the framework for multiparty elections in 1994.

57. Döring, "Freundschaftsform Ökonomie?" 86.

58. Ibid., 84; Matthes and Voß, "Die Beziehungen der DDR zur Volksrepublik Mosambik in der Afrikapolitik der DDR," 127–28.

59. See Matthes and Voß, "Die Beziehungen der DDR zur Volksrepublik Mosambik in der Afrikapolitik der DDR," 408–9.

60. Mamdani, *Citizens and Subjects*, 135.

Bibliography

Arendt, Hannah. *Imperialism: Part Two of the Origins of Totalitarianism*. New York: Harvest, 1968.

Cabral, Amílcar. *A Acção armada e os métodos militares 21: O oitavo ano da luta de libertação nacional*. N.p.: Avante, 1988.

Césaire, Aimé. *Discourse on Colonialism*. Translated by Jessie Pinkham. New York: Monthly Review Press, 1972.

Chatterjee, Partha. *Nationalism and Colonial Thought: A Derivative Discourse?* Minneapolis: University of Minnesota Press, 1993.

Döring, Hans-Joachim. "Freundschaftsform Ökonomie? Zur Rolle und Funktion der Kommerziellen Koordinerung (KoKo) in den Beziehungen der DDR zur Volksrepublik Mosambik." In Döring and Rüchel, *Freundschaftsbande und Beziehungskisten*, 68–87.

Döring, Hans-Joachim, and Uta Rüchel, eds. *Freundschaftsbande und Beziehungskisten: Die Afrikapolitik der DDR und der BRD gegenüber Mozambik*. Frankfurt: Brandes und Apsel, 2005.

Engel, Ulf, and Hans-Georg Schleicher. *Die beiden deutschen Staaten in Afrika: Zwischen Konkurrenz und Koexistenz, 1949–1990*. Hamburg: Institut für Afrika-Kunde, 1998.

Fitzpatrick, Matthew. "The Pre-History of the Holocaust? The *Sonderweg* and *Historikerstreit* Debates and the Abject Colonial Past." *Central European History* 41, no. 3 (2008): 477–503.

Howe, Herbert, and Marina Ottaway. "State Power Consolidation in Mozambique." In Keller and Rothchild, *Afro-Marxist Regimes*, 43–65.

Isaacman, Allen, and Barbara Isaacman. *Mozambique: From Colonialism to Revolution, 1900–1982*. Boulder, CO: Westview Press, 1983.

Jinadu, L. Adele. "Soviet Influence of Afro-Marxist Regimes: Ethiopia and Mozambique." In Keller and Rothchild, *Afro-Marxist Regimes*, 225–56.

Johnson, Robert Craig. "COIN [Counterinsurgency]: The Portuguese in Africa, 1959–1975." *Chandelle: A Journal of Aviation History* 3, no. 2 (June-July 1998): http://worldatwar.net/chandelle/v3/v3n2/portcoin.html (accessed May 28, 2009).

Keller, Edmund J., and Donald Rothchild, eds. *Afro-Marxist Regimes: Ideology and Public Policy*. Boulder, CO: Lynne Rienner, 1987.

Kundrus, Birthe. "Blind Spots: Empire, Colonies and Ethnic Identities in Modern German History." In *Gendering Modern German History: Themes, Debates, Revisions*, edited by Karen Hagemann and Jean H. Quataert, 86–106. New York: Berghahn, 2007.

———. "From the Herero to the Holocaust? Some Remarks on the Current Debate." *Afrika Spektrum* 40, no. 2 (2005): 299–308.

Lourenço, Eduardo. *O Labirinto da saudade*. Lisbon: Dom Quixote, 1978.

Mamdani, Mahmood. *Citizens and Subjects*. Princeton, NJ: Princeton University Press, 1996.

———. *When Victims Become Killers: Colonialism, Nativism, and the Genocide in Rwanda*. Princeton, NJ: Princeton University Press, 2001.

Matthes, Helmut, and Matthias Voß. "Die Beziehungen der DDR zur Volksrepublik Mosambik in der Afrikapolitik der DDR." In Döring and Rüchel, *Freundschaftsbande und Beziehungskisten*, 39–52.

Mignolo, Walter D. *Local Histories/Global Designs: Coloniality, Subaltern Knowledges, and Border Thinking*. Princeton, NJ: Princeton University Press, 2000.

Newitt, Malyn. *A History of Mozambique.* Bloomington: Indiana University Press, 1995.

Ragozat, Ulrich. *Die Nationalhymnen der Welt: ein kulturgeschichtliches Lexikon.* Freiburg im Breisgau: Herder, 1982.

Rui, Manuel. *Sim, Camarada.* Lisbon: Edições 70, 1975.

Salazar, Oliveira. *Discursos e notas políticas: 1935–1937.* Vol. 2. Coimbra: Coimbra Editora, 1937.

Santos, Boaventura de Sousa. "Between Prospero and Caliban: Colonialism, Postcolonialism, and Inter-identity." *Luso-Brazilian Review* 39 (2002): 9–43.

Weiss, Peter. *Gesang vom Lusitanischen Popanz: Mit Materialien.* Frankfurt: Suhrkamp, 1974.

Winrow, Gareth M. *The Foreign Policy of the GDR in Africa.* Cambridge, UK: Cambridge University Press, 1990.

Young, Robert J. C. *Postcolonialism: An Historical Introduction.* Oxford: Blackwell, 2001.

Zimmerer, Jürgen. "Kein Sonderweg im Rassenkrieg? Der Genozid an den Herero und Nama 1904–08 zwischen deutschen Kontinuitäten und der Globalgeschichte der Massengewalt." In *Das Deutsche Kaiserreich in der Kontroverse,* edited by Sven Oliver Müller and Cornelius Torp, 323–40. Göttingen: Vandenhoeck und Ruprecht, 2009.

13

Germany, Palestine, Israel, and the (Post)Colonial Imagination

Martin Braach-Maksvytis

Historians have often noted the almost "pathetic glorification" of the nascent Israeli state by West German observers in the early 1950s and the mid-1960s.[1] This glorification expressed itself in the glowing adulation for the "valiant" Jewish pioneers who "were making the desert bloom," and who were turning an "old and neglected Palestine" into a "modern, civilized and civilizing state" that could serve as a shining example to the "backward and stagnant" Arab world. A common explanation holds that this attitude emanated from a strong current of a guilt-infused form of philosemitism that reached its zenith during the Arab-Israeli Six Day War in 1967.[2] In other words, West Germans saw in their unconditional support of "all things" Israeli the opportunity to atone for the crimes that had been committed *in their name* by the National Socialist regime against the Jews. The emphasis is deliberate, because as late as 1961 only 6 percent of Germans would admit to a shared responsibility for the destruction of the Jews, while 88 percent categorically denied being somehow vicariously guilty (*irgendwie mitschuldig*).[3] While surveys indicate a gradual decline in the persistence of anti-Semitism in West German society during this period, in 1965 only 34 percent of Germans rejected the proposition that "it would be better for Germany not to have Jews living in their country."[4]

We are confronted with a paradox: on the one hand, the West German adoration for Israel, on the other hand, the persistence of anti-Semitic discomfort at the prospect of a small (surviving) Jewish minority living in Germany. How do we account for these two simultaneously occurring phenomena? I argue that these seemingly contradictory sentiments need to be read against the background of Palestine and Israel as an imaginary colonial space. Questions of German national identity, politics, society, and race need to be embedded in this context. Such a reading transcends established lines of demarcation in German historiography and reveals West Germans to be *frustrated colonialists*, whose solidarity and admiration for Israel were less an expression of atonement for National Socialist crimes than a form of a *redemptive proxy colonialism* that was part of the German cultural and physical rebuilding process. As such, I question generally accepted arguments that locate the essence of the "special relationship" between Germany and Israel exclusively in the common historical inheritance of the Holocaust. What has yet to be analyzed is the additional powerful inheritance between Germans and Jews based on a common colonial imagination that the debates about German postcolonialism have so far overlooked. I advance this paradigm in response to what Omer Bartov has identified as serious shortcomings in postwar scholarship, namely, the "general tendency to write the history of the Germans and the Jews separately, even though many German Jews saw themselves first and foremost as Germans, at least as long as the Nazis did not force them to think otherwise."[5]

Bartov's claim can also be applied to the trajectory of recent studies into the complex linkages between German colonialism in east Africa and the Holocaust.[6] C. S. Davis's recent dissertation reminds us that German Jews (or Germans of Jewish descent), such as State Secretary Bernhard Dernburg and Colonial Director Paul Kayser, occupied the highest levels of administrative power in the German colonial bureaucracy between 1890 and 1910. Their central role in the administration of the German colonial empire raises important questions about the intersection of racism, anti-Semitism, and colonial violence and introduces a complex counterpoint to the argument that German "colonialism (in East Africa) laid the ideological groundwork for the Holocaust."[7] Nor can the significant participation of German-speaking Jews in Zionism and the colonization of Palestine be excluded from the wider German public interest in colonial enterprise.

We also need to acknowledge that Zionists operating within the German *Kulturbereich* were keen observers of German colonial strategies, settlement planning, and agriculture not only in Germany's overseas territories but also on the European continent.[8] To name but two examples: Otto Warburg, a leading German Zionist, brought his expertise gained as an adviser in the German colonial service to the Zionist project; and Arthur Ruppin, a key figure in German Zionism and the head of the World Zionist Organization's Palestine Office from 1907 onward, advocated the establishment of a binational state in Palestine that "was a translation ... of the distinctively illiberal settlement model of the Prussian colonization of his native Posen."[9] There was substantial interest in the German Jewish and non-Jewish German communities across a broad political spectrum in the Zionist colonization of Palestine—as the quest for the establishment of a Jewish homeland was commonly referred to prior to 1933.[10] In the first instance, of course, the Zionist project attracted attention by advancing a "solution" to the "Jewish Question." Yet at the same time, successive Weimar governments supported Zionism as a vehicle to spread German language, culture, and economic influence to the Middle East.[11] Although the complex reciprocal relationship "between the German discourse on nationalism, identity, and Nazism, and the Jewish discourse on identity, Zionism, and the Holocaust" has been recognized, the legacy of a shared colonial imagination has not.[12]

Strands of this common colonial imagination persisted in West German politics, culture, and society, particularly after the German defeat in the Second World War. The Allied occupation and the loss of the "Eastern Territories" emulated and indeed reignited the postcolonial trauma German society had experienced in the years of the Weimar Republic. Against this background the German relationship with the nascent Israeli state lends itself to an exploration of German postwar mind-sets and the importance of nationalism, philosemitism, (post)colonialism, and orientalism in the context of postwar West German nation-building.

The structure of this chapter is informed by these themes and their connections to the *redemptive-proxy-colonialism paradigm*. Proxy colonialism is how the German postcolonial imagination and the Zionist "metanarrative"[13]—the hegemonic claim of Zionist ideology over Israeli history, identity, and culture—intersected in a continuation from the shared German Jewish colonial imagination and created multiple narratives through which Germans articulated and transmitted their (still) existing colonial fantasies.[14] Germany was not the only country to engage with the foundational Zionist discourse of heroic pioneer settlers in this fashion, but it was the only country in which the semantic adoration and material support for Israel had an overt redemptive function, essential for the ongoing processes of national identity formation and rehabilitation. It is my contention that within the long trajectory of Germany as a frustrated colonial nation, Germans saw Israel as the "colonial success story" that they had always hoped they themselves would achieve. We can thus regard Germany's proxy-colonial relationship with Israel as a continuance of the German "imperial dilemma" that Birthe Kundrus notes "always revolved around something that Germany didn't have."[15] Israel, therefore, functioned as a kind of psychological compensation in the absence of tangible evidence of Germany's colonial prowess in its short-lived colonial history. German observers could project their colonial fantasies onto the Jewish state, while at the same time distancing themselves from the Holocaust and the failed and tainted internal and external "colonial genocidal projects" of the Nazis.[16] Proxy-colonial sentiments therefore allowed Germans to retain mentalities of cultural superiority that had existed prior to the years of National Socialism.

The colonial imagery that accompanied the creation of the State of Israel and the seeming confluence of two young emerging democratic nations "starting from scratch" offered Germans more than just passing points of similarities and identification. By exalting in the successes of the young, vigorous, and energetic Jewish pioneers, Germans could take part in a belated and guilt-free "colonial project" that paralleled their own efforts at nation-building. They could do so at a time when their erstwhile colonial rivals were engaged in a process of protracted, complicated, and often violent disentanglement from their former colonies.

Mutual Dependencies and (Post)Colonial Subtexts

In the postwar years two parallel but frequently intersecting narratives emerged in the proxy-colonial relationship between West Germany and Israel. The first was the "official" narrative of the West German government that stressed the "compelling moral obligation"[17] of Germans and the Federal Republic in relation to Israel after the Holocaust. The second was the "popular" narrative that focused virtually exclusively on the new "terra incognita"[18] of Israel as well as the Zionist-cum-Jewish "struggle" within a "hostile" Arab world.

The official narrative is commonly cited as evidence for the pro-Israel sympathies of the Adenauer government (1949–63).[19] It can be read as a signpost to the complicated and delicate foreign policy path the West German government had to negotiate between the conflicting moral obligations toward Israel and the political and economic importance the German government(s) attached to maintaining good relations with the Arab states. The narrative was also increasingly informed by the Federal Republic's responsibilities as a member of the Western alliance and security concerns in the context of the East-West conflict.[20] Nonetheless, the "moral obligation" to the Jewish state remained the paramount component of the German discourse in defining the "special relationship" or "special bilateralism" between the two nations.

In material terms the "official" narrative found its expression in the conclusion of the "*Wiedergutmachungsabkommen*" or "restitution and reparations agreement" between Germany and Israel in September 1952. Under its terms the Federal Republic would pay the state of Israel more than 3 billion German marks in commodities and services over a period of twelve years.[21] The financial and material aid would become a crucial cornerstone in the consolidation of the Jewish state in the critical years from 1950 to 1967. It would also help Germany reenter the community of nations and "atone" for the crimes committed by the National Socialists against Jews. Read differently, the political, economic, and geographical consolidation of the State of Israel in this period was intrinsically linked to the nation-building efforts of the Adenauer government. The continuing survival of the Jewish state thus functioned as a fundamental building block in the political and cultural rehabilitation of the West German nation and the shaping of its national identity.[22] The mutually dependent relationship found its logical extension in the establishment of secret military links between the two countries as early as 1955 that would include the training of elite Israeli army units in West Germany, the exchange of intelligence information, and the trade of armaments over the next ten years.[23]

The relationship left little room to consider the effect the establishment of Israel had on the indigenous Palestinian Arab population. Arab League objections that the creation of Israel "had 'solved' a European problem on the backs of the Arab inhabitants of Palestine ... were met with incredulity."[24] The "moral imperative" that underscored the official German narrative with regard to Israel did not extend to the more than seven hundred thousand Palestinian Arabs who had become refugees in the course of the establishment of the State of Israel.[25]

Despite the limited choices available to the West German government in the immediate postwar environment, it is possible to read a (post)colonial subtext into Adenauer's double standards of morality or the official narrative that informed the relationship with Israel. If we consider Jürgen Osterhammel's insistence on the deep embeddedness of colonial thinking in the mindset of former colonizing nations, we can identify more than a moral or politically expedient dimension in the support advanced by the West German government to Israel.[26] With Germany deemed "a moral and cultural leper" in the international community after the Second World War, the political and cultural functionality of a "rapprochement" with Israel bears similarities to the German quest for the return of its colonies in the course of the Weimar Republic. We need to recall here that in the discourse of imperialist logic, "to be a people without culture" meant to occupy a subaltern role on the scale of Western civilization and to be ultimately "a people without history" who could be ruled and dominated.[27] With the allied occupation, the division of Germany, and the specter of the Morgenthau plan fueling their anxieties, Germans experienced yet another "shameful national humiliation" akin to what they had experienced in the wake of the First World War, Versailles, and the loss of their colonies.[28] Against the growing threat of the cold war, what West Germans feared most was to be abandoned, forgotten, and left behind by the club of cultured and civilized nations.[29] When introducing the restitution treaty between Germany and Israel on March 4, 1953, to the West German parliament, Chancellor Konrad Adenauer clearly echoed these concerns: "The name of our fatherland must regain the esteem appropriate to the historic accomplishment of the German people in culture and economic matters."[30]

We also need to consider here whether the residues of German colonial history and the colonial imagination influenced the decision making of key German politicians involved in the rapprochement with the Jewish state. Adenauer, for example, had been a vice president of the German Colonial Society from 1931 onward and had urged in 1927 that it was essential for the German Reich to gain colonies in order to have more space for the German people. He argued that a colonial Mandate would be a first practical step in this direction. Adenauer maintained, though, that one should never forget to aim for the outright possession of colonies.[31] That same year Adenauer had also joined the influential German Pro-Palestine Committee (PPK) founded in 1926. Made up of prominent German Jews, non-Jews, Zionists, and non-Zionists that included Thomas Mann and Albert Einstein, the committee promoted Jewish colonization in Palestine as an excellent means "for the economic and cultural development of the Orient, ... the spread of German economic relations as well as the rapprochement among the peoples."[32] During his famous meeting with the Israeli prime minister David Ben Gurion in New York in 1960, Adenauer embraced Ben Gurion's plan for a joint German-Israeli development of the Negev and, while on a private visit in Israel in 1966, he declared, "I too was a member of the Zionist movement."[33]

Consider also Eugen Gerstenmaier, who as president of the German Federal Parliament had passionately rejected the objections of Arab states to German restitutions to Israel. In 1963 he heralded Israel as "a great experiment of modern state creation and as an enormous economic and colonization achievement in our time."[34] Three years earlier, in his capacity as the first president of the Africa Society, he noted that the era of colonialism had "not just been an era of exploitation but above all an era of great colonial and therefore cultural achievements."[35]

More than thirty years later, the former German ambassador to Israel Rolf Pauls urged the continuance of German material support to Israel, because the region was on the verge of an "unheard of renaissance," with Israel's scientific, technological, civilizing, and motorizing power at its core. Germany, he maintained, should be part of this "new birth" of Israel as a key power in the Middle East. Apart from aiding Israel, it would also open up a completely new path for Germany into the Middle East. Pauls stressed that this endeavor was neither "colonial" nor "imperial" but in "the best and most modern sense civilizing." By highlighting the importance of the German Jews in the development of German "Zivilisationskultur" prior to 1933, he proposed that they would play the same "civilizing" role in the Near East.[36]

Pauls's comments warrant consideration at length because of his proximity to the inner circle of Adenauer's advisers at the time of the conclusion of the treaty with Israel. As the first West German ambassador to Israel (1965–68), he also provides a crucial personal link between both countries. While his speech was firmly grounded in the rhetoric of Germany's "special relationship" with Israel, the projection of Israel as a modern and civilizing entity in an—by implication—uncivilized Middle East reveals thought patterns not dissimilar to those that underscored visions of Germany's "peaceful penetration" in the Ottoman Empire prior to the First World War. The idea of a culturally more advanced nation bringing the "blessings" of Western civilization to those that are less mature or developed in science, technology, and culture is a key ingredient in colonialist ideology.[37] In addition, by stressing the superior civilizing character of Israel, Pauls directly inverted a paradigm extensively used by the Nazis that defined the "Jewish influence" on German culture and society as a "colonial" threat. New research suggests that this paranoia substantially informed Nazi genocidal policies and locates the Holocaust in "a mentality borne of a frustrated imperial nation struggling against a perceived colonizer."[38] What I am suggesting here is that Pauls's advocacy of German participation in Israel's civilizing mission even as late as 1995 functions as a distancing tool from Nazi crimes while at the same time manifesting the persistence of latent colonial desires transposed onto the Jewish state.

Colonial Imaginations and Proxy Colonialism

The persistence of aspects of colonial ideology and colonial fantasies is particularly evident in the "popular" discourse that accompanied the gradual establishment of links between West Germany and Israel. Postwar German perceptions of the Jewish state were informed by a broad variety of sources and publications, such as pamphlets, articles, and monographs by authors from across the political and religious spectrum, including those of German-Jewish survivors who had settled in Israel or had remigrated to Germany.[39] Their impressions and views, garnered in part during individual visits or as part of small delegations to Israel, were supported by reports in the West German media that generally endorsed the government line on Germany's moral obligations toward Israel.[40]

The admiration for and romanticization of the emerging Jewish state is evident in the titles of publications available throughout the 1950s and early 1960s. They often echo the Zionist metanarrative that glorifies their endeavors over the previous three decades: "Years ago there was only desert here"; "The desert will live"; "The desert rejoices in David's land"; "Homeland, plough sword and bridge: Israel's emergence from dark times"; "Israel in battle with swamp and desert."[41] All accounts refer to the superior civilizing skills and industrious mettle of the Jewish pioneers, who were making the "wasted" land arable again. Their settlement achievements were deemed even more remarkable in the light of Arab "belligerency" and "hostility." While reflecting the rapid economic and social transformation of Palestine, German perceptions of the desert's "taming" were part of a wider and still prevailing Western discourse that associated the desert with chaos and disorder (because of the wandering sands), as well as madness (because of the immense heat).[42] In the context of the persistence of colonial thought patterns, Europeans, or in this case Israel, felt entitled to impose order on this chaos.

A typical example is the assessment made by Professor Franz Böhm, who, as the former chief negotiator in the *Wiedergutmachungsprozess*, was one of the first high-ranking West German parliamentarians to visit Israel in 1955: "If one visits Israel today, one finds itself in a European pioneer world, in a state with a wide social security net, outstanding health services and an exemplary education system." Böhm's glowing account is full of superlatives, such as "astonishing civilizing efforts," "exemplary pedagogic, social-political and charitable effort," "blossoming Jewish state," and "proud development." The success of the Jewish pioneers in transforming "a for centuries neglected" and "decaying" country "virtually overnight" captured his imagination and admiration. Israel's task now is to become a shining industrial and social example, "a flowering Swiss civilization oasis in a still very backward Orient."[43] Given that Böhm was a political contemporary of Rolf Pauls, one is struck here by the similarities in their statements made forty years apart!

Similarly in awe of the rapid transformation of the "old and neglected" Palestine into a civilized, agrarian, and industrious Jewish state was the German writer and translator Wolfgang Cordan, who had traveled through the Middle East two years earlier: "It is a great spectacle that the observer encounters in Palestine, in Eretz-Israel, in the Promised Land. The ancient people, united as the youngest nation, demonstrate to a divided world... of what men are capable if possessed by an idea. Israel proves in the final analysis that the world constitutes itself out of will and imagination. It proves the dominance of the spirit over matter.... It is the will of the united that makes the desert bloom." Cordan regarded the "new State of Israel as a part of the Orient... an experiment that could lead to the reconciliation of two substantially different civilizations." For him the Orient has regained its importance because of the renewed attention by the West, which has awakened it.[44]

Erich Lüth, a key activist for German-Jewish reconciliation, repeated this theme on his second journey to Israel in 1955 when he marveled at the transformation of the desert: "Myriads of fine roots grasp the dust and transform it back into soil.... And the earth begins to breathe. It is almost as if death awakens from its rigor. The week of creation experiences a new morning." Telling for the close identification between the German postwar reconstruction efforts and the construction of the Jewish state was Lüth's compliment that Israel's economic miracle was "greater and more real... than that of the Federal Republic."[45]

Such glowing descriptions of the social, economic, and cultural achievements of the Jewish state contrasted sharply with the stereotypical dismissal or negation of the reality of the Arab states, the Arab Islamic culture, and the indigenous Palestinian Arabs, who had remained in Israel or fled to the refugee camps. In Böhm's account Arabs are only mentioned when he compares Israel's Western qualities to Arab "negligence," "dirt," and "corruption." For in Israel, "gone is the oriental dirt, the neglect, the corruption, the 'Paschawirtschaft,' the exploitation of the peasants by the feudal landlords and the great landowners."[46]

For Cordan only the words of Ben Gurion held the "absolute truth" about the character of the Arab states: "The Arab states have no interest in the welfare of their own people. They don't care whether their people live in desolation, poverty, dirt, sickness, and ignorance."[47] He reasoned that the presence of a modern and democratic state in the Levant was the true reason that Arab notables commenced the war with Israel and why they would fear peace. Implicit in Cordan's statement was "the factual denial of disputed interests (*objectiven Interessengegensatz*) between Israeli Jews and the Palestinians," which is characteristic of most accounts written during this period.[48]

Whereas Böhm ignored the issue completely, Lüth recognized Palestinians only as "refugees" for which the Arab League was to blame. He maintained that they were better cared for in the refugee camps than most of the population in their (Arab) host countries. Lüth blamed the continuing skirmishes between Jewish settlers and Arab "aggressors" on the Arab League and "the law of the desert." What is more, he perceived the "occasional" Israeli retaliation and aggression as part of the same phenomenon: the (corrupting influence) "of the Arab mentality and the law of the desert." Lüth was convinced that "the practical work methods" of the Israelis could solve all "the enormous social problems" of their Arab neighbors. In fact, they could not wish for a better taskmaster (*Lehrmeister*) because "these people are not only modern and cultured with all their rich gifts. In their deepest roots they are also people of the desert, created and sent, to make the earth fruitful."[49]

The editor of the *Darmstädter Echo*, Hans Reinowski, was equally effusive about the civilizing influence of the Jewish State: "The Arab masses will recognize one day that the free and democratic order created by the Israelis can provide them with a better, more humane, and easier existence than the existing feudal order with its artificial mass movement, in which they have to vegetate in poverty, deprivation and without legal rights. . . . In time, perhaps, they will achieve greater freedom from their rulers. In many aspects, they are bound to follow the more experienced, skilful, cleverer and spirited Israelis."[50]

What authors such as Lüth and Reinowski were advocating was nothing less than a return to the "peaceful crusade" formula that had served as the guise for Western colonial ambitions nearly one hundred years earlier. Only now it was to be carried out "by proxy" in the form of the Jewish settlers. Their descriptions also emulated the arguments that leading German-speaking Zionists such as Theodor Herzl and Max Nordau had advanced when placing Jews "on the European side of the fence (and) on the western side of the east/west dichotomy."[51] By heralding Israel's exemplary function in the Middle East, Lüth and Reinowski were also drawing on quintessential aspects of colonialist thought that designated non-Europeans as mentally, physically, and culturally inferior and therefore in need of guidance and guardianship.[52] In fact, their comments and those of other German observers that stressed the civilizing role of Israel in the Middle East bore more than a passing resemblance to the discourse that had informed German colonization efforts in Poland prior to the First World War. As Philipp Ther has pointed out, a large section of the German public regarded the settlement and colonization efforts in the east as part of a historical and national mission to extend the benefits of German culture and civilization to the "primitive" and "lazy" Poles and Slavs.[53]

Accounts by German authors also frequently contained orientalist references that juxtaposed the "superior" civilizing qualities of the "new Jew" with the "inferior" and "redundant" abilities of the Arabs. Implicit to the close identification of Western observers with the political, social, and cultural setup of Israel "as a democracy" was the rejection and dismissal of the various forms of Arab nationalism. Moreover, the unresolved question of German national identity allowed West German commentators to transfer their negative feelings toward a tainted German nationalism onto the various manifestations of Arab nationalism and its key representatives.[54] Adenauer, for example, privately referred to Egypt's President Nasser as a "little Hitler" during the Suez crisis in 1956![55]

Against this background Palestinians and their society in Israel now served most German observers as a quaint reminder of the Oriental past of the country. Whether they were sitting at the side of the road or on the hills with their goat herds, Palestinians were only noted as a mere backdrop in a rapidly changing landscape, "immovable like bronze statues."[56] In contrast to the growing development and Westernization of Israel, the Arab "reality" was observed as stagnant and decaying, albeit at times with orientalist romantic overtones: "Settlements, farms and plantations of the Jews demonstrate the civilizing potency of world Jewry, while time seems to stand still in the Arab world of Fellaheen and Bedouins."[57]

Redemptive Proxy Colonialism

How much the "moral imperative" of the Holocaust was an active ingredient in the fusion of philosemitism, orientalism, and latent colonial desires during the 1950s and 1960s can be gathered from the frequent expressions of doubt, hesitancy, and uncertainty of the German travelers about how they would be received in Israel. Lüth's reaction encapsulates these sentiments: "For us Germans their can be no 'tourism' to Israel, only pilgrimages.... Our journey had to be inconspicuous, without demands, with all due sensitivity and silence. That was simply a case of human tact. We could not open old wounds, disturb anyone or push into conflict [those] who had not come to rest."[58]

Journeys were defined primarily by the physical manifestations of the successful Zionist colonial endeavor: the kibbutz, the symbol of Jewish rebirth; the new settlements and the major cities such as Tel Aviv. Marietta Böhm, who had accompanied her husband to Israel, expressed surprise that "only the present spoke to me, that what I saw with my own eyes, *the modern people* which surrounded me. I did not succeed to feel the breath of the past. I was standing on the soil on which the Biblical life of the Old Testament had taken place, on which Jesus and his apostles had walked later, but I could not feel it. We were presented with several chances to visit Christian holy places. But they provided no more interest than any other tourist site."[59]

What most preoccupied the postwar German observer of Israel were the rapid transformation of the "ancient" Palestine and the reaction of the Holocaust survivors to their presence. Consequently, the effusive descriptions of Jewish achievements were symbiotically tied to the quest for individual, national, and German redemption. Gilad Margalit has noted that during the 1950s the West German press turned German Jews "into the most humanistic and progressive element in the whole of Israeli political culture and as a true representative of the European spirit."⁶⁰ The glowing accounts and images of a young, vigorous "new Jew," often with a rifle at the ready, signaled a striking reversal of the common anti-Semitic depictions of Jews as "weak," "effeminate," "degenerative," "parasitic," "foreign," and "alien" elements within German society prior to 1945. The "new Jew of the present," as the journalist Joachim Schwelien noted in the *Frankfurter Allgemeine Zeitung*, did not "resemble at all the stereotype of the past," and this made him "able to live (*lebensfähig*)."⁶¹

Schwelien's assessment points to an additional dimension in the (post)colonial narratives that Germans employed when describing the achievements of the Jewish state. Saul Friedländer, in his seminal study on Nazi Germany and the Jews, has noted that German anti-Semitism combined the *völkisch* phobia of racial degeneration with the religious belief in redemption that justified the expulsion and physical annihilation of European Jews.⁶² Read against Friedländer's paradigm of "redemptive anti-Semitism," redemptive proxy colonialism in a sense fulfilled the aspirations of the former. It is a truism in the postwar German relationship with Israel that for all the lament of the loss of the German-Jewish population and praise for its place in German culture, virtually no invitation or encouragement to return was ever proffered to those Jews that had fled Germany.⁶³ What is more, by extending financial, economic, and rhetorical support to Israel, Germans could not only find absolution for the murderous evil of the Nazis but also redeem the German nation in the eyes of the civilized Western world. Erich Lüth had no doubt that "the creation of the Jewish State can lead us Germans also to liberation and rebirth (*Befreiung und Wiedergeburt*)—if we would only learn to interpret the signs and miracles."⁶⁴

Within the redemptive-proxy-colonial discourse the Jewish pioneers in Israel attained an "abstract" quality that echoed the reversal of public German attitudes toward Jews in the immediate postwar years of the Federal Republic. This "philosemitic syndrome" within German society became an important "moral legitimator of the democratic character of the second German Republic during the period of its establishment and the attainment of sovereignty."⁶⁵

While serving the same redemptive and nation-building function, the philosemitic descriptions of the Jewish pioneers in Palestine were inscribed with a different language and imagery. The effusive accounts of the Jewish conquest of a "barren" land and their civilizing prowess had their origins less in an inversion of Jewish stereotypes than in the transferal of German colonial desires. Descriptions by non-Jewish German observers merged seamlessly with the Zionist metanarrative that carefully controlled and propagated images of Israel's rapid political, military, cultural, and economic development. Paradoxically, it was the "general amnesia about (German) colonialism" that allowed Germans to transpose their colonial fantasies so readily onto the Jewish state.[66] What I am referring to here is the persistence of the German colonial legend identified by Uwe Timm in West German public consciousness between 1945 and 1980. Part of this legend was the image "of the hard-working Germans who built roads and railroads in Africa and taught the blacks their ABC. That this legend survive[d] so stubbornly can probably also be explained by the fact that—after the horrors of German fascism—Germans thought that in this area at least they had an edge on other peoples."[67]

German adulation for Israel hence recognized the "German qualities" in the construction of the Jewish state that made Israeli society into "the Prussians of the Near East."[68] The Jewish pioneers were achieving what German colonizers had always hoped they would achieve and, indeed, were doing so with crucial material and German financial aid. Understood this way, Germans could assign "Germanic" qualities to the Jews in Israel that substantial sections of the German population were loath to extend to them at home. In this sense the words of one of the foremost Zionist thinkers, Ahad Ha'am, proved prophetic: "What Herzl understood is that only by leaving Germany and settling in the Jewish state could the Jew finally become a real German."[69]

Notes

My profound gratitude goes to A. Dirk Moses for his close reading of this chapter and his invaluable suggestions. I am also indebted to Volker Langbehn and Mohammad Salama for their constructive comments.

1. See Kloke, *Israel und die deutsche Linke*, 46.
2. Stern, *The Whitewashing of the Yellow Badge*, 402; Büttner, "German Perceptions of the Middle East Conflict." My chapter drew part of its inspiration from Büttner's insightful article.
3. Bergmann, "Sind die Deutschen antisemitisch?" 121.
4. Ibid., 115.
5. Bartov, "Defining Enemies, Making Victims," 797.

6. See Volker Langbehn's and Mohammad Salama's introduction to this volume.

7. Davis, "Colonialism, Anti-Semitism, and Germans of Jewish Descent in Imperial Germany, 1884–1912," 22.

8. Penslar, *Zionism and Technocracy*; Berkowitz, *Western Jewry and the Zionist Project, 1914–1933*.

9. Aschheim, *Beyond the Border*, 10; Reichman and Hasson, "A Cross-Cultural Diffusion of Colonization."

10. See Diner, "Sozialdemokratie und koloniale Frage."

11. Nicosia, "Weimar Germany and the Palestine Question."

12. Bartov, "Defining Enemies," 771.

13. Pappe, "Critique and Agenda."

14. See, e.g., Fetscher, "Lambarene und der Dschungel der Deutschen"; and Michels, "Germany's Colonial Past as TV Scandal."

15. See Kundrus in this volume.

16. On Nazi colonialism see Furber and Lower, "Colonialism and Genocide in Nazi-Occupied Poland and Ukraine."

17. See Adenauer, *Erinnerungen, 1953–1955*, 155.

18. On "terra incognita" see Erich Lüth's preface to Berendsohn, *Aufbauarbeit in Israel*, 5. Lüth was the head of Friede mit Israel.

19. See Geller, *Jews in Post-Holocaust Germany, 1945–1953*.

20. Jaeger, *Die Quadratur des Dreiecks*, 19–23.

21. Segev, *The Seventh Million*, 227–52.

22. On the function of "philosemitism . . . as a constitutive element in the intellectual development of the Federal Republic in its formative years" see Stern, *The Whitewashing of the Yellow Badge*, xxiv.

23. Spiro, "'Für Israels Sicherheit paktieren wir sogar mit dem Teufel'"; Nassauer and Steinmetz, "Die Goldene Hochzeit der Waffenschmieden"; Seelbach, *Die Aufnahme der diplomatischen Beziehungen zu Israel als Problem der deutschen Politik seit 1955*, 100–103.

24. Schölch, "Die Gegenwart der Geschichte," 47.

25. The figures are taken from Morris, *Righteous Victims*, 252.

26. Jürgen Osterhammel, as cited in Friedrichsmeyer, Lennox, and Zantop, *The Imperialist Imagination*, 18.

27. Wolf, *Europe and the People Without History*. On this point compare, too, Flitner, "Vom 'Platz an der Sonne' zum 'Platz für Tiere,'" 258.

28. See Rogowski, "'Heraus mit unseren Kolonien!'"

29. Maier, "The American View," 60.

30. Quoted in Vogel, *The German Path to Israel*, 69.

31. Konrad Adenauer in a response to a 1927 survey of two hundred eminent public figures on the question of whether Germany should be engaged in *Kolonialpolitik*. Reprinted in Gründer, *"—da und dort ein junges Deutschland gründen,"* 327.

32. See Walk, "Das Deutsche Komitee Pro Palästina, 1926–1933."
33. Jelinek, *Zwischen Moral und Realpolitik*, 60–61; Vogel, *The German Path*, 183.
34. Gerstenmaier made this remark in his opening address to the exhibition "Monumenta Judaica—2000 Jahre Geschichte und Kultur der Juden am Rhein," Oct. 14, 1963, in Cologne. Speech excerpt reprinted in *Zeitschrift für Kulturaustausch* 13, no 3 (1963).
35. Quoted in Seidler, "Wissenschaftsgeschichte nach der NS-Zeit," 27.
36. Pauls, "Brücken bauen."
37. Osterhammel, *Colonialism*, 108–10.
38. Moses, "Empire, Colony, Genocide," 24–25.
39. For a detailed assessment of the attitudes and responses of the German left toward Israel see Kloke, *Israel und die deutsche Linke*.
40. See Margalit, "Israel Through the Eyes of the West German Press, 1947–1967"; and Medzini, "Israel's Changing Image in the German Mass Media."
41. Bertram, "Vor Jahren war hier eine Wüste," 18; "Die Wüste wird leben" and "Die Wüste jubelt in Davids Land," both cited in Meier-Cronemeyer, "Israel, zwischen Legende und Wirklichkeit," 225; Reinowski, *Heimat, Pflugschar, Schwert und Brücke*; Kaufmann, "Israel im Kampf mit Sumpf und Wüste," 510.
42. Gerhard and Link, "Der Orient im Mediendiskurs—aktuelle Feindbilder und Kollektivsymbolik," 286–87.
43. Böhm, "Israel einst und heute," 1–6.
44. Cordan, *Israel und die Araber*, 148, 7, 144.
45. Lüth, *Ein Deutscher sieht Israel*, 28, 25.
46. Böhm, "Israel einst und heute," 1.
47. Cordan, *Israel und die Araber*, 147.
48. Kloke, *Israel und die deutsche Linke*, 48.
49. Lüth, *Ein Deutscher sieht Israel*, 73, 75, 26.
50. Reinowski, *Heimat, Pflugschar, Schwert und Brücke*, 321.
51. Khazzoom, "The Great Chain of Orientalism," 499.
52. Osterhammel, *Colonialism*, 108–9.
53. See Ther, "Deutsche Geschichte als imperiale Geschichte."
54. Büren, "Die arabischen Staaten in der außenpolitischen Konzeption der Bundesrepublik Deutschland," 17.
55. Schwanitz, "Ägypten," 18.
56. Lüth, *Ein deutscher sieht Israel*, 57.
57. "Wüste-Wasser-Tänze," *Der Spiegel*, May 29, 1948, as cited in Margalit, "Israel Through the Eyes of the West German Press," 237.
58. Lüth, *Ein deutscher sieht Israel*, 15, 17.
59. Böhm, "Eine Reise nach Israel," 14 (my emphasis).
60. Margalit, "Israel Through the Eyes of the West German Press," 247.

61. Joachim Schwelien, "Israel kann nicht vergessen," *Frankfurter Allgemeine Zeitung*, May 16, 1961, as cited in Margalit, "Israel Through the Eyes of the West German Press," 240.
62. Friedländer, *Nazi Germany and the Jews*, 73–112.
63. Stern, "German-Jewish Relations in the Post-War Period," 92.
64. Lüth, *Ein deutscher sieht Israel*, 15.
65. Stern, *The Whitewashing of the Yellow Badge*, xxi, xviii.
66. Friedrichsmeyer, Lennox, and Zantop, "Introduction," 24.
67. Uwe Timm, as quoted in ibid.
68. Margalit, "Israel Through the Eyes of the West German Press," 244.
69. Quoted in Yigal Ilam, "Deconstruction and Reconstruction," as cited in Khazzoom, "The Great Chain of Orientalism," 500.

Bibliography

Adenauer, Konrad. *Erinnerungen, 1953–1955*. Stuttgart: Deutsche Verlags-Anstalt, 1966.
Aschheim, Steven E. *Beyond the Border: The German-Jewish Legacy Abroad*. Princeton, NJ: Princeton University Press, 2007.
Bartov, Omer. "Defining Enemies, Making Victims: Germans, Jews, and the Holocaust." *American Historical Review* 103, no. 3 (June 1998): 771–816.
Berendsohn, Walter A. *Aufbauarbeit in Israel*. Berlin: Bernard and Graefe, 1953.
Bergmann, Werner. "Sind die Deutschen antisemitisch? Meinungsumfragen von 1946–1987 in der Bundesrepublik Deutschland." In *Antisemitismus in der politischen Kultur nach 1945*, edited by Werner Bergmann and Rainer Erb, 108–30. Opladen: Westdeutscher Verlag, 1990.
Berkowitz, Michael. *Western Jewry and the Zionist Project, 1914–1933*. Cambridge, UK: Cambridge University Press, 1997.
Bertram, Christof. "Vor Jahren war hier eine Wüste." *Christ und die Welt*, Aug. 6, 1959, 18.
Böhm, Franz. "Israel einst und heute." In Böhm and Böhm, *Eine Reise nach Israel*, 1–7.
Böhm, Franz, and Marietta Böhm. *Eine Reise nach Israel*. Düsseldorf: Kalima-Druck, 1955.
Böhm, Marietta. "Eine Reise nach Israel." In Böhm and Böhm, *Eine Reise nach Israel*, 8–24.
Büren, Rainer. "Die arabischen Staaten in der außenpolitischen Konzeption der Bundesrepublik Deutschland." In *Araber und Deutsche: Begegnungen in einem Jahrtausend*, edited by Friedrich H. Kochwasser and Hans Robert Roemer, 11–33. Tübingen: Erdman, 1974.

Büttner, Friedemann. "German Perceptions of the Middle East Conflict: Images and Identifications During the 1967 War." *Journal of Palestine Studies* 6, no. 2 (winter 1977): 66–81.

Cordan, Wolfgang. *Israel und die Araber: Versuch einer Anschauung*. Frankfurt: Büchergilde Gutenberg, 1954.

Davis, Christian Stuart. "Colonialism, Anti-Semitism, and Germans of Jewish Descent in Imperial Germany, 1884–1912." PhD diss., Rutgers University, 2005.

Diner, Dan. "Sozialdemokratie und koloniale Frage: Dargestellt am Beispiel des Zionismus." *Die Dritte Welt*, nos. 1–2 (1974): 58–87.

Fetscher, Caroline. "Lambarene und der Dschungel der Deutschen." In Flitner, *Der deutsche Tropenwald*, 225–43.

Flitner, Michael, ed. *Der deutsche Tropenwald: Bilder Mythen Politik*. Frankfurt: Campus, 2000.

———. "Vom 'Platz an der Sonne' zum 'Platz für Tiere.'" In Flitner, *Der deutsche Tropenwald*, 244–62. Frankfurt: Campus, 2000.

Friedländer, Saul. *Nazi Germany and the Jews: The Years of Persecution*. London: Phoenix, 1998.

Friedrichsmeyer, Sara, Sara Lennox, and Susanne Zantop. "Introduction." In *The Imperialist Imagination: German Colonialism and Its Legacy*, edited by Sara Friedrichsmeyer, Sara Lennox, and Susanne Zantop, 1–29. Ann Arbor: University of Michigan Press, 1998.

Furber, David, and Wendy Lower. "Colonialism and Genocide in Nazi-Occupied Poland and Ukraine." In Moses, *Empire, Colony, Genocide*, 372–402.

Geller, Jay Howard. *Jews in Post-Holocaust Germany, 1945–1953*. Cambridge, UK: Cambridge University Press, 2005.

Gerhard, Ute, and Jürgen Link. "Der Orient im Mediendiskurs—aktuelle Feindbilder und Kollektivsymbolik." In *Der Islam im Aufbruch? Perspektiven der arabischen Welt*, 2nd ed., edited by Michael Lüders, 277–97. Munich: Pieper, 1993.

Gründer, Horst. *"—da und dort ein junges Deutschland gründen." Rassismus, Kolonien und kolonialer Gedanke vom 16. bis zum 20. Jahrhundert*. Munich: Deutscher Taschenbuch, 1999.

Jaeger, Kinan. *Die Quadratur des Dreiecks: Die deutsch-israelischen Beziehungen und die Palästinenser*. Schwalbach am Taunus: Wochenschau, 1997.

Jelinek, Yeshayahu A., ed. *Zwischen Moral und Realpolitik: Deutsch-israelische Beziehungen 1945–1965; Eine Dokumentensammlung*. Gerlingen: Bleicher, 1997.

Kaufmann, Julius. "Israel im Kampf mit Sumpf und Wüste." *Frankfurter Hefte*, no. 7 (1955): 510–13.

Khazzoom, Aziza. "The Great Chain of Orientalism: Jewish Identity, Stigma Management, and Ethnic Exclusion in Israel." *American Sociological Review* 68, no. 4 (Aug. 2003): 481–510.

Kloke, Martin W. *Israel und die deutsche Linke: Zur Geschichte eines schwierigen Verhältnisses.* Frankfurt: Haag and Herchen, 1990.

Lüth, Erich. *Ein Deutscher sieht Israel.* Hamburg: Gesellschaft für Christlich-Jüdische Zusammenarbeit in Hamburg, 1955.

Maier, Charles. "The American View: A Comment." In *The Cultural Legitimacy of the Federal Republic: Assessing the German "Kulturstaat,"* edited by Frank Trommler, 57–66. Washington: American Institute for Contemporary German Studies, 1999.

Margalit, Gilad. "Israel Through the Eyes of the West German Press, 1947–1967." In *Jahrbuch für Antisemitismusforschung II*, edited by Wolfgang Benz, 235–48. Berlin: Metropol, 2002.

Medzini, Meron. "Israel's Changing Image in the German Mass Media." *Wiener Library Bulletin* 26, nos. 3/4 (1972/1973): 8–13.

Meier-Cronemeyer, Hermann. "Israel, zwischen Legende und Wirklichkeit." *Gewerkschaftliche Monatshefte* 18 (1967): 225–34.

Michels, Eckard. "Germany's Colonial Past as TV Scandal: The WDR Documentary 'Heia Safari' (1966/67)." Paper abstract for "Germany's Colonialism in International Perspective" conference, San Francisco State University, Sept. 6–9, 2007: www.sfsu.edu/~german/GCC/Abstracts/Michels_Heia%20Safari.pdf. (accessed July 31, 2007).

Morris, Benny. *Righteous Victims: A History of the Zionist-Arab Conflict, 1881–2001.* New York: Vintage, 2001.

Moses, A. Dirk, ed. *Empire, Colony, Genocide: Conquest, Occupation, and Subaltern Resistance in World History.* New York: Berghahn, 2008.

———. "Empire, Colony, Genocide: Keywords and the Philosophy of History." In Moses, *Empire, Colony, Genocide*, 3–54.

Nassauer, Otfried, and Christopher Steinmetz. "Die Goldene Hochzeit der Waffenschmieden: 50 Jahre deutsch-israelische Rüstungskooperation." *Das Parlament*, no. 15 (April 11, 2005): 9.

Nicosia, Francis R. J. "Weimar Germany and the Palestine Question." *Leo Baeck Institute Year Book* 24 (1979): 321–45.

Osterhammel, Jürgen. *Colonialism: A Theoretical Overview.* 2nd ed. Princeton, NJ: Marcus Wiener, 2005.

Pappe, Ilan. "Critique and Agenda: The Post-Zionist Scholars in Israel." *History and Memory* 7, no. 1 (June 1995): 66–91.

Pauls, Rolf. "Brücken bauen: Als erster deutscher Botschafter in Israel." In *Zeit-Fragen: Israel und die Bundesrepublik Deutschland; Dreißig Jahre diplomatische Beziehungen*, edited by Renate Schlief-Ehrismann, 71–75. Bonn: Haus der Geschichte and Argon, 1996.

Penslar, Derek J. *Zionism and Technocracy: The Engineering of Jewish Settlement in Palestine, 1870–1918.* Bloomington: Indiana University Press, 1991.

Reichman, Shalom, and Shlomo Hasson. "A Cross-Cultural Diffusion of Colonization: From Posen to Palestine." *Annals of the Association of American Geographers* 74, no. 1 (March 1984): 57–70.

Reinowski, Hans J. *Heimat, Pflugschar, Schwert und Brücke: Israels Aufstieg aus dunkler Zeit.* Darmstadt: Reba, 1960.

Rogowski, Christian. "'Heraus mit unseren Kolonien!' Der Kolonialrevisionismus der Weimarer Republik und die 'Hamburger Kolonialwoche' von 1926." In *Phantasiereiche: Zur Kulturgeschichte des deutschen Kolonialismus,* edited by Birthe Kundrus, 243–62. Frankfurt: Campus, 2003.

Schölch, Alexander. "Die Gegenwart der Geschichte: Deutsche, Israelis, Palästinenser." In *20 Jahre Deutsch-Israelische Beziehungen,* edited by Karlheinz Schneider, 45–63. Berlin: Deutsch-Israelischer Arbeitskreis für Frieden im Nahen Osten, 1985.

Schwanitz, Wolfgang G. "Ägypten: Zweierlei Deutsche im Kalten Krieg." *Comparativ,* no. 18 (2006): 11–29.

Seelbach, Jörg. *Die Aufnahme der diplomatischen Beziehungen zu Israel als Problem der deutschen Politik seit 1955.* Meisenheim: Anton Hain, 1970.

Segev, Tom. *The Seventh Million: The Israelis and the Holocaust.* New York: Hill and Wang, 1993.

Seidler, Christoph. "Wissenschaftsgeschichte nach der NS-Zeit: Das Beispiel der Ethnologie." Master's thesis, Albert-Ludwigs-Universität, Freiburg, 2003.

Spiro, Shlomo. "'Für Israels Sicherheit paktieren wir sogar mit dem Teufel': 50 Jahre Deutsch-Israelische Beziehungen der Nachrichtendienste." *Das Parlament,* no. 15 (April 11, 2005): 8.

Stern, Frank. "German-Jewish Relations in the Post-War Period: The Ambiguities of Anti-Semitic and Philosemitic Discourse." In *Jews, Germans, Memory: Reconstructions of Jewish Life in Germany,* edited by Y. Michal Bodemann, 77–98. Ann Arbor: University of Michigan Press, 1996.

——. *The Whitewashing of the Yellow Badge: Antisemitism and Philosemitism in Postwar Germany.* Oxford: Pergamon, 1992.

Ther, Philipp. "Deutsche Geschichte als imperiale Geschichte: Polen, slawophone Minderheiten und das Kaiserreich als kontinentales Empire." In *Das Kaiserreich transnational: Deutschland und die Welt 1871–1914,* edited by Sebastian Conrad and Jürgen Osterhammel, 129–48. Göttingen: Vandenhoeck und Ruprecht, 2004.

Vogel, Rolf. *The German Path to Israel.* London: Oswald Wolff, 1969.

Walk, Joseph. "Das Deutsche Komitee Pro Palästina, 1926–1933." *Bulletin des Leo Baeck Instituts* 15, no. 52 (1976): 162–93.

Wolf, Eric R. *Europe and the People Without History.* Berkeley: University of California Press, 1982.

Contributors

Shelley Baranowski (Ph.D. Princeton University, 1980) is Distinguished Professor of History at the University of Akron, Akron, Ohio. She is the author of *Strength Through Joy: Consumerism and Mass Tourism in the Third Reich*; *The Sanctity of Rural Life: Nobility, Protestantism, and Nazism in Weimar Prussia*; and *The Confessing Church, Conservative Elites and the Nazi State*. She also coedited, with Ellen Furlough, *Being Elsewhere: Tourism, Consumer Culture, and Identity in Modern Europe and North America*. Her most recent book, *Nazi Empire: German Imperialism and Colonialism from Bismarck to Hitler*, was published in September 2010.

Russell A. Berman (Ph.D. Washington University, St. Louis, 1979) is the Walter A. Haas Professor in the Humanities at Stanford University, with appointments in the departments of German studies and comparative literature. He is the editor of the journal *Telos*, and he has written on many topics in modern literature and culture theory. His books include *Between Fontane and Tucholsky: Literary Criticism and the Public Sphere in Imperial Germany*; *The Rise of the Modern German Novel: Crisis and Charisma*; *Modern Culture and Critical Theory: Art, Politics, and the Legacy of the Frankfurt School*; *Cultural Studies of Modern Germany: History, Representation, and Nationhood*; *Enlightenment or Empire: Colonial Discourse in German Culture*;

Anti-Americanism in Europe: A Cultural Problem; and *Fiction Sets You Free: Literature, Liberty, and Western Culture*.

Martin Braach-Maksvytis (graduate student, Department of History, University of Sydney) is writing a dissertation called "Germany, Palestine, Israel, and the (Post)-Colonial Imagination." He has taught undergraduate courses at the School of German and Russian Studies at the University of New South Wales on Weimar and postwar German history and was a researcher at the School of Economic History at the University of Sydney. He is coauthor of the articles "Bureaucracy and the Economy in Japan and Germany in the Post-War Era," in Vera Mackie et al., eds., *Japanese Studies, Cultures, Critiques,* vol. 2, *Identity Politics and Critiques in Contemporary Japan* and "Bureaucracy and the Railway in Germany and Japan," in Olle Krantz and Lena Andersson-Skog, eds., *Perspectives on Institutional Change in the Communication and Transport Industries in the Nineteenth and Twentieth Centuries*.

Timothy Brennan (Ph.D. Columbia University, 1987) is professor of cultural studies and comparative literature, and English at the University of Minnesota. His books include *Secular Devotion: Afro-Latin Music and Imperial Jazz*; *Wars of Position: The Cultural Politics of Left and Right* (Columbia University Press, 2006); *At Home in the World: Cosmopolitanism Now*; *Empire in Different Colors*; *Salman Rushdie and the Third World: Myths of the Nation;* and Alejo Carpentier's *Music in Cuba*, which he edited, introduced, and cotranslated. Between 1997 and 2003, he was the editor of Cultural Margins, a book series at Cambridge University Press. He has edited "Narratives of Colonial Resistance," *Modern Fiction Studies* (1989); "Blacks in Albion," the *Literary Review* (1990); and coedited "Intellectual Labor," *South Atlantic Quarterly*. His essays on literature, imperial culture, cultural politics, and intellectuals have appeared in a variety of academic and nonacademic publications including the *Nation,* the *Times Literary Supplement, Critical Inquiry,* the *Toronto Star, The Cambridge Companion to Postcolonial Studies,* the *Chronicle of Higher Education,* and the *London Review of Books*.

Malte Fuhrmann (Ph.D. Freie Universität, Berlin, 2005) is researcher at the Orient Institute Istanbul and has published *Der Traum vom deutschen Orient: Zwei deutsche Kolonien im Osmanischen Reich, 1851–1918*. He is the author of several articles on German imperialism, European-Ottoman relations, and Eastern Mediterranean port cities. He coedited the special issue "Hafenstädte: Mobilität, Migration, Globalisierung," *Comparativ* 17, no. 2 (2007) with Lars Amenda and the special issue "The Late Ottoman Port Cities: Subjectivity, Urbanity, and Conflicting Orders," *Mediterranean Historical Review* 24, no. 2 (2009) with Vangelis Kechriotis. He also edited, together with Ulrike Freitag, Nora Lafi, and Florian

Riedler, *The City in the Ottoman Empire: Migration and the Making of Urban Modernity*. He is currently working on a book entitled *Being European in the Late Ottoman Port Cities*.

Ulrich van der Heyden (Ph.D. Humboldt Universität zu Berlin, 1984, and Ph.D., 1997, and Habilitation, 2002, Political Sciences, Freie Universität, Berlin, 1997) is a historian in African and colonial studies, as well as a political scientist with a concentration on Africa, adjunct professor at the Otto Suhr Institute for Political Sciences of the Free University Berlin, and seminar research associate for missionary studies at Berlin's Humboldt University. He has written or edited more than 40 monographs and some 140 papers, along with hundreds of book reviews and popular science articles. He is the acting director of the Berlin Society for Missionary History and is editor or coeditor of seven book series: Cognoscere Historias, Die DDR, und die Dritte Welt; Missionsgeschichtliches Archiv: Studien der Berliner Gesellschaft für Missionsgeschichte; Berliner Beiträge zur Missionsgeschichte; Spektrum: Berlin Series on Society, Economy, and Politics in Developing Countries; Schlaglichter der Kolonialgeschichte; and Studien zur Kolonialgeschichte. His latest monographs are *Martinus Sewushan, Nationalhelfer, Missionar, und Widersacher der Berliner Missionsgesellschaft im Süden Afrikas* and *Auf Afrikas Spuren in Berlin: Die Mohrenstraße und andere koloniale Erblasten*.

Kristin Kopp (Ph.D. University of California, Berkeley, 2001) is assistant professor of German studies at the University of Missouri, Columbia. She is the author of *Germany's Wild East: Positioning Poland as Adjacent Colony*, which will be published in 2011. She is also coeditor, with Klaus Müller-Richter, of *Die Großstadt und das Primitive: Text, Politik, Repräsentation* and, with Werner Michael Schwarz, of *Peter Altenberg: Ashantee—Afrika und Wien um 1900* [Peter Altenberg's *Ashantee*: Africa and Vienna at the Turn of the Century (a reprint of Altenberg's 1897 text accompanied by contextualizing essays)].

Birthe Kundrus (Ph.D. Universität Bielefeld, 1993) is professor of history at the University of Hamburg. She is the author of *Kriegerfrauen: Familienpolitik und Geschlechterverhältnisse im Ersten und Zweiten Weltkrieg* and *Moderne Imperialisten: Das Kaiserreich im Spiegel seiner Kolonien*. She is also the editor of *Kolonialphantasien: Zur Kulturgeschichte des Deutschen Kolonialismus* and *Die Deportation der Juden aus Deutschland: Pläne-Praxis-Reaktionen, 1938–1945*, and she is the regional editor for Germany in Prem Poddar, Rajeev S. Patke and Lars Jensen, eds., *A Historical Companion to Postcolonial Literatures: Continental Europe and Its Empires*. She has published on German history, especially National Socialism and the German empire, but also on the history of violence and genocide. One of her latest essays is

"Blind Spots: Empire, Colonies, and Ethnic Identities in Modern German History," in Karen Hagemann and Jean H. Quataert, eds., *Gendering Modern German History: Rewriting Historiography*. She is currently involved in a major new research project that investigates the German occupation of Poland during the Second World War as a precursor to the Nazi war of racial annihilation against the Soviet Union and will be published as *Laboratorium der Gewalt: Polen unter deutscher Besatzung, 1939–1945*.

Volker Langbehn (Ph.D. University of Minnesota, 1998) is associate professor of German at San Francisco State University. He is the author of *Arno Schmidt's Zettel's Traum: An Analysis* and has published articles on Friedrich Nietzsche, Christa Wolf, Arno Schmidt, Fritz von Unruh, Novalis and Gert Heidenreich, and the visual representation of German colonialism. He is the editor of *German Colonialism, Visual Culture, and Modern Memory*. His current book project, tentatively titled *The Visual Representation of Cultural Identity in European Mass Culture Around 1900*, focuses on visual representations of indigenous people in European mass culture.

Ulrike Lindner (Ph.D. Ludwig-Maximilians-Universität, Munich, 2001) is senior researcher at the Faculty of History of the University of Bielefeld. She has published *Gesundheitspolitik in der Nachkriegszeit: Großbritannien und die Bundesrepublik Deutschland im Vergleich*, for which she received the Prize of the German Historical Institute, London. She has coedited *Ärztinnen, Patientinnen, Frauen im deutschen und britischen Gesundheitswesen des 20. Jahrhunderts* and *Deutsche Geschichte in Quellen und Darstellung: Besatzungszeit, Bundesrepublik, und DDR, 1945–1969*, vol. 10. Another coedited volume, *Hybrid Cultures, Nervous State: Germany and Britain in the (Post)Colonial World* is forthcoming. She recently finished her Habilitation, "Colonial Encounters: Germany and Great Britain as Imperial European Powers in Africa before World War I," which addresses British and German colonialism in sub-Saharan Africa. She has published articles on German-British comparative history, the history of the European welfare states—including gender issues—and more recently, the relations and cooperation between German and British African colonies as well as the the transfer of knowledge between colonizers.

Luís Madureira (Ph.D. University of California, San Diego, 1991) is a professor in the University of Wisconsin–Madison's Department of Spanish and Portuguese. His major areas of specialization include Luso-Brazilian colonial and postcolonial studies, as well as modernism and modernity in Latin America, Africa, and the Caribbean. He has written two books, *Imaginary Geographies in Portuguese and Lusophone-African Literature: Narratives of Discovery and Empire*, which studies figurations of empire, nation, and revolution in Portuguese and Lusophone African literatures, and *Cannibal Modernities*, a reexamination of the Brazilian and Caribbean avant-gardes from a postcolonial perspective. In addition, he has published several articles on topics ranging from Luso-Brazilian literature and cinema to early modern travel narratives and postcolonial theory. He is currently conducting research on theater and citizenship in Mozambique on a Fulbright fellowship.

Kitty Millet (Ph.D. University of Minnesota, 1996) is associate professor of Jewish studies, specializing in comparative Jewish literatures and modern Jewish thought at San Francisco State University. She publishes regularly on Jewish writing in the Americas as well as Holocaust studies. In addition to the forthcoming anthology that she is coediting with Wlad Godzich, *Open Question: The Holocaust and Its Effects on the Humanities*, she is also at work on her manuscript "Literature's Identifying Marks and the Anagnorisis of Holocaust Witness."

A. Dirk Moses (Ph.D. University of California, Berkeley, 2000) is professor in history and civilization at the European University Institute, Italy. He is the author of *German Intellectuals and the Nazi Past*, editor of *Empire, Colony, Genocide:Conquest, Occupation, and Subaltern Resistance in World History* and *Genocide and Settler Society: Frontier Violence and Stolen Indigenous Children in Australian History* and coeditor of *Colonialism and Genocide* and *The Oxford Handbook of Genocide Studies*. He is an editor of the *Journal of Genocide Research*. In 2010, he became chair in global and colonial history at the European University Institute in Florence, Italy.

Hartmut Pogge von Strandmann (D.Phil. Oxford University, 1969/70) is professor of modern history at Oxford University and Emeritus Fellow of University College, Oxford. He has published *Ins tiefste Afrik: Paul Pogge und seine präkolonialen Reisen ins südliche Kongobecken* and *Imperialismus vom Grünen Tisch: Deutsche Kolonialpolitik zwischen wirtschaftlicher Ausbeutung und "zivilisatorischen Bemühungen"* and coedited *The Revolutions in Europe, 1848–1849: From Reform to Reaction* and *The Coming of the First World War*. He has also written about German colonialism and European imperialism, the revolutionary history of 1848, 1918, and 1989, German-Soviet relations in the interwar period, the First World War, Wilhelmine Germany, Walther Rathenau, and Anglo-German liberalism.

Mohammad Salama (Ph.D. University of Wisconsin, Madison, 2004) is assistant professor and coordinator of the Arabic program at San Francisco State University. He has a forthcoming book, *Islam, Orientalism, and Intellectual History: Modernity and the Politics of Exclusion Since Ibn Khaldun*, and has just completed a book tentatively called "Wounded Modernities: Studies in Modern Arabic Literatures." His main areas of research include theories of modernity, comparative social, intellectual, and cultural trends in colonial and postcolonial Europe and the Middle East, modern Arabic literature, colonial and postcolonial thought, Egyptian visual and cultural studies, and intellectual history.

Index

Adenauer, Konrad, 139, 298–300, 304, 308n17, 308n31, 310
Afro-Americans, 38
Anarchism, 6, 11, 23n14
Angola, 200, 275–8, 284–7, 290n49
anticolonial discourse, xv, 168; *see also* colonial discourse; postcolonial discourse
anti-Semitic tradition, xvi,
anti-Semitism, ix, 39, 55, 58, 63, 65, 72, 77, 178, 183–5, 207–8, 294–6, 306, 308n7
Arendt, Hannah, 9, ix, xvi, xviii, xx, xxivn3, xxvn11, xxvin30, 8, 25n54, 53, 65n6, 66n43, 72–86, 86n1, 86n5–7, 86n12, 86n14–7, 87n18, 87n20–5, 87n28, 87n35, 37, 147, 157n3, 177–181, 184, 186n4, 186n13, 187n16, 187n26, 269n52, 270n66, 282–3, 290n32, 290n37; *see also* Boomerang thesis; *The Origins of Totalitarianism*; Pan-Germanism; Pan-Slavism
Aristocratic radicalism, 27
Armenia, xiv, 62–63, 134
Armenians, genocide of, 139, 173, 207
Asia Rising, 18
Atatürk, Mustafa Kemal, 137
Aurochs, 98–101, 104, 109, 114n12

Basel Mission, 228–230, 238n83
Ben Gurion, David, 300, 303
Berlin Missionary Society, 225, 227, 232
Berman, Russell A., xv, xvi, xix, xx, xxii-iii, 26n66, 52, 73, 116n49, 139–140, 142n44, 159n22, 254–5, 266n1, 267n11

Best, Werner, 61, 66n38
Bismarck Archipelago, 126, 233
Bismarck, Otto von, 11, 53, 124, 126, 130, 149, 170, 187n15, 193–4, 197–200, 202, 205, 208n2, 209n14, 209n15, 209n19, 233, 236n27, 284
Bitburg controversy, xi; see also *Historikerstreit* (historian's dispute); *Sonderweg*
Bleichröder, Gerson von, 196, 203
Blond Beast, 16, 26n58
Boehmer, Elleke, 156, 159n29
Böhm, Franz, 302–3, 305, 309n43, 309n47, 309n50
Boomerang thesis (Arendt), 67, 73–5, 136, 179; see also *The Origins of Totalitarianism*; Pan-Germanism; Pan-Slavism
Boxer Uprising, 232; see also China
Brandenburg, Friedrich Wilhelm of, 219
Brest-Litovsk, Treaty of, 54
British Church Missionary Society, 264; see also Diner, Dan
British Foreign Office, 261–3; see also German Foreign Office
Bushiri Uprising, 199, 227

Cabral, Amílcar, 276–7, 284, 289n2
caesura, xvii, 33, 93, 106–8, 113
Cameroon, 13, 33, 176, 201, 228–9
capitalism, 10, 64, 156, 165, 170, 178
Carpentier, Alejo, 8, 275
Césaire, Aimé, 8, 24n27, 84, 87n40, 282, 290n31
Chatterjee, Partha, 288
China, xxi, 18, 33, 133, 140n4, 168, 181, 193, 204, 208, 230–2, 239n99, 239n102, 239n105–6, 239n111–3; see also Boxer Uprising

Christian mission, xxi, 215–220, 222, 226–8, 230–2, 234, 239n99, 239n104; see also civilizing process
civilizing process, xxi, 201–2; see also Christian mission
colonial discourse, xiv, xix, 4, 37, 150, 154, 156–7, 172, 180–1, 255, 257, 259, 306; see also anticolonial discourse; postcolonial discourse
colonial fantasies, xix, xxvin35, 156–7, 167, 296–7, 301, 307
colonial literature, 155–6, 159n28, 216
colonialism without colonies, 37, 156
Committee of Union and Progress, CUP, 62; see also Ottoman Empire; Turkey; Turks
communism, 24n37, 178, 180–1
continuity, x, xii-xiv, xvi-xx, xxiii-iv, xxvn7, 26n66, 33–4, 52, 72–3, 93, 111, 123–4, 147–8, 150, 164, 167, 169, 172, 177–183, 206, 255, 266, 279–281, 283; see also continuity thesis; discontinuity; eugenics; genocide; genocide studies; Herero and Nama war; Herero genocide; Holocaust; race theory; racial hygiene; racism; rupture
continuity thesis, vii, xiv, xvii-xix, xxvn7, 52, 72, 147–8, 177, 182–3; see also continuity; discontinuity; eugenics; genocide; genocide studies; Herero and Nama war; Herero genocide; Holocaust; race theory; racial hygiene; racism; rupture
Cooper, Frederick, 39, 154, 159n24
cosmopolitanism, 5, 7

Dar-es-Salaam, 225
decolonization (process of), xx, 8, 37, 39, 54, 75, 85, 171, 175, 184

Dernburg, Bernhard, 36, 201, 204–5, 210n47, 256, 267n16, 295
Deutsch-Türkische Vereinigung, DTV, 134–5; *see also* German-Turkish Association
Diner, Dan, 73, 84–5, 88n48; *see also* British Church Missionary Society
discontinuity, xii-xiii, xvi-xix, xxiii, 73, 206; *see* continuity; continuity thesis; eugenics; genocide; genocide studies; Herero and Nama war; Herero genocide; Holocaust; race theory; racial hygiene; racism; rupture
Du Bois, W. E. B., 84, 87n40, 168–9
Dutch East India Trading Company, 219

Eastern Europe, xix, 29, 33, 54, 74, 77, 110–11, 138, 146–155, 159n23, 172, 174, 184, 186n13
Eichmann, Adolf, 78–80, 82, 184
entangled history, 255, 267n9; *see also* German exceptionalism; "native policy"; secondary colonialism
Enver, İsmail, Pasha, 135–6, 138
Epp, Franz Xaver, Ritter von, 56
Erziehung zur Arbeit (educate to work), 201
eugenics, ix, 21, 51, 96, 98, 102–4; *see also* continuity; continuity thesis; discontinuity; genocide; genocide studies; Herero and Nama war; Herero genocide; Holocaust; race theory; racial hygiene; racism; rupture

Fabri, Friedrich, 128–9, 133, 187n15, 220
Fanon, Frantz, 84
Foucault, Michel, xv, 7–8, 23n20, 24n25, 24n37

Frankfurt School, 177
Freikorps, 54
Frelimo [Frente para a Libertação de Moçambique (Front for the Liberation of Mozambique)], 277, 284, 288, 289n7
Freytag, Gustav, 150

Geheimschrift (Esoteric Writing), 13
Generalplan Ost (General Plan East), xix, 96, 151–3, 155, 157, 158n15, 158n17; *see also* Poland
genocide studies, xii, 84, 138; *see also* continuity; continuity thesis; discontinuity; eugenics; genocide; Herero and Nama war; Herero genocide; Holocaust; race theory; racial hygiene; racism; rupture
genocide, ix-xiii, xv-xvi, xviii, xix, 51–2, 57, 61–2, 64, 73, 78–9, 81–2, 84–6, 86n1, 87n38, 110, 112, 116n49, 138–9, 147–9, 173, 184, 206, 222, 266n7, 279, 281–3, 289, 290n34; *see also* continuity; continuity thesis; discontinuity; eugenics; genocide studies; Herero and Nama war; Herero genocide; Holocaust; race theory; racial hygiene; racism; rupture
German East Africa, 13, 204, 224–5, 227, 258, 264
German exceptionalism, 255, 266; *see also* entangled history; "native policy"; secondary colonialism
German Foreign Office, 130, 263; *see also* British Foreign Office
German Labor Front (*Deutsche Arbeitsfront*), 56–7
German nationalism, xxiii, 5, 254, 304
German postcolonialism, xxii

German Pro-Palestine Committee, 299
German Southwest Africa, xv, xix,
    13, 35, 147, 149, 157, 206, 221–2,
    256, 258, 260–1, 263, 266, 266n7,
    268n38
German-Turkish Association, 134,
    136; see also Deutsch-Türkische
    Vereinigung
global imperialism, xvii
globalization, ix, xiii, 39, 112, 169–170,
    175, 185
Goldhagen, Daniel Jonah, xxiii, xi
Goltz, Colmar von der, Freiherr, 131–2,
    135
Göring, Hermann, 61, 95–6, 99–100,
    104–5, 110–11, 113
Greece, xiv, 33, 127, 169, 172; see also
    Hellenic Kingdom
Große Politik (Great Politics), 5
Grosse, Pascal, x, 147–8
Guinea-Bissau, 276–7, 284

Hallstein Doctrine, 287
Hansemann, Adolph von, 198–9, 203
Heck, Lutz, 96–104, 109–111, 113
Hellenic Kingdom, 127–8, 130; see also
    Greece
Herero and Nama war, ix, 111, 222,
    258, 260, 264, 266n7; see also
    continuity; continuity thesis;
    discontinuity; eugenics; genocide;
    genocide studies; Herero genocide;
    Holocaust; race theory; racial
    hygiene; racism; rupture
Herero genocide, x, 112, 266n7, 281; see
    also continuity; continuity thesis;
    discontinuity; eugenics; genocide;
    genocide studies; Herero and Nama
    war; Holocaust; race theory; racial
    hygiene; racism; rupture
Himmler, Heinrich, 59, 80, 146, 149

Historikerstreit (historian's dispute),
    xi, 112; see also Bitburg controversy;
    Sonderweg (special path)
Hitler, Adolf, ix, xi, xviii, xxiii, 55–6,
    58–9, 62, 64, 72, 74, 77, 81, 83, 100,
    109, 115n34, 137, 142n48, 151, 177–8,
    184, 206, 281, 290n49, 304
Holocaust, vii, ix-xii, xv-xvi, xviii-xxiv,
    51–2, 64–5, 72–3, 78–80, 82–6,
    88n45, 93, 102, 106, 111–113, 115n26,
    115n32, 116n49, 139, 147–8, 151–2,
    173, 186n13, 206–7, 279–83, 289,
    295-7, 301, 305; see also continuity;
    continuity thesis; discontinuity;
    eugenics; genocide; genocide
    studies; Herero and Nama war;
    Herero genocide; race theory; racial
    hygiene; racism; rupture
Holocaust historiography, ix, 86n1
Honecker, Erich, 284
Huelle, Paweł, 154, 158n21
human rights, 75, 84, 169–170

internationalism, xx, 170, 177, 179–182,
    185
Islamism, xx, 73
Israel, xxi-xxii, 84, 139, 183–4, 294–
    306, 308n18, 308n23, 309n39

Jäckh, Ernst, 132–6, 138
Jews, xviii-xix, xx, 39, 51–3, 57, 59–60,
    62–4, 77–80, 94–5, 99, 101–113,
    115n34, 152, 173, 178–9, 183–5, 283,
    294–5, 298–300, 303–7
Johnson, Lyndon, 276
Johst, Hanns, 146, 149–150
just war, 4

Kaiserreich, xiv, 30, 33, 38, 52, 56, 58,
    61, 64, 95, 114n2, 123–4, 138, 177
Katyn, 180, 182

Kiatchou, 230–2
Kieniewicz, Jan, 153
Kohn, Hans, 76
Kolonialabteilung (Colonial Department), 204
Kolonialamt (Colonial Office), 204
Kolonialrat (colonial council), xxi, 200, 203–5
Kupka, Frantisek, 15–6

Lacoue-Labarthe, Philippe, xviii, 106–110, 113
Lassalle, Ferdinand, 11
Lebensraum (living space), xv, xix, xx, 51–4, 57–9, 95, 206
Lemkin, Raphael, 78, 114n18
Leninism, 288
Lettow-Vorbeck, Paul von, 56
Leutwein, Theodor, 202
Liebknecht, Wilhelm, 10–11
Lomé Convention, 286
Loomba, Ania, 154, 156
Ludendorff, Erich, 54
Lugard, Frederick, 259
Lusophone Africa, 275–8, 286
Lüth, Erich, 302–6, 308n18

Machel, Samora, 277, 287
Maji Maji War, 227
Mamdani, Mahmood, x, xvi, 282–3, 288, 290n34
Mann, Thomas, 299
Marschall von Bieberstein, Adolf Freiherr, 131, 134
Meinertzhagen, Richard, 257
Merensky, Alexander, 225–6, 237n56
Meyer, Konrad, 153
Middle East xx, xxii, 63, 130, 173, 182–5, 296, 300, 302, 304; *see also* West Asia
Mignolo, Walter, 285

mixed marriages, 36, 260, 262, 268n37, 268n42, 269n48
Mozambique, xix, 204, 275–7, 279, 284–5, 287–9, 291n56
MPLA [Movimento para a Libertação de Angola (Movement for the Liberation of Angola)], 277–8
Muslim Brotherhood, xx, 182–3

national identity, 107, 295, 297–8, 304
National Socialism, x-xi, xix-xx, xxii, 51, 64, 77, 112, 147–8, 157, 178, 181–2, 184, 223–4, 266n7, 269n52, 297
Nationale Volksarmee (National People's Army), 277
"native policy", 257, 267n16; *see also* entangled history; German exceptionalism; secondary colonialism
Nazism, x, xiv, xviii, 22, 23n10, 30, 52–3, 57, 59, 73–4, 77–8, 80, 96, 104, 108, 111, 178–9, 185, 296
Neto, Agostinho, 277
New Guinea, 197–9, 204, 233–4
Nietzsche, Friedrich, ix, xiii, xvii, 3–17, 19, 22n1, 22n6, 23n8, 23n10, 23n20, 24n25, 24n37, 24n38, 25n45, 25n48, 25n49, 25n54, 26n58, 130, 168
North German Missionary Society, 229–230

orientalism, xxii, 23n20, 33, 123, 172–3, 296, 305
Origins of Totalitarianism, The (Arendt), xvi, xviii, xx, xxvi, n30, 8, 25n54, 72, 77, 78, 86n12, n14–5, 87n18, 87n20, 87n28, 87n38, 157, 157n3, 177–180, 186n4, 187n16; *see also* Boomerang thesis; Pan-Germanism; Pan-Slavism
Ottoman Empire, xiv-xv, 52, 62, 125–130, 133–135, 138–9, 141n23, 141n34,

Ottoman Empire (*continued*)
173, 182, 300; *see also* Committee of Union and Progress, CUP; Turkey; Turks

PAIGC [Partido Africano para a Independência de Guiné-Bissau e Cabo Verde (African Party for the Independence of Guinea-Bissau and Cape Verde)], 277
Palestine, 63, 126, 182–4, 294–6, 298
Pan-Germanism, 73–4; *see also* Arendt, Hannah; Boomerang thesis; *The Origins of Totalitarianism*; Pan-Slavism
Pan-Slavism, 73–4; *see also* Arendt, Hannah; Boomerang thesis; *The Origins of Totalitarianism*; Pan-Germanism
Pauls, Rolf, 300–2
Peters, Carl, 56, 199, 202, 257, 264
Philhellenism, 127, 130, 137
philosemitism, 294, 296, 305, 308n22
Poland, xv, xix, xxv, 33, 60, 62, 93, 96, 110, 146–151, 153–155, 157, 158n10, 158n17, 174, 186n13, 206, 304; *see also* Generalplan Ost (General Plan East)
Portugal, xix, 170–171, 200, 276–78, 284–6, 289n3, 289n7, 290n49
postcolonial discourse, xiv, 8; *see also* anticolonial discourse; colonial discourse
postcolonial imagination, 296; *see also* postcolonial relationship; postcolonial studies
postcolonial relationship, xxi, 124; *see also* postcolonial imagination; postcolonial studies
postcolonial studies, xx, 5–7, 22, 30, 139, 158n20, 165–7; *see also* postcolonial imagination; postcolonial relationship
Prus, Bolesław, 11
Prussia, 11, 33, 52–5, 57, 60–2, 95, 124, 127–8, 131, 149, 151, 158n10, 174–6, 219, 296, 307

Qingdao/China, 32
Quijano, Aníbal, 285

race theory, 95, 98, 100–103, 109, 113; *see also* continuity; continuity thesis; discontinuity; eugenics; genocide; genocide studies; Herero and Nama war; Herero genocide; Holocaust; racial hygiene; racism; rupture
racial hygiene, 58, 65, 138; *see also* continuity; continuity thesis; discontinuity; eugenics; genocide; genocide studies; Herero and Nama war; Herero genocide; Holocaust; race theory; racism; rupture
racism, xxii, 42n42, 52–3, 57, 74–6, 78, 85, 102–103, 179, 207, 260, 282, 295; *see also* continuity; continuity thesis; discontinuity; eugenics; genocide; genocide studies; Herero and Nama war; Herero genocide; Holocaust; race theory; racial hygiene; rupture
Rangordnung (hierarchical order), 14
Rathenau, Walther, 204, 207
redemptive anti-Semitism, 306,
redemptive proxy colonialism, xxi, 295–6, 305–6
Renamo [Resistência Nacional Moçambicana (Mozambique National Resistance)], 288
restitution and reparations agreement, 298

Rhenish Missionary Society, 222–3, 232–4
Rohrbach, Paul, 132–3, 141n25, 219, 257
Roman Empire, 52, 75, 171–2, 176
Rosenberg, Alfred, 108–111
Rothberg, Michael, 85
Rui, Manuel, 278
rupture, x, xix, xx, xxiii-xiv, 82, 84, 123, 177; *see also* continuity; continuity thesis; discontinuity; eugenics; genocide; genocide studies; Herero and Nama war; Herero genocide; Holocaust; race theory; racial hygiene; racism

Salazar, António Oliveira, 276–7, 284, 286, 290n49
Samoa/South Pacific, 32, 197–8, 233
Schama, Simon, 93–5, 98
Scottish Free Church, 227
Scramble for Africa, 170, 179, 194, 285
Second World War, xv, xxii, 81, 146, 171, 184, 206, 286, 296, 299
secondary colonialism, 254; *see also* entangled history; German exceptionalism; "native policy"
Semicolonialism, 125
Sienkiewicz, Henryk, 154
Simango, Uria T., 284
slavery, 12, 195, 201, 261
Slavs, 53–4, 57, 60, 76, 106, 112, 151, 304
Solf, Wilhelm, 32, 205
Soll und Haben (Gustav Freytag), 150
Sonderweg (special path), xi, xix, xxvn12, 138, 207, 278–9, 281, 289n17; *see also* Bitburg controversy; *Historikerstreit* (historian's dispute)
Steinmetz, George, x, 77, 155, 186n12
Strength through Joy (*Kraft durch Freude*), 57
subaltern, 7, 94–6, 285–6, 299

Surynt, Izabela, 153

Togo, 13, 201, 229–230
transcultural, xii, 234
transnational imperialism, xiv
transnational, xii, xiv, 30, 72–3, 75, 85, 140, 164–7, 169–170, 172, 174, 179–181, 185, 186n1, 255–7
Trotha, Lothar von, xxvn7, 32, 207, 258, 264, 280–1
Turkey, xiv, 81, 137–9, 169, 173; *see also* Committee of Union and Progress, CUP; Ottoman Empire; Turks
Turks, 127, 129, 132–7, 207; *see also* Committee of Union and Progress, CUP; Ottoman Empire; Turkey

Uerlings, Herbert, 146, 156–7

Versailles Treaty, 168, 171, 230, 258
Vieira, Luandino, 278
von Bülow, Franz Josef, 265

Wannsee Conference, 63
Warneck, Gustav, 227
Weber, Max, 171, 199
Weimar Republic, xxii, 38, 56, 58, 139, 177, 205, 296, 299
West Asia, 123–4, 130; *see also* Middle East
Wilsonianism, 175
Wisent, 98–9, 104
Woermann, Adolph, 198, 203
World War I, 15, 18, 41n22, 51–2, 54–8, 62, 64, 124, 139, 193, 223, 255, 258–9, 265, 279

Zimmerer, Jürgen, ix, xxivn4, 40n2, 60, 72, 157n2, 157n5, 211n51, 260, 268n37–8, 279–281
Zionism, 184–5, 295–6

GPSR Authorized Representative: Easy Access System Europe, Mustamäe tee 50, 10621 Tallinn, Estonia, gpsr.requests@easproject.com

www.ingramcontent.com/pod-product-compliance
Lightning Source LLC
Chambersburg PA
CBHW050855300426
44111CB00010B/1260